CW01240300

Also by K. Natwar Singh

E.M. Forster: A Tribute
The Legacy of Nehru
Tales from Modern India
Maharaja Suraj Mal
Curtain Raisers: Essays, Reviews and Letters
Profiles and Letters
Yours Sincerely
The Magnificent Maharaja
Heart to Heart
My China Diary (1956-88)
Walking With Lions: Tales from a Diplomatic Past

ONE LIFE IS NOT EN

ONE LIFE IS NOT ENOUGH

~an autobiography~

K. NATWAR SINGH

RUPA

Published by
Rupa Publications India Pvt. Ltd 2014
7/16, Ansari Road, Daryaganj
New Delhi 110 002

Sales Centres:

Allahabad Bengaluru Chennai
Hyderabad Jaipur Kathmandu
Kolkata Mumbai

Copyright © K. Natwar Singh 2014
Photos courtesy: author archives

All rights reserved.
No part of this publication may be reproduced, transmitted,
or stored in a retrieval system, in any form or by any means,
electronic, mechanical, photocopying, recording or otherwise,
without the prior permission of the publisher.

ISBN: 978-81-291-3274-1

First impression 2014

10 9 8 7 6 5 4 3 2 1

The moral right of the author has been asserted.

Printed by Replika Press Pvt. Ltd, India

This book is sold subject to the condition that it shall not,
by way of trade or otherwise, be lent, resold, hired out, or otherwise circulated,
without the publisher's prior consent, in any form of binding or cover
other than that in which it is published.

To Hem, without whom not

CONTENTS

Preface   ix

1. The Early Years   1
2. I Join the Indian Foreign Service   24
3. Mao Tse Tung's China   43
4. Back to South Block   61
5. At the United Nations   68
6. My Father   104
7. Once a Nehruite…   107
8. I Marry a Princess   128
9. Working with Indira Gandhi   132
10. Emergency   159
11. My Years in Zambia   170
12. In Pakistan   187
13. The Two Summits   217
14. Nineteen Eighty-Four   229
15. The Rajiv Gandhi Years   237
16. The Tragedy of Sri Lanka   252
17. The China Breakthrough   265
18. The Decline of the Congress   273
19. The Demise of the USSR   302

20. Sonia Gandhi	307
21. The Millennium Years	325
22. The Volcker Conspiracy	345
Epilogue	371
Appendices	376
Acknowledgements	397
Index	398

PREFACE

> *An unexamined life is not worth living.*
>
> —Plato

I believe that life is a journey without maps. Many leaves have turned in my garden. There is now no losing or winning, there is only self-realization. Each dawn is no longer a promise.

I have made and unmade my life more than once. Immortality and reincarnation do not interest me. I worship truth and courage. I believe that no 'chosen people' exist. The rich will prosper and the poor will not inherit the earth. I share the indignation of the African-American writer, Frank Hercules, who wrote, 'In my view the great obstacle to human beings was not theological sin or spiritual wickedness but congenital stupidity' on account of the low evolution of the human species.

I am a short-term pessimist and a long-term optimist. I am convinced that mankind will eventually make it. Hurdles will be many. The moral crises, the breakdown of institutions, the eroding work ethic, blatant consumerism and wholesale corruption must be combated with vigour and resolution. It will be a long and exhausting undertaking but we should achieve our objective. Private decencies must be transferred to public activities.

PREFACE

My schadenfreude is reserved for those who live on a heap of lies. Am I on good terms with myself? At times I feel ashamed of myself, for doing what is expedient and not what is right. I have, to the best of my ability, avoided moral shortcuts. I ferociously oppose any assault on my honour or integrity. Defiance is a prominent part of my character. A price has to be paid for defiance. I have, without regret, paid the price more than once.

I do not subscribe to the gospel of equality. France pronounced in 1789 that liberty, fraternity and equality would cure the inequities of humankind. Liberty has been achieved, so also a diluted fraternity. Equality is a receding dream. No level playing fields exist. With apologies to the great Jean Jacques Rousseau, man is not born free. Equality between human beings is impossible, although they could achieve a measure of fraternity.

I believe in the great man theory. I am with Thomas Carlyle, Bertrand Russell and Isaiah Berlin, who subscribe to this theory. There would have been no freedom movement without Gandhi. He created the circumstances, they did not create him. But I reject Carlyle's assertion that 'The history of the world is but the biography of great men'. Some so-called great men have their hands deep in blood.

My nature is rooted in solitude. Boris Pasternak, the author of *Dr Zhivago*, called silence 'the best sound on earth'. But solitude is in short supply in our chaotic and noisy world. There exist niches within us and shelters in the world where silence prevails.

Like E.M. Forster, I give two cheers for democracy, 'one because it admits variety and two because it permits criticism'. Our democracy may be flawed but it has taken root. In spite of wholesale corruption and the mess left by the UPA government, I firmly hold that what is right with India is infinitely greater than what is wrong.

What are my vices? Conceit, overconfidence, occasional

obstreperousness, zeal, suffering the foolish, leaping before looking.

I have a passion for history, which is not shared by a very large number of my compatriots. In the last one hundred years we have produced only three eminent historians, D.D. Kosambi, Irfan Habib and Romila Thapar. All three, left of centre.

From history I learnt that progress is not inherent in history. Dropping atomic bombs on Hiroshima and Nagasaki is not a sign of 'progress'. Two deadly world wars in a generation are melancholy examples of 'progress'. No one denies the earth-shattering achievements in science and technology. Conscience and compassion are missing. Science is neutral on spirituality, ethics and morality.

The father of the atom bomb, J. Robert Oppenheimer, paid a heavy price for opposing the development of the hydrogen bomb. A genius was thrown to the wolves by the American establishment.

I believe in prayer. I meditate every morning. I have with reverence read our sacred books which are sublime. Religion as practised has no attraction for me. I need no pujari to stand between me and the Cosmic Master, who makes the earth go round, the stars shine and guides our destinies. This ends in my being an unapologetic determinist. My mentors are the Buddha, Ashoka, Guru Nanak, Abraham Lincoln, Mahatma Gandhi, Swami Vivekananda, Nelson Mandela. Not Niccolò Machiavelli or Karl Marx.

I believe in friendship. It is one of the greatest joys of life. I have at times let my friends down as they have let me down. Friendship rests on trust and reliability. It is not a social contract. The heart signs no contracts. Friendship is not a bargain.

Friends ask me, 'How do you spend your time after being so busy and active in your life?' I answer with a French phrase, 'Vieillir c'est les autres'. Only other people grow old. I enjoy old age, I read, write, relax. I listen to music, watch tennis and cricket on TV. I spend time with my grandchildren (who consider their grandparents dedicated old bores). Sometimes I sit and think. At other times I just sit.

As I was finishing this book I had a surprise visit from Sonia Gandhi and her charming daughter, on 7 May 2014. It was an extraordinary encounter. Even bizarre. They were apprehensive about my autobiography touching raw nerves.

On Sunday, 6 May, Priyanka called me to ask if she could meet me. I agreed, and invited her to my house. Attractive and with an engaging personality, she shares her mother's sartorial elegance. Unlike her mother and brother, she is a natural communicator; the exactness of her expression is an asset. She is, as far as I know, free from the chattering fidgetiness so common among ladies of south Delhi. On that hot day, she came in what I may call feminine mufti. We talked about Amethi and Raebareli. About her kids. They were growing very fast.

Initially she was a bit subdued, even hesitant, but she soon came to the point. Her mother had sent her to meet me. She recalled the interview I had given to the *Economic Times* on 28 April about my autobiography. Would I be writing about the events that took place in May 2004 before the swearing-in of the UPA government? I said I intended to. No one could edit my book. I would not skirt the truth, nor would I hit below the belt. Certain proprieties cannot be ignored. Just then Sonia walked in. 'What a surprise!' I said. Her overtly friendly and gushing greeting bewildered me. It was so out of character. It was a giveaway. Swallowing her pride, she came to her 'closest' friend to surrender her quiver. It took her eight-and-a-half years to do so.

My book has aroused unexpected interest. I am flattered. Also mildly worried. The expectations are sky high.

PREFACE

Understatement, restraint, objectivity have a paralysing effect on an autobiography. Mine is as subjective as it could be.

Duniya ek ajab saraye-faani dekhi,
Har baat yahan ki aani-jaani dekhi.
Jo aake na jaaye wo budhapa dekha,
Jo jaake na aaye wo jawaani dekhi.

We are things that make and pass into the sea upon an unknown mission. —H.G. Wells

1

THE EARLY YEARS

Bharatpur. A town struggling to be a city and the capital of a medium-sized princely state. This is where I was born on 16 May 1931.

In 1805, the ruler of Bharatpur, Maharaja Ranjit Singh, withstood five attacks by Lord Gerard Lake on the town. Thereafter, decline set in. Bharatpur had half a dozen leading families, including mine: feudal, conservative, stubborn and a touch wild. Having mastered the art of survival, this small group had generally flourished. My ancestors served the founders of the Bharatpur dynasty for generations. This was at the end of the seventeenth century. A year after I was born, my father, Govind Singh, was appointed Nazim and District Magistrate of the beautiful and historic town of Deeg, adjacent to Bharatpur. Deeg is an outpost of Braj Bhumi and Govardhan is less than fifteen miles from it. The post was a coveted one, and he was one of only three Nazims in the entire state. The family moved to Deeg to live in a large and ugly house, though one not devoid of comfort. Electricity had not yet reached Deeg; neither had motor cars. We owned a grand-looking buggy with fancy upholstery, drawn by a horse which had been specially chosen by my father.

My parents were married in 1914, when my mother, Prayag Kaur, was thirteen years old, not unusual for that time. She could neither read nor write, like other ladies of her time. She was stubborn, self-willed and moody, yet also magnanimous. She suffered from depression. My father looked after my mother for over fifty years, even though he could have married again, as was the custom in those days. My mother was not an easy person to get on with, but my father never lost his temper or serenity, and remained steadfast by her side.

Father's tenure as Nazim was eventful, and he earned the respect and affection of the townspeople by handling tricky and complex situations with patience, yet firmness. His work notwithstanding, Father utilized his time at Deeg well. Since he didn't have much by way of academic distinction then (though he was an excellent horse rider and an energetic hockey player), he used this period to study law.

My earliest memory is of sitting on the lap of my grandfather. His white flowing beard was receiving disrespectful treatment from a spoilt brat, not yet five. Baba-saab, as we called him, was, I later learnt, quite a character. He married three times, and fathered thirteen children, of whom nine survived. His sister was married to Maharaja Jaswant Singh of Bharatpur. She had a son who, before he reached the age of ten, was poisoned. Sinister intrigue was a chronic feature in princely India. Accomplished plotters, like dark shadows, were ever present. Baba-saab was short, sturdy, strong. He was born in 1870 in our ancestral village, Jaghina, adjacent to Bharatpur. His idiosyncrasies were fascinating. The family barber was in awe of the patriarch who would not bend his head while getting his hair cut. The poor man used to get down on his knees to trim the hair at the back of his head.

THE EARLY YEARS

Baba-saab died in 1936, aged seventy-five. His death was unexpected and caused much grief. I was too young to mourn, and was mystified to see my father with a shorn head. My mother was crying. Why? Why this sudden gloom? Thakur Singh, the one-eyed servant of long standing, had the not-so-exciting task of looking after Chote Kunwar-saab—that's me. In my baby language I asked Thakur Singh why my father had no hair on his head. I remember his answer even now: 'Baba-saab Bhagwan ke paas chale gaye (Baba-saab has gone to heaven).' This meant nothing to me. Mother's mourning lasted several days. Salt-free meals were cooked for thirteen days. For me, this was an ordeal. I wanted salt. I was denied it. The family priest dictated. The family obeyed. Such was the stranglehold of tiresome rituals.

An event I vividly recall was a religious tour we took soon after Baba-saab's death. I must have been around five years old then. My uncle, Colonel Ghamandi Singh, a minister in the Court of Wards administration, lent my father a bus for this Braj Yatra. Our family, along with several servants, travelled in comfort for over a week. Our first halt was Govardhan, a town seeped in Krishna lore. We did the rounds of several temples. I still remember how spotlessly clean they were. Even at that innocent age I could feel the hallowed atmosphere of these sacred towns with wonderful names—Gokul, Nandgaon, Barsana, Mathura, Vrindavan. Here, religion, rites and rituals reigned. The Bharatpur state had vast properties in all these towns which the retainers kept spotlessly clean. My father performed all the pujas at these places, with us brothers watching, entranced.

◆

The youngest of four brothers, I had a lonely childhood because my three older brothers were studying at Mayo College, Ajmer.

Aristocratic families kept very much to themselves and there was no socializing. The outside world was very outside indeed. I did not even know who my cousins were till I was nearly ten years old. During these years I was home-schooled. Private tutors were hired to teach me Hindi and Urdu.

Life took a major turn when I was about seven. A new chapter opened up in our lives when my father was summoned by the state's British Diwan, Sir C.P. Hancock, ICS, and told that he would have to move to Bharatpur as assistant guardian to the young Maharaja Brijendra Singh, who had returned to India after spending six years in England. Captain Alexander, who had earlier served in the North-West Frontier Province (NWFP), was to be the Maharaja's guardian. Father was thirty-seven years old then. In Bharatpur, we stayed in a palatial house called Ijlas-e-Khas.

Brijendra Singh, known to his family as Indu, had been orphaned at the age of ten, and was a strong-willed, ill-tempered and moody—but generous—eighteen-year-old prince. On reaching the age of twenty-one, he would be the absolute ruler of a quarter million people, mostly villagers. Though my father soon realized his young ward's unpredictability, he remained loyal to the House of Bharatpur which had done much for his ancestors. He understood that he had been selected by the British for this job because of the faith they placed on his integrity and sound judgement.

Father was a practical man. He was not given to aimless self-analysis; nor did he pretend to be intellectually inclined. His mind was uncluttered, but not fenced. He was proud of his lineage but was not loud-mouthed about it.

Father's duties were not onerous; nevertheless, he was required to be in attendance throughout the day. From time to time, his patience and tact would be tried by the uncontrollable

THE EARLY YEARS

young Maharaja who could flare up even when unprovoked. Father would plead with him but not argue, and the responsibility of disciplining the Maharaja was Captain Alexander's, whose shadow fell everywhere—the Raj was omnipresent.

◆

From April to early October, the Bharatpur durbar shifted to Shimla, the summer capital of the Raj, nearly 250 miles away. The royal retinue comprised my father, four aide-de-camps, a large administrative staff and an energetic team of rickshaw-pullers and horses. Shifting the Maharaja, along with his staff, horses, pets and hangers-on, was a major undertaking.

On the way to Shimla, we stopped in New Delhi for the night. I recall us going to 12 Hardinge Avenue (now Tilak Marg) to pay our respects to the Sardarni Sahiba of Rajasansi, a wealthy estate in the Punjab. This formidable great-aunt of mine was perched on a huge platform, which was very ornamental and stately. She was my grandfather's sister and my father's aunt. Our names were called out and we trooped in one by one, receiving one gold coin each. Nearly fifty years later, my wife's niece, Jaya, married Sardarni Sahiba's great-grandson, Gurpal.

The Bharatpur estate in Shimla was extensive, with lots of fruit trees growing in spacious gardens, and tennis courts—both grass and hard. Though our lifestyle was quite luxurious, I did not enjoy Shimla. The novelty of the hills soon wore off. I remember being confined to our cottage. It rained most of the time. To relieve my boredom, my father engaged an English teacher to teach me English. The outcome was not encouraging and the young teacher gave up, to my great relief. Mother didn't much enjoy Shimla either as she was constantly ill; so much so that doctors and nurses were in and out of our cottage on a regular basis.

A servant of ours at Shimla, Havaldar Bhole Singh, was a memorable character. He had fought in Mesopotamia during World War I. He was severely wounded and had been awarded several medals, which he showed me with pride. He used to wear them on 'ceremonial' occasions. One time, the ribbons of the medals needed replacements. He and I proceeded to the Army and Navy shop on the Mall where the shop owners were all British. Bhole Singh saluted them smartly and inquired about the price of the ribbons. One of the sahibs had also fought in the war. Impressed by Bhole Singh's record, he gave him the ribbons for free! Bhole Singh was thrilled. From then on, I looked upon him with awe. He would regale me with his war exploits, which resembled those of Brigadier Gerard, who is one of the most entertaining characters created by Arthur Conan Doyle.

To some extent, the Maharaja would indulge me, affectionately addressing me as Bacchu, and give me toys. That, however, didn't rid me of my nervousness, as he was extremely short-tempered. In fact, he got annoyed when my eldest brother, Bharat, beat him at tennis. Bharat was immediately sent back to Bharatpur. Whims, not wisdom, were the Maharaja's constant companions. He was an inspired bully but, in the presence of the British Diwan, he was subdued and well behaved.

We would return to Bharatpur in time for the Dusshera festival, usually in October, which was quite an occasion. The Maharaja rode on an elephant in a silver howdah, along with the British Diwan, in his full royal regalia—zari achkan, sword, a turban adorned with jewels—and the procession passed through the main bazaar. Father, too, was part of the procession, also dressed up. The entire street would be milling with people who had poured in from all parts of the state to pay homage to their Raja. The divine right of kings was then accepted without reservation.

THE EARLY YEARS

Despite a population of thirty-five thousand, Bharatpur did not have a cinema hall. Father, Mother, my maternal grandmother and I once drove all the way to Agra to see the Hindi film *Achut Kanya*, starring Ashok Kumar and Devika Rani. We had reserved a box in the cinema hall. My mother and grandmother observed strict purdah and special arrangements were made by the cinema owner to ensure their privacy. Our car stopped at a side gate. Kanats had been installed on both sides of the alighting point to block out intruding eyes. I was hugely excited. Forty years later, I saw Devika Rani in Bangalore.

The great event of the year in Bharatpur was the annual duck shoot in December. The Viceroy, Lord Linlithgow—'heavy of mind and heavy of body', as Jawaharlal Nehru described him—would arrive with a large retinue. All work would come to a standstill during his two-day trip. The butts would be selected with care by the Maharaja himself, and the Viceroy would be installed in the best possible location. The beaters, who would make the ducks take off, would stand waist-deep in freezing water. The shoot would last nearly four hours, and the bag was several thousand ducks. The Bharatpur nobility turned up in breeches, tweed jackets and sturdy shoes. Each one was introduced to the visiting British nobility, but received only frigid smiles.

The Bharatpur state had many Muslims, mostly Meos. They were converts to Islam, although they participated in Hindu festivals. Father came into close contact with them, and was instrumental in establishing a rapport between the communities, so much so that the state remained peaceful for the next fifteen years. The Meos held him in high esteem. When I contested the Lok Sabha elections of 1984 from the area, most of the elderly Meos I met spoke of Father with nostalgic admiration. I was immensely moved. It was perhaps because of this admiration that I received nearly 65 per cent of the Meo votes.

The days of my undisciplined childhood at Bharatpur soon came to an end. Due to our proximity to the House of Bharatpur, I was awarded a scholarship. I thus joined my brothers at Mayo College, excited but apprehensive. On the train to Ajmer, I was inconsolable and cried most of the night.

Mayo College was founded by the Viceroy, Lord Mayo, in 1875, with the aim of replicating Eton and Harrow on Indian soil. The students, in the first quarter of the institution's existence, came exclusively from the nineteen princely states of Rajputana (Rajasthan). The prescribed dress for students was achkan, churidar pyjama and turban. World War II started on 3 September 1939. The college Principal, V.A.S. Stow, was a high Tory who gave us a lecture on the virtues of the British Empire. The college policy for admission changed, albeit grudgingly, to admit boys from outside Rajputana. Basically, Mayo remained elitist, exclusive and a den of snobbery. Not only was it exclusive, it was also grand. None of the other four Chiefs Colleges—in Lahore, Indore, Rajkot and Raipur—could match the aristocratic ambience, style, panache and the quintessential quirkiness of Mayo.

In my time, there were one hundred and five students, while their retainers and servants exceeded three hundred! My class fellows included the young Maharaja of Kishengarh and the Maharaja Kumar of Baria. My most exotic and interesting classmate was Said bin Taimur, the uncle of the present King of Oman. Maharaja Kumar Hanwant Singh of Jodhpur lived all by himself in the New Jodhpur House. He brought his car, his polo ponies and a vast number of servants. He was the senior monitor, and was admired and feared.

My love of reading led me to the school library which was

THE EARLY YEARS

wanting for readers—Mayo was keener on sports than on academic excellence. My studies, too, were progressing satisfactorily. It was in school that I became passionately interested in general knowledge. I started a scrapbook in which I drew maps and stuck newspaper cuttings and magazine photos of politicians, sportsmen and writers, as well as Shankar's cartoons. I still have it. I must be among the very few who have the newspaper cuttings reporting Tagore's death in 1941, with tributes from Gandhiji and Nehru, as also the eight-column front-page spread about Gandhiji's arrest in August 1942. At the time, the only newspaper allowed into school was *The Statesman*, which was favoured by the Raj. The *Hindustan Times* was taboo. Nevertheless, a few copies were regularly smuggled in.

My first brush with authority was caused by the Mahatma. During one of my vacations, I had cut out a picture of Gandhiji from the *Hindustan Times* and hung the framed photograph in my room. Principal Stow, on one of his surprise visits, came into my room and saw it on my wall. His imperial soul was outraged. 'Where did you get this wicked man's picture?' he thundered. I mumbled something incomprehensible. He pronounced that the picture must be removed. He would write to my father about my subversive activities. Though my father was no Gandhian, he ignored Stow's complaint.

◆

My world came crashing down on a sultry afternoon during the summer holidays in 1944. My father informed me that I would be withdrawn from Mayo and sent to Scindia School, Gwalior. I felt miserable but the family code could not be violated—sons and daughters did not argue with their parents.

Decades later, I discovered the truth about my uprooting.

VICEROY'S TRIBUT[E]
DR. TAGORE

POET'S SERVICES TO CO[UNTRY]

CAL[CUTTA]
"I AM deeply grieved to learn of the death of y[... in a] message received from the Viceroy by [...] "This marks the end of a long life of service inspir[ed by a] nobly conceived and actively pursued, and will [be an] example for generations to come. In him India ha[s lost one of her] greatest sons who, through his manifold gifts [...] helped to raise her in the estimation of the world. P[lease accept sin]cere condolence in your irreparable loss."

MR. GANDHI'S TRIBUTE

On hearing of Dr. Tagore's death, Mr. Gandhi said: "In the death of Rabindranath Tagore we have not only lost the greatest poet of the age but an ardent nationalist who was also a humanitarian. There was hardly any public activity on which he has not left the impress of his powerful personality. In Santiniketan and Sriniketan he has left a legacy to the whole nation, indeed, to the world.

"May the noble soul rest in peace and may those in charge at Santiniketan prove worthy of the responsibility resting on their shoulders."

TRUE PATRIOT

Mr M. A. Jinnah has issued the following statement: "I am grieved to hear of the death of Dr. Rabindranath Tagore. I had the privilege of knowing him from my younger days, and last time I had the honour of meeting him was in London in 1929. His very frank and illuminating discussions were a great source of encouragement. Above all, he was a true patriot and always ready to understand and appreciate the opposite point of view. My deepest and sincerest sympathies go out to his family in their bereavement. It is an irreparable loss to India. Tagore will live with us through his work."

PT. NEHRU'S MESSAGE

Pandit Jawaharlal Nehru in a telegram sent to Mr. Rathindranath Tagore from the Dehra Dun Central Jail says: "Gurudev's passing away has left us all, who have grown up in the shadow of his towering genius and mighty personality and enveloped by his great tradition, forlorn and in the dark. India's greatest star illumining not only our own country but the world with a synthesis of the rich wisdom of the past and of the present has set, and our hearts are empty. Yet his voice rings in our ears and the flaming message of his recent utterances will be our guiding star.

"In line with great Indian sages of the past he has left us an imperishable inheritance and even at the moment of his passing away, we think with pride and gratitude, love and reverence of this magnificent life and its achievement. That precious inheritance we shall treasure, and I earnestly trust that every Indian will consider it his duty to help in the development and growth of Santiniketan and Viswabharati which embody Gurudev's ideal."

SERVICE TO COUNTRY

"With the passing away of Dr. Rabindranath Tagore, the world has parted with a colossus not merely in public life but in literature, philosophy and art," says Sir Ramaswami Mudaliar, Commerce Member, Government of India.

"He was physically and intellectually moulded on a gigantic scale; more than any other person of his [time...]

for ever remain [...] characters of go[...] the country. H[is...] nation for nearl[y...] will continue to [...] It was he who [...] language an[d...] On behalf of the [...] cutta, I convey [...] at his death. H[e...] of an age, but h[is...] in the heart of [...] centuries to com[e...]

GRIEVOUS LOSS

Referring to th[e...] Calcutta High [Court, Justice] Derbyshire, the [...] "It is a very gr[ievous loss...] probably someon[e...] than myself wil[l...] memory. I gath[er...] gentlemen conne[cted...] would probably [...] respect to the m[emory of Dr.] Tagore, and I p[ropose in] view that the c[ourt rise for] the day at 2 o'c[lock..."]

REMARKABLE V[ERSATILITY]

Sir S. Radhak[rishnan said] the greatest fig[ure in the] Indian renaissan[ce...] qualities we h[ave seen in] generations. H[e ranges] from Valmeeki [to...] versatility was r[emarkable,] and prose writ[er, painter,] composer, his a[rt is of] the first quality[...] great prophet an[d...] a guide for [...] Millions outside [this] country and its [people read] his writings. I [lose a personal] friend. That h[e died at a time when] country means [...] appointed with [...] pect that we can[...] would be to st[rive for the] ideal of this gr[eat man and] them against e[very attempt to] jugate the coun[try."]

"FIGURE OF RO[MANCE"]

Mrs. Sarojini [Naidu said: "His] genius, his bea[uty, his] wit, the charm [of his...] gracious person[ality, in a] lifetime a uni[que...] figure of roman[ce. Now he is] gone he will b[ecome a] legend, a fairy [tale...] his song [...] ration after g[eneration...] the first flower [...] and as enchant[ing as] the moonlit str[eam..."]

APOSTLE OF C[ULTURE]

Mr. M. R. Ja[yakar said: "India has] lost her noblest [apostle of] civilization, one [...] and respected o[ver the] world. The do[minant note of his] teaching was [...] tween India's [...] it was offered [to all and not] aggressive for [...] assimilation. [...]

CREMATION OF DR. TAGORE

BRAHMA SAMAJ RITES

VAST CROWD AT BURNING GHAT

CALCUTTA, Aug. 7.

The cremation of Dr. Tagore started at about 8-15 p.m. The rites at the burning ghat were performed according to the procedure followed by the Adi Brahma Samaj.

Mr. Subirendranath Tagore, son of the late Surendranath Tagore and grandson of the poet, did the *mukhagni* (adding fire to the mouth of the deceased on the pyre) and the body was then set ablaze. Mr. Rathindranath Tagore, the only son of the poet, was unable to participate in the last rites owing to ill-health, although he accompanied the bier and stayed at the ghat for some time.

The ashes of Dr. Tagore, which have been carefully preserved, will be taken to Santiniketan.

The death of the poet was the talk of the day in the city, and everything, even the news of the international situation, paled into insignificance. The Indian section of the population of the city was literally in mourning, and all amusements—cinema shows and theatrical performances—were abandoned.

Those who called at the poet's house during the day or attended the funeral included the Chief Minister of Bengal, Mr. A. K. Fazlul Huq, Sir M. Azizul Haque, Sir Jadunath Sircar, Sir S. S. Bhatnagar, Sir A. H. Ghuznavi, Dr. S. P. Mookerjee, Dr. R. C. Mojumdar, Mr. Sarat Chandra Bose, Mr. Nalini Ranjan Sarker, Mr. Kiran Shankar Roy, Dr. W. A. Jenkins, Mr. U. N. Sen, and Mr. H. N. Dutta.

WREATH FROM GOVERNOR

During the afternoon people continued to arrive at the poet's house in procession, flowers and wreaths in their hands, to pay homage to Dr. Tagore. Among the crowd were numerous Chinese and Buddhists. Numerous wreaths were also sent by prominent individuals and institutions, including one from the Governor of Bengal, sent through an A.D.C.

Before the body was taken downstairs Vedic hymns were chanted and Mr. Ramananda Chatterjee conducted a short divine service.

With the body placed on a decorated bier, the funeral procession started at 3-30 p.m. and proceeded through Upper Chitpore road, Vivekananda Road, Chittaranjan Avenue, Caloottola Street, College Street, Cornwallis Street, Grey Street, B. K. Pal Avenue and Strand Road. The procession reached the Nimtolla burning ghat at 5-45 p.m., covering a distance of about five miles in two hours. Wreaths at the burning ghat were placed, among others, on behalf of the Czecho-Slovakian Government in London, the Czecho-Slovakian Association in Calcutta, Calcutta University, the Home Minister of Bengal, Sir Nazimuddin, the Arabic Persian Society, the Bengal Moslem Sahitya Samity, Calcutta University Law College and the Bengali ex-Service Association by Mr. B. N. Roy Choudhury.

CROWDS SWELL

As the twilight set in, crowds at the Nimtolla burning ghat swelled to immense proportions. Trams and buses and an unending stream of motor cars conveyed the mourners to the bank of the river, and a large number of people crossed the river in country boats from the other bank. Some of these boats were able to get near the burning ghat while a number of them lay anchored in mid-

MAHATMA GA
WORKING COM
MEMBERS ALSO

"BLITZ" REPRESSION STARTS

LATHI CHARGE AT BOMBAY

BOMBAY, Aug. 9.

MAHATMA GANDHI WAS ARRESTED AT ABOUT 5 O'CLOCK ON SUNDAY MORNING.

The Congress President, Maulana Azad, Pandit Jawaharlal Nehru, Sardar Vallabhbhai Patel, Mrs. Sarojini Naidu and other members of the Congress Working Committee were also arrested at about the same time.

others arrested are Miraben, Mr. Mahadev Desai, Gandhiji's ......, and the President and the Secretaries of the Bombay Provincial Congress Committee. Nearly 20 local leaders have been arrested so far.

Mahatma Gandhi and the party, including the Working Committee members, are being taken by a special train, presumably, to Poona.

Three police cars arrived at Birla House, where Mahatma Gandhi was staying, at 5 a.m. and waking up the watchman entered the premises.

As usual, Mahatma Gandhi woke up at 4 in the morning for his prayer. Following last night's two-hour speech at the A.I.C.C. and the writing of some letters till late at night, Mahatma Gandhi felt rather exhausted and, therefore, said his prayers in bed.

Shortly after 5 a.m. Mahatma Gandhi was informed that the Police Commissioner, Mr. Butler, had arrived and wanted to see Mr. Mahadev Desai. Mr. Butler had brought with him three warrants of arrest and detention under the Defence of India Rules for Mahatma Gandhi, Mr. Mahadev Desai and Miraben. In reply to Mahatma Gandhi's inquiry, accompany the police to the special train

OTHER LEADERS

An hour after the police officer presented Sardar Vallabhbhai Patel with a warrant of arrest for him and his daughter, Maniben Patel, he left his residence taking his personal belongings. In the same building Acharya J. B Kripalani, General Secretary of Congress, was also arrested. They were taken by car to the special train waiting at Victoria Station.

Maulana Abul Kalam Azad, the Congress President, and his Secretary, Ajmal Khan, both were arrested at Mr. Bhulabhai Desai's residence, where they were staying and were taken to the special train.

Simultaneously police parties went round the city arresting members of the Congress Working Committee and other Bombay Congressites.

DELHI LEADERS ARRESTED
Ansari, Ahmad And Nigam

DELHI, Sunday.

Mr. Faridul Huq Ansari, Dr. Yudhvir Singh, Mir Mushtaq Ahmad and Prof. Nigam, local Congress workers, were arrested this morning.

The Congress office in Chandni Chowk was raided by the police this morning. Mr. Faridul Huq Ansari and Prof. Nigam, who were in the office, were arrested. A large crowd which had collected before the Congress office followed the arrested leaders to the Kotwali

DHI ARRESTED
ITTEE

"CONGRESS WILL DO OR DIE"

GANDHIJI ADDRESSES A.-I.C.C.

PARTING INSTRUCTIONS TO THE NATION

INDIANS ASKED TO FEEL AS FREE MEN

Gandhiji addressed the A.-I.C.C. session for two hours on Saturday. In his parting instructions to the nation, Gandhiji called on all Indians to begin to feel that they are free men.

Gandhiji asked Indian Princes to act as trustees of their people and not be autocrats. The time for them to change had come. He asked them to act wisely while he was alive. When he was gone, Pandit Nehru would have no patience with them.

BOMBAY, Aug. 9.

Addressing the A.-I.C.C. last evening for two hours Mahatma Gandhi said: "I take up my task of leading you in this struggle not as your commander, not as your controller, but as the humble servant of you all; and he who serves best becomes the chief among them. I am the chief servant of the nation; that is how I look at it." He added: "I want to share all the shocks that you have to face."

Gandhiji referred to the interpretations put in foreign countries on his utterances during the last three weeks, and said: "I know that in the course of the last few weeks I have forfeited the privilege of the friendship and the trust of many of my friends in India and abroad, so much so that they now have begun, some to doubt my wisdom and some even to doubt my honesty. My wisdom is not such a treasure which I cannot afford to lose, but honesty is a precious treasure to me."

Gandhiji then referred to the friendship which had grown between him and many Viceroys, and in particular, between him and Lord Linlithgow. "It is a friendship which has outgrown mere official relations. I hope Lord Linlithgow will bear me out but personally, I think there has sprung up between him and me a friendship. This is not a secret."

Gandhiji then referred to the deep friendship he cherished for the late C. F. Andrews and said: "At the present moment the spirit of Andrews is sweeping me and Andrews seems to me to be the highest that I have known among the English. With Andrews I enjoyed a relationship closer than which I have not enjoyed with any Indian. There was no secret between us; we exchanged our hearts every day. Whatever was in his ..."

... tion. I know my purpose; I know what freedom is. English teachers have taught me its meaning. I must interpret that freedom according to what I can see and what I have experienced."

APPEAL TO CRITICS

Urging all his critics to search their hearts before accusing him of dishonesty, Gandhiji said: "I want Englishmen and all the United Nations to examine their hearts and search their hearts; what crime has the Congress committed in demanding independence today? Is it wrong to do so? Is it right to distrust that organization? I hope Englishmen won't do it. I hope it won't be done by the President of the United States and by the Chinese Generalissimo, Marshal Chiang Kai-shek, who is still fighting desperate battles with Japan for his existence."

After having owned Jawaharlal as comrade, I hope he won't do it. I fell in love with Madame Chiang Kai-shek. She was my interpreter and I have no reason to doubt that she was a faithful interpreter to her husband. Gandhiji added" that she had not as yet said that we were wrong in demanding our independence. I have great regard for British diplomacy which has enabled them to hold the Empire so long. But now others ha..."

(Continued on page 5, col. 3)

LATE NEWS

FIRING IN BOMBAY

BOMBAY, Aug. 9.

The Government of Bombay have issued the following *communique*: "Riotous action by Congress demo...

RESS DECLARED UNLAWFUL

BOMBAY, Aug. 9.

It is understood that the Congress Working Committee, the All-India Congress Committee, and the Provincial Congress Committees are being declared unlawful bodies under the Criminal Law Amendment Act.—A.P.I.

DELHI ORDER

P.C.C. DECLARED UNLAWFUL

NEW DELHI, Sunday.

The Chief Commissioner of Delhi in a notification has declared unlawful the All-India Congress Committee, the Working Committee of the All-India Congress and the Delhi Provincial Congress Committee under the Criminal Law Amendment Act, as in his opinion "these associations interfere with the administration of law and the mainte..."

Pages from K. Natwar Singh's scrapbook (Also see pages 10-11)

ONE LIFE IS NOT ENOUGH

The Maharajas of Bharatpur and Gwalior were close friends. At one of their tête-à-têtes, the Maharaja of Gwalior casually asked the Maharaja of Bharatpur to send some boys to Scindia School. As a result, I joined Scindia. Badan Singh, a boy whose father had been killed by a tiger, was also sent there.

In mid-July, escorted by my brother, Bhagwat Singh, Badan and I travelled to Agra by car, from where we caught the train to Gwalior. I was in deep depression. Badan, two years younger, was less morose. My brother attempted to console me but without much success. I was enjoying Mayo, my friends were there, as were my brothers. Why, why was I being sent away?

At Gwalior Railway Station, we were met by the school bus which took us up to the fabulous Gwalior Fort where the school was located. When I alighted, my heart sank. It was such a small place. Where were the sports fields? And where were the pavilions? And those hideous barracks, so reminiscent of the military establishments of the Raj.

This was a veritable nightmare! The nights were horrific. I slept badly. Living in a dormitory was like living in a hospital ward. My dormitory companions were, to me, a wholly new species. They hailed from parts of India of which I had absolutely no knowledge. I had never met anyone from Madras or Calcutta or Mysore before that.

Badan, too, was miserable. We met each day and plotted our escape. On the first Sunday, we explored the massive fort to select a suitable spot to make our escape. We concluded that the parapet behind Shivaji House was a possibility. We had to scale down a thirty-foot wall. A slip would be fatal. However, we were desperate enough to ignore the risks. The following Sunday, we executed the plan and managed a flawless exit. With ten rupees each in our pockets, we set forth and bought third-class tickets to Agra, from where we got on to another train to Bharatpur.

On edge, we hardly spoke to each other through this journey. Hungry, tired and, of course, scared, we reached Bharatpur. We took a tonga and arrived at Ijlas-e-Khas, where I had lived for four years but which now housed the Maharaja Badan Singh School. The headmaster, Keshav Dev, was well known to us, and he fed us and gave us fresh clothes. Dead tired, we slept soundly.

By the morning, the suspense was over. Keshav Devji had sent word about the arrival of his teenage 'guests' to my father, and we were instructed to proceed to Deeg immediately. The thirty-mile drive was enveloped in silent gloom in anticipation of the 'reception' we would receive. What a homecoming it was! The welcoming committee included my father, who had a cane in his hand, as well as the Maharaja and his daredevil brother, Giriraj Singh (Bacchu), also with a cane. Both Badan and I were given three lashes each, in sight of the entire palace staff. More than the punishment, it was the humiliation that stayed with me for a long time.

Then followed the chilling command issued by the Maharaja: 'You both will leave for Gwalior tomorrow. Learn to behave yourselves.'

The firmness with which my father dealt with my conduct made it abundantly clear to me that I could not have my way. So, back to school we went.

After I returned, I immediately discerned a change in the atmosphere in the dormitory. I was, to my surprise, being treated like a minor hero. My escapade had certainly earned me notoriety, but also admiration and an indefinable deference. 'How did you do it?' 'Were you not afraid?' 'Did you really climb down?' I embroidered my tale with each telling and began to enjoy myself, becoming reconciled to my new surroundings. I even wrote an article in the fortnightly school review about our daredevil escapade—my first literary effort.

Gradually, memories of Mayo faded.

My housemaster, N.G. Thakar, a Sanskrit scholar from Pune, taught me English and was someone I came to respect. He taught me to read books, not just collect them. Our course books included *A Tale of Two Cities* by Charles Dickens and *Julius Caesar* by William Shakespeare. Much later, when I was working in Indira Gandhi's Secretariat, I proposed his name for the Padma Shri, which he richly deserved. He was an intellectual Gandhian, and a secular nationalist with an attractive personality.

The important visitors to the school included C. Rajagopalachari, Viceroy Wavell, the educationist Maria Montessori, Jawaharlal Nehru, Padmaja Naidu, V.K. Krishna Menon and Amjad Ali's father, Ustad Hafiz Ali Khan. The Hutheesings (Krishna Hutheesing was Jawaharlal Nehru's younger sister) were frequent visitors. Their two sons, Harsha and Ajit, were in Jayaji House, as was I. The matinee idol of the forties, Leila Chitnis, too, came to see her two sons, both good friends of mine. Almost all the masters and senior boys fell instantly in love with her. She was not only stunningly beautiful; she had elegance, style, sex appeal and a regal bearing.

By the beginning of 1945, I was very much at the centre of school activities—studies, sports, hobbies, debating, dramatics. Did I have no spats? I certainly did, but I mostly emerged unscathed. First I became house prefect, then school prefect with near-dictatorial powers unknown even to Members of Parliament. Trousers replaced shorts. I had a tiny room to myself where I stuck large, coloured posters of Gandhiji, Pandit Nehru, Netaji Subhas Chandra Bose and Jayaprakash Narayan on the walls.

◆

On 25 June 1945, Lord Wavell called a conference of all political

THE EARLY YEARS

leaders in Shimla. Mahatma Gandhi was also invited by the Viceroy for the conference, and word spread that he would be travelling by the Frontier Mail, which stopped in Bharatpur for a few minutes. I told my father that come what may I would go to Bharatpur to see Gandhiji at the station. This posed a dilemma for my father: had he not been an important part of the Maharaja's establishment, he would have had no problem in allowing me to do so, but his allegiance was to his ruler, the Maharaja. My going to the Bharatpur Railway Station would in no way go unnoticed by the British CID.

Finally he relented. Wearing a khadi kurta-pyjama and a Gandhi cap, I reached the station where there was bedlam, with a lot of local Congress leaders awaiting the arrival of the train with garlands. Five rupees in hand, the amount the Mahatma charged for an autograph, I carried a photograph of Gandhiji in the hope of getting it signed by him. It was scorchingly hot. The train arrived punctually at 3.15 p.m., and even before it came to a halt, there was a mad rush to locate the great man's third-class compartment. I was pushed around and got nowhere near his coach. The minutes were ticking by. In desperation, I jumped between two carriages, crawled to the other side and pulled myself up to the window. There he was, shaven-headed, watch tucked into the waistline of his loincloth. He was much darker than I had thought him to be. 'Bapuji, your autograph please,' I kept shouting till a man came to the window and told me not to shout. 'No autograph. Bapu is fasting. It is his day of silence.' I later discovered that the man who admonished me was none other than Pyarelal, Gandhiji's personal secretary. The train moved. I jumped and nearly landed on my back, the photograph still in my hand. The Gandhi cap, too, survived.

And, sure enough, my teenage presence at the railway station had been noted, with the report eventually reaching my father.

He could have sat on it but it would never have crossed his mind to do so. He caught the Maharaja in one of his less explosive moods and showed him the report. The Maharaja's response was something along these lines: 'You should be more strict with Natwar. Ask him to keep clear of these Congress-wallahs.'

◆

On 6 and 8 August 1945, American planes dropped atom bombs on Hiroshima and Nagasaki respectively, killing thousands of people. The nuclear age had come.

In a lecture, our science teacher described in detail the horrors of their action. Scindia School was not only a left-of-centre secular institution, it was defiantly anti-Raj, even though it was situated in a princely state. Nationalism was in the air. On the midnight of 15 August 1947, the entire school was glued to the radio to hear Nehru's speech, which still resonates sixty-five years after that day. The next day, Principal Shukla hoisted the Indian tricolour on a specially erected pole. I was then in Class C3, and was to take the Senior Cambridge examination by the end of the year. Among the students, I was the number one nationalist, and my closest friends too shared my views on politics. We loathed both Muhammad Ali Jinnah and Lord Mountbatten and while we were angry with Gandhiji for agreeing to the Partition of India, our reverence for him remained undiminished.

The euphoria of Independence did not last too long in Gwalior. I sensed a sudden change in the behaviour of some of the Muslim boys in my class: they became apprehensive and subdued. Aley Hassan, the only Muslim teacher, decided to migrate to Pakistan. Word also spread that Hindu–Muslim riots had broken out in the city. Perched on the fort, we could see smoke from the burning houses enveloping the city. In school, to our horror, we discovered that at least two teachers were staunch supporters of the Hindu Mahasabha—I had an unpleasant argument with one in the school dining room.

When I went home for the Dusshera holidays, I noticed that not a single Muslim was to be seen in Deeg. The city and its neighbourhood had been home to several thousand Meo Muslims who had, by and large, lived in peace with their Hindu brethren. Sporadic communal incidents did occur, but these were few and far between. I asked my father about Halim and Rehmani, who worked in his office, and also about two Muslim tennis markers at the club. I got no satisfactory answer. What transpired would, in today's language, be described as an ethnic cleansing. The killings of the Muslims of Bharatpur echoed in the United Nations' Security Council in January 1948 when the Pakistan foreign minister, Sir Muhammad Zafarulla Khan, referred to the plight of his community and the treatment meted out to them. Simply put, the Muslims were hunted—trains were stopped, passengers pulled out, stripped and shot. It was a moment of sadness that, as a young boy, I saw India partitioned, and human lives lost on both sides.

◆

I sat for the Senior Cambridge examinations in December 1947. In those days, the question papers came from Cambridge by sea, and the answer papers, too, took that same route back. The results were declared in May 1948. Outcome: a good second division.

◆

I was back home for the winter holidays. On 30 January, Father and I were at our haveli listening to the 5 p.m. news on the radio. Suddenly, the programme was interrupted by an earth-shaking announcement: Gandhiji had been assassinated! Father put down his teacup and said, 'Beta, bahut bura hua (son, what has happened is very bad).' He respected Gandhiji, but was not reverential about the great man. He was also not a demonstrative person, but he was visibly upset and it took him a while to regain his composure. For the next couple of hours, he sat almost motionless and silent. He decided that no dinner was to be cooked that evening. The mysterious hold Gandhi had over millions did not leave my father untouched. To him, Gandhi was more saint, less politician.

We remained glued to the radio. He was deeply moved by Nehru's speech: 'The light has gone out…' and I was mesmerized by it. Nothing more appropriate, more memorable, nothing so eloquent could have been said by anyone about Gandhi.

◆

In July 1948, I joined St. Stephen's College, Delhi, for the BA (Hons) degree course in history. The next three years were among the happiest and most rewarding of my early life. Everything that could go right did go right. I entered the portals of St. Stephen's as a young man of nineteen, self-confident, brimming with élan, arrogance and self-righteousness. At times, I must have been insufferable.

I took to St. Stephen's even more enthusiastically than a duck does to water. It did not take me long to fathom why the college had acquired its reputation—it was focussed on all-round excellence. During World War I, Tagore and Gandhiji stayed with Principal Rudra, along with C.F. Andrews, who was then teaching at the college (then located at Kashmere Gate). The sports master was the chain-smoking S.K. Bose, who taught philosophy, was a raconteur par excellence, a rabid cricket buff and a devout bachelor. If you excelled at games, Bose-sahib would save your neck if you were ever in trouble. Such was his authority and influence that even the Principal David Raja Ram never addressed him by his first name, Sudhir. It was always Bose-sahib. Another college institution was Sukhia. Generations of Stephanians remember him fondly. His pedas, barfi and samosas were sold next to the the college café.

Our constitutional history professor, Ian Shankland, used to follow Constituent Assembly debates avidly. At the end of every week, he would make us write a summary of what was discussed. This brought them alive for us.

The first term lasted from July to October. On a very wet 15 August 1948, I walked to the Red Fort to hear Jawaharlal Nehru's address to the nation. One among a massive crowd, I could just manage a glimpse of a small figure in white, about half a mile from where I was standing. We were all soaking wet, yet no one left the meeting.

I did well at college, excelling not only at studies—with an eclectic and extensive reading list—but also at extra-curricular activities such as debates and discussions. I felt blessed. Come final year, I won more prizes than any Stephanian had for decades. I was elected President of the Students' Union, got the Westcott Memorial Prize for the highest marks in history and the Krishna Prasad Memorial Prize for outstanding all-round achievement. I won colours in tennis, hockey, football, cricket and athletics. I was the college and university tennis champion and the Delhi state junior tennis champion.

Was I the perfect student? Mercifully not. If I were, I would not be of any interest to anyone. I acquired a reputation of being the chief ragger in college. Ragging was then a civilized affair and not the brutal crusade it became in later years. In

July 1949, we selected as our target a third-year student who had just shifted into the residence in Rudra South. I led the ragging squad, disguised as a teacher. Right in the middle of our ribaldry, misfortune struck in the form of my house tutor, Mr Ramsden. Not only did he give us a dressing down, we were produced before the Principal the next day. We apologized. This was not good enough for Principal Raja Ram. Seven of us were sent down for two weeks. Where were we to go, and what were we to tell our parents? Strategically, I decided not to disturb my father's peace of mind. Instead, I spent two happy weeks at my friend Atul Gupta's house on Tughlaq Lane. I returned to college after our vanavas as an undergraduate celebrity.

In my final year, as President of the Students' Union, I travelled to Bombay to take part in the meeting of the National Students' Federation. Inaugurated by Minoo Masani, the author of *Our India*, the first Indian bestseller, the meeting soon became rowdy when communist youth leaders nearly beat him up. I was one of the students who smuggled him out the back door. The concluding session was addressed by Jawaharlal Nehru and Jayaprakash Narayan at the Cricket Club of India. The latter took a dig or two at the Prime Minister when speaking about corruption in public life.

In my time, St. Stephen's was prudish and puritanical when it came to sex. Even the use of the words 'venereal disease' in a debate got me into trouble with Principal Raja Ram, who asked me not to use such language. My protestations that I was quoting Benjamin Disraeli made no difference to him. He was well known for his malapropisms. He once introduced Countess Mountbatten as Mountess Countbatten!

Contact with girls from Miranda House, the 'sister' college to St. Stephen's, was initially forbidden, though, slowly and steadily, chinks appeared in the twin citadels. The silver lining was the telephone, with which we could speak to girls at Miranda during the day. Debates and dramatics, too, broke the barriers, but chastity remained a cause and a creed.

I fell in love, proverbially at first sight, with Sagari, the most alluring and beautiful girl in Miranda House; I met her during an inter-college debating contest. A sophisticated South Indian who set fire to the hearts of uncultured North Indians, she and I got to know each other well and wrote rather chaste letters to each other for a number of years. I kept hers with me till I got married. Her memory still endures.

On 26 January 1950, India became a republic. The first Republic Day parade was held in what is now Shivaji Stadium. My brother, Bharat Singh, was adjutant of the President's Bodyguard, and escorted President Rajendra Prasad to the stadium. He had arranged a pass for me to be present as well. Even after so many years, I vividly remember the occasion.

In April 1951, we had our final examinations; I managed a first division, standing second in Delhi University.

2

I JOIN THE INDIAN FOREIGN SERVICE

I completed my civil services examination on 16 October 1952, and then immediately left for Cambridge University. It was the pre-jet age, and it took me twenty-four hours to reach London—we stopped at Karachi, Basra, Cairo, Rome, Zurich and Paris before finally arriving. It was my first trip abroad, and my return ticket cost Rs 2,200. From London, I took a train to Cambridge. I hailed a cab and asked the driver to drop me at Corpus Christi College. Corpus was founded in 1352, and was celebrating its six hundredth anniversary. At Corpus, I was greeted in a friendly manner by the Hall Porter: 'My name is Albert. Welcome, sir. How is your brother, Bhagwat Singh?' My room was on staircase P in the Old Court which had been built in the early part of the fifteenth century. I soon acquired a gown, which all students were required to wear throughout the day, and a second-hand bicycle for a princely twelve shillings.

Although I had a first-class degree in history from one of India's leading colleges, I was admitted as an undergraduate to Corpus Christi College. The Master of the college then was Sir George Thompson, who had been awarded the Nobel Prize

I JOIN THE INDIAN FOREIGN SERVICE

for Physics in 1937. My history tutor was John Roach. When I took my first tutorial to him, he said, 'You'll have to do better than this.' By the third tutorial, Roach said that there was some hope for me. The lectures and bi-weekly tutorials left me much time to do as I pleased. Among my other history teachers were Sir Herbert Butterfield, Sir G.R. Elton and J.H. Bury. The great Whig historian, George Trevelyan, who had just retired and lived in an ugly house on Trumpington Street, was admired and respected.

In the middle of the term, the Prime Minister of Ceylon, Dudley Senanayake, who had been at Corpus Christi in the 1920s, the Prime Minister of Pakistan, Khawaja Nazimuddin, as well as C.D. Deshmukh, representing Nehru, had come to the college. It could be said the governance of the subcontinent lay in the hands of Cambridge alumni.

At the end of term, I got a job in the local post office for nine pounds a week to help the establishment sort out the Christmas mail. However, I did not join the post office but made my maiden trip to Europe, visiting Holland, Belgium and West Germany. When I returned to college, a telegram was waiting for me asking me to appear for an interview at the Union Public Service Commission (UPSC) office in Dholpur House in Delhi on 9 January 1953.

A fellow passenger on the flight to Delhi was V.K. Krishna Menon, then High Commissioner of India to the United Kingdom. I introduced myself, he was pleasant, and even gave me a crash course for my forthcoming interview. I was to encounter him a decade later in New York when he was leading the Indian delegation to the United Nations. By that time he had succeeded in becoming the most disliked Indian in the United States.

On the appointed day, wearing my best suit, I reached Dholpur House at 10 a.m. in my brother's Jaguar. I was called in for the interview at around 11 a.m. Eight gentlemen sat around a semi-circular table. At the centre sat the Chairman, R.N. Bannerji, ICS, then the Home Secretary.

I sat opposite the Chairman, my heart pounding. The interview commenced with a loaded question, 'In your application you only mentioned the IAS and IFS and not the other services. Are you so sure of getting into either of the two?' I answered, 'Sir, I am not sure, but I am confident.'

I was then asked what my plans were if I did not qualify. I told them I would finish my Tripos at Cambridge and then look for a job. The next question: 'Man is born free but is everywhere in chains. Who said that?' My reply: 'Rousseau, sir.' Then: 'In your view, is man in chains?' I said: 'No, sir. I am not in chains.'

I had been warned that at some point a 'trap' question would be asked. Sure enough, the 'trap' was laid with finesse. I was asked if I had read a particular book, which I had not. In nine cases out of ten, the temptation would have been to bluff and say yes, but an affirmative answer would have done me in. But I did not get intimidated and negotiated the 'trap' with some sangfroid. The next question was deceptively easy: 'What are the three events in the last twelve months that have made an impact on you?' 'Can I, sir, be given a minute or two to think before answering?' This, I was later told, had made a favourable impression on the selection board.

The ordeal of the interview over, I proceeded to Bharatpur. One night, we were about to sit down for dinner when my elder brother, Bhagwat Singh, switched on the radio to hear the 9 p.m. news. Halfway through, the announcer started reading out the names of those who had been selected for the IAS and IFS. My name was amongst them—the first Rajasthani in the country to qualify for the Indian Administrative Service and the Indian Foreign Service.

I JOIN THE INDIAN FOREIGN SERVICE

◆

14 April 1953—a new beginning, a new adventure, a new promise. All probationers—seven from the IFS and thirty-two from the IAS—reported at Metcalfe House for our six-month training. The IFS probationers were told that Prime Minister Jawaharlal Nehru would meet each of us individually.

The meeting with the Prime Minister was a formal affair. We arrived at gate number 2 of South Block, and were taken to the room of the personal secretary to the Prime Minister. Although I had met Pandit Nehru a few times at Teen Murti House, when his sister, Krishna Hutheesing, was in Delhi (her sons, Harsh and Ajit, were close friends of mine), I was decidedly nervous. As I stepped into the room, the Prime Minister got up from his chair and shook my hand. Over the next few minutes he asked me about my home, family, etcetera. He was, I later realized, giving me a chance to calm my nerves. 'Now, let's get down to business,' he announced after a while.

'Kya humein Cheen se koi khatra hai (Does China pose a danger to us)?'

'Jee, hai bhi aur nahin bhi hai (yes and no), because our next-door neighbour is our best friend and worst enemy,' was my audacious reply.

'Mujhe Chanakya neeti sikha rahe ho (you are teaching me politics)?' the great man said, half in jest.

The next few questions related to South Africa and the Second Five-Year Plan.

At the end of the interaction, to my utter amazement, he saw me off at the door. It was the supreme gesture of good manners and magnanimous grace by a statesman of world stature.

◆

All thirty-nine of us probationers were eligible bachelors and much in demand. I distinctly remember a Rashtrapati Bhavan car arriving to take an IFS probationer to meet the President, Dr Rajendra Prasad. He ended up marrying the President's granddaughter.

In the first week of August, the IAS and IFS probationers were sent on a tour of Kashmir. We called on the Chief Minister, Sheikh Abdullah, at his Srinagar residence which overlooked the Dal Lake. In the past few months, he had not been listening to Jawaharlal Nehru and refused to come to Delhi. Nehru had unnecessarily given him a very long rope. All of us, while in Srinagar, felt uneasy. Two flags flew over the Chief Minister's house and other buildings: the Indian tricolour and the Kashmir flag.

In early September, the IFS probationers sailed for London—four headed to Cambridge, one to Oxford and one to the Arabic school in Shamlan, Lebanon, and one to Harvard. Hence, I was back in Corpus Christi College after nearly ten months.

My status had changed. I was not an undergraduate, nor a postgraduate. All that I was required to do was to study Chinese.

The college had arranged for a Chinese tutor to induce me to take some interest in learning the language, the most difficult language that exists. Thrice a week I went to Mr Tang's home for an hour. He was a Buddhist with a controlled disdain for the communist regime in China. We never talked politics. I was a conscientious pupil. He tried, I tried, but without success.

It was during this period that I became friends with E.M. Forster. I had first seen him in the winter of 1952 at a meeting of the Tagore Society in Cambridge. By that time, Forster had become something of a cult figure. His rooms in King's College were a literary pilgrimage for many young men and women from all over the world, particularly from India. But friendship, not fame, was his priority. He was aware of the influence his writings had on a vast number of people all over the English-speaking world. He was at the time among the best-known British novelists in the world. Fame came to him; he did not seek it. He felt uneasy with fame.

He was almost fifty years older than me, and at the peak of his career. He lent me several books, including J.R. Ackerley's *Hindoo Holiday*, Christopher Isherwood's *Lions and Shadows* and Goldsworthy Lowes Dickinson's *The Greek View of Life*. While at Cambridge, I read most of Forster's books as well as his essay, 'What I Believe', included in *Two Cheers for Democracy* (1939). His most well-known sentence was: 'I hate the idea of causes, and if I had to choose between betraying my country and betraying my friend I hope I should have the guts to betray my country.' Here I differed with Forster. I believe that it is entirely possible to love one's country as well as one's friend. The conflict of loyalties can be surmounted without damaging either. But it was his passion for friendship and personal relationships which greatly appealed to me. His two-word epigram, 'only connect', had a profound and lasting influence on me. It is largely to him that I owe such awakening as has befallen on me.

In 1954, I remember asking Forster if he would agree to *A Passage to India* being made into a film. He said, 'No. I would have no control over its production.' As an exception, in 1960, he allowed Santha Rama Rau to write a script for a stage production of the novel in London and New York. Several years after Forster's death, David Lean produced the film. Forster would have been appalled.

If I had not met Forster I would never have known Ahmed Ali, the author of *Twilight in Delhi*, R.K. Narayan, Raja Rao, Narayana Menon, Mulk Raj Anand and Santha Rama Rau. Each of them looked at life differently, but their destination was the same—to live decently on their own terms. Knowing them, reading them, meeting them was not only a pleasure, it was something more. These remarkable people certainly saved me from a sordid vision of life and also shielded me from lugubrious formality.

I made two other friends at Cambridge: John Vaizey at Queens and Brian Abel Smith at Clare College. Both were from the top drawer, earning firsts in economics. Brian became Professor of Social Administration at the London School of Economics. John Vaizey was undoubtedly among the most brilliant and witty men I have ever known. He was a member of the Labour Party for many years, but then became disenchanted by it. In 1976, he became a Life Peer. His last book, *The Squandered Peace: The World 1945-75*, provides a grim picture of the post-1945 international scene. He was prophetic about the decline of the UN. My favourite Vaizey book is *In Breach of Promise*. It is a collective portrait of five exceptionally talented British politicians. John died within a year of the book's publication in 1984, aged fifty-five.

In the biography of his friend, Goldsworthy Lowes Dickinson, Forster wrote what I consider the most entrancing summing up of why Cambridge is so special and unique. It is an extension of 'only connect'.

> As Cambridge filled up with friends it acquired a magic quality. Body and spirit, reason and emotion, work and play, architecture and scenery, laughter and seriousness, life and art, these pairs which are elsewhere contrasted were fused into one. People and books reinforced one another, intelligence joined hands with affection, speculation became passion and discussion was made profound by love...

At the end of our stay in Cambridge, we spent six weeks at the Foreign and Commonwealth Office in London. Besides us, there were probationers from Pakistan, Malaya, Ceylon and Hong Kong;

several of them became Foreign Ministers of their countries. The course was instructive in some ways and disappointing in others. Most of the senior officials were still living in the past and were not quite reconciled to the independence of India, Pakistan and Ceylon. The only worthwhile lecture was by Harold Nicolson, whose book, *Diplomacy*, is a classic.

◆

I returned to India in late September 1954 to join the Ministry of External Affairs (MEA). For reasons unknown to me, I was deputed to accompany various foreign delegations to different parts of India. The first was a large Chinese cultural delegation which gave breathtaking performances in Delhi, Bombay, Madras and Calcutta.

King Saud bin Abdulaziz Al Saud of Saudi Arabia brought a huge delegation, with several planes transporting his hedonistic entourage. Maulana Azad made one of his rare appearances at Palam airport. He was fluent in Arabic and spent some time talking with the King.

The King, along with his 'delegation', which comprised several young princes, travelled to Agra by train. In Agra, they ventured into a street with an unsavoury reputation, and paid the ladies in gold biscuits. When this princely adventure was brought to the notice of His Majesty, he asked for the names of the culprits. He said to the protocol officer, 'Give me their names and I will send their heads to Bandit Nehru'—the letter 'p' does not exist in the Arabic language. The matter was not pursued.

In March 1955, the King of Cambodia, Norodom Sihanouk, came on a state visit to India. Cambodia is a Buddhist country; its most famous landmark, Angkor Wat, was built in the twelfth century by Hindu artisans from Tamil Nadu. Prime Minister

Nehru went to Palam airport to receive him. The plane circled the airport a few times and then landed. After receiving the King, Nehru asked him what had happened. The King responded by saying that the French pilot's map did not show Palam airport; instead it showed Safdarjung airport. The map had been published in 1936, and no effort had been made to revise it!

The King brought in his entourage five Buddhist monks. To receive them, we too took five of our Buddhist monks. The two groups spoke to each other in Pali. The leader of the Indian group of monks asked his Cambodian counterpart about their food preferences. The Cambodians said they wanted to eat beef. The Indian monks all but collapsed.

In December 1955, the General Secretary of the Communist Party of the Soviet Union, Nikita Khrushchev, and Nikolai Bulganin, the Prime Minister of USSR, arrived on a state visit to India. They got a genuinely warm welcome, both in Calcutta and in Delhi. The two leaders also spent a weekend in Srinagar. At a reception hosted by Sadr-e-Riyasat Karan Singh, Khrushchev, without consulting his Foreign Minister, Andrei Gromyko, announced that the whole of Kashmir was a part of India. No other country had said so.

I was attached to the Soviet delegation as baggage officer. The delegation was a large one—at least one-third of the members were from the KGB. They had brought vast amounts of luggage. My duty was to make sure that the baggage was secured. On the day of their departure, to my horror I discovered that a few pieces of their precious cargo had been misplaced. I went to see my counterpart at the Soviet delegation, Sergey Ivanov, who asked me to go to Comrade Bukov, who shooed me off to Comrade Zukov, who disdainfully said to me, 'Go to Comrade Fuckov...!'

The visit of the Soviet leaders was a substantial one. Several important agreements were reached. Indo-Soviet relations were deepened and strengthened. The visit was carefully monitored by the Americans and the Chinese.

◆

It was around this time that I ran into Nirad C. Chaudhuri at a dinner at St. Stephen's College. Nirad-babu was the shortest and the most garrulous man I had ever met. While still at Cambridge, I had read his outrageous attack on Forster and his novel, *A Passage to India*. Nirad-babu had written an article in *Encounter*, a monthly magazine edited by well-known English poet Stephen Spender, damning Forster and his novel. On returning to India, I wrote an article in the *Illustrated Weekly of India*, countering the the *Encounter* article. To my surprise, Nirad-babu had read it.

I found Nirad Chaudhuri garrulous and his outbursts disagreeable. However, in the next few months, we met several times and gradually got to know each other well.

As a writer, he had no equal in India. It was worthwhile putting up with his idiosyncrasies. There was no doubting his erudition and scholarship. He was a walking-talking encyclopaedia. His *Autobiography of an Unknown Indian* is among the best written by an Indian in the twentieth century. It earned him worldwide fame, but little money, and he always lived in a modest flat at Mori Gate with his wife and three sons.

In early 1955, the BBC and the British Council invited him to visit England for two weeks. Nirad-babu had never been out of India. He was fifty-seven years old then. Before leaving, he asked me if I could arrange a meeting for him with Forster. Recalling his attack on Forster, I was surprised but still wrote to him. Forster wrote back, 'Now I get your line about Mr Chaudhuri. I had a letter about him from the British Council earlier in the day.

They suggested our meeting, and I replied to them that if he cared to write to me direct, I should hope to fix something. It is up to him to write, I think, after the way he "snubbed my poor Aziz".' He did meet Nirad-babu, though, and, after the meeting, he wrote, 'I liked Mr Chaudhuri—thought him so first hand...'

In 1970, Nirad Chaudhuri migrated to England and settled in Oxford. I met him in London in 1974. His financial position was then precarious and I helped him in a modest way.

In 1987, when I was back in India, the second volume of his autobiography, *Thy Hand, Great Anarch!*, had been rejected by Chatto & Windus. The book was a thousand pages long and no publisher was willing to take the risk of bringing out such a tome by an author whose fame was fading. Around that time, a British publishers' delegation came to Delhi led by Graham C. Greene, the nephew of novelist Graham Greene and the head of Chatto & Windus. I told Greene that Chatto had turned down Chaudhuri's book. Chaudhuri was ninety years old and the least the publishers could do was to give him a birthday present. Greene had no knowledge of the rejection. On his return, he made sure that the book was published, with not one deletion. *Thy Hand, Great Anarch!* demonstrated Nirad-babu's stylistic decline and did not do well. Both volumes of his autobiography have a common flaw—Nirad-babu's version of Indian history does not include South India, and seldom does he mention Islam.

I also did some high-level log-rolling behind the scenes to get Chaudhuri a doctorate from Oxford University. At a lunch in London in June 1988, I sat next to Roy Jenkins, the Chancellor of Oxford University, and spoke to him at some length about Nirad-babu. He was vaguely familiar with the name, but had not realized that Nirad-babu lived in Oxford. I suggested to Jenkins that Oxford should give him some recognition. Jenkins made no commitment but, later, Nirad Chaudhari was given an honorary

I JOIN THE INDIAN FOREIGN SERVICE

degree by Oxford University. He lived in Oxford till his death in 1999, aged a hundred and one.

◆

In January 1956, as part of my IFS training, I had to spend four months in Tamil Nadu. The Madras government had provided me and my two IFS colleagues with a cook and three servants. We spent a fortnight at Tanjore, but took no interest whatsoever in Tanjore paintings. We also visited Kumbakonam, the home of the world-famous mathematical genius Srinivasa Ramanujan. The word Kumbakonam has a Machiavellian connotation. It found its way into the Oxford dictionary as 'the act of being cunning', but the entry was subsequently removed when the people of the town objected.

The Collector was Kunchi Thappatham. He had risen from the ranks and took his job very seriously. One story doing the rounds was about his twenty-fifth wedding anniversary. At a reception he gave on the occasion, one of his guests asked him how it felt to be with the same woman for so long. He answered, 'When I married her, she was awfully simple; now she is simply awful.'

From Tanjore, I went to Mysore to meet R.K. Narayan, not yet famous then. With some difficulty, I reached his newly constructed single-storey house in Yadavagiri. I opened the wicket gate and called out, 'Is anybody home?' A man wearing a shirt and lungi appeared. I told him I was looking for R.K. Narayan. 'You are talking to him,' he said. I said my name was K. Natwar Singh, and E.M. Forster had spoken highly about his novels. On hearing who I was and why I had come, he asked me if I was Khushwant Singh's brother!

I got back to Delhi on 1 May and immediately left for

Bharatpur by the Frontier Mail. Father always came to the station when any one of his four sons arrived. I looked for him. He was not there, which worried me. I had a foreboding that something was wrong. When I reached Govind Niwas, I saw him reclining on a sofa in the drawing room. He looked pulled down. He told me he had suffered a mild heart attack. I was stunned and numbed with anxiety. He had never been ill in his life, except for an attack of pleurisy in 1935. It was Mother who was constantly ill. I immediately postponed my departure for Peking. I asked him why he had not informed me; I would have been with him in less than twenty-four hours. His reply was that of an exceptionally loving parent: 'Had it been serious I would have asked you to be with me. It was a mild attack.' He was stoic and generally in control of himself.

◆

My posting to Peking was announced soon after—as Third Secretary in the Embassy. My diplomatic career had begun. I will speak about my time in China in greater detail in the next chapter.

On my return to India from Peking in May 1958, I had expected to be attached to the China division but that, to my disappointment, was not to be. I was appointed Undersecretary in the IFS (B). The department was an administrative oddity, and only those who did not have godfathers were dumped there. I could easily have asked Krishna-masi—Pandit Nehru's sister—to do some log-rolling on my behalf but chose not to ask for such a favour.

My immediate boss was the ferociously acerbic but competent and clear-handed Leelamani Naidu, the daughter of the irrepressible Sarojini Naidu. She initially treated me with sneering disdain, but her behaviour changed dramatically once she learnt that I knew Krishna Hutheesing. Leelamani Naidu's ill temper and chaotic functioning were legendary. No one had the temerity to contradict her as she had direct access to the Prime Minister. The only officer who did stand up to her was Muhammad Yunus, who had been in jail with Nehru.

Tony Agate was also one of my senior officers. One day, I sent him a file sanctioning the leave application of the section officer. Tony sent the file back with LBW written on it. I went to him and asked what a cricketing term was doing on a leave application. He asked how a dope like me got into the IFS. LBW meant 'Let the Bastard Wait'.

In the interim, I had become a member of the Gymkhana Club, and occupied suite number 22 in the residential area of the club. It was an ideal place to live—swimming in the morning, tennis in the afternoon, billiards in the evening. The library was a significant attraction, and it was during this period that I not only had plenty of time to read but also to review books—something that M.O. Mathai, the all-powerful private secretary to the Prime Minister, tried to warn me off.

One day at the Gymkhana, M.F. Husain turned up and asked if he could borrow my newly bought Fiat car for a few hours. I readily agreed. The few hours turned into forty-eight hours. During this time, I was more worried about my car than Husain, who I knew didn't have a license. When he finally returned, I asked him what happened. 'I just felt like going to Kanpur,' he said.

It was sometime in late November that I was visiting Mrs Hutheesing at Teen Murti House. S. Mulgaonkar, the editor of the *Hindustan Times* and a friend of Krishna-masi, was also present. Indira Gandhi joined us, followed shortly after by M.O. Mathai. I was talking about the book Mulgaonkar had asked me to review. Mathai told me sternly that as, an officer of the IFS, I could not write for newspapers. 'Book reviewing is not the same thing as writing for newspapers,' I retorted. Mathai was not satisfied: 'Have you taken permission from the government to review books?' he asked. At this point Krishna-masi intervened: 'Look here, Mac, Natwar is like my son. Lay off.' And he did. He was a man with a chip on his shoulder, and quite often misused his power.

S. Gopal, in his biography of Nehru, writes, 'Mathai exercised vast and irregular power... Nehru was informed that Mathai could not account for his great wealth and without doubt had received money from C.I.A. as well as businessmen in India. It can indeed be safely assumed that from 1946 to 1959, the C.I.A. had access to every paper passing through Nehru's Secretariat.'*

◆

In early May 1960, I became private secretary to the Secretary General (SG), R.K. Nehru. I was not overworked. I continued reviewing books and writing articles. I regularly played tennis and even got elected to the Delhi Gymkhana Executive Committee. However, I was in danger of getting an inflated idea of my importance. So I mended my ways. Treading on sensitive toes was not a risk worth taking. Innovation and originality were frowned upon and mediocrity was a virtue. And this was more than evident in the calibre of the ICS officers. The four top secretaries—R.K. Nehru, M.J. Desai, B.N. Chakravarty and Y.D. Gundevia—were all ICS men. In his autobiography, Jawaharlal Nehru was severely critical of the ICS which was disdainfully called 'neither Indian nor civil nor service'. Independent India catapulted them to high positions that would have eluded them under the Raj.

---

*Sarvepalli Gopal, *Jawaharlal Nehru: A Biography*, New Delhi: Oxford University Press, 1979

I JOIN THE INDIAN FOREIGN SERVICE

With the exception of Subimal Dutt, almost all lacked gravitas, and none of them stood up to the Prime Minister. Y.D. Gundevia, the only Parsi in the service, did once in a while quiz the boss in a somewhat irreverent way, and got away with it. The most outstanding member of the ICS was Sir Girija Shankar Bajpai. He had been appointed Secretary General of the Ministry of External Affairs in 1948. The Prime Minister had high regard for his judgement and experience.

◆

In mid-June, R.K. Nehru took over as Secretary General of the Ministry of External Affairs, succeeding Sir N.R. Pillai, a well-meaning brown sahib.

A private secretary's job combines discretion with responsibility, and R.K. Nehru had complete confidence in me. However, he was, in several ways, a difficult person and, having served under him in China, I was familiar with his work habits. He agonized over seemingly insignificant things. When he was required to send a note to the PM, a dozen drafts would land in the wastepaper basket. And he was unduly fastidious about his appearance.

The SG's office was fifteen yards from that of the PM's, and every once in a while Nehru would walk into the SG's room. Once or twice, he had peeped into my cluttered room, shared by my two stenographers.

I unintentionally invited the PM's wrath in the first week of July 1960. The SG was to leave for Mongolia to participate in their National Day celebrations. The evening before his departure, I cleared all the files, except one. In it was the PM's letter to the King of Nepal, a four-page epistle. I put it in my cupboard thinking I would read the letter next morning and then send it to the Foreign Secretary.

The next morning, I accompanied the SG to Palam. He was to catch a flight to Hong Kong and, as it was delayed, I stayed chatting with the ebullient Mrs Rajan Nehru, the SG's wife. A few minutes later, I saw a vaguely familiar man approaching our table. He uttered five chilling words: 'Panditji is calling you, sir.' My heart skipped a beat as I immediately remembered the Nepal file. I drove to South Block at break-neck speed, at the entrance of which I was met by a peon who, too, politely reminded me: 'Panditji is waiting for you, sir.' I ran up the stairs, two steps at a time, to my room, pulled out the file from the locked cupboard and rushed to the PM's personal secretary, S.P. Khanna. On seeing me he said, 'Natwar Singhji, the PM will throw something at you if you go in. He was very angry. Give the file to the FS.' On reaching Foreign Secretary M.J. Desai's room, I was once again told of the PM's ire and was instructed to leave the file there.

A day later Badar Tyabji, the Secretary (administration), told me what had transpired. While I was merrily chatting at the Palam lounge, dramatic events had been unfolding in South Block. At 9.30 a.m. the Prime Minister arrived in his South Block office. Instead of sending for the Foreign Secretary, he went to his room. 'M.J., what do you think of my letter to the King of Nepal?' M.J. said that he had not seen it. 'Sir, the Nepal file has not so far been put up to me.' (This is classical bureaucrat talk). The Prime Minister was slightly put out and asked Khanna, his private secretary, why the file hadn't reached the Foreign Secretary. Khanna told him that the file was sent to the SG. At this Nehru was livid: 'Why was it sent to the SG? He has nothing to do with it.' Khanna informed him that all files coming from the Prime Minister were sent to the SG, whose private secretary (that is, I) passed it on to the Foreign Secretary and others. Khanna, normally an unflappable individual, then rushed to my room but found me gone. My steno told him that I had gone to the airport. Khanna asked him where the file was and then demanded that my cupboard be opened. He was informed that it was locked and I had the key. By now, the Foreign Secretary and the other secretaries had assembled in the Prime Minister's room for their morning 'prayer' meeting. Khanna then informed the Prime Minister that the key was with Natwar Singh, who had gone to see the SG off at Palam. The Prime Minister had a minor explosion. 'Break open the cupboard. And ask the police to get hold of him!' and he banged the table. To relieve the tension, Tyabji, said, 'Sir, Natwar must have found your letter to the King very interesting and kept it to read it at leisure.' By now, the PM was in no mood for jokes: 'I have not written the letter for Natwar Singh's pleasure. Get hold of him. I can't have my work disrupted in this fashion.'

Petrified at the prospect of coming face to face with the PM, I changed my exit route from my room after this incident, and resumed the old route only a week later. As I was passing by his room one day, Prime Minister Nehru stepped out as well. I greeted him with folded hands with a book between my palms. He stopped, returned my greeting, and asked me what the book was. I said it was Amaury de Riencourt's *The Soul of China*. 'I have read his *The Soul of India*,' the Prime Minister announced.

'So have I, sir.'

He took a few steps towards the staircase and remarked: 'Rather Spenglerian, I thought.'

Having never read Oswald Spengler, all I could do was to smile nervously.

He walked on and as he started to descend the staircase he looked back and said with a beautiful smile and a twinkle in his eyes: 'Nehru Imperator, hmm!'

It was rare for a young IFS officer to have breakfast with

the PM but I was afforded that privilege twice during Krishnamasi's trips to Delhi. On the first occasion, he was avuncular but absorbed in his thoughts. The only time he showed some interest was when I said a word or two about my stay in China. On the second occasion, when Krishna Menon, Indira Gandhi and Feroze Gandhi were also present, he looked grim. In awe or nervousness, I don't remember which, I kept refusing everything I was offered. 'Ye sharma sharmi kyon (why so shy)?' he asked me abruptly, and put an apple on my plate. At the end of the breakfast, Indira Gandhi told me, 'Papu is very upset. One of his pet dogs is very ill.' This touched me.

◆

In 1961, Queen Elizabeth II was the chief guest at the Republic Day parade. Lord Mountbatten had got Nehru to agree to the Queen and President Rajendra Prasad jointly taking the salute. This was an atrocious proposal. I spoke to several of my colleagues about it. There was unanimous disapproval. I also spoke to S. Gopal, the son of Dr S. Radhakrishnan. Sensing the mood, Nehru dropped the idea. What bothered me even more was the pernicious influence of the Mountbattens on Nehru, so much so that he was literally eating out of their hands. He was oblivious to Mountbatten's glaring shortcomings. His wife, Edwina, had fallen in love with Nehru, and he with her. When Edwina Mountbatten died in early 1960 in Borneo, Nehru paid her a tribute in Parliament. This was unprecedented.

3

MAO TSE TUNG'S CHINA

After spending two days in Hong Kong, I left for the border town Shum Chun to take a train to Canton, where I spent a miserable night in a hotel which needed to be pulled down. Next day, on 28 June 1956, I took the train to Peking. I had a first-class compartment to myself. On the side table rested a thermos flask filled with hot water, and a packet of green tea but no milk or sugar. I later became addicted to it. People in China drink vast amounts of green tea. I hardly saw an obese Chinese in my two-year stay in China!

The only book I had with me was Edgar Snow's classic, *Red Star Over China*. It was the first book to make known the names of Mao Tse Tung, Chou En-lai and the great silent military leader, Marshal Chu Teh, to the Western world. The book was published in 1937 when Snow was twenty-six years old. He was the first foreign correspondent to interview Mao who had, after the Long March—six thousand miles—made Yunnan his military headquarters. In the 1968 edition of the book, Edgar Snow wrote: 'It provided not only for non-Chinese readers, but also for the entire Chinese people—including all but the communist leaders themselves—the first authentic account of the Chinese Communist Party.' During the Cultural Revolution, Snow was the only journalist to stand next to Mao at the annual parade (1 October 1970). It was a signal to the Americans but they missed the significance, as Kissinger admits.

On reaching Peking's uncrowded station, I was met by a member of the Embassy staff. My luggage was modest—one large leather suitcase and a small handbag. The overcoat, I carried on my arm.

The staff car deposited me at Hsin Chiao Hotel where, I later discovered, low-level diplomats, peripatetic travellers and several intelligence agents to keep an eye on the diplomats were put up. Hsin Chiao was Spartan. That suited me—I was at that time a show-off puritan.

The next morning I went up to the almost empty dining room for breakfast. The menu was in Chinese. Just as I was beginning to despair, a lady wearing a colourful dress walked in and sat down three tables away from mine. I could not take my eyes off her. She was very beautiful. Not so discreetly, I kept looking at her. Where had I seen her? Could she be Han Suyin? No, of course not. What would she be doing in China? Yet, she looked familiar. I scribbled a note on the back of the menu: 'I am starving and cannot get my breakfast. Are you Han Suyin? If so, could you help me order my breakfast?' As I fretted about my impetuosity, an answer arrived: 'Yes, I am Han Suyin. Come and join me.' Thus began a friendship that lasted more than fifty years.

Her novel, *A Many-Splendoured Thing*, published in 1952, became a world bestseller. It is one of the most moving and tragic love stories of our time. Suyin wrote superb English. Her 'ruffled disquiet' never left her. She helped me, to some extent, understand China. On an excursion to the Summer Palace outside Peking, we circled the luminous lake in front of the Palace in a small boat. The setting was heavenly. I uttered a banality: 'Here one finds the peace that passeth all understanding.' Suyin said, 'The peace that passeth all misunderstanding.'

After our unorthodox introduction, I frequently met Han Suyin. She took me to the Forbidden City, the Temple of Heaven and the Beihai Park. She also reduced my ignorance of ancient and Mao's China. She told me about how she had met a 'wonderful Indian in Nepal', with whom she instantly fell in love. Ours was a platonic friendship. We gave each other time and silence. We did not fall for each other but over the decades, we exchanged hundreds of letters. We met frequently, in Hong Kong, Singapore, New Delhi, London, New York, Lausanne and Geneva.

The man she fell for was Colonel Vincent Ratnaswamy, a Catholic, married with children. I got to know him and liked him very much. He was solid, steady, unhurried, a splendid listener and non-intruding. Vincent divorced his wife to marry Suyin (not easy for a Catholic). She in turn divorced her English husband, Leonard Comber, a police officer.

Suyin had an acute identity complex. Her heart was Chinese but her head (after marrying Vincent) was Indian. The Chinese used her and she used them in return. She wrote a dreadful biography of Mao Tse Tung; it was far too reverential. I wrote about it in my book, *Profiles and Letters*, in 1997. I also reviewed her book *The Mountain Is Young* for the *Illustrated Weekly of India*. She approved of the review and wrote me a thousand-word letter on it, which I had not expected.

In her autobiography, *My House Has Two Doors*, she wrote, 'I had [an]other good friend in Peking...and Natwar Singh, a young Embassy Secretary, a delightful companion for rambles and a devotee of the English writer E.M. Forster. He was learning

Chinese, but appeared in no hurry to become an expert...'*

◆

The Embassy was a seven-minute drive from the hotel. It was located in what was known before 1949 as the Legation Quarter, the exclusive preserve of European, American, Russian and Japanese Embassies. The only Chinese allowed entry were servants.

On my first day at the office, I was introduced by Ashok Bhadkamkar, the head of the Chancery, to my senior colleagues—I.J. Bahadur Singh, Panu Guha, A.R. Ram and V.V. Paranjpe. The Ambassador, R.K. Nehru, and his wife, Rajan Nehru, gave me tea in the afternoon. No one was even remotely interested in me or knew what to do with me. Each morning, the Ambassador held an 'officers meeting'. Attendance was de rigueur. V.V. Paranjpe read out important news items from *The People's Daily* and *Ta Kung Pao*. His choice of the news items was arbitrary. Since he was the only Chinese-speaking member of the Embassy, Ambassador Nehru's reliance on Pai (as we all called him) was total. A polyglot, Pai spoke Marathi, Hindi and English besides Chinese. His mastery of the language was the envy of the entire diplomatic corps. He was Nehru's translator in his meetings with Mao Tse Tung and Chou En-lai in 1954. Besides his linguistic accomplishments, Pai had one other asset. He could consume vast quantities of maotai and other alcoholic brews without ever getting drunk.

I have singled out Pai because he was an original. Carefree, unpunctual and slightly quirky, he fitted into no bureaucratic niche. One evening at his house, I noticed a few sheets of paper lying on the floor. These turned out to be the record of a Mao

---

*Han Suyin, *My House Has Two Doors*, New York: G.P. Putnam, 1980

Tse Tung–R.K. Nehru meeting. I handed them to Pai who flung them on to his cluttered writing table. I was curious to know where the other sheets were. He asked me to look in his overcoat. I did as he said. They were there all right, but not in very good shape. Was Pai a security risk? No. No outfit could use him as their agent. He was too outspoken and unpredictable.

As I began to spend more time in our Embassy in China, I read up on Chinese history. I bought and read the Chinese classics too: *All Men Are Brothers* (translated from the Chinese by Pearl S. Buck), *The Dream of the Red Chamber* by Cao Xueqin, and books about Hiuen Tsang and Confucius. I also met the greatest living Chinese novelist, Lao She. His book, *The Rickshaw Boy*, became a bestseller in America. The Embassy also selected Dean Chang, a scholar and a dear old man who had seen better days, to teach me Chinese.

◆

I vividly recollect the first time I saw Chairman Mao Tse Tung. This was at a banquet for the Prime Minister of Laos. He wore a light grey baggy Mao suit. Other leaders, including President Liu Shaoqi, Chou En-lai and Marshal Chu Teh, were in blue suits. Mao was taller than all of them. Mao was a thinker, a poet, a scholar, an intellectual, a revolutionary, a Marxist and a ruthless man with an iron will. His knowledge of his country's history was deep and he reached out to history. No one disagreed with him. The power of his mind was second to none, with the exception of Lenin.

Mao Tse Tung was transforming China—the lives of five hundred million Chinese and their way of thinking. His aim was to produce a society which would be a model for all communist countries. He put an end to chaos, squalor and corruption. The cost of this transformation, in human terms, was no doubt high but no one had an inkling of this in the 1950s. It is only now we know that Mao was responsible for the murder of seventy million Chinese. One could, as a detached observer, complete an entire encyclopaedia of suffering under Mao.

I set about educating myself on Mao's China. A few weeks before my arrival in Peking, Mao Tse Tung had made a speech at a meeting of the Politburo of the Central Committee in which he had dealt with ten major relationships and set forth the ideas underlying the general line of building socialism (read communism, Mao style) with greater speed.

Two very important speeches made by Mao during my stay were on 'The Correct Handling of the Contradictions' and on 'Let a Hundred Flowers Blossom, Let a Hundred Schools of Thought Contend'. I recollect writing to E.M. Forster about the latter. His reply was that there was always the hundred and first.

Mao was a tremendous innovator and a prophet who made Marx stand on his head. It was the Chinese peasants, he said, and not the industrial class, who would make the revolution. This was a revolution within a revolution. Stalin thought poorly of Mao's political views. He called him a 'cave Marxist'. But, to me, Mao's insights were both novel and original.

Indian delegations poured into China. The first was led by the communist, E.M.S. Namboodiripad, who was accompanied by P. Sundarayya and P.C. Joshi. The Ambassador held a reception for them at which dozens of Chinese officials turned up. The most prominent was Soong Chingling. She spotted me and asked how I was. The Ambassador, curious, asked Madam Soong how she knew me. The once gorgeous-looking lady said, 'Yes. I saw much of him during my visit to India last year.' The CPI delegation met Chairman Mao Tse Tung, Chu Teh, Chou En-lai and Liu Shaoqi. P.N. Sharma, the well-known photographer, too was at the reception. He took lots of pictures, including one of mine. Later I invited him to lunch at the hotel. He showed me a photograph of himself with Chairman Mao, Chou En-lai, Liu Shaoqi and Marshal Chu Teh. Sharma was in the centre of the photo. I got to know him well in the years to come. He was a good but naïve person and his marriage to a Russian girl was a disaster. He gradually faded away and died in obscurity.

Among the people who came for the National Day— 1 October 1956—was the world-famous Mexican muralist David Alfaro Siqueiros. He and his wife called at the Embassy. He enthralled us by his animated conversation. He had met Nasser and was looking forward to seeing Nehru. Their interpreter exasperated them and he asked for a substitute. Siqueiros had an interesting past. He was an ideological painter. He had fought in the Spanish Civil war where he got to know Ernest Hemingway. He was a friend of John Steinbeck, author of *The Grapes of Wrath*. He had joined the Communist Party in 1924. He asked me if I knew Satish Gujral who had learnt painting 'at his feet'. I said I had met him but did not know him well. It was after many years that I learnt of his role in the assassination of Leon Trotsky in 1940.

In September came a delegation headed by R.K. Patil. It included a mix of personalities. D.K. Barooah of the Congress, particularly, proved to be a ready wit. One day he asked his interpreter, 'Are these the Western Hills?' When she confirmed, Barooah teasingly asked, 'Before or after Liberation?' He later told me that he was fed up with repeatedly being told that all good things were a gift from Chairman Mao after Liberation. H.K. Malaviya, a senior member of the delegation, was impressed with Mao's China. According to him, the change that had been wrought about in the very humanity of China by Mao was nothing short of remarkable. However, he was unimpressed by the 'gramophone record refrain'. To him, the Party's propaganda machine was overactive and needed to be restrained. His other observation was curiously appealing. According to him, in China, they did not allow grass to grow under one's feet even though they did not mind that the grass grew on people's roofs. In India, Malaviya observed, grass was allowed to grow all over the place. The Ambassador did not take undue interest in the Patil delegation. They were, for him, a Category B bundle.

So much of the diplomat's time was spent at Peking airport, which was then a poor man's version of our Palam. Between July and October, Indian diplomats were constantly at the airport to welcome the Prime Ministers of Laos, Nepal and Pakistan as well as President Sukarno of Indonesia. In addition, came two high-powered Indian delegations to attend the 1 October festivities and the military and cultural march past. The dapper General J.N. Chaudhuri led the defence delegation.

On 29 September came the large delegation under the leadership of Lok Sabha Speaker, Ananthasayanam Ayyangar. After lunch for the Speaker, I rushed back to the airport for the arrival of President Sukarno, who was received by Mao Tse Tung himself. I broke all the rules of protocol and was all over the place taking photographs, including one of Mao from very close. No one objected. The security was unobtrusive, but alert. They knew who I was and let me get away with my improper conduct. Chairman Mao stood apart from Chu Teh, Liu Shaoqi, Chou En-lai, Soong Chingling, Deng Xiaoping who looked even shorter than me. President Ahmed Sukarno came out of the plane in military uniform, medals, baton and black Indonesian cap. The contrast between Mao and Sukarno was stark. While Mao was indifferent to sartorial elegance, Sukarno needed frills to impress, and impress he did. President Sukarno was an intellectual but no revolutionary. Nevertheless, he had his uses. At the banquet

Chairman Mao gave for Sukarno, he held forth for fifty minutes. Mao spoke for five minutes.

On 1 October, the D-Day, it poured from morning till noon. The parade, spectacular in spite of the rain, lasted four hours. The diplomat's enclosure was to the right of the Tiananmen Gate. On the balcony sat Mao, Sukarno and the Nepali Prime Minister, as well as other top leaders. The march pasts, the athletic displays by acrobats were spectacular. So was the military march past. The participants also carried huge portraits of Marx, Lenin, Stalin and Mao. Those of us sitting in the diplomatic enclosure were provided umbrellas and hot Chinese tea was served in the large rooms below the enclosure. However, our parliamentary delegation suffered. They felt the cold and were provided overcoats and umbrellas. The parade was, however, not witnessed by the inhabitants of Peking as all roads leading to Tiananmen Square were blocked.

Chairman Mao Tse Tung received the parliamentary delegation at midnight of 30 October at his residence in Chung Nan Hai. An audience with the Chairman was a unique event. Mao Tse Tung never called on anyone. President Nixon called on him during his historic visit to China in February 1972. Mao did not return his call. No Emperor in China's history had ever wielded the power Mao did.

My notes made after the meeting even after fifty-eight years have not lost the liveliness of the occasion. With the Chairman were Liu Shaoqi and the Mayor of Peking, Peng Chen. We were fifteen in number. The Chairman and the Speaker sat facing each other. The meeting lasted close to one hour. Ananthasayanam Ayyangar talked much more than Mao. However, he had been briefed by the Ambassador beforehand and did not deviate from his brief.

Mao—'I can see changes on the globe and visualize that the West is withering away. We are not bothered about the UK and Europe, but about the USA. At the moment the USA is not afraid of China but it is afraid of the Soviet Union. At the moment we are far behind USA technically, and it will take us about fifty years to catch up with them. Unlike you, we have made the mistake of having a vast army of nearly three million and that has hampered progress in other fields. Do you think we have too large an army?'

The speaker's reply was tactful and sensible.

Speaker—'We haven't studied the military aspect and neither have we seen any of your military installations. We went wherever our hosts took us. We didn't wish to embarrass them by asking them to show places that they might not like us to visit.'

Mao—'No, we wouldn't have been embarrassed and we have nothing to hide from you.'

Speaker—'Our armed forces delegation that is here, told me that you had not kept anything from them when you received them. They were very satisfied with their visit.'

Mao—'I asked them the same question, but they didn't tell me if they thought that our army was too large, that's why I'm asking you.'

Speaker—'We need to defend our territories and that's the main purpose for having an army. India faces no dangers, but your problems are different and as per force, you had to keep this large army. Like us, you too have a large population and it was your manpower that saved the day in the Korea war.'

I was surprised to hear that Mao Tse Tung said that China had been spending 33 per cent of its budget for defence purposes. This was too much. In the next few years they hoped to bring it to 20 per cent and then to 12 per cent.

Mao—'We want peace and development in our country. At this moment, we can produce only medium-sized machinery, not big and precision machinery. This we must build.' He said this in reply to the speaker's remark that India and China lead the world in handicrafts.

Mao not once said that China was on top in anything. This studied modesty is typical of all Chinese leaders, and in contrast to our leaders who all the time pat themselves on the back and throw their achievements in the face of others. The Chinese tone is like, 'we have done little, we wish to learn from you.' Mao listened with interest to all that the speaker had to say, about our Five Year Plan and the freedom movement. Mao said that they had been misinformed about the freedom movement in India and it was only now that they realized that the struggle led by Gandhi and Nehru was a mass movement.

I think he said this tongue-in-cheek. Nehru in 1954 had told him about the freedom movement. He said that they understood the works of Gandhi better today.

Speaker—'Gandhi believed in soul force and to him, means were more important than the ends.'

Mao—'Non-violent, non-cooperation were also struggles. Was it a philosophy of revolution?'

Speaker—'Your progress is so fast that you will soon catch up with us.'

Mao—'Not necessarily.'

Ambassador—'We will go ahead together.'[*]

---

[*]K. Natwar Singh, *My China Diary: 1956-88*, New Delhi: Rupa Publications India, 2009

Was he being polite—the popular slogan, 'Hindi-Chini bhai bhai', was still being mouthed—or was he ignorant? Did he seriously wish to see a united India? Most certainly not. He was being disingenuous. In his discussions with Nehru in October 1954, he had not called the Partition a mistake nor had spoken about a united India.

♦

On 7 July 1957, I flew to Ulan Bator, Mongolia—the world of Chengis and Kubla. I was excited to visit this remote country. A vast landmass, juxtaposed between Russia and China, where one million people lived. The Gobi desert was below us, forbidding, treeless. I was surprised to see patches of water in it.

After nearly two hours the clouds parted, the mist disappeared and out popped Ulan Bator. It looked green and beautiful, like the meadows of England. There was no runway. The airfield was full of grazing cattle and the pilot had to bring the plane down very low to scare them away. We landed on the second attempt. It was cold and windy. We were received by a gentleman who later turned out to be the Czech Ambassador. I felt sorry for him—first he had been posted to Afghanistan and now Mongolia.

The Chinese Ambassador to Mongolia arrived in the afternoon. It was so cold that even with my overcoat on, I was shivering. The Ambassador thought this undignified. He had a young Mongolian interpreter, who had learnt Hindi in Moscow.

The Foreign Minister held a reception for us at the Foreign Office. It was a big room with heavy furniture obviously brought in from Moscow. He spoke French and Russian; few Mongolians knew Chinese.

In Mongolia, one got a pleasant feeling of unreality. The fifteenth century rubbed shoulders with the twentieth. One saw horses all over the place. On them the Mongols had conquered half the existing world. They built an empire but neglected to build a nation.

◆

Around this time, the Suez Canal issue was gathering momentum. A strongly worded statement was issued on Independence Day. It read: 'The Egyptian people built the Suez Canal on their own territory with their own blood. All international treaties concerning Suez Canal cannot but recognize that the Suez Canal is an integral part of Egypt and that the Suez Canal Company is an Egyptian Company. The Asian and African countries had declared at the Bandung Conference (April 1955) that colonialism in all its manifestations was an evil which should speedily be brought to an end.'

During the Suez crisis in 1956, tens of thousands of young Chinese assembled outside the British Embassy. Some carried megaphones, others life-size placards with irreverent cartoons of John Bull and Anthony Eden. The slogans were standard—'Down with British Imperialism'; 'Down with French Imperialism'; 'Down with America'; 'Down with Israel, Enemy of the Brave Arab People'. The protesters were mostly students. I watched these noisy scenes from the other side of the road. Photographers were plenty and so were the newsreel teams. The newspapers were full of the developments in Egypt. Egypt had opened an Embassy in China only a few weeks earlier. The Egyptian Ambassador had even been received by Chairman Mao. Jawaharlal Nehru's statements condemning the invasion of Egypt by Britain, France and Israel were lauded by the leadership. The demonstrations continued for several days and nights. No attempt was made by them to enter the British Embassy. The frenzy was orchestrated.

Close on the heels of the Suez Canal crisis came the news of the Soviet intervention in Hungary. Mao fully supported the Soviet invasion. Chou En-lai made a hurried trip to Moscow, Warsaw and Budapest to assure the Soviets, Poles and Hungarians of China's support. He also cautioned the Polish leadership to use restraint.

The Prime Minister's refusal to place Hungary at par with Suez created an outrage in India. Jayaprakash Narayan wrote (on 5 November 1956), 'If you [Nehru] do not speak out, you will be held guilty of abetting enslavement of a brave people by a new imperialism more dangerous than the old because it masquerades as revolutionary.' Krishna Menon made matters worse by stating in the Security Council that events in Hungary were a domestic affair. He went further. On his own, he abstained from voting on a resolution condemning the Soviet Union for the use of force, justifying his action with an abrasive speech. The Prime Minister stood by Krishna Menon to the chagrin even of senior officials of the Ministry of External Affairs. Jawaharlal Nehru did himself no good by defending the indefensible.

Chou En-lai then visited India, in December, to hold talks with Nehru. In India, Chou En-lai also met the Dalai Lama, who was in India for the 2,500th anniversary of the birth of the Buddha. While both Nehru and Chou advised His Holiness to return to Lhasa, the Dalai Lama did not want to return to Tibet because China was flooding the country with Han people—the Tibetans would soon be in a minority. Nehru innocently committed a serious mistake by making the Tibetan leader sit between himself and Chou En-lai.

◆

On 18 September 1957, Vice President S. Radhakrishnan arrived in the Chinese capital. He was received by all the top Chinese leaders, including President Liu Shaoqi, Prime Minister Chou En-lai, Soong Chingling and the Mayor of Beijing, Peng Chen. Even Chairman Mao returned to Beijing a day early from a trip to receive the Vice President.

Radhakrishnan called on Mao. His hand was bandaged as he had hurt his finger while getting into a car at Phnom Penh. After shaking hands, he patted Mao on the left cheek. Mao, as well as the other Chinese officials present, were taken aback by this unusual familiarity. However, the philosopher quickly diffused the situation by saying, 'Mr Chairman, don't be alarmed, I did the same thing to Stalin and the Pope.'

The Mao-Radhakrishnan talks went off smoothly. Radhakrishnan observed that 'if India and China stood together the world would take note of it'. To this, Mao replied that if India and China stood together for twenty years, no one would be able to make them go on different paths.

At the banquet Mao gave for Radhakrishnan, he picked a piece of meat with his chopsticks and put it in the plate of his vegetarian guest. This was the ultimate act of expressing deep friendship. I watched with horror, but the Vice President dealt with this culinary outrage with extreme tact. He did not touch the meat but helped himself to a dozen vegetarian dishes.

◆

Thanks to my teacher, Dean Chang, an old Buddhist, my study of Chinese had picked up. I had become proficient enough in the language to be able to read Mao in the original. I still remember one of his dictums: 'When necessary bend like a willow, when necessary stand unbending like an oak.'

Before the year ended, I had the good fortune to meet the

legendary painter, Chi Pai-shih. It was not easy to locate this nonagenarian national treasure, and a meeting was finally arranged by Vice Minister Chen Chen Tho. For years, no one had taken any notice of Master Chi until Chou En-lai paid him a visit on his ninety-third birthday in January 1953. Life changed for the man after that, and he became a celebrity overnight. He was given a comfortable house to live in, as well as servants to look after his daily needs.

I remember arriving at his house on a very cold morning in mid December. I was greeted by a smartly dressed young man who turned out to be his son. I was taken into Master Chi's study. For a moment or two, I could not spot him, rolled up as he was in a warmly padded cotton gown, with a black cap on his head. His beard was skimpy and his spectacles resembled those of Gandhiji. The Master's son mentioned that his father had been recently ill.

The old man did not seem to notice me. It was only after his son shouted in his ear that he suddenly came to and offered me tea. My first question was inane. I asked who his favourite contemporary Chinese painter was. He named Chen Pan Ting, a man I had never heard of. When I asked if he had seen any Indian paintings, Master Chi said that he had seen some Indonesian paintings in a book President Sukarno had sent him. He had recently been awarded the International Peace Award by the World Peace Council. But, when asked what he thought of the award, he mentioned that he did not think his paintings had any 'peaceful content'. Chi painted objects from real life, including shrimps, crickets and fish. His son explained that Chi 'patiently studied the activities of these small creatures and acquired an infinitely sympathized understanding of their beings and outer forms'. Chi also wrote poetry and relished reading the Thang poets: Li Po and Tu Fu. I bought two of

Chi's paintings for a total of one hundred and fifty yuan. Today, they are priceless.

Cultural life, too, was rich. Mei Lanfang, the legendary star of the Peking Opera, was a major attraction. He only played female parts. A refined, polite and cultured person, he gave me tickets to his shows on two occasions. He was full of praise for Kamala Lakshman, the legendary danseuse, who had come to China to give several dance performances, all to packed houses. Mei Lanfang had met Uday Shankar in New York in 1930. A reunion took place in Peking in 1957 when Shankar came to Peking to perform.

At the reception after one of the shows, I exchanged a few words with Prime Minister Chou En-lai. And, at the end of the event, I committed a protocol blunder by making Chou En-lai and Mayor Peng Chen wait. I had quite forgotten that the reception was given by Chou En-lai and not by us. I kept chatting with one of the Chinese officials and did not notice others leaving. To my horror, I realized that the Prime Minister was waiting for me to leave. Peng Chen and Marshal Ho Lung had their disapproving eyes on me. I ran out, cursing myself.

A day or two later, I accompanied the charge d'affaires for his meeting with Chou En-lai. It was a meeting made memorable by a curious incident. When Chou En-lai asked about the results of the recently concluded Kerala Assembly elections, the charge d'affaires said that we had not received any results. The Prime Minister, however, without referring to any notes, rolled out the details party wise!

Chou En-lai was the most engaging, sophisticated and brilliant diplomat among his peers. With the passing of each year, his prestige only grew. While he only implemented the foreign policy laid down by Mao Tse Tung, he was nevertheless the most visible Chinese leader on the international scene.

I, along with Meira Mallik and Darshan Bhutani, spent six months learning Chinese as a day scholar at the Peking University, the best known in China—Peita is its Chinese name. The campus is beautiful, with willow trees bending gracefully in the wind. Mao Tse Tung was a librarian in Peita in 1918-1920. Peita's alumni have the reputation of being student rebels. The last example of their rebellion was in June 1989, when they occupied Tiananmen Square and demanded the end of totalitarianism. Deng Xiaoping ruthlessly suppressed the revolt.

Classes started at 7 a.m. I drove two IFS colleagues in my Volkswagen to Peita. Not one of our teachers spoke English. The course was demanding. All three managed to pass the final examination. The Chinese students lived in overcrowded dormitories and ate while standing in the dining room, as chairs were in short supply. They lived very Spartan lives and were not permitted to mix with foreign students. Our course included the writings of Mao Chu Si—Chairman Mao. The great man's prose was like glue, and for newcomers a challenge. 'A revolution is not the same as inviting people to dinner, or writing an essay or painting a picture... A revolution is an insurrection, an act of violence by which one class overthrows another,' he wrote in 1954. In 1938, he declared, 'Every Communist must grasp the truth, "political power grows out of the barrel of a gun".' It is one of his best-known statements and one of the most deadly.

In February 1958, I had got reasonably good marks both in the written and the oral tests for advanced Chinese. The results were sent to the School of Foreign Languages of the Ministry of Defence. The Director of the school asked for the qualifications and names of the Chinese examiners. Ashok Bhadkamkar, councillor in the Embassy, replied, 'We do not know the qualifications of the examiners but the names are Mao Tse Tung and Chou En-lai.'

4

BACK TO SOUTH BLOCK

My posting in China lasted for twenty-two months and, on 2 May 1958, I left Peking, both happy as well as sad. Mao Tse Tung's China had impressed me; it had also depressed me. I caught a P&O ship in Hong Kong after spending a memorable day with Han Suyin. After seventeen days, I reached Bombay and stayed with Krishna Hutheesing for a couple of days.

◆

On 31 March 1959, I escorted the IFS probationers of the 1958 batch for their meeting with Jawaharlal Nehru in his South Block office. He had by now given up the practice of meeting probationers individually. During this meeting, the Foreign Secretary, Subimal Dutt, walked in and whispered something to Nehru, and the Prime Minister announced that he had to leave for Parliament to attend to an important matter. The probationers and I were left to speculate, but the mystery was soon resolved: His Holiness the Dalai Lama had crossed the Indo-Tibet border on the same morning with a large party and was seeking political asylum in India. The Chinese people reacted ferociously. Chairman Mao called Nehru 'half-man and half-devil' and the Chinese task was to wash off his face so that it wouldn't be frightening, like a devil's.

The Dalai Lama arrived in Delhi after a few days' rest in Tezpur, Assam. He was put up at Hyderabad House, and I was attached as liaison officer. The Dalai Lama spoke no English but this linguistic shortcoming in no way diminished his presence and charm: his smile was enchanting and his eyes seemed to be an extension of his smile.

I escorted him to his meetings with the Vice President, Dr S. Radhakrishnan, and the Home Minister, Pandit Gobind Ballabh Pant.

In spite of the decades that have elapsed since, the Pant-Dalai Lama meeting is still fresh in my memory. The Home Minister—wise, astute and unhurried—was an influential and powerful member of Nehru's government, second only to the Prime Minister. Apart from the interpreter and myself, there were only a couple of other people present in the room. The Dalai Lama, mature beyond his years, expressed his anxiety and deep concern about the plight of his people and China's total disregard for human rights. Pantji listened and said that the people and government held His Holiness in high esteem; granting him political asylum was a public acknowledgement of that. At this stage, Pantji paused, pointed a finger in my direction, and asked, 'Tum kaun ho (who are you)?' It turned out that he was referring to the person sitting behind me. The Dalai Lama's face turned red when the man identified himself as a PTI reporter. He and the Home Minister were discussing top secret affairs. I had expected the Home Minister to ask the intruding reporter to leave the room but he did not do so. Instead, Pantji requested the Dalai Lama to continue.

As the meeting concluded, the Home Minister asked the reporter to stay back and, in icy tones, conveyed his severe displeasure, warning him against reporting about the meeting. The man left in deep shock, and nothing appeared in the press.

I was at first puzzled that Pantji had allowed the reporter to stay in the room even after he had been identified. Then the penny dropped. Had he asked the reporter to leave the room, he would have run to the nearest telephone to file the story immediately. Pandit Pant knew that. He dealt with a somewhat tricky development with breathtaking sure-footedness. He won my whole-hearted respect that morning.

China receded into the background for a short while when US President Dwight D. Eisenhower arrived on a state visit in December, the first American President to do so. However, the euphoria of Eisenhower's visit did not last long. Ominous clouds were gathering on the Sino-Indian horizon. The breaking point had not been reached, yet the future looked bleak. Chou En-lai invited Nehru to visit China. Due to other commitments, Nehru had to decline, but he invited Chou to visit India instead. Chou En-lai accepted Nehru's invitation to come to New Delhi for talks to resolve the Sino-Indian border dispute, arriving on 20 April 1960, accompanied by the outspoken Foreign Minister, Marshal Chen Yi. However, he could not resist reminding Nehru that this was his third visit to India, whereas Nehru had been to China only once. The reception at Palam airport was correct but cool. Chou En-lai's speech was more friendly than that of Jawaharlal Nehru's. I quote S. Gopal on this visit:

> It was against this background of general ill-will towards India that [C]hou came to Delhi in April. It was to be the last meeting of these two men, with so much in common—

intelligence, finesse, sensitivity to wider issues; easily, at that time, the world's two most intellectual Prime Ministers. But [C]hou had always a clearer idea than Nehru of where power and interest lay, and by now they had become paired antagonists locked together. Only the stylized courtesies were maintained in a chill atmosphere.*

I had been deputed as liaison officer attached to the Chinese Prime Minister. R.N. Kao was the security officer. While I have written at length about this doomed visit in *My China Dairy*, I will mention one or two incidents here.

Nehru told the Chinese PM that some of his senior Cabinet ministers would call on him. Being the shrewd man that he was, Chou insisted that he would call on them instead. I accompanied Chou when he met Vice President S. Radhakrishnan, Home Minister Gobind Ballabh Pant and Finance Minister Morarji Desai. Though not one of them was familiar with the complexities of the Sino-Indian border, they chose to go into the specifics. The Vice President and the Finance Minister thus succeeded in irritating the Chinese Prime Minister. The Vice President began by saying that the Sino-Indian border problem should be settled during Prime Minister Nehru's lifetime. The Chinese leaders found this incomprehensible. The Vice President said that the two countries had no conflict in two thousand years and war would be no solution. To this the Foreign Minister of China, Marshal Chen Yi, replied that China did not want war. He had first-hand knowledge of war. For thirty years the Communist Party of China had fought against the Chiang Kai-shek government and the Japanese imperialists. He himself had seen his wife and son being executed across a river. The Vice President then asked what 400

---

*Sarvepalli Gopal, *Jawaharlal Nehru: A Biography*, Volume 3, New Delhi: Oxford University Press, 2012

square miles of territory was compared to the friendship of 400 million Indians. Premier Chou En-lai replied what were a few thousand acres of land compared to the friendship of 600 million Chinese. The Vice President was no match for Chou En-lai.

The Vice President was somewhat condescending and his generalizations were laced with philosophical sentimentality. Morarji Desai was at his self-righteous worst. He was abrasive and uncouth and I was aghast at his behaviour. After the unpropitious encounter with Morarji Desai, Chou En-lai said to me, 'I am discussing the border question with Prime Minister Nehru. Why are my courtesy calls being used to lecture me?' I had this query conveyed to the Prime Minister.

It was on the third day of the visit that a cartoon depicting Chou En-lai as a snake appeared on the front page of a national newspaper. In another cartoon, he was shown with a broad grin, coming out of Teen Murti House after a session with Nehru. The two cartoons were offensive by any standard, and the normally imperturbable Chou was livid: 'If I come out smiling, I am criticized. If I do not smile, I am criticized. Why do such things appear in your newspapers?' he asked me. My response was that we had a free press, and that even Nehru had been lampooned. With some asperity, Chou En-lai asked, 'Do you think this proper?' I kept quiet.

The failure of those talks is one of the most painful episodes of Indian history. They broke down irretrievably. The fact was that Chou En-lai outwitted the Indian Prime Minister because he had the facts on his fingertips and set off a chain of events that spiralled into the disastrous Indo-China War of 1962.

On 25 April at 10.30 p.m. Chou En-lai addressed a hastily summoned press conference which ended at 1 a.m. the next day. It began with a lengthy statement, which enumerated what were called the six points of proximity.

These were:

1. There exist disputes with regard to the boundary between the two sides.
2. There exists between the two countries a line of actual control up to which each side exercises administrative jurisdiction.
3. In determining the boundary between the two counties, certain geographical principles such as watersheds, river valleys and mountain passes, should be equally applicable to all sectors of the boundary.
4. A settlement of the boundary question between the two countries should take into account the national feelings of the two peoples towards the Himalayas and the Karakoram Mountain.
5. Pending a settlement of the boundary question between the two countries through discussion, both sides should keep to the line of actual control and should not put forward territorial claims as pre-conditions, but individual adjustment may be made.
6. In order to ensure tranquillity on the border so as to facilitate the discussions, both sides should continue to refrain from patrolling along all sectors of the boundary.

The joint communiqué issued on the last full day of the visit, 25 April 1960, was notable for a major omission—it made no reference to the Five Principles of Peaceful Coexistence. It was believed India was not agreeable to its inclusion since, in its view, the occupation of Indian territory by China was a violation of the principles and their inclusion would amount to condoning it. The communiqué said that the two Prime Ministers explained 'their respective stands on the problems affecting the border areas', noted the failure of the talks 'in resolving the differences that

(*above*): K. Natwar Singh's father, Govind Singh, and mother, Prayag Kaur

(*below*): K. Natwar Singh with his brothers Girdhar Singh, Bharat Singh and Bhagwat Singh, 1950

(*above*): Govind Niwas, Bharatpur
(*above right*): Scindia School, Gwalior

(*above*): Mayo College, Ajmer

(*left*): St Stephen's College, New Delhi
(*below*): Corpus Christi College, Cambridge

(*above left*): Delhi State Junior Tennis Champion, 1949; (*above right*): Graduating from St Stephen's College, 1951

(*below*): As part of the tennis team, Corpus Christi College, 1954

(*above*): Hem, at the Red Fort, 1964

(*facing page top*): K. Natwar Singh and Hem, with Indira Gandhi as a witness at their wedding, 21 August 1967

(*facing page below*): Maharani of Patiala, K. Natwar Singh, Indira Gandhi, Hem, and Maharaja of Patiala, 21 August 1967

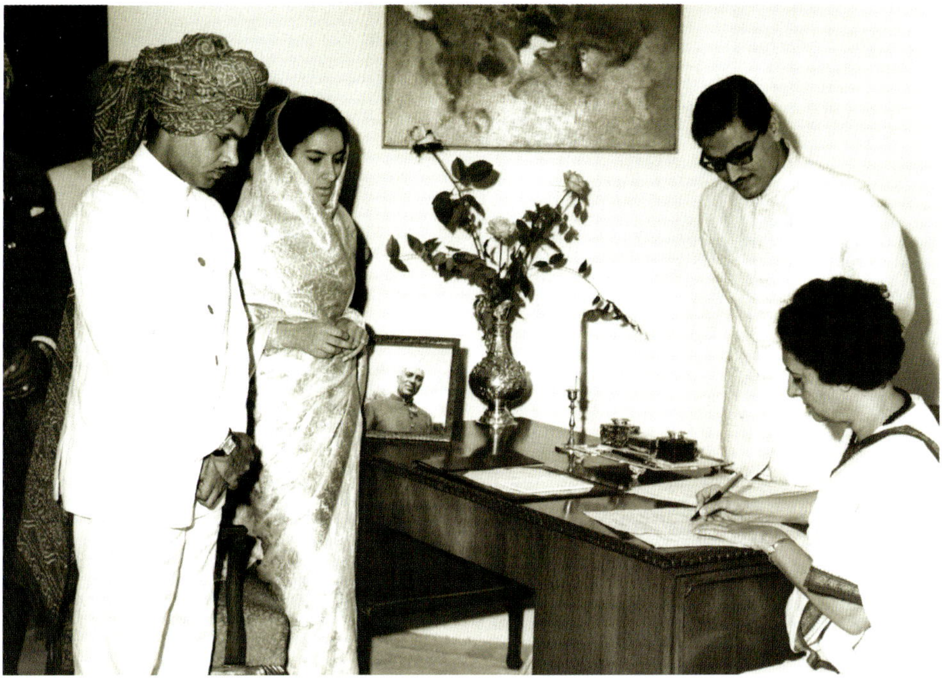

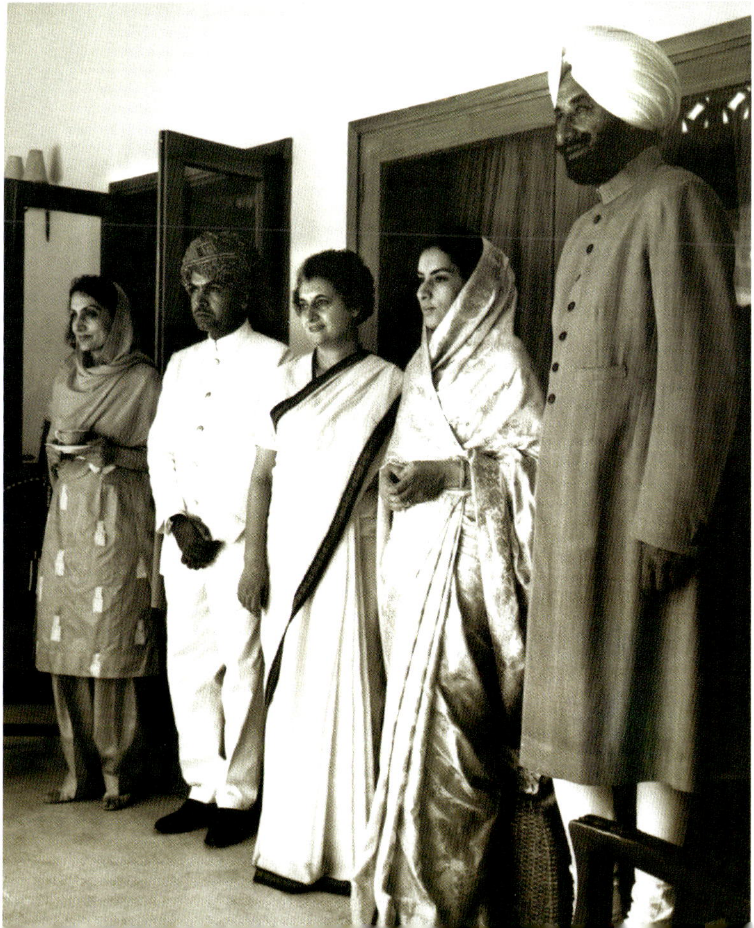

(*above*): Hem and K. Natwar Singh with K. Natwar Singh's mother Prayag Kaur holding Jagat, 1968

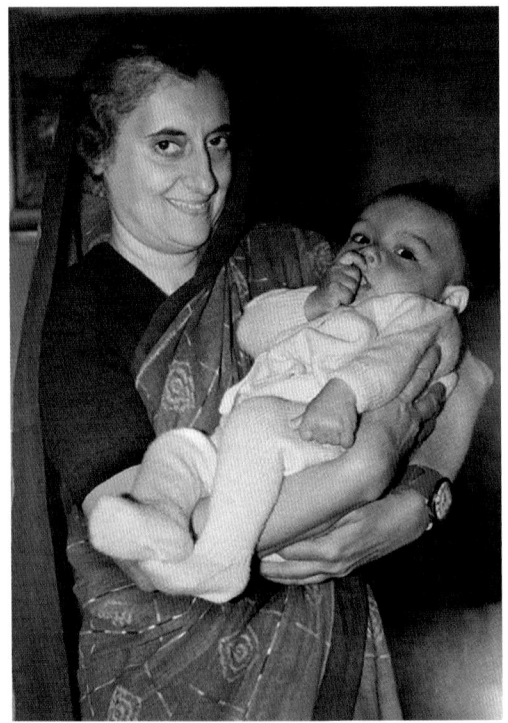

(*below*): K. Natwar Singh and Hem with Jagat, 1968

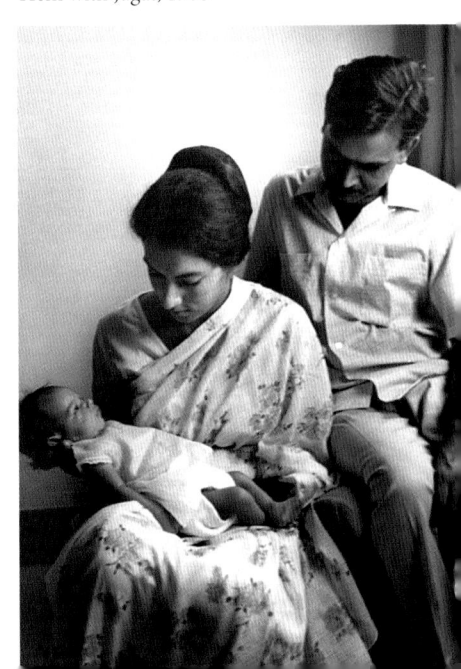

(*above*): Indira Gandhi with Jagat, 1969

(*above*): Moti Bagh Palace, Patiala

(*right*): (left to right) Maharaja Yadavindra Singh, Hem, Maharaja Amarinder Singh, Harpriya Kaur, K. Natwar Singh, Preenet Kaur, Raja Malvinder Singh; front row: Major Kanwaljeet Singh Dhillon, Maharani Mohinder Kaur, Rupinder Kumari

(*above*): Ritu and Jagat
(*right*): With Hem, Jagat and Ritu, London, 1974

Jagat with his sons, Himmat and Hanut

had arisen' and the consequent need for further examination of the factual material.

Nehru himself conceded that he had unwisely not taken Parliament into confidence earlier. For this error, he paid heavily in 1962.

5

AT THE UNITED NATIONS

WE THE PEOPLES OF THE UNITED NATIONS DETERMINED

- to save succeeding generations from the scourge of war, which twice in our lifetime has brought untold sorrow to mankind, and
- to reaffirm faith in fundamental human rights, in the dignity and worth of the human person, in the equal rights of men and women and of nations large and small, and
- to establish conditions under which justice and respect for the obligations arising from treaties and other sources of international law can be maintained, and
- to promote social progress and better standards of life in larger freedom,

AND FOR THESE ENDS

- to practice tolerance and live together in peace with one another as good neighbours, and

- to unite our strength to maintain international peace and security, and
- to ensure, by the acceptance of principles and the institution of methods, that armed force shall not be used, save in the common interest, and
- to employ international machinery for the promotion of the economic and social advancement of all peoples.

WE HAVE RESOLVED TO COMBINE OUR EFFORTS TO ACCOMPLISH THESE AIMS

Accordingly, our respective Governments, through representatives assembled in the city of San Francisco, who have exhibited their full powers found to be in good and due form, have agreed to the present Charter of the United Nations and do hereby establish an international organization to be known as the United Nations.

Having completed three years at headquarters, I was posted to London as Private Secretary to Vijaya Lakshmi Pandit, the High Commissioner. She turned me down as I was close to her sister, Krishna Hutheesing, with whom she didn't get along. Both sisters had a well-developed streak of self-destructiveness, which made them say and do things which, in calmer moments, they no doubt regretted. Their temperaments were very different, but both were given to inspired indiscretion. Instead of London, the ministry posted me to the Permanent Mission to the UN, a much more worthwhile job.

I arrived in New York on 21 August 1961 and spent nearly five years there. For any diplomat, the UN is the best university the globe has to offer.

I landed in New York with an inbuilt prejudice against the Yankees. My intellectual centre of gravity was Cambridge, England, rather than Cambridge, Massachusetts. Not only that, I was also hugely critical and disdainful of US foreign policy. Manhattan, with its bridges, buildings, its frenetic pace, its glamour, intensity, wealth, Broadway, the Empire State Building and the skyscrapers, was impressive. However, I was not overwhelmed, and for several months took a supercilious and superficial view of the city. Yet, New York grew on me and I fell for the city.

The sixteenth annual session of the General Assembly was to begin on 19 September 1961. Just two days short of this, the Secretary General, Dag Hammarskjöld, perished in a plane crash near Ndola (Zambia). This cast a pall of gloom over the session, particularly as Dag was much admired. He was subtle, cultured, widely read and intuitively wise enough to espouse the cause of history. He stood up to Nikita Khrushchev in a debate on Congo in the General Assembly in November 1960 when Khrushchev had vilified him: 'If he himself cannot muster the courage to resign in, let us say, a chivalrous way, we shall draw the inevitable conclusions from the situation. There is no room for a man who has violated the elementary principles of justice in such an important post as that of the Secretary General.' Hammarskjöld replied the next day: 'The representative of the Soviet Union spoke of courage. It is very easy to resign. It is not easy to stay on. It is easy to bow to the wish of a big power. It is another matter to resist. By resigning, I would...at the present difficult and dangerous juncture throw the Organization to the winds. I have no right to do so...' The General Assembly gave him a five-minute standing ovation.

The vacancy caused by the death of Dag Hammarskjöld was filled by the gentle Buddhist, U Thant of Burma. One or two misguided Indian aspirants cut very sorry figures. Krishna Menon was keen for Arthur Lal, one of his favourite Indian Ambassadors, to get the job, but he found no takers, and the proposal was

AT THE UNITED NATIONS

dead the moment it was made. Next, he attempted to push the name of M. Chacko, a Malayali Christian, who held a junior post in the UN. This proposal provoked uninhibited laughter. Another undeclared person who was keen to get to the thirty-eighth floor of the UN building was Braj Kumar Nehru. In his autobiography, *Nice Guys Finish Second*, he claims that Krishna Menon, of all people, asked him if he would like to be Secretary General, and regrets woefully his mistake in showing no interest in the job. How a man of such experience and wisdom could convince himself that he was done out of the job by his own folly is beyond me. Anyone acquainted with the functioning of the UN would be aware of the unwritten rule that the UN Secretary General must come from a small country.

◆

R.K. Narayan was in town. He opened several doors for me. We had re-established contact when he came to Delhi in March 1961 to receive the Sahitya Akademi Award for the best book in English for his novel, *The Guide*. At the time, I had asked him if there was anything I could do for him while he was in Delhi. He was keen to meet Prime Minister Jawaharlal Nehru and see the Mughal Gardens in Rashtrapati Bhavan. Somehow, I managed both. I took him to Teen Murti House, where Pandit Nehru confessed that he had not read any of R.K.'s novels, though his niece, Tara, had. He introduced Indira Gandhi to R.K. as well. R.K. had been very pleased and excited by the meeting. He asked me to send him the photographs taken on the occasion. This was atypical because normally he avoided publicity. That is why, a few years later, I was surprised when he did not mention it in his autobiography, *My Days*. I spoke to R.K. about it. He said it never occurred to him to exploit the occasion and, in any case, he could not have woven the incident into the narrative. All I could say was that modesty need not be carried to such extremes.

In the late summer of 1962, actor-director Dev Anand was in New York. He contacted me as he had heard that I was a friend of R.K. Narayan. He asked if I could give him a letter of introduction as he wanted to adapt R.K.'s novel, *The Guide*, into a film. I obliged. R.K.'s reply was encouraging: 'It was awfully good of you to have given my address to Dev Anand, who wrote to me and then met me and we have arrived at a very satisfactory arrangement for the production of *The Guide* both in Hindi and English.'

Through R.K. I came to know James T. Farrell, the marvellously unkempt author of *Studs Lonigan*, which he wrote at the age of twenty-six. R.K. also introduced me to Santha Rama Rau. For over a decade and a half, Santha was the best-known Indian writer in English in the US. Her father, Sir Benegal Rama Rau, had been the Indian Ambassador to the US. Santha was herself educated in the US and settled in New York after marrying Faubion Bowers, himself an author. It was as good a beginning as I could hope for in a new environment and uncharted territory.

Santha became a close friend. Her marriage was, to use an Americanism, on the rocks. She consumed vast amounts of alcohol, beginning at breakfast. As a result, her writing suffered. She needed a shoulder to lean on and selected mine. To her, I was an understanding fellow Indian. In our friendship, emotion took precedence over passion. She was vulnerable; the least I could do was try to help her. It was a beautiful friendship. We were, on many aspects of life, on the same side.

Santha introduced me to Raja Rao of *Kanthapura* fame. She was regularly reviewing books for the *New York Times Book Review* and the *Saturday Review*. She suggested to them that I should be included on their list of book reviewers. I reviewed books for both between 1962 and 1966.

I remember Santha taking R.K. and me to a party hosted by John Gunther (famous for his 'Inside Books') and his wife at their magnificent apartment. Assembled were many well-known, beautiful, powerful, glamorous, rich, bitchy authors, actors, diplomats and eccentric musicians. Santha introduced me to Moura Budberg, the mistress of H.G. Wells. A little later, I saw her talking to another beautiful lady and asked her who she was. 'Greta Garbo, you dope,' said Santha. Garbo was a legend, seldom seen in public. R.K. told me that he was teaching Garbo yoga.

Santha passed away in New York in 2011 at the age of eighty-five. I often think of our wonderful platonic friendship. She was one of the least vain women I have known.

◆

The General Assembly session was electrified by speeches given by President John F. Kennedy and Che Guevara. The world was besotted with both, albeit for different reasons. Kennedy's inaugural speech: 'Ask not what your country can do for you…' still resonates. I remember the elegance and vigour of his personality and his charisma. Che Guevara was already a cult figure then. He spoke at some length, chiding and needling Adlai Stevenson, the US delegate, for the Bay of Pigs fiasco. Kennedy's was not an easy act to follow, but the huge General Assembly Hall was packed for Che.

In November, Pandit Nehru, accompanied by Indira Gandhi, arrived in the US for talks with President Kennedy, who had spoken of Prime Minister Nehru's 'soaring idealism'. Kennedy remarked that Nehru's was the worst visit of any leader he had hosted. The PM was jaded, tired and made a dull after-dinner speech. His address to the UN General Assembly too was serviceable, though uninspiring. B.K. Nehru had arranged for the boldest and the brightest in Kennedy's White House to be at the breakfast with PM Nehru. They were all very excited about meeting him. But the PM remained silent. It was clear that he was past his prime. He was exceptionally affectionate when I asked him to sign some photographs of his that I had taken. This was the last time that I saw him.

On 19 December 1961 all hell broke loose at the UN, and the Americans moved a resolution in the Security Council condemning India's liberation of Goa and two other Portuguese enclaves. The British delegate invoked a sixteenth-century Anglo-Portuguese treaty which laid down that an attack on one country would be considered an attack on the other. What surprised us in the Indian delegation was that two great democracies were defending Portuguese colonialism. The Soviet delegate, Z.A. Zorin, vetoed the resolution that was condemning India's getting rid of Portuguese colonialism. The reaction in the Western world against India was virulent.

As B.K. Nehru later wrote:

> There was hardly any necessity for me to explain our case to the State Department; they knew it well and undoubtedly sympathised with our predicament. I went to the President to give him our point of view. This also was really unnecessary because he knew our case as well as I did. When I said that I hoped he was not annoyed with us, like the rest of the country seemed to be, he said, 'Not at all. I am not in the least bit annoyed because I understand your case. You have done now what you should have done fourteen years ago. But you spent those fourteen years preaching morality to us and telling us how wrong it is to use force in one's

own interests. Now you have done exactly what any other country would have done and used violence to further your interests. The result is that the country is saying that the minister (preacher) has been caught coming out of the brothel and people are clapping. And, Mr Ambassador, I wish to tell you that I am clapping with them.'*

By the time the sixteenth session concluded, I was beginning to learn the messy art of multilateral diplomacy. One of the requirements was to be able to think on your feet and come up with instant answers during interviews on complex issues. Throughout my diplomatic career, I was repeatedly told that a good diplomat should think twice before saying nothing. At the UN, the lesson was to speak, and speak even when speech made little sense. Debates in the special political committee kept me busy. The ones on South Africa's apartheid policy and the Arab-Israel conflict produced more heat and less light, but were rightly taken seriously. The Palestine debates were acrimonious and noisy. The seating arrangement also contributed to the simmering tension. Iceland, India, Indonesia, Iran, Iraq and Israel sat in the same row, in alphabetical order. The last two were fiery antagonists, and strong words were exchanged. The Arabs could not match Abba Eban's—the Israeli diplomat and politician—oratorical skills. In an interesting turn of events, they accused Israel of providing beautiful women to certain African countries to ensure that they sided with Israel. Alas, no such allurements were offered to the Indian delegate on the committee!

◆

*B.K. Nehru, *Nice Guys Finish Second: Memoirs*, New Delhi: Penguin Books India, 1997

Even as events in the UN continued apace, New York was creeping into my consciousness. I went house-hunting and finally found one—404, E66 Street between First and York Avenues. It was in an upper-crust area, and only a twelve-minute walk from the UN offices. I didn't face the problems that some of my African colleagues at the UN had while looking for accommodation. While at the UN there was absolutely no discrimination on the grounds of skin colour, the same could not be said of smart hotels, restaurants, theatres and hospitals. For African diplomats, at the time, diplomatic level playing fields did not exist. Finding apartments was a humiliating experience. An African delegate, Harry Stow, told me of his ordeal: no fewer than eighteen apartment owners shut the door on him when they saw that he was black. It made him bitter.

In December, the General Assembly set up a committee to specifically deal with colonies, protectorates, etcetera. It was to be known as the Committee on Decolonization, or the Committee of Seventeen. India was to be one of the seventeen, and Indian Ambassador C.S. Jha was unanimously elected Chairman. The establishment of the committee was inspired by a proposal made at the fifteenth session of the General Assembly by Nikita Khrushchev in 1960.

The committee soon took over the work of the Trusteeship Council. The members included the US, the UK, the USSR, and several African and Latin American countries. C.S. Jha was succeeded by Soli Coulibaly from Mali. A soft-spoken man, Coulibaly came from one of the poorest countries in the world. I was India's representative on the committee.

The committee soon acquired teeth. Its deliberations were followed with extraordinary interest in all colonial territories. Between February and September 1962, it examined the situation in twelve territories, eleven of them in Africa. The twelfth was

AT THE UNITED NATIONS

Singapore and Malaysia.

In the summer, the committee toured three countries in Africa, which I had never visited before. Our first halt was Morocco. The first session was held in Tangier. From Tangier, Gibraltar is a few hours away. We spent half a day in Rabat el Fatif, where we called on the young Sultan. It was during that trip that Moroccan cuisine became a personal favourite, particularly couscous. The country was beautiful; the Kasbah had its own character, and its narrow lanes reminded me of Chandni Chowk.

Our next destination was Casablanca. I asked to see the villa where Winston Churchill and Franklin D. Roosevelt had stayed in January 1943. It was at this historic location that Churchill and Roosevelt met two French Generals, Charles de Gaulle and Henri Giraud, to broker peace. Eventually, de Gaulle would send Giraud into oblivion. In what came to be known as the Casablanca Declaration, the Allied powers declared that they would not rest until they had achieved the 'unconditional surrender' of the Axis powers.

Our last stop was Marrakech. In this glorious, enchanting, alluring city—even though snakes and scorpions were not in short supply—one could witness the most wonderful sunsets over the Atlas mountains. I stayed there in the fabulous Al-Mamounia Hotel where Roosevelt and Churchill, too, once stayed, and met. I have not been to Morocco since 1962, but the spell cast on me by the country has not deserted my memory. It's among the most agreeable countries to holiday in.

We flew over the Sahara before touching down at Addis Ababa, the capital of Ethiopia and headquarters of the Organisation of African Unity. The highlight of our three-day stay was an audience with His Imperial Majesty, Elect of God, Conquering Lion of the Tribe of Juda, King of Zion, Negusa Nagast—King of Kings—the Emperor of Ethiopia, Haile Selassie I.

All members of the committee were enthused at the prospect of meeting so legendary a personality. His appearance at the League of Nations before World War II and his defiance of Mussolini had won him accolades in the non-Fascist, non-Nazi world. The protocol at the Emperor's palace was elaborate and strictly adhered to. The Ethiopian representative on the committee briefed us on how to approach the Emperor, how to withdraw, and how to stand—we were forbidden from putting our hands in our pockets. Coming from an Indian princely state, I was not overawed, but the others were. The Soviet, Polish and Yugoslav representatives were alarmed and apprehensive. Bowing before a feudal was unthinkable. In the end, however, bow they did. One East European delegate asked me how he should address Haile Selassie. I told him, 'Comrade Emperor will do.'

I stayed with Ambassador R.G. Rajwade. He came from the twenty-one-gun-salute state of Gwalior, and was thus accustomed to the demands of Maharajas. He regaled me with an account of his first audience with the Emperor. Before an Ambassador can begin his formal duties, he has to present his credentials to the Head of State. Rajwade went decked up in a black achkan, churidar pyjamas and a turban. The Emperor received Ambassadors sitting on his golden throne, with two Ethiopian lions sitting next to him. Most Ambassadors not only dreaded this ordeal, they panicked when they saw the two lions licking their lips. India's Ambassador behaved differently. He walked up to His Imperial Majesty, read his speech and handed to the emperor his letters of credence, signed by the President of India. He then withdrew. At this stage, the two lions got up to follow the Ambassador. This was the moment when all the other Ambassadors broke into a cold sweat and were all but ready to run. Rajwade did nothing of the sort; he walked nonchalantly. This was too much for the Chief of Protocol, used as he was to seeing Ambassadors collapse with fear. He said to Rajwade, 'Your Excellency, do you not see the two lions who are following us?'

Rajwade replied, 'Excellency, Mr Chief of Protocol, I recognize no lions. I have eyes only for the Lion of Juda.' From then onwards, he was shown unusual respect by the Emperor's establishment.

Our committee did not receive the lion treatment. We were too insignificant. At our audience, the Emperor walked in with two Chihuahuas, who hardly noticed the lowly diplomats. These tiny quadrupeds were treated with much deference by the Emperor's staff. We were made to stand in alphabetical order. His Majesty said a few words in Amharic and withdrew. Kifle Wodajo, the Ethiopian delegate in the committee, almost crawled while approaching his Emperor. He walked backwards, bowing, without looking at the Emperor. It was quite an experience for our Western friends. Even in 1962, all traffic stopped when the Emperor was on his way to a function. My driver stopped the car, got out, and lay down flat on the ground, as did all others in the vicinity.

The committee then proceeded to Dar es Salaam, the capital of Tanzania. Julius Nyerere was then heading the government of the newly independent country. He was by any standards a man of consequence. While an eloquent speaker, he was somewhat tautological—he had been a schoolmaster at one time. A committed socialist, Nyerere possessed all the qualities needed for him to become an African statesman—he almost did. Several petitioners from Southern and Northern Rhodesia (now Zimbabwe), Nyasaland (now Malawi), Basutoland (now Lesotho), Bechuanaland (now Botswana), Zanzibar, Mozambique, Southwest Africa and Angola appeared before the committee in the Tanzanian capital. None had been permitted by the colonial powers to travel to New York. The stories of the miseries inflicted on them by the whites were heartrending. Jayaprakash Narayan, in suit and tie, also appeared before the committee.

One incident in Dar es Salaam has remained in my memory. For a minor stomach upset, I was advised to go to the main hospital. The nurse who attended me was a foolish Englishwoman. Her manners matched her accent. 'You there, what's wrong with you?' she bleated. I told her off. Sheepishly, she apologized. Tanzania was no longer a colony but the colonial odour had not dissipated.

I returned to New York via Athens, Rome, Geneva and London. Except for London, I was seeing these cities for the first time.

My African journey made me even more critical of the colonial powers. Whites, who in their respective countries would have been porters and petty traders, lived in Africa like pashas. Their treatment of Africans was so appalling it almost made me sick. In Africa, their behaviour was shameful. What was extraordinary was that, even in 1962, the British were justifying their policies of oppression—from Fiji to Mauritius, from Trinidad and Tobago to Rhodesia. They were lecturing us on human rights, having paid no heed to them for three hundred years. I constantly crossed verbal swords with the British delegates on the committee. In one of my speeches I quoted Bernard Shaw:

> There is nothing so bad or so good that you will not find Englishmen doing it; but you will never find an Englishman in the wrong. He does everything on principle. He fights you on patriotic principles; he robs you on business principles; he bullies you on manly principles; he supports his king on royal principles and cuts off his king's head on republican principles. His watchword is always Duty; and he never forgets that the nation which lets its duty get on the opposite side to its interest is lost.

AT THE UNITED NATIONS

♦

In the first week of October 1962, C. Rajagopalachari (Rajaji) arrived in New York. He was leading the Gandhi Peace Foundation delegation which was to press for a total ban on nuclear tests. At that time, Rajaji's professional relations with Pandit Nehru were strained, but their personal relationship remained unimpaired. The PM had instructed the concerned embassies to extend all support to Rajaji. India was short on foreign exchange and the delegation was sanctioned limited hard currency. Wherever possible, Ambassadors were asked to put up Rajaji and his colleagues. The Ambassador to the UN was B.N. Chakravarty. He had been Rajaji's private secretary when Rajaji was Governor of West Bengal, fifteen years earlier. Rajaji should have stayed with Chakravarty, who had recently taken up his new assignment. However, since Chakravarty was then living in a hotel, he asked me if I could accommodate Rajaji in my apartment, which I willingly agreed to.

Rajaji spent nearly five days in New York. This was his first visit outside India, with the exception of Ceylon. I was curious to see how the old world would cope with the new world. He arrived wearing a brown achkan and, to my great surprise, woollen trousers. The trousers were discarded the next day—he found them too uncomfortable. It was back to dhotis.

I saw much of Rajaji at close quarters and what I saw I liked. His lifestyle resembled that of a rishi. He never put on an act. His manners were impeccable and his speech gentle and soft. He was never condescending or patronizing. Like Nehru, he was always punctual.

I asked him to write his autobiography or dictate his reminiscences. He had played such an active, at times decisive, role in recent Indian history; he owed it to the nation to leave behind an account. I reminded him that Mahatma Gandhi and Jawaharlal Nehru had written their autobiographies. He said he really did not have enough time. I told him that he would have had plenty of time when he was Governor General. With a smile on his face, he said he spent much of his time patching up the quarrels between the PM and the Deputy PM.

Another day, we discussed the Partition of India. To provoke him, I said Lord Mountbatten sold Partition to Nehru and Sardar Patel. Rajaji replied, 'Let me tell you, Natwar Singh, I sold Partition to Mountbatten. The Attlee government had already made up its mind to transfer power, but did not know how to go about it.' Mountbatten had asked Rajaji how to break the impasse. He said Partition was the only solution. I said that Gandhiji had been against Partition. Why had he suddenly given in? This had come as a great shock even to my teenage self. Rajaji said Gandhiji had been aware of what was going on in the minds of Pandit Nehru and Patel and other members of the Working Committee. Only Maulana Abul Kalam Azad, Khan Abdul Ghaffar Khan and Jayaprakash Narayan had been against Partition. Gandhi had been very disillusioned. He left Delhi for Calcutta before 15 August. His dream of a united India lay shattered.

Rajaji suffered from asthma. During his first imprisonment in 1921, he was locked up in a cell from six in the evening to six in the morning. There was no electricity, the cell was full of mosquitoes, and the humidity aggravated his asthma. I was taken aback when he told me he had thought of committing suicide. In those days medicines were not available in India for curing ailments. It was only by following a very strict diet and by relying on his enormous willpower that he got over his affliction.

The only time I had an argument with him was about Goa. Rajaji strongly condemned our action of sending in troops to liberate Goa. I vigorously defended the government's decision, but he did not hold it against me.

A stream of people came to meet Rajaji in New York. The first was Vincent Sheen, the author of *Lead Kindly Light*, a biography of Gandhi. Sheen claimed that he had asked Pandit Nehru to send Rajaji as Ambassador to Washington. Rajaji felt he was not cut out for the post. It was many years later that I came across the letters that Sheen had exchanged with Pandit Nehru discussing the matter. From them, it became clear that his appointment as Ambassador to Washington had been seriously considered. It was also clear that Rajaji would have been a complete misfit as an Ambassador.

The other people Rajaji met during his sojourn were Robert Oppenheimer, the father of the atom bomb, and Louis Fischer, the author of a biography of Mahatma Gandhi. He had stayed with Mahatma at Wardha in 1942 and his book became a bestseller. Norman Cousins, editor of the influential weekly magazine *Saturday Review*, the advocate of world peace, U Thant; Adlai Stevenson; and Sir Muhammad Zafarulla Khan, whom he had known before Partition, also visited.

From New York, Rajaji went to Washington to meet President Kennedy. Kennedy had been briefed about Rajaji's mission. From all accounts, Rajaji's advocacy was lucid and to the point. The President said he agreed in principle with Rajaji but there existed serious problems. The US could not unilaterally stop nuclear tests; the USSR, too, must stop testing. How far Rajaji influenced Kennedy is not known.

Before leaving New York, Rajaji gave me his book, *The Voice of the Uninvolved*. In it, he wrote, 'As a memento of the happy days I spent in your apartment in New York and in grateful memory of your hospitality and help.'

I was Ambassador to Poland when the news of his death

reached me on 26 December 1972. He was ninety-four years old. I felt sad—it had been such a pleasure and privilege to know him, to correspond with him, to discuss books, authors and politics. I acquired wisdom rather slowly; some of it I definitely imbibed from Rajaji.

◆

The Security Council met on Tuesday, 23 October 1962. The atmosphere was charged, the tension was scorching, and the debate riveting. That day, I was in the Security Council chamber where the Cuban crisis was being debated. Adlai Stevenson asked Zorin, 'Do you, Ambassador Zorin, deny that the USSR has placed and is placing medium- and intermediate-range missiles and sites in Cuba? Yes or no? Don't wait for the translation.' He then produced photographs of the sites. Zorin faced an impossible situation; his government had kept him in the dark. The Cuban Missile Crisis lasted thirteen agonizing days and the world came very near a nuclear war. Kennedy kept his nerve to the end and the Soviet Union lost out. Khrushchev's position in the Politburo was weakened.

China's attack on India could not and did not take precedence over the Cuban Missile Crisis at the UN. We were getting small doses of patchy information. I remember reading in one of the New York papers that Prime Minister Nehru had allegedly said, on or around 16 October 1962, at Madras airport on his way to Sri Lanka, that he had asked the army to push the Chinese out of Indian territory. Even in the midst of the Sino-Indian border war the question of demitting the People's Republic of China to the UN came up. Our instructions were to support China's entry. It was a courageous decision, but not many at the UN appreciated it. Neither did the Chinese government. While

AT THE UNITED NATIONS

Pandit Nehru had disdain for realpolitik, the Chinese practised it in full measure.

In the UN, one got a good idea of which way the winds were blowing. Even the non-aligned countries, including Egypt, Indonesia and Ghana, did not openly support us. B.K. Nehru has claimed in *Nice Guys Finish Second* that Jawaharlal Nehru, late in 1962, had received a note from the Chief of the General Staff, Lt Gen. Verma in which he predicted a war with China. PM Nehru took no notice of Verma's note. He actually said that he did not expect a war with China during his lifetime! PM Nehru had invested much in his China policy and, when it failed, he panicked for the first time in his life. His letters to President Kennedy asking for military help made even a hardcore Nehruite like me wince in embarrassment (see Appendix 1). What made matters worse was the American media, which relished sniping at Pandit Nehru and ridiculing him.

The mood in the Permanent Mission was sombre, even depressing. At the UN, our image had taken a severe beating. This became evident at the meetings of the Commonwealth and non-aligned groups. One man who relished our discomfiture was Foreign Minister Jaja Wachuku of Nigeria. I had dubbed him the poor man's Krishna Menon. He belittled India and enjoyed doing so. (See the chapter on Nehru.)

◆

Cipher code books for our missions in South America were sent to half a dozen missions by special courier from New York. I was Head of Chancery and decided to act as courier in February 1963. No member of my family had ever been to South America. As a British colony, we had no contact with the continent. While I did not exactly feel like Columbus, I looked forward to this trip. My first halt was Port of Spain, the capital of Trinidad and Tobago, home to thousands of Indians, Calypso music and world-famous cricketers. There I bought two books by V.S. Naipaul, *The Middle Passage* and *A House for Mr Biswas*. I arrived in Rio in pouring rain and followed the well-worn tourist track—first a walk on the Copacabana beach, crowded with beautiful women in skimpy bikinis. Ambassador V.H. Coelho had put a car at my disposal and I was driven up a hill on top of which a huge statue of Jesus Christ looked down on the city, the slums of the Carioca and the blue Atlantic beyond. Buenos Aires was elegant, expensive, and an exciting blend of cultures. There were lots of Italians in the city and it was a haven for ex-Nazis. Soon after my trip, Israeli authorities captured Adolf Eichmann, the butcher of Auschwitz, in Buenos Aires. On the flight to Santiago, we flew over the snow-covered Andes. Chile is the eastern spine of the continent of South America. As the waves of the Pacific Ocean lapped at my feet, I felt as if I would drop off the edge of the world. One unpleasant fact was that the shadow of the US fell over the entire continent. These counties had no foreign policy of their own. Cuba was the exception.

I returned to New York ten days later. South America had been warm; New York was freezing. The civil rights movement was gathering momentum in the Southern states. Gregory Peck's powerful portrayal of a white lawyer defending a black man in *To Kill a Mockingbird* highlighted the blatant iniquities of democratic America. Racialism had not 'gone with the wind'. Except at the UN, African Americans were servants, bus drivers, entertainers, caddies and athletes. Arthur Ashe was the first black tennis player to appear on the tennis court at Forest Hills. Even in 1963, African Americans were considered inferior, immoral and unclean. With Kennedy in the White House, the African Americans saw hope, if not salvation.

By the summer of 1963, however, the patience of the African Americans was running thin. Martin Luther King Jr. was emerging as the black leader who not only accepted Gandhi's non-violent approach but had the commitment and courage to practise it. In the very large US Mission to the UN, there were only one or two African Americans at the diplomatic level. In the US Foreign Service, the number of African Americans was twenty-six. As the summer advanced, so did the civil rights struggle. One event on 3 May 1963, covered extensively on television, changed America. In Birmingham, Alabama, the police commissioner—a man called Conner—set his ferocious police dogs on a group of African Americans, including King, who were then engaged in a peaceful demonstration. On 4 May, a photo appeared on the front page of the *New York Times* showing a police dog lunging at an African American woman. That day, America changed. The world—with the exception of the bigots of South Africa and America's Deep South—was appalled.

Next to Martin Luther King Jr., the man who was most articulate and passionate about black rights was the young author, James Baldwin. A writer of penetrating power, he soon became a bestselling author. His book, *The Fire Next Time*, made the whites of the South squirm.

One of great events of the second half of the twentieth century occurred on 28 August 1963. Martin Luther King Jr., speaking to a crowd of a quarter million in front of the Lincoln Memorial in Washington DC, delivered one of the most inspiring and powerful speeches of the century. Even after five decades, the speech inspires. 'I have a dream that one day every valley shall be exalted, every hill and mountain shall be made low, the rough places will be made plain, and the crooked place will be made straight...

'When we let freedom ring, when we let it ring from every

village and every hamlet, from every state and every city, we will be able to speed up that day when all of God's children, black men and white men, Jews and Gentiles, Protestants and Catholics, will be able to join hands and sing in the words of that old Negro spiritual, "Free at last! Free at last! Thank God Almighty, we are free at last!".' I was among the tens of millions who saw him deliver this speech on TV and shall never forget 23 August 1963.

I met Dr King only once, in December 1964, at a reception hosted by Ambassador Adlai Stevenson at the US Mission. He was on his way to Oslo to receive the Nobel Prize for Peace. I had a word with him then, asking when he would be sending his chapter for *The Legacy of Nehru*, a book of tributes which I was then editing.

In March 1968, Martin Luther King Jr. was shot dead in Memphis, Tennessee. His death marked the closure of one of the most vibrant chapters of the American civil rights movement, and is one of the darkest episodes of American history.

◆

For the 1963 session of the UN General Assembly, the PM selected Mrs Pandit to lead the delegation. Because of the London episode, I was not particularly pleased by her arrival. I also remembered how, in April 1960, when Krishna-masi was staying with her sister in London, she wrote me a letter criticizing Mrs Pandit's lifestyle: 'It is an astounding set up—no office—shopping, parties—hair dressers—more parties—cancellation of programmes due to ill health, but no social cancellations.' In another letter, she said that Mrs Pandit '...has played another foul trick on me and stabbed me in the back. I am coming to Delhi on the 31st evening by plane—10.30 or something with

AT THE UNITED NATIONS

Raja [her husband], and am going to have it out once and for all with the PM.'

On a visit to West Germany in 1959, she was presented with a two-seater Mercedes, which she accepted. Mrs Pandit got to know of this and wrote to her brother that it would create a wrong impression if Krishna-masi was to accept the car. Krishna-masi never forgave her elder sister for what she called her 'betrayal'. The Prime Minister didn't want to get involved in the tiff between the two sisters. Eventually, Lal Bahadur Shastri, whom Pandit Nehru had deputed to sort the mess out, found a solution whereby Krishna-masi could keep the car but would have to pay import duty for it.

I had become a close friend of Rita Dar, Vijaya Lakshmi Pandit's youngest daughter. Rita's husband, Avtar Dar, was the number-two man in our Embassy in Washington. Rita was good-looking, amusing and vivacious, with a gift for diplomatic hijinks. One day, out of the blue, she telephoned to congratulate me on a book review I had done for *The New York Times*. She also said that she would be coming to New York to be with her mother during the session of the General Assembly. They would be staying at Carlyle Hotel, the elegant sanctuary of the diplomatic elite. Within a day or two, I was asked to become an ADC-cum-secretary to her mother. I was astounded. I had not even gone to receive her at the airport. I asked Rita how I had been selected to serve her mother. I also told her that I was not really looking forward to the assignment. She said she had not the foggiest idea and asked me not to worry. 'Mummy is the nicest person in the world. You will adore her.'

I cannot say that I was not a little tense when I arrived at the hotel to see the leader of the Indian delegation who greeted me with a haughty authority combined with grace. I addressed her as 'madam'.

'Stop calling me madam. What do you call Betty [Krishna]?'
'Masi,' I said.

'You can call me that too,' she replied. For the next few weeks, I spent several hours each day with her. She had last been at the UN nearly nine years earlier in 1953 when she had been elected President of the UN General Assembly. In that interval, the UN had changed. The white faces no longer dominated, as Afro-Asian members were now in a majority. Everyone at the UN was deferential to her, keen to exchange a few words with this beautiful, sophisticated woman. I soon began to enjoy myself. I met the famous and the influential in her company. She looked ten years younger than she was—elegant, stylish, vibrant, and with an amazing voice. The Nehru aura was very much in evidence. This was one of the reasons for the rivalry between the two sisters, Krishna and Vijaya Lakshmi—the elder sister was good-looking while the younger was not. Krishna-masi also lacked the touch of magic that made her elder sister so formidable a social and diplomatic star. The fame that Mrs Pandit enjoyed irked Mrs Hutheesing no end. She tried to drown her frustration in alcohol, which did her no good. She had always treated me like a son. When she died of a heart attack in London in 1967, my grief lasted many months. Her autobiography, *With No Regrets*, is a charming book.

Zulfikar Ali Bhutto, the Foreign Minister of Pakistan at the time, was leading his country's delegation at the 1963 session. Mrs Pandit had known his father, Shah Nawaz Bhutto. But the young Bhutto was cast in a different mould. He was a product of Berkeley and Oxford, a fine debater, abrasive, arrogant and sartorially striking. He had a passion for beautiful women, most of whom fell for him. He was an outstanding Foreign Minister who outwitted us in weaning China away from the US without annoying the US.

AT THE UNITED NATIONS

In his speech, he made a blistering and venomous attack on India. On the issue of Kashmir, he was offensive beyond words. Vijaya Lakshmi's Pandit's immediate reaction was to exercise her right of reply. It required a combination of tact and persuasion to dissuade her from doing so. I told her that nothing would please Bhutto more than to get a reaction from her. So, instead, she asked one of the senior secretaries to reply, to the considerable discomfiture of the Pakistanis.

◆

On 22 November 1963, I was driving to the UN and listening to the news. Suddenly, the regular programme was interrupted and it was announced that President Kennedy had been shot in Dallas, Texas. I stepped on the accelerator. On reaching the UN, I ran up to the delegates' dining room where Mrs Pandit was lunching with friends. She had already heard the news, but asked me to keep her informed on any developments. Very soon, the news of Kennedy's death was confirmed. It was a tragedy that generated grief throughout the world.

For our Embassy in Washington, the pressing question was who would represent India at the funeral. The first message from Delhi to B.K. Nehru said that he should lay a wreath on Kennedy's coffin! How completely out of sync could the MEA be? B.K. Nehru's suggestion that the Prime Minister personally attend the funeral was ignored. It was finally decided that Mrs Pandit would represent India. I accompanied her to Washington on 24 November. The state funeral of the late President was impressive, sombre and meticulously planned. Most eyes were wet when Mrs Kennedy received the US flag, which had been wrapped round the coffin, from her brother-in-law, Robert Kennedy, at the gravesite in Arlington Cemetery. More than fifty Heads of State and government attended the burial. I kept asking why Jawaharlal Nehru did not attend. After all, Kennedy, in the middle of the Cuban Missile Crisis, had gone out of his way to aid us in the disastrous Sino-Indian War.

In the late afternoon, a reception was held in the White House by Jacqueline Kennedy. I attended with Mrs Pandit and B.K. Nehru. Several leaders, including Charles de Gaulle of France, came over to Mrs Pandit to have a few words with her. What is imprinted in mind is the composure, self-control and the poise of Mrs Kennedy. The morbid thought occurred to me that if a bomb was to go off in the room, several countries would be left without a government.

We returned to New York on 26 November. Eulogies were paid to Kennedy at the UN. Mrs Pandit asked me to draft her memorial tribute. That speech was one of my best efforts, to which she made only one or two minor corrections. The seventeenth session dragged on for another three weeks, going through the motions. The diplomatic marrow had frozen. The session ended without even a whimper.

◆

A pleasant memory of that year is the unannounced arrival of M.F. Husain, who stayed with me. Husain was not yet a celebrity, but would soon be. He was free as a bird; temperamental, unpredictable, unpunctual and unconcerned, except for his art. He was also generous to a fault. And what a talent for risqué Urdu jokes! He survived mostly on fresh air, biscuits, tea and, occasionally, a piece of chicken. He did then wear shoes and did not carry a three-foot-long paint brush.

I asked him if he had brought any paintings with him. He had not. Then he startled me by announcing that he would paint them in my apartment, which he did; thirty in all. We exhibited them in a large hall in the Permanent Mission, as he could not find a gallery to showcase his work. He painted portraits of Pearl S. Buck; R.K. Narayan, who happened to be in New York at the time; Ved Mehta, the blind Indian author; and two of mine.

Few knew that this free bird had a very thin skin. One day, he came to meet me in my office. The security guard asked who he was and whom he wished to see. When I got home in the evening, I did not find Husain there. Instead, there was a short note saying he had decided to leave New York because he could not tolerate being cross-examined by guards. That was that. I was a little irritated that he hadn't waited for me. Even unconventionality must be tempered by restraint.

My elder brother, Bhagwat Singh, arrived in New York sometime later. He had come for a three-month holiday but, in fact, he made New York his home for the next forty-seven years—the original man who came to dinner. He had done his Tripos in Economics from Cambridge in 1949. Immediately after, Burmah Shell employed him while he was still in England. He was posted to Calcutta but did not last long there. To his horror, he observed that the whites had their meals on a platform in the dining room while the Indians sat at a lower level. What was even more galling was that the whites were served before Indians. This, three years after Independence. At least one of the Englishmen had been with him at Cambridge. We Bharatpur people do not put up with racist behaviour. My brother, to his credit, resigned and returned to Bharatpur. No other Indian did. They willingly did jee huzoori to third-rate Englishmen. Exclusive clubs still existed then—Indians were not allowed entry to, let alone become members of, the Calcutta Club. It was only in the mid-1950s that the whites realized that times had changed.

◆

In one of my meetings with Santha and Raja Rao, Raja remarked that Forster would be eighty-five years old on 1 January 1964. Santha immediately suggested that we do a book of tributes on him, which should be published on that date, and that I should edit the volume. I said that it would be presumptuous of me to undertake such a task. Santha firmly announced, 'No arguments, Natwar, you are going to do it and for my sake. Now, let's get down to names.' Over the next day or two, we agreed on Mulk Raj Anand, Narayana Menon, Ahmed Ali, Raja Rao, R.K. Narayan, Santha and me. (R.K. Narayan, to my annoyance, declined.) Santha was to find a publisher and I was to write to Forster. On 1 May came Forster's reply: 'What an agreeable idea, and may I be here [in New York] in 1964 the more fully to appreciate it? It would be excellent to include my tribute to Gandhiji, for I don't think it was widely known. My kindest regards to Santha Rama Rau when you see her.'

Santha got in touch with Forster's American publishers, Harcourt, Brace and World. They were interested only in the sales. Except for Santha, none of the other authors were known in America. So I asked Forster if he would permit us to include some of his writings on India in it. He promptly agreed, saying that he did not wish to sign any contract, neither did he want any payment.

E.M. Forster: A Tribute hit the bookshops on Forster's birthday. Its publication created a minor literary ripple. The bay windows of bookshops on Fifth Avenue and Second Avenue displayed the book for over a month. It went into a second print run within two weeks of publication and was widely reviewed.

◆

AT THE UNITED NATIONS

Manhattan overflowed with the tormented, the eccentric, the nymphomaniacs and the experts in all varieties of sex. It was sophisticated, chic, arty and elegant. It was outrageous, bawdy, witty, catty, snobbish, cultivated, earnest, radiant, seductive. On Fifth Avenue were the best and the classiest restaurants and the finest bookshops. There was Broadway for plays, the Lincoln Theater for music, Central Park for dates and for loitering. In the museums, one could spend a lifetime. The Harlem slums were far away. It was a city of stockbrokers, newspaper barons, lunatics, snooty clubs, efficient publishers, bestsellers and superb hotels. The pursuit of happiness, in reality, was chasing a receding target; the city's attractions and allures were irresistible. The American dream was flawed, but was exciting even in its flawed state.

The UN created a committee of hospitality, which was funded by wealthy American ladies, enabling delegates to travel outside New York. It was a praiseworthy example of American generosity. In the middle of January 1964, I joined one of these all-expenses-paid flying safaris to California in the company of a dozen delegates from Asia, Africa, Europe and South America. California was, for me, virgin territory. The flight from New York to San Francisco took over five hours and the time difference was three-and-a-half hours. I was thus over thirteen hours ahead of the clocks of Govind Niwas, Bharatpur. New York was below freezing when we left, San Francisco was about twenty-one degrees Celsius.

We were escorted by a young woman, Jane, a beauty with an engaging personality. Conscious of her unusual physical endowments, she did not allow anyone to get over-familiar. It was a sight to observe middle-aged Ambassadors, free from the restraints of their UN duties, making undiplomatic passes at the exquisitely attractive Jane, who spoke Ivy League English and Condé Nast French. We became intimate and lifelong friends.

Our hotel, the Fiarmont in San Francisco, was luxurious

and famous. The roller-coaster streets gave the city a profile so different from that of Los Angeles. In 1945, the UN was born in San Francisco and Kennedy had won the democratic nomination here in 1960. I was pleasantly surprised to see the Forster book edited by me on display in several bookshops, which was a balm to the ego. I actually noticed a girl buy a copy and could not resist telling her that I was the editor of the book. She looked sceptical. I turned the book around and there was my photograph with Forster on the back cover. She almost shrieked. Inevitably, she asked me to sign it.

From San Francisco, we flew to Los Angeles or, to give its full name, El Pueblo de Nuestra Senõra la Reina de los Ángeles del Rio de Porciúncula. A most civilized and highly cultured family was my host. Leonard Freedman was teaching at the University of California, LA. He not only made me comfortable but subjected his family to considerable discomfort in doing so. He gave me his book, *Issues of the Sixties*, which helped me appreciate, comprehend and understand America from a different and deeper perspective.

I had to cut short my tour and return to New York as a Security Council debate on Kashmir was likely. I was thus deprived of seeing the Mecca of hedonism—Las Vegas.

I had been elected rapporteur of the Committee on Decolonization. One of the petitioners, whose presentation was brilliant by any standards, was Lee Kuan Yew of Singapore. In 1962, he appeared before the committee stating that Singapore should remain a part of Malaysia. The following year, he convinced us why Singapore should separate from Malaysia. Only a man of his penetrating brilliance could do so. In decades to come, I got to know him well. We met at Commonwealth summits in New Delhi, Jamaica, Ottawa, Kuala Lumpur and in Singapore. Indira Gandhi did not take to him. He was openly critical of her leftist economic policies, and did not hesitate to say so to her face. He, on the other hand, had turned a sleepy, colonial third-world city into a world-class business hub; an unparalleled achievement. That he did so in less than two decades is all the more remarkable. But Singapore is a controlled democracy which permits no laxity, indiscipline, democratic chaos or unbridled media freedom. I often ask myself, would I want to settle down in Singapore? The answer is an emphatic no. For a holiday, yes. I would feel claustrophobic, its municipal righteousness would get on my nerves, and its treatment of illegal immigrants would outrage me. Kenneth Kaunda of Zambia also appeared before the committee and broke down, describing the brutal racism of the whites. Blacks were denied entry into shops. I immediately took to him and even gave him a mini tour of Manhattan. Ambassador C.S. Jha paid him no attention. Two years later, he became Prime Minister of Zambia. Ambassador Jha was at the New York station to receive him along with the Ambassador. On spotting Jha he asked, 'Where is Natwar?'

The Australians were active and responsible members of the committee. For a short while, the Australian representative was Sir James Plimsoll, a wise man and an open-minded diplomat. He was succeeded by J.K. McCarthy, who had spent the better part of his working life as a district officer in Papua New Guinea which was administered by Australia under the Trusteeship Agreement approved by the UN General Assembly on 13 December 1946.

The Australian delegates cooperated with the committee, but did not permit petitioners from Papua New Guinea to travel to New York. In July, the Australian government invited the Iranian representative and me to visit Papua New Guinea. We were invited in our personal capacities.

Papua New Guinea was uncharted territory for me. On arrival, everything was a surprise. Parts of Papua New Guinea were still living in the Stone Age. Cannibalism, though no longer rampant, had not altogether disappeared. I was introduced to a man who had been locked up for seven years for killing a man and eating his heart. He had felt no remorse but had walked to the nearest police post to give himself up. But such instances were extremely rare in the mid-1960s.

In Papua New Guinea, we witnessed a unique panorama of the transformation of a primitive people. They believed in the supernatural and worshipped unknown totems—bow-and-arrow tribes confronted by modernity and technology. Till the 1930s, most had lived in isolation. Savagery and violence were common. There were no roads or railways; and no cattle or horses. The only domesticated animals were pigs brought to the island by the Japanese during World War II. Our hosts took us to the remotest, most densely forested areas and to mountainous regions six to eight thousand feet above sea level. One either walked or used aeroplanes. Most tribal men and women were scantily dressed; the women bare-breasted, the men with noses pierced with refined bones, bodies smeared with grease, and no footwear. Our single-engine plane landed on a strip the size of a football field. At times, it was totally enveloped in thick clouds. I was adventurous, but there were occasions when I felt that our pilot was taking unnecessary risks. If we crashed, it would take weeks to discover the debris. Building even the handkerchief-sized tarmacs was a time-consuming undertaking. Bricks, machines, steel and cement were all transported by air. The Australians had done a fantastic job. Their rule was paternalistic but it had brought education, healthcare, sanitation to a people who, even in 1964, were living in the tenth century. We visited several schools—the children were neatly turned out (for our benefit, no doubt) and learning English!

In Port Moresby, I saw a poster of a Hindi film! The cinema

hall was next to the hotel we were staying in and blaring music kept us awake for the better part of the humid night. The Governor of Papua New Guinea invited us for dinner. He and his prickly wife loathed Port Moresby, the capital. They were there on sufferance. My colleague, Nabib, asked if he could use the toilet. Madame Governor said that the word should never be used in her house. Nabibi was told to ask if he could go for a walk.

We spent a night in Mount Hagen, more than six thousand feet above sea level. The administrator was an ex-Australian Air Force man. He and his wife were the only whites living several hundred miles away from the nearest town. The mail arrived once a week, weather permitting. There was no doctor for three hundred miles. Life-threatening accidents and illness were not infrequent, in which case the patient had to be ferried by air in a four-seater plane. I asked the administrator if he did not feel utterly lonely. He said that his job kept him busy throughout the year. He could, at certain hours, contact Port Moresby, but not mainland Australia. After retiring from the RAAF, he had needed a job. After dinner Nabibi asked if he could go for a walk. The administrator said, 'Can I join you?' Nabibi changed his mind.

Among the places we visited was the beautiful harbour town of Rabaul, Japan's primary naval and military base in the South West Pacific during World War II. From Rabaul, we went to Guadalcanal, where Kennedy's boat, PT 109, had been cut into two by a Japanese bomb. He survived.

At each place we had a set drill. The local official introduced us as UN diplomats from India and Iran. In most interior outposts and villages, the people had not heard of either of any of these countries. Our questions were standard: do you want i) independence ii) self-determination or, iii) to live under the present dispensation? The translation exercise was frustrating—English to pidgin to the district dialect and finally to the village sub-dialect. Monumental patience was needed. Our listeners were bewildered; their answers came in grunts, and the translation process was then reversed. The Foreign Service official did not try to interfere or coach the mostly naked chiefs even once; they were, in any case, more interested in our aeroplane than in the UN or us. Comprehension was beyond the carefree, sexually uninhibited tribals. At times, a feeling of infinite melancholy settled on me. Why had the Almighty given such a raw deal to the inhabitants of this inaccessible and remote island?

At the end of two weeks, the two of us concluded that Australia was not a colonial power in the traditional sense. It was making serious efforts to prepare Papua New Guinea for self-rule. Within a decade, Papua New Guinea joined the UN as a sovereign state.

On the return flight from Port Moresby to Sydney, I had a seat next to Tom Mboya, the young Kenyan leader. He was likely to succeed Jomo Kenyatta as the President of Kenya. He was assassinated in a Nairobi market. Mboya was then thirty-eight. His book, *The Challenge of Nationhood*, has not been forgotten.

◆

My travels during 1964 were, by any count, impressive. The West German government invited me to visit their country. They laid out the red carpet: first-class air travel, lodgings in good hotels, and a liaison officer to escort me everywhere I went. I arrived in Bonn on 5 July and, out of courtesy, I called on Ambassador P.A. Menon. His first question was why I had not informed him earlier of my coming to Bonn. I told him I was a guest of the German government with two others, all members of the Decolonization

AT THE UNITED NATIONS

Committee. Neither I nor the Permanent Mission saw any reason for troubling the Ambassador. It was an unpleasant encounter. I had last been in Germany in December 1952. Then, the ravages of war had been very evident. By 1964, the workaholic Germans had rebuilt most of their war devastated country. The eyesore was the forbidding Berlin Wall built in 1961—one more unfortunate whim of Nikita Khrushchev's.

Cologne looked different from what it had been in 1952. The cathedral had been repaired and the bridge over the Rhine had been rebuilt. Berlin, too, had a new look—no war debris, no pedestrians with torn coats and worn shoes. The hotels were doing well, as were the nightclubs, and the alluring waitresses were flirtatious and skimpily dressed—if the skirts had been any shorter, they needn't be worn any longer.

After a few days, I could not but help conclude that hardly any Germans had been Nazis. Not one I spoke to seemed to be aware of the concentration camps. Here was mass amnesia on an unprecedented scale. Hitler's name was never mentioned. I was not going to miss the Berlin sports stadium where the 1936 Olympic Games had been held. I asked the guide if she knew that Hitler had refused to shake hands with Jessie Owens, the greatest athlete at the games, because he was black. She feigned ignorance. I also paid a visit to East Berlin. Access was restricted by the Berlin Wall. The contrast between West and East Berlin could not have been greater.

I was keen to go to Bad Godesberg, where Chamberlain had met Hitler on 22 September 1938. The meetings had been held at Hotel Dresden. I also did a touristy round of Hotel Petersberg where Chamberlain and his party were put up. The Rhine flowed calmly as the fate of Europe was being decided. Both establishments were kept as they were in 1938, including the beige-coloured table. I had read enough history to know that on this very spot, twenty-six years earlier, Hitler had humiliated the British appeaser by telling him what he intended to do to Czechoslovakia. At the Dresden Hotel, history was not only made, it was also given a beating.

The most pleasant part was a day spent in Heidelberg. Situated on the left bank of the Necker, it was one of the most picturesque places I have visited. Its university is the oldest in Germany. It gained fame in the nineteenth century for the students' duelling competitions. I bought a copy of Goethe's *Faust.*

◆

On 3 July, I left for a round-the-world trip: London, Rome, Moscow, Delhi, Bharatpur. In Delhi, I spent forty-five minutes with Indira Gandhi. Her father had died a few months earlier. In January 1964, Mrs Pandit had written to me about a stroke her brother had suffered. Her concern for his ill health was genuine. The fortunes of the Nehru family had also changed. Lal Bahadur Shastri had succeeded Nehru and appointed Swaran Singh as Minister for External Affairs. He could have given the job either to Indira Gandhi or to Mrs Pandit, but both would have overshadowed him. Mrs Pandit had retired to Dehradun, where she was working on her autobiography, *The Scope of Happiness.*

I got to Bharatpur on the tenth, and saw Kakaji and Maji after three years. I had sent my father the Forster book. He was very pleased and had marked portions of it.

In the next leg of the journey I stopped in Singapore, and then in Suva, the capital of Fiji, where, to the discomfort of the British governor, I asked if he would be the Mountbatten of Fiji. The country became independent three years later. I spent two memorable days in Honolulu and came back to New York via San Francisco.

AT THE UNITED NATIONS

In 1965 the Security Council had several debates on Kashmir. In the debate held in July, Zulfikar Ali Bhutto made an offensive and abusive speech and called Jawaharlal Nehru names. We in the mission, including Ambassador Parthasarathi, felt enough was enough. If Zulfikar Ali Bhutto used similar language the next day, the Indian delegation would walk out. It was an unprecedented proposal but Ambassador Parthasarathi persuaded even the least demonstrative person like Sardar Swaran Singh, the External Affairs Minister, to accept it. Sardar Swaran Singh decided to speak to Lal Bahadur Shastri whose diplomatic reply was, 'Sardar Saab, you are on the spot. I leave it to your judgement.'

The next day, when Zulfikar Ali Bhutto spoke along the same lines, the Indian delegation walked out. The matter Kashmir wasn't taken up again for a decade and a half. No photograph of the walkout exists.

6

MY FATHER

7 September 1965. I was about to leave for the UN when the cipher assistant walked into my room. He handed me a telegram, avoiding looking me in the eye. It said, 'Father deceased...'

I was stunned. It took me a while to gather myself. I informed Ambassador Parthasarathi, who was then in the Security Council, and left promptly for India.

During the ten-hour flight, I did not sleep a wink. I found it difficult to believe that Father was no more. He was just sixty-five; he had been seriously ill only twice in his life. In Bharatpur, the medical facilities were primitive. The local doctors had done all they could, but in vain.

I arrived in New Delhi on the morning of 8 September and caught the train to Bharatpur. Memories of Father overwhelmed me as I made my way home.

Alighting from the train at Bharatpur, I was surprised to see my elder brother, Bharat Singh. He had come from Ahmednagar, where he was posted. We had travelled in the same train without meeting even once.

My home, Govind Niwas, was in mourning. Mother was

MY FATHER

inconsolable. She had not eaten anything since Father had died. I felt even worse because none of us four brothers had been with Father at the time of his death.

My five-year-old nephew, Kishan Singh, lit the funeral pyre. The ashes were immersed in the Mansiganga, in Goverdhan.

I asked myself what had brought on the fatal heart attack. Perhaps it was his worry for my elder brother, Girdhar Singh.

The Indo-Pak war had started on 6 September and Girdhar was near Sialkot, involved in a lethal tank battle. Girdhar-bhai got to know of Father's death nineteen days after he had passed away.

I recalled so many happy days with Father. Since I was the youngest son, he tended to spoil me. He had been tremendously happy at my getting a first division in my BA (Hons.) examination and was overjoyed at my making it to the IFS. In the summer of 1961, I had had my appendix removed and did not inform him. As soon as he got to know, he had left for Delhi to see me. He had reprimanded me for not informing him.

I had spent two days with him only six weeks prior to his death. I recalled him waving to me as the Frontier Mail pulled out of the station. It had never occurred to me then that I would never see him again.

I have been prone to tears all my life. Inexpressible joy and sorrow turn into tears. So do states of helplessness or despair. My incommunicable loneliness haunted me for a long time. My world had collapsed. I had lost my bearings, my main anchor in life had disappeared. Forty-nine years later I still miss him, the quality of his character, the austerity of his life. I remember him and will continue to do so till I become ashes.

7

ONCE A NEHRUITE...

The woods are lovely, dark and deep,
But I have promises to keep,
And miles to go before I sleep,
And miles to go before I sleep.

—Robert Frost

His life was gentle, and the elements so mixed in him that nature might stand up to say to all the world, 'This was a man.'
—William Shakespeare

'To call someone a great man is to claim that he has intentionally taken (or perhaps could have taken) a large step, one far beyond the normal capacities of men, in satisfying, or materially affecting, central human interests.'*

Jawaharlal Nehru's life is as well documented as those of Mahatma Gandhi and Winston Churchill's. Both Pandit Nehru

---

*Isaiah Berlin. *Personal Impressions*, Henry Hardy (ed.), New Jersey: Princeton University Press, 1998.

and Churchill wrote superb English and loved the sounds of words and phrases. It is, therefore, not necessary to elaborate on the already well-known aspects of his life. Only to say that modern India is Jawaharlal Nehru's creation. He laid the foundations of a democratic, secular, pluralistic and inclusive nation-state and succeeding Prime Ministers strengthened those foundations. His imprint on the development of India has endured. At times, he involved himself with administrative trivia. He judged people by his own standards. His grip on and understanding of the masses was second only to that of Mahatma Gandhi's. Nehru, with all his shortcomings, was a great Prime Minister. Most aspects of our national life have a Nehru imprint. He erred. So did Lenin, Roosevelt, Churchill and Mao Tse Tung. If one takes an overall view of his character, life and achievements, he emerges a great man. Malice and pettiness did not touch him. His vision inspired millions.

I have been a Nehruite all my life. For decades I was mesmerized by his courage, his penchant for living dangerously. His stellar role in the freedom movement was second only to that of Gandhiji, who gave it a spiritual dimension. Nehru provided the intellectual dimension.

Within a fortnight of Nehru's passing on 27 May 1964, I decided to edit a book of tributes to him. I approached his American publishers and they, without hesitation, agreed to publish *The Legacy of Nehru*. The first question was: who would the contributors be? Raja Rao, Santha Rama Rau and I drew up a list. I wrote to some of his great contemporaries. They responded immediately with their reflections and reminiscences. Dr Radhakrishnan permitted me to use the message to the Indian nation, broadcast on 27 May, as the foreword to the volume. The contributors included C.B. Attlee, former Prime Minister of the UK; Nobel Laureate Pearl S. Buck; Martin Luther King Jr;

Norman Cousins, the editor of the prestigious *Saturday Review*, Ilya Ehrenburg, the well-known writer from the Soviet Union; Bertrand Russell; Arnold Toynbee, the great historian; U Thant, Secretary General of the United Nations; and Adlai Stevenson, former Governor of Illinois and Permanent Representative of the US in the UN. The book appeared on 27 May 1965, Pandit Nehru's first death anniversary. I also included parts of Pandit Nehru's last will and testament, written in sublime English.

In his over quoted 'Tryst with Destiny' speech, he conceded that the freedom movement had ended in partial failure. All through the movement, the aim and destination was the achievement of an independent, undivided India. Few remember that Pandit Nehru's first Cabinet of fifteen ministers included six non-Congressmen: S.P. Mookerjee, B.R. Ambedkar, Sardar Baldev Singh, John Mathai, C.H. Bhabha and R.K. Shanmukham Chetty. It is futile to debate the pros and cons of Partition. As Pandit Nehru conceded, Partition was the lesser evil.

M.A. Jinnah never went to jail, never participated in any street protests, never faced a lathi charge. He was a single-minded person clear about his goal. He outwitted the entire Congress leadership with the exception of Sardar Patel. It is often said that Sardar Patel would have made a better Prime Minister. He probably would have, had he lived longer. He died on 15 December 1950, three years after Independence. Who would have succeeded him? Jawaharlal Nehru without a doubt.

One very striking fact has been ignored. There was no national debate on the Partition of India. A divided Congress Working Committee passed a resolution accepting Partition. Gandhiji's reservations were ignored, so were those of Jayaprakash Narayan, Maulana Azad and Khan Abdul Ghaffar Khan. Gandhiji was not in Delhi on 15 August; he had left for Calcutta to douse the communal fires burning there. The resolution of the CWC accepting Partition was sent to AICC and was voted upon on 14 June 1947. The result was 157 for, twenty-nine against, twenty-three abstentions.

My aim here is to judge Pandit Nehru as Foreign Minister. Here, his record is less impressive. In his speech of 7 September 1940, as the Vice President of the Interim National Government, he said:

> We propose, as far as possible, to keep away from the power politics of groups, aligned against one another, which have led in the past to world wars and which may again lead to disasters on an even vaster scale. We believe that peace and freedom are indivisible and the denial of freedom anywhere must endanger freedom elsewhere and lead to conflict and war. We are particularly interested in the emancipation of colonial and dependent countries and peoples, and in the recognition in theory and practice of equal opportunities for all races. We repudiate utterly the Nazi doctrine of racialism, wheresoever and in whatever form it may be practised. We seek no dominion over others and we claim no privileged position over other peoples. But we do claim equal and honourable treatment for our people wherever they may go, and we cannot accept any discrimination against them.
>
> The world, inspite of its rivalries and hatreds and inner conflicts, moves inevitably towards closer co-operation and building up of a world commonwealth. It is for this One World that free India will work, a world in which there is free co-operation of free peoples and no class or group exploits another...
>
> In spite of our past history of conflict, we hope that an independent India will have friendly and co-operative relations with England and the countries of the British Commonwealth...

In South Africa racialism is the State doctrine and our people are putting up a heroic struggle against the tyranny of a racial minority...

We send our greetings to the people of the United States of America to whom destiny has given a major role in international affairs...

To that other great nation of the modern world, the Soviet Union, which also carries a vast responsibility for shaping world events, we send greetings...

China, that mighty country with a mighty past, our neighbour, has been our friend through the ages and that friendship will endure and grow. We earnestly hope that her present troubles will end soon and a united and democratic China will emerge, playing a great part in the furtherance of world peace and progress.*

His world stature between 1950 and 1955 was recognized by one and all. He was a peacemaker and a staunch opponent of a nuclear winter. He was respected and admired the world over as a man of vision and wisdom. He put India on the map of the world in more ways than one. What is now called the Third World looked up to him. In Commonwealth summits his voice counted. Even Winston Churchill, the arch enemy of Indian Independence, conceded as much.

Now I come to the widening chinks in his foreign policy armour. His three cardinal errors were: his disastrous handling of the Kashmir issue, his misplaced trust of the leaders of the People's Republic of China and his turning down of the Soviet proposal to give India a permanent seat in the United Nations Security Council.

Selected Speeches of Jawaharlal Nehru, Volume 1, Jawaharlal Nehru Memorial Fund, 2001

All three have been millstones around the necks of the people of India and successive governments since 1947.

◆

A man who was so much more than the sum of his parts, Jawaharlal Nehru was also a great author. Through his writings he reached out to history. But the private Nehru remains elusive even in his widely read books. The veil is lifted now and then in his autobiography, *Glimpses of World History* and *The Discovery of India.*

Some of the questions related to the very private Jawaharlal Nehru are answered in his selected works. A project brought to fruition by the Jawaharlal Nehru Memorial Fund, the first volume of the series appeared in 1972. Fifty have been published and ten more are to come. These volumes totalled 9,292 pages and have been edited by Sarvepalli Gopal who has done a superb job, combining research with professionalism. For those interested in the evolution of Jawaharlal Nehru's thinking, the Indian freedom movement, and his seventeen years as Prime Minister, these books are indispensable.

Jawaharlal Nehru spent nearly ten years in jail between 1922 and 1945. He occupied his time by keeping his mind and body in good shape. He read voraciously and wrote copiously. He says, 'I am a lover of words and phrases and try to use them appropriately. Whatever my opinions might be, the words I use are meant to express them intelligibly and in ordered sequence.'* In jail, he kept a regular diary in which are reflected his moods, his political highs and lows and his inner turmoils. It was tremendous exercise in self-discipline. Pandit Nehru was at his best in adversity, when the flame of life burnt low.

---

*Selected Works of Jawaharlal Nehru, Jawaharlal Nehru Memorial Fund, 2001

In the 1930s, nothing was going well. Freedom was nowhere in sight; he was at odds with Gandhiji and the Congress; his wife was terminally ill; his widowed mother had had a stroke; daughter Indira, not in robust health, was being shunted from one school to another; he himself was in jail. Would there ever be a break in the clouds? One entry reveals the state of Pandit Nehru's mind during this period: 'January 12, 1935. A terrible and unexpected shock. Early in the morning a telegram came from Nan [Vijaya Laxmi Pandit] from Allahabad that Jivraj Mehta had telephoned from Bombay to say that mother had had a stroke and was unconscious... I collapsed and wept and found some difficulty in pulling myself together...'

'I have seldom felt quite so lonely and cut off from the world as I have felt here. It is solitary confinement with a vengeance.'* There was no self-pity, and he gave no quarter to hate. And, more than anything, there were no moral trade-offs. This was the measure of the man.

He gave us hope and pride. For him, ideas were not mere abstractions. He made them come alive—alive in our minds, inspiring us, shaping and influencing our lives. I now deeply regret not drawing him out on literary matters when the opportunity presented itself.

◆

One cannot but applaud Pandit Nehru's achievements. His accomplishments were not confined to foreign policy, finance or Five-Year Plans. He laid the foundations of our nation; its democracy, secularism, pluralism and an independent non-aligned foreign policy. For over sixty-six years, a broad national

---

*Selected Works of Jawaharlal Nehru, Jawaharlal Nehru Memorial Fund, 2001

consensus on foreign policy existed. Only recently has that consensus been questioned. Not only politics, but economics and finance, science, technology, health, human development, rail and road, Parliament and planning, reform and regeneration, administration and atomic energy are his gifts. He worked sixteen hours a day, spent time on matters which could have been dealt with by his officials—even mundane matters would attract his attention. Every letter was promptly replied to, even if it addressed trivial matters.

Taking the Kashmir issue to the Security Council of the United Nations was a monumental mistake. By doing so, he converted a domestic matter into an international one. What was even more erroneous was his going to the Security Council under Chapter VI of the UN Charter, which addresses itself to disputes. He should have taken the Kashmir problem to the Security Council under Chapter VII, which deals with aggression. In the case of Kashmir, he allowed his personal feelings to cloud his professional judgement; a major failing for a statesman of his stature. Members of the Council rightly said that, by doing so, India had accepted that a dispute exists.

On 22 October 1947, Pakistan invaded the Jhelum Valley in Kashmir. India learnt of this incursion two days later and Pandit Nehru spoke to Lord Mountbatten, who had stayed on as the Governor General of Independent India, about it. Mountbatten, as well as the three chiefs of the army, air force and navy were all Englishmen and maintained their own agenda. In Pakistan, too, the army, air force and navy chiefs were Englishmen. These chiefs of the two states were in touch with each other and were secretly informing Mountbatten of day-to-day events. Mountbatten kept Nehru in the dark. Not only that, he used the British High Commission in Delhi to send messages to British Prime Minister Clement Attlee and King George VI—all behind the back of a government of which he was the Governor General. It was Pandit Nehru's error to have invited Mountbatten, the last Viceroy of India, to become the first Governor General of India. Jinnah was more realistic. When Mountbatten suggested that he become the Governor General of Pakistan as well, Jinnah firmly turned him down. Mountbatten nominated a Chairman of the Defence Committee that played a critical role in policymaking, a role from which he should have been excluded. Pandit Nehru did not object personally and these matters, which should have been discussed in the Indian Cabinet, did not come up. Thus, the Defence Committee took over the duties of the Indian Cabinet with the full knowledge of the Prime Minister.

Mountbatten was a constitutional figurehead, yet it was he who advised Pandit Nehru to take up the Kashmir issue to the United Nations. He was even against sending Indian troops to Srinagar until the Maharaja of Kashmir had signed the Instrument of Accession to India. Disregarding his advice, Pandit Nehru and Patel decided that Indian troops should be flown to Srinagar immediately. They arrived just in time to save Srinagar from falling into the hands of the Pakistani invaders.

After the draft of the communication which India was to send to the UN Security Council was prepared, Mountbatten suggested that the Indian draft be shown to Liaquat Ali Khan, the Prime Minister of Pakistan. It was so outrageous a proposal that even Pandit Nehru refused to oblige him. Sardar Patel was not in favour of even a limited reference on Kashmir to the United Nations, which he called 'Dis-United Nations'. Pandit Nehru had the good sense to show the draft to Gandhiji, who made a vital correction by cutting out in pencil the words 'independent status'.

It is now well known that Jawaharlal Nehru deeply regretted accepting the advice that Mountbatten gave him. At a meeting called by Mountbatten on 25 February 1948, Pandit Nehru said,

'That it had been an act of faith by the Government of India, at a time when the situation was rapidly deteriorating to make their reference to the Security Council in the first place. If this faith was now proved to be misplaced, the consequences would have to be borne by those who had made the reference.' Sardar Patel, who was also present at that meeting, did not mince his words. He said that Pandit Nehru, in particular, had reposed great faith in the United Nations. But the Security Council had been meddling in power politics to such an extent that very little of that faith had been left uneroded. He pointed out that it had been the Governor General who had induced the government to refer the issue to the United Nations in the first place. Mountbatten had no choice but to accept what Sardar Patel said.

Not only this, Pandit Nehru even agreed to a plebiscite in Kashmir for ascertaining the views of the people. He also agreed to a representative of the UN Secretary General to conduct these elections. Furthermore, he mentioned that he had no objections to taking the Kashmir issue to the International Court of Justice at The Hague.

The Indian delegation to the first meeting of the Security Council was led by Sir Gopalaswami Ayyangar. He was a PCS officer of the Madras Presidency who was appointed Diwan of Kashmir in 1937 and had served there till 1943. He was a wise and soft-spoken man of unimpeachable integrity. But he was not familiar with the manner in which the Security Council functioned. The Pakistan delegation was led by Sir Muhammad Zafarulla Khan, the Foreign Minister and a very eminent lawyer who had decided to migrate to Pakistan after Partition. Gopalaswami Ayyangar put forward his case in a mild manner. Zafarulla got the better of him. Sheikh Abdullah was also a member of the delegation. It is now well known that even in 1948 he had an independent Kashmir at the back of his mind.

An American writer has written that Indians had made Abdullah a member of the delegation in the expectation that he would be an effective spokesperson for India's cause. They could not have calculated that he would undercut their position by calling for Kashmir's independence in a private conversation with the US delegate in the Security Council Warren Austin. Nehru had put all his Kashmiri eggs in the Abdullah basket.

At the Security Council, the Kashmir issue became entangled in the Cold War between the two superpowers, the USSR and the US. But for the Soviet Union's support, India would have been isolated in the Council. From the very beginning, the dice was loaded against us. Pakistan was being aggressive and being openly supported by the UK and the US. Between 1948 and 1957, the Security Council passed several resolutions which took a neutral view on Pakistan's invasion of Kashmir. India's request that Pakistani troops vacate Kashmir, too, was not taken seriously.

In 1957, Krishna Menon addressed the Security Council for nine hours. The speech made him a hero in India, but had little impact on the Security Council. Even members friendly to India commented: 'If you have such a good case, then why is it necessary to make a nine-hour-long speech?' At least four members of the Security Council were half asleep by the end of it.

It was only after Jawaharlal Nehru's death in May 1964 that it became possible to view the Kashmir issue in a different way.

◆

The Indo-China boundary conflict arose primarily because the two concepts—the Chinese one of strategic borders and India's of historic borders—could not be reconciled.

While the Chinese were prepared to use diplomatic and, if necessary, military methods in pursuit of their concept, the Indian approach from 1950 was primarily declaratory and ineffectively military.*

Pandit Nehru, the idealist, did not really gauge the hard-headed pragmatism of Mao Tse Tung, Chou En-lai and other Chinese leaders, and how it affected China's policies vis-à-vis the border and India from the time when the Chinese Army occupied Tibet in 1951. Pandit Nehru consistently maintained that India should revive the ancient cultural ties it shared with China and keep them alive. He, as well as his officials, all but ignored the rapid building of infrastructure in Tibet, leading up to the border with India, and the regular reprinting of maps by China which showed large parts of India as its own. The country's focus, Pandit Nehru asserted, should be on maintaining internal peace, particularly in the Northeast. And, hindsight demonstrates that in taking Chou En-lai at his word—when he dismissed India's concerns regarding matters at the border as mere misunderstandings which could easily be sorted out by dialogue—and not by taking anything in writing from Chou En-lai, Pandit Nehru displayed poor judgement.

The Panchsheel Treaty, the Five Principles of Peaceful Coexistence, was signed between the two countries in June 1954.

> The principles and considerations which govern our mutual relations and the approach of the two countries to each other are as follows:
>
> (i) Mutual respect for each other's territorial integrity and sovereignty;

---

*C.V. Ranganathan and Vinod C. Khanna, *India and China*, Delhi: Har Anand Publications, 2000

(ii) Mutual non-aggression;
(iii) Mutual non-interference in each other's internal affairs;
(iv) Equality and mutual benefit; and
(v) Peaceful coexistence.

At this time Nehru remarked about China:

> I am not at all sure of what China may do ten or twenty years hence. But to protect ourselves against possible developments, we have to do other things and not try to put up a useless Maginot Line. In particular we have to have peace, quiet and contentment on our side of the border. I am worried more about the Naga trouble from this point of view than about anything that the Chinese may do.

In October 1954, the Prime Minister visited China, and was welcomed in Peking by a million people lined up on both sides of the road as Pandit Nehru and Chinese Premier Chou En-lai drove by in an open car. Pandit Nehru genuinely thought that it was a spontaneous and popular welcome. The fact is that it was organized spontaneity. If the Chinese government had so decided, not a single person would have been on the roads. In later years, when I read the record of the talks, it became clear that there was no real meeting of minds and, most importantly, the border question, too, was not raised.

On his return, Pandit Nehru stopped in Calcutta. The first letter he wrote on his China experience was to Edwina Mountbatten, and shared with her the content of his discussions with the Chinese leaders. Strictly speaking, this was against the oath of secrecy he had taken. At the time, of course, no one knew of this letter, and only came to light later when his selected works, edited by S. Gopal, were published.

The roots of Indo-Soviet cooperation go back to the 1920s. As early as 1923, Lenin was conscious of Mahatma Gandhi and India's struggle for independence. Nehru had visited the Soviet Union in 1927 for the tenth anniversary of the Russian Revolution. In 1928, he published his first book, *Soviet Russia*. Throughout the 1930s, he made favourable comments on the Soviet Union and Soviet policies under Stalin. This he did in good faith, ignoring the bloody purges of thousands of party leaders and generals between 1937-38.

The Soviet Union did not reciprocate Nehru's friendly gestures. By this time, the Cold War had already started. The world was divided into two camps. Nehru stuck to non-alignment. Stalin's Soviet Russia refused to accept that Nehru was the leader of an independent and sovereign country. Not only that, the Russians continued to assert that India was politically and economically a lackey of Western imperialists and looked upon India's membership of the Commonwealth with disdain. Stalin also lent active support to the Communist Party of India, which was leading a liberation struggle in Hyderabad. It was only after Lord Mountbatten's departure that Sardar Patel ended the rebellion in Hyderabad and the Nizam acceded to India.

To Nehru, friendship with the Soviet Union was an important part of his policy. Good relations with the USSR would enhance Nehru's world influence. Neither superpower could ignore him.

It was only after Stalin's death that a slight change in Soviet policy towards India became discernible. The Soviets had appreciated India not signing the peace treaty on Japan as well as its attitude during the Korean War. The Soviets also began to look at Nehru's non-alignment policy with an open mind. Nehru's visit to the Soviet Union in 1955 was a landmark moment in the histories of the two countries. He received a very friendly and enthusiastic welcome not only from the government but also from the people of the Soviet Union.

In 1955 when Nehru was in the USSR, he had a discussion with Bulganin, the number two man in the Politburo.

> Bulganin: We are agreed about the American airmen and we will inform our Chinese friends. We are grateful to be informed about Krishna Menon's activities about the Four Power Conference. Regarding your suggestion about the Four Power Conference we would take appropriate action. While we are discussing the general international situation and reducing tension, we propose suggesting at a later stage India's inclusion as the sixth member of the Security Council.
>
> JN: Perhaps Bulganin knows that some people in USA have suggested that India should replace China in the Security Council. This is to create trouble between us and China. We are, of course, wholly opposed to it. Further, we are opposed to pushing ourselves forward to occupy certain positions because that may itself create difficulties and India might itself become a subject of controversy. If India is to be admitted to the Security Council it raises the question of the revision of the Charter of the UN. We feel that this should not be done till the question of China's admission and possibly of others is first solved. I feel that we should first concentrate on getting China admitted. What is Bulganin's opinion about the revision of the Charter? In our opinion this does not seem to be an appropriate time for it.*

---

*Selected Works of Jawaharlal Nehru, Volume 29, Jawaharlal Nehru Memorial Fund, 2001

Nikita Khrushchev and Nikolai Bulganin, too, were very warmly welcomed in India when they visited in December 1955. The Soviet Union consistently helped us in the Security Council on Kashmir, where the US-led Western countries supported Pakistan, as also on our liberation of Goa.

The Soviet Union was placed in an awkward situation during the Sino-Indian border conflict. It took a neutral stand on the border dispute and wished that the matter be settled between the two countries. The Chinese reaction to Soviet Union's neutralism was severe and condemnatory. They felt that in a dispute between a socialist and a non-socialist country, it was imperative for the Soviet Union to support the former.

In April 1955, the PM attended the Bandung Conference. Pandit Nehru had succeeded in getting China invited, against the wishes of some of the pro-Western countries, many of which did not recognize the People's Republic of China. In all good faith, Pandit Nehru took Chou under his wing and introduced him to a large number of leaders. Chou later exploited, in full measure, these connections he had made. Instead of being grateful to Nehru Chou En-lai thought he was patronizing him.

However, even as Pandit Nehru stuck to his position of maintaining good relations with China, the constant incursions into Indian territory in Aksai Chin and China's overall expansionist intentions, and the slow eroding of the 'Hindi Chini bhai-bhai [The Indians and the Chinese are brothers]' slogan, matters reached a boiling point.

In 1959, the Dalai Lama, as well as the large entourage accompanying him, crossed the Chinese border with India and sought refuge. The immediate and the most serious fallout of India playing host to the greatest Buddhist in the world was that Sino-India relations, already strained, began to fall apart. Throughout 1959, Peking kept the heat on Pandit Nehru, provoking numerous incidents on the border. Pandit Nehru, for the first time during his tenure, faced pointed criticism within the Lok Sabha, even from members of the Congress, for what they called his inept handling of the situation. The press, too, was unforgiving. The fears, both within the Parliament and on the streets, wasn't unfounded and the enormity of the bilateral freeze became clear when the Chinese Ambassador to India, Pau Tse-hi, called on the Foreign Secretary, S. Dutt. I was asked to attend the meeting and take notes, but the need did not arise. Ambassador Pau handed a sealed envelope to S. Dutt and left. It was a deliberate act of gross diplomatic discourtesy.

As Chinese military activity on the border increased with disquieting speed, Pandit Nehru's responses did not satisfy Parliament. This was a wholly new experience for him, for his authority had never been challenged. Among the officials, too, unease was discernible. Some of us junior officials argued heatedly about the faith the Prime Minister had placed in Chou En-lai. Nevertheless, his statement in the Rajya Sabha, which was widely reported, was disquieting. He confessed that he had 'foolishly' not kept Parliament informed of the developments and made an irresponsible statement that not a blade of grass grew in Aksai Chin.

'But nothing can be a more amazing folly than for two great countries like India and China to get into a major conflict and war for the possession of a few mountain peaks, however beautiful the mountain peaks might be, or some area which is more or less uninhabited.'*

In October 1962, China launched a full-fledged war and we were comprehensively defeated. Our army was ill-equipped.

---

*Sarvepalli Gopal, *Jawaharlal Nehru: A Biography*, New Delhi: Oxford University Press, 1979

The General in-charge, B.G. Kaul, was a favourite of Krishna Menon. Menon had convinced Nehru over the years that the real enemy was Pakistan, not China. The Chinese troops had favourable terrain on their side of the border. They were extremely well-trained, armed and equipped. Their information about our weaknesses was up to date. Having achieved their objective, they withdrew and declared a unilateral ceasefire, sparing us further humiliation and damage. Not one non-aligned nation supported us. It was President Kennedy who, preoccupied with the Cuban Missile Crisis, promised and delivered aid promptly. Pandit Nehru's letters to Kennedy are pathetic. B.K. Nehru, who was then Ambassador to the US, reports in his memoirs that he felt a sense of shame when he was delivering Pandit Nehru's messages to Kennedy.

The conflict also took a great toll on Pandit Nehru's health. I have extracted here parts of a letter Vijaya Lakshmi Pandit wrote to me where she expresses concern for her brother's well-being:

> Ever since I came home from the U.S. I have been worried sick about the P.M.'s health. He looked so ill I could hardly bear to look at him. It was obvious he was heading for a breakdown and was driving himself mercilessly in spite of it. He was alone in the house due to Indu's absence and though he was accompanied by a doctor on his tour this poor little man was so junior he literally trembles every time he had to approach P.M. There was no question of advice or assistance.
>
> The day P.M. and Indira left for Bhuvaneshwar I could have wept. He got up at 5.00 a.m after a late night & left at 6.45 a.m. going straight on from Bhuvaneshwar by helicopter—a rattling broken down affair to some other place for a perfectly silly engagement. After that there were meetings of the A.I.C.C. Next morning he couldn't get up.

The doctor call this a spasm—momentarily for a few hours he was not able to use his left foot and hand but by the night this righted itself. His blood pressure was terrifically high and he had to be put to bed...

I was in Delhi for four days and was glad to find that visitors were not allowed except for two minutes and only about two a day...

The problem now is going to be how to restrain Bhai. You know his sense of responsibility and the way in which he wants to take everybody's mistakes on himself—this obviously, must stop. He is required for a long time and must be made to understand it...

The Indian doctor is not firm and also sometimes frightened to annoy a big person. Indira is swayed in all sorts of directions and gives in. I do not quite know who is to take care of this precious life. As you know I am somewhat of a *persona non grata*. One can but pray.

Yet, despite all this, there was no stauncher patriot than Jawaharlal Nehru, and these passages from his last will bear testament to it:

> When I die, I should like my body to be cremated. If I die in a foreign country, my body should be cremated there and my ashes sent to Allahabad. A small handful of these ashes should be thrown in the Ganga and the major portion of them disposed of in the manner indicated below. No part of these ashes should be retained or preserved.
>
> My desire to have a handful of my ashes thrown in the Ganga at Allahabad has no religious significance, so far as I am concerned. I have no religious sentiment in the matter. I have been attached to the Ganga and the Jumna rivers in Allahabad ever since my childhood and, as I have

grown older, this attachment has also grown. I have watched their varying moods as the seasons changed, and have often thought of the history and myth and tradition and song and story that have become attached to them through the long ages and become part of the flowing waters. The Ganga, especially, is the river of India, beloved of her people, round which are intertwined her racial memories, her hopes and fears, her songs of triumph, her victories and her defeats. She has been a symbol of India's age-long culture and civilization, ever-changing, ever-flowing and ever the same Ganga. […] I am proud of that great inheritance that has been, and is, ours, and I am conscious that I too, like all of us, am a link in that unbroken chain which goes back in the dawn of history in the immemorial past of India. That chain I would not break, for I treasure it and seek inspiration from it. And, as witness of this desire of mine and as my last homage to the great ocean that washes India's shores.

The major portion of my ashes should, however, be disposed of otherwise. I want these to be carried high up into the air in an aeroplane and scattered from that height over the fields where the peasants of India toil, so that they might mingle with the dust and soil of India and become an indistinguishable part of India.

◆

The most effective pose is one in which there seems to be the least of posing, and Jawahar had learned well to act without the paint and powder of an actor... What is behind that mask of his? ...What will to power?...He has the power in him to do great good for India or great injury... Men like Jawaharlal, with all their capacity for great and good work, are unsafe in a democracy.

—*Modern Review* 1936, written by Jawaharlal Nehru under the pseudonym 'Chanakya'

Friends and Comrades,

The light has gone out of our lives and there is darkness everywhere. I do not know what to tell you and how to say it. Our beloved leader, Bapu as we called him, the Father of the Nation, is no more. Perhaps I am wrong to say that. Nevertheless, we will never see him again as we have seen him for these many years. We will not run to him for advice and seek solace from him, and that is a terrible blow, not to me only, but to millions and millions in this country. And it is a little difficult to soften the blow by any other advice that I or anyone else can give you...

And while we pray, the greatest prayer that we can offer is to take a pledge to dedicate ourselves to the truth, and to the cause for which this great countryman of ours lived and for which he has died. That is the best prayer that we can offer him and his memory. That is the best prayer we can offer to India and ourselves.

—From Jawaharlal Nehru's address on Gandhiji's death, 30 January 1948

8

I MARRY A PRINCESS

1967 was one of the most significant years of my life. I got married. The justification I give for my prolonged bachelorhood is a quotation from E.M. Forster—'All those that marry do well. All those that refrain do better.' This was, to some extent, off the mark. I did not completely rule marriage out. Neither did I share the view of Beatrice Webb, who considered marriage the wastepaper basket of emotions. However, the phrase that marriages were made in heaven, I thought, was banal and silly. Married people did not live in heaven. A perfect marriage, I thought, was a mirage. I was wrong.

Foreign services the world over provide endless opportunities for philandering. The temptations are many and opportunities even more. I had my fill of affairs. These were international in scope and short-lived.

I first set my eyes on my future wife, Hem, the daughter of the Maharaja of Patiala, at a dinner hosted by Dinesh Singh, a Minister of State in the Ministry of External Affairs and Indira Gandhi's close counsellor at the time. Although he was a man with a swollen head, I personally owe him a huge debt for his lasting and profound contribution to my future happiness and well-being.

Each one of us has an idea of beauty. I cannot define mine, but I can recognize it straightaway. She was elegantly dressed and beautiful. She carried herself with poise and style. Her figure was eye-catching and her dignity radiant. She moved with silent grace. Sardul Vikram Shah, Dinesh Singh's brother-in-law and Chief of Protocol, formally introduced me to her. She gave me an indifferent regal nod. Someone else approached her and I moved on. My mind, though, was on her and my eyes followed her everywhere. Towards the end of the dinner, I asked her if I could telephone her. I had taken a calculated risk. She neither said yes, nor no. It was high-class restraint. We were total strangers. Her world and mine were like chalk and cheese. Had I been presumptuous? Had I crossed the line of propriety?

I fell in love with Hem. Our near clandestine courtship lasted fourteen months. I was pleasantly surprised to discover her interest in books. She did not flaunt her princely persona. That was real class.

On her birthday, 1 June 1967, I invited her to lunch at a restaurant with an atrocious name, Gaylord, near the Regal Cinema in Connaught Circus. We had got to know each other well. I thought the courtship had lasted long enough. After serious and anxious reflection, I decided to propose marriage.

We had got through the first course. I could not bear waiting any more. On an impulse, I said that I had a birthday present for her. 'Thank you, what is it?' she asked.

'It's not it. It's me. I am asking you to marry me.' She gave an uncomprehending look. It was a highly unorthodox way to propose. She was silent for a moment or two. If she said 'no', my world would come tumbling down. If she said 'yes', I would be on cloud nine. She did neither. She said, 'I will think about it.'

Hope and despair was mixed. It was foolish for me to expect an immediate acceptance. I realized that brought up as she was in an elitist, exclusive environment, she could hardly be expected to come up with an instant acceptance.

For three weeks, she kept me in harrowing suspense. On 21 June, she accepted my proposal. It was one of the most memorable days of my life.

Her family disapproved of me. To them, an IFS officer working in Indira Gandhi's secretariat was not good enough. But Hem stuck to her decision. A date was fixed.

A month before the wedding, I got measles. The date had to be changed. This caused unrestrained, maddening ribaldry. Friends were hugely amused.

I had asked Indira Gandhi to be a witness at my civil marriage. My mother-in-law to be had asked two of her political friends—Chief Minister Parmar of Himachal Pradesh and Lok Sabha MP Nath Pai—to do so too, as three witnesses were required by law.

We were married at Patiala House, 9, Tees January Marg on 21 August 1967. Magistrate R.K. Anand did the honours. This was followed by a Sikh wedding. A day later, my in-laws, Maharaja Yadavindra Singh and Maharani Mohinder Kaur, held a reception at the Ashoka Hotel. It was quite an occasion. Indira Gandhi and her Cabinet colleagues came, as did most of the well-known people in Delhi. It was called the wedding of the year.

I embarked on marriage with joy and ecstasy. So did Hem. We lived in a small house opposite Lodi Gardens. Hem was used to living in palaces but she handled the transition from palace to a D-1 house without any complaint or fuss. But marriage is not a ticket to eternal bliss. Hem and I realized how strong-willed we both were. In addition, I was insufferably self-righteous, with a slight chip on my shoulder. Two people living so close do

(above): K. Natwar Singh, Jawaharlal Nehru and President Dwight D. Eisenhower, 1961

(below): Front row: Premier Chou En-lai, Marshal Chu Teh, Dr S. Radhakrishnan, Chairman Mao Tse Tung, Ambassador R.K. Nehru, President Liu Shaoqi. K. Natwar Singh is seen in the back row, third from right

With C. Rajagopalachari, New York, 1962

(*above*): With E.M. Forster, Cambridge, 1954

(*left*): Jawaharlal Nehru, R.K. Narayan and K. Natwar Singh, Teen Murti House, 1961

(*above*): With Raja Rao, New York, 1963

(*left*): With M.F. Husain painting his portrait, New York, 1963

(clockwise from top right):
K. Natwar Singh, R.K. Narayan and Mulk Raj Anand;
With Nirad Chaudhuri, Oxford;
With Ahmed Ali, Karachi;
With Thakazhi Sivasankara Pillai, Thakazhi;
With Amaury de Riencourt and Han Suyin, Geneva

With Santha Rama Rau, New York

(*left*): With Madame Soong Chingling, 1955
(*below left*): R.N. Kao, with P.N. Dhar
(*below*): P.N. Haksar

With Lord Mountbatten, London, 1975

With His Holiness, The Dalai Lama. Also seen in the picture is Vikas Swaroop

(*above*): With Dev Kant Barooah, Congress President, and Indira Gandhi, 1974

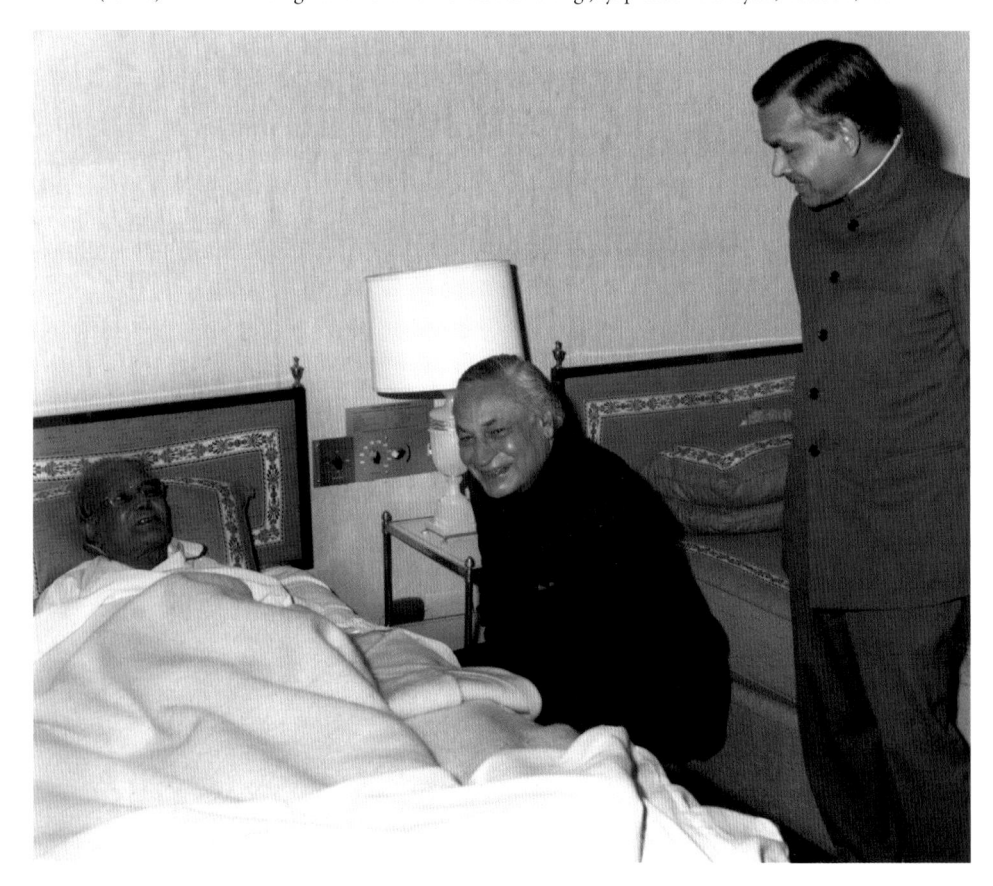

(*below*): K. Natwar Singh and B.K. Nehru visit an ailing Jayaprakash Narayan, London, 1977

get on each other's nerves. It is inevitable that at times discord overtakes harmony. Adjustments are unavoidable and these were made, not always without pain.

9

WORKING WITH INDIRA GANDHI

Indira Gandhi was a great leader; not the solemn, serious martinet she is made out to be. Seldom is it mentioned that this graceful, sparkling, engaging human being was a caring humanist, that she was endowed with charm, elegance and good taste. She enjoyed the company of artists, authors, poets and painters. Her sensibility was adorned with self-deprecating humour. She possessed what the French so delicately describe as je ne sais quoi—a certain style.

Before becoming Prime Minister, she had gathered around her a group of people (Dinesh Singh, Romesh Thapar, Rajni Patel and I.K. Gujral) who were derisively called the 'kitchen Cabinet'. This group acquired substantial influence after she became Prime Minister. From 1966 to 1969, Indira Gandhi was in office but not in power. The actual power rested in the hands of the 'syndicate'—S. Nijalingappa, Atulya Ghosh, K. Kamaraj, Morarji Desai and S.K. Patil.

Mrs Gandhi's first foreign visit after becoming Prime Minister was to Washington and New York. At the time I was in New York and had just been given transfer orders to Delhi.

Air India was on strike, so I asked her if I could return to Delhi with her.

After my return, I was predictably posted to the United Nations' division of the Ministry of External Affairs. On 19 May 1966, I was told that I was being shifted to the Prime Minister's Secretariat. The appointment came as a surprise and to this day I don't know how it came about. The Ministry of External Affairs was also mystified. Eyebrows were raised 'Why Natwar', he is only a Deputy Secretary. A new post was created for me and I was not quite sure what my duties would be.

The Prime Minister's Secretariat was the most powerful establishment in the country. It was a very small team in comparison to today's PMO—the Prime Minister, her Principal Secretary L.K. Jha, Joint Secretary Sushital Banerjee, Information Adviser George Verghese, Sharada Prasad and me. The Prime Minister's Secretariat, unlike other ministries, did not function on a strict hierarchical principle. Only the most important matters were put up to the Prime Minister. The rest of us dealt directly with her. This reduced delays and gave the officers responsibility they would not have had in other ministries.

The Prime Minister was not familiar with the rules and regulations under which she had to function. She needed constant propping up. She was uncomfortable in Cabinet meetings and even more so in Parliament. Cabinet ministers were also not used to dealing with a woman Prime Minister and did not feel at ease in her presence. Her first major decision on 6 June 1966, the devaluation of the Indian rupee, was treated with derision. The Congress President, K. Kamaraj, considered it a sell-out. Mrs Gandhi herself soon realized that she had been misguided by her advisers. She was, however, a quick learner and a great leader, who was not averse to taking risks. After this, she did not trust anyone outside her immediate circle.

One of my duties was to be present when foreign dignitaries met the Prime Minister. I accompanied her to most functions. For me, this was a lesson in diplomacy at the highest level. The Prime Minister was a good listener. And with each encounter, her confidence increased. Economic subjects bored her. She also did not look forward to occasions such as laying foundation stones or attending wedding receptions.

◆

Soon after Indira Gandhi became Prime Minister, in May 1966, Mao Tse Tung launched the Cultural Revolution in China. Mao had been feeling that he was being isolated by some of his senior comrades, particularly Liu Shaoqi, Peng Chen and Peng Dehuai. The Revolution lasted almost ten years and China was torn apart from east to west and from north to south. The Red Guards, who answered to none, save Mao, were let loose. Their relentless attack on very senior members of the Communist Party led some to commit suicide; houses were ransacked, ancient monuments were destroyed and universities were shut. The British Embassy was burnt down and all the glass windows of the Indian Embassy were shattered by students pelting stones.

Two young officers of our Embassy in Peking were on a picnic in the western hills. They had taken some photographs when they were arrested and treated harshly. They were not only detained, but it was announced that they would receive capital punishment. This was, of course, part of the psychological war that Mao and his Red Guards were using to demoralize everyone. It was only after a great deal of pressure and protest that the Chinese government decided to let them leave. But, before they could be flown out, they were put in a truck and exhibited before a crowd of two hundred thousand people. They were pushed and kicked and spat upon. Such treatment was contrary to every known diplomatic rule.

◆

October 1966 was the tenth anniversary of the meeting between Jawaharlal Nehru, Josip Broz Tito and Gamal Abdel Nasser at Brioni. Tito and Nasser came to Delhi for the occasion. The opening of the conference was in Rashtrapati Bhavan. As soon as Indira Gandhi started her inaugural speech, the microphone failed, much to my horror.

◆

President S. Radhakrishnan's five-year term was to end in May 1967. He had been openly critical of the Prime Minister's style of functioning and, in his broadcast to the nation of 25 January 1967, on the eve of Republic Day, he overstepped the bounds of constitutional propriety when he said, 'Even after making allowance for all the difficulties we cannot forgive widespread incompetence and gross mismanagement of our resources.' Indira Gandhi was upset and annoyed by this and decided not to give Radhakrishnan a second term—the eminent philosopher paid the price for patronizing a powerful politician. I was sitting next to her when she said, 'I am not giving him a second term.' Dr Zakir Hussain was elected the next President. He was a man of sterling qualities, and was a well-known educationist who had worked with Mahatma Gandhi before Independence. He was highly respected for the refinement of his character and his genuine humility.

◆

The 1967 Lok Sabha elections were held early in the year. Polling in the country took place between 15 and 21 February 1967. There is one incident of that time that stands out vividly in my mind. On 8 February 1967, the Prime Minister was addressing a huge election rally in Bhubaneswar when a few hundred people started heckling her. Stones were hurled, and she was hit by one on the nose. She started bleeding but continued her speech. Later, a medical examination showed a minor crack in her nasal spine—her upper lip was also bruised. Her doctor had not accompanied her and, to my horror, I discovered that no one present knew her blood group.

The election results were announced on 26 February and the Congress just about scraped through with a bare majority. The Swatantra Party, under the leadership of C. Rajagopalachari, consisting largely of former princes and some people from the corporate sector, did exceptionally well. The Congress was unable to form governments in the state assemblies of Bihar, UP, Punjab, Rajasthan and Bengal. Many of the Congress leaders were defeated, including K. Kamaraj, C. Subramaniam, Sachin Chaudhuri and S.K. Patil.

When the Cabinet formation was under way, Kamaraj wanted the Prime Minister to include Morarji Desai as her Home Minister and Deputy Prime Minister. L.K. Jha, the Prime Minister's Principal Secretary, had worked under Morarji Desai for a number of years and also supported him. By and large, the bureaucracy tilted towards Morarji Desai. After some hesitation, the Prime Minister accepted Morarji Desai as Finance Minister and Deputy Prime Minister but made it clear that this did not imply that Morarji Desai was number two in the Cabinet. Morarji Desai also assured the Prime Minister of his cooperation.

In his autobiography, *First Draft*, B.G. Verghese has written:

The 1967 election was a watershed. The Congress' single party dominance was challenged, especially in the States. Federalism took on new meaning as Centre-state differences could no longer be resolved within the family by reference to the Congress Working Committee or AICC. A new political vocabulary and norms of conduct came into vogue. Terms like gherao, bandh, hartal, zero hour, defection, aya ram gaya ram, floor test, Rashtrapati Bhawan or Raj Bhawan parades, shouting brigade, booth capturing, young turks became part of the new lexicon.*

After the elections, I wrote a paper on foreign policy based on an idea propounded by B.G. Verghese in his paper 'Mandate for Change', which spoke of the democratization of foreign policy. In my paper I highlighted the shortcomings of our foreign policy. India continued to view the world and its problems in a simplistic and moralistic manner, rather than in empirical terms. My paper posed certain questions. What did the policy of non-alignment mean in 1967? Did our policy towards Pakistan and China need a fresh look? Should we not take a closer look at Southeast Asia, Japan, New Zealand and Australia? I also emphasized that we should pay more attention to Africa and Latin America. I took the risk of recommending that India become a nuclear power and questioned the nuclear monopoly of the five Permanent Members of the United Nations Security Council. The foreign policy of a country, to be effective, I said, 'must be backed by power'. This was contrary to conventional wisdom. Treading on dangerous ground, I questioned the wisdom of our policy on Israel, which was static, rigid and unimaginative—Israel was being treated as a diplomatic leper. I also recommended the revision

---

*B.G. Verghese, *First Draft: Witness to the Making of Modern India*, Tranquebar Press, Chennai, 2010

of India's Arab policy. While I was aware that the feelings and sentiments of our Muslim community had to be borne in mind, it was important that we not forget that not a single Arab country supported our stand on Kashmir. I was firm that what Pakistan needed was a dose of benign neglect; for nothing bothered Pakistan more than our indifference.

Neither B.G. Verghese's nor my efforts bore fruit. Verghese soon left the secretariat and my paper was put in cold storage.

◆

In March 1967, the Svetlana incident caused a slight dent in Indo-USSR relations. Svetlana was the daughter of Joseph Stalin. She fell in love with Brajesh Singh, a committed communist who had lived in Moscow for many years. Brajesh Singh then fell seriously ill and doctors recommended a shift to a warmer climate. He was not permitted to return to India. So Brajesh Singh stayed in Moscow, where he died. Svetlana, however, was permitted to come to India to immerse Singh's ashes in the Ganga River.

On 23 March 1967, the American Ambassador Chester Bowles brought a memo for Indira Gandhi, which Svetlana had given to a member of the American Embassy on 6 March. He requested the Prime Minister to look at it. Indira Gandhi told the American Ambassador that the Soviets were putting the blame on India for allowing Svetlana to leave India. On 7 March, Svetlana had lunched with the Russian Ambassador and asked if she could remain in India. Her request had been promptly rejected. The Ambassador had handed back her passport and an air ticket to Moscow and had asked Svetlana to leave the next day. Svetlana then got into a taxi and drove to the US Embassy to seek asylum. She was persuaded to take a flight to New York. The Soviets were furious and our Ambassador in Moscow was given a dressing down by Foreign Minister Andrei Gromyko.

◆

In July 1967, the Prime Minister's secretary L.K. Jha was appointed Governor of the Reserve Bank of India. Jha was replaced by Parmeshwar Narain Haksar. For me it was a welcome change, for I had not warmed up to Jha. He had not taken kindly to my joining the Prime Minister's Secretariat without his being consulted. Haksar was a forceful character with a powerful intellect. He inspired us with his Nehruvian vision of India and his ability. Ideologically, he was Left-leaning and in his youth he had been an active communist. Within a few months, Haksar made the Prime Minister's Secretariat the most powerful institution in the Government of India, reducing the authority of the Cabinet Secretariat. Soon he became the Prime Minister's closest confidante and adviser. Haksar also helped create the Research and Analysis Wing (RAW), India's first-ever foreign intelligence bureau. By the end of 1967, he was the most powerful civil servant in India.

But the Prime Minister's troubles within her party did not cease. The economic scenario was far from satisfactory. While the Green Revolution had changed the agricultural scene, the food situation was a constant worry. The worst hit state was Bihar, where there was acute famine. The Prime Minister visited Bihar and also travelled to Punar near Muzaffarnagar to meet the architect of the Bhoodan Movement, Vinoba Bhave. I also accompanied her. She also met Jayaprakash Narayan. Driving through the countryside, I was distressed to see the havoc that the famine had inflicted on the people of Bihar.

◆

Indira Gandhi enjoyed foreign trips. Her elegance, sangfroid, sophistication and ease of manner impressed one and all. Wherever she went, she was greeted with cheers, even enthusiasm. In September–October 1967, the Prime Minister went on official visits to Poland, Bulgaria, Romania and Yugoslavia on the advice of Haksar. These were satellite states of the Soviet Union, but each had a distinct profile and all of them held India in high esteem. At the end of the East European tour, the Prime Minister spent two days in Cairo, during which she held extensive discussions with President Gamal Abdel Nasser. Israel had inflicted lethal blows on Egypt during the Six-Day War in June 1967. Nasser had offered his resignation after the defeat, which was not accepted. He was the tallest Arab leader, vastly popular, and much respected if not admired by other Arab countries. For Egypt, he was indispensable. He appreciated Indira Gandhi coming to Cairo as a gesture of solidarity. He desired closer relations with India and suggested that the two countries should collaborate in the areas of manufacturing and strengthen import-export ties. Nasser also explained the Arab attitude towards Israel—he insisted that there was no possibility of any Arab state recognizing Israel.

In 1968, Nasser visited India. A reception was held in his honour at the Red Fort in New Delhi, at which the Egyptian national anthem was played. Later, Nasser told the Prime Minister that the band had played the wrong anthem! They had mistakenly played the anthem from King Farouk's time, who had been deposed in the 1952 revolution led by Nasser.

Nasser died of a heart attack in 1970; he was fifty-two. Israel's comprehensive victory in the Six-Day War had affected Nasser in the same way that India's defeat in 1962 at the hands of China had affected Nehru.

♦

Mrs Gandhi was the first Indian Prime Minister to visit South America in 1968. The trip lasted three weeks. During her visit there, the British Ambassador to Argentina asked his Indian counterpart, 'How much did you spend on collecting such large crowds to welcome your Prime Minister?' The answer was, 'Not a penny.' Most South American countries knew little about modern India—many even assumed that Indira Gandhi was the daughter of Mahatma Gandhi. People were curious to see a female Prime Minister from India, 'a country of snake charmers and rope tricks'.

In each capital, she spoke of the Indian freedom movement, our foreign policy—with particular emphasis on Kashmir—and the economic problems of developing countries. 'We can face them not merely with idealism, not merely with sentimentality, but clear thinking and hard-headed analysis,' she said at the university of Buenos Aires.

A pleasant diversion in Buenos Aires was a meeting with Victoria Ocampo, a poet and editor of the well-known Spanish literary magazine, *Sur*. Rabindranath Tagore had stayed with her for six weeks in 1924 at her huge estate, San Isidro, outside Buenos Aires. She had translated *Gitanjali* into Spanish. For a short while, he seemed to have fallen in platonic love with 'Vijaya', the name he gave the beautiful Victoria. He wrote some of his most lyrical poems on his voyage back to India. Mrs Gandhi, in her capacity as Chancellor of Visva-Bharati University made her an Honorary Doctor of Literature. Victoria was now old, with failing eyesight. I was more than glad to meet so celebrated a lady.

In several South American universities Tagore's poems were read and taught. Mahatma Gandhi's statues were installed in at least four countries of South America.

♦

When the Soviets violated the sovereignty and territorial integrity of Czechoslovakia in June 1968, Mrs Gandhi did not condemn them publicly. However, she conveyed her discomfiture through diplomatic channels. This was appreciated by the Soviet leaders. During the Bangladesh crisis they supported her and made sure that China did not intervene on Pakistan's side. I visited the Soviet Union twice to hold discussions with the Foreign Minister of Russia and I couldn't help but reach the conclusion that the nation was a genuine friend of India.

On 28 August 1968, unbounded happiness arrived in our lives with the birth of our son, Jagat, at the Willingdon Hospital, delivered by Dr Gaur Sen. Congratulatory letters, telegrams and telephone calls poured in. Indira Gandhi sent an affectionate handwritten note. My family and friends added to our joy. Jagat slept most of the day and howled most of the night. I learnt to tie his nappies. Hem and I took turns to take him in our arms, walking up and down the small veranda. Jagat was indeed a lovely baby. For us, he could do no wrong. All parents think their children are special. Jagat certainly was.

A year later, our daughter, Ritu, arrived. Indira Gandhi wrote a charming letter on the occasion, 'You certainly have done better planning than many of us. My heart has always yearned for a daughter, so I can imagine your joy in Jagat's having a baby sister.'

♦

Indira Gandhi faced multiple challenges in June 1969. The most serious one was the attempt by the Syndicate, which was led by Congress President S. Nijalingappa and supported by Morarji

Desai, to wrest power. During the AICC meet at Faridabad that year, Nijalingappa made a withering attack on Indira Gandhi's functioning and her economic policies. The stakes were very high. She had to act quickly to counter the threat. As a first step to securing her position, Mrs Gandhi wrote to the Deputy Prime Minister, Morarji Desai, telling him that she would very much like him to continue in his role as minister and that he could choose any portfolio, except finance. It was a bold decision. As expected, Morarji Desai felt insulted and resigned from the Cabinet. Next, she nationalized fourteen banks, a step which was widely welcomed in the country. The Prime Minister had demonstrated acute political acumen in meeting the direct challenge of the Syndicate head-on. Though I was not involved in the high-level discussions, all of us in the secretariat were aware of what was happening. Those were tense days and though the Prime Minister outwardly kept her composure, I could see how worried she was. In this crisis she relied heavily on P.N. Haksar, her principal adviser.

◆

In August 1969, the Prime Minister paid a brief visit to Kabul, along with Rajiv and Sonia Gandhi. There she met Khan Abdul Ghaffar Khan for the first time after 1947. In the evening, the Prime Minister asked me to go to Badshah Khan's house to ask when it would be convenient for him to receive her. He said that he would himself come to meet her at 4 p.m. I was fifteen seconds late in arriving to escort him, at which he showed his annoyance, saying that I should have been on time.

One afternoon, Mrs Gandhi had some free time and decided to go for a drive, along with me. A few miles outside Kabul she saw a dilapidated building surrounded by a few trees, and asked the Afghan security officer what it was. Bagh-e-Babur, he told us, and Mrs Gandhi decided to drive up to it. The protocol department went into a tizzy as no security arrangements had been made. Regardless, we headed towards Babur's grave. She stood at the grave with her head slightly lowered and I behind her. She said to me, 'I have had my brush with history.' I told her I had had two. 'What do you mean?' she asked. I said that paying homage to Babur in the company of the Empress of India was a great honour.

On 2 October 1969, Badshah Khan arrived in Delhi for Mahatma Gandhi's centenary. The Prime Minister, Jayaprakash Narayan and several of her Cabinet colleagues were at the airport to receive him. This was the first time after June 1947 that he was setting foot on Indian soil. It had been decided that the Prime Minister and Badshah Khan would travel in the same car. Jayaprakash Narayan also made a move to get into the car. When a security officer attempted to stop him, I saw JP get very angry for the first time. He pushed the man aside and entered the car.

Badshah Khan treated Indira Gandhi like a daughter and the fact that she was the Prime Minister of India made no impression on him at all. Badshah Khan was a law unto himself. He was invited to deliver the Jawaharlal Nehru Memorial lecture on 14 November 1969 on the lawns of Teen Murti House. He spoke for one hour, but did not once take Jawaharlal Nehru's name. It was a deliberate omission—he had not forgiven Nehru for agreeing to Partition.

◆

Dr Zakir Hussain suddenly passed away on 3 May 1969. Indira Gandhi was not in Delhi at that time, nor was Haksar. Dr Hussain's demise not only left a void, but had serious political ramifications.

The immediate problem which faced the Prime Minister was to choose his successor. At the Congress Parliamentary Board meeting in Bangalore in June, the majority had opted for N. Sanjiva Reddy, the Speaker of the Lok Sabha, as President. The Prime Minister had initially backed Reddy but later changed her mind as he was very close to the Syndicate.

V.V. Giri, the Vice President, was also in the running for the Presidency. However, he did not find much support—even the Prime Minister was not enthusiastic about his candidature. But when she consulted the senior members of her Cabinet, their advice was that in the prevailing circumstances, Giri was the best choice. The Prime Minister's close advisers were Chief Minister Dwarka Prasad Mishra of Madhya Pradesh; Uma Shankar Dixit, a member of the Congress Working Committee and a confidante of the Nehru family; and P.N. Haksar. The election of the President led to intense lobbying. By then it was clear that the Syndicate was determined that the Prime Minister's candidate should lose. They fully backed Reddy and strenuously campaigned for him. A third candidate was C.D. Deshmukh, who had been the Finance Minister in Jawaharlal Nehru's government. All members of the Prime Minister's Secretariat were in Parliament House, where the voting took place. V.V. Giri won by a thin majority. Two speeches were prepared for the Prime Minister—one to be delivered if V.V. Giri won, the other if he lost. All the officials of the Prime Minister's Secretariat were present in Parliament House when the result was announced late at night.

November was a month of unprecedented political jockeying and unseemly name-calling by the Syndicate. On 1 November, while the Prime Minister was in a meeting with President Antonin Novotný of Czechoslovakia at Rashtrapati Bhavan, one of her secretaries, Yashpal Kapoor, took her the news that Nijalingappa had expelled her from the Congress for indiscipline. When

I conveyed this to her, she told me not to bother about it. Outwardly she was calm, but I could imagine her inner turmoil. She, a granddaughter of Motilal Nehru, and the daughter of Jawaharlal Nehru, was being expelled from the party. This led to a split in the Congress, and Indira Gandhi formed a new party, the Congress (R). Kamaraj became the head of the parent Congress Party, the Congress (O).

◆

The pressure on the government to abolish privy purses was mounting by the late 1960s. At the time of Independence, too, Nehru and Sardar Patel had not seen eye to eye on this matter: Nehru wanted to abolish all privileges, including privy purses, but Sardar Patel (and Lord Mountbatten) felt that since the states had acceded to India, they were entitled to their interests being protected. It had, therefore, been decided that the princes would retain their privileges, properties and privy purses.

In 1967, the All India Congress Committee met in Shimla. Chandra Shekhar, the leader of the Young Turks, tabled a resolution seeking the abolition of privy purses. The resolution was passed, even though only twenty-five members were present. Prime Minister Indira Gandhi was taken by surprise, as she had not been present at the meeting. However, for three years the resolution was not implemented. The matter came up again in Parliament in early 1970. The non-abolition of the privileges and privy purses was attracting continuous criticism and could no longer be ignored. Negotiations were started with the princes and a decision was taken to amend the Constitution to abolish the privileges.

The rulers were unable to accept this. They established a mechanism called the 'concord'—an odd assortment of some misguided rulers, including my mother-in-law, the Maharani of Patiala. Three individuals mainly represented the concord—the Begum Sahiba of Bhopal, the Gaekwad of Baroda and the ruler of Dhrangadhra. My father-in-law and most of the larger states, except Baroda, refused to join.

The government was under pressure to find a solution. K.C. Pant, Minister of State in the Home Ministry, was nominated to hold discussions with the rulers. Then a member of Prime Minister Indira Gandhi's Secretariat, I was asked to represent the Secretariat in these discussions. I personally took a number of princes to meet the Prime Minister. I also kept the Prime Minister informed of the ongoing discussions. Eyebrows were raised when it became known that I was to negotiate and parley with the princes. It was said that in 1948-49, Sardar Patel had negotiated with the princes. That was indeed the case but 1970 was not 1948.

Mrs Gandhi wished for an amicable settlement. She wanted to resolve the issue amicably and avoid a confrontation, and she wrote a letter to all the princes to this end. A large number of them responded to the Prime Minister's letter but some did not, particularly the members of the concord. The Prime Minister and K.C. Pant held several meetings with the trio representing the concord.

A Bill was drafted for the Amendment of the Constitution in 1969. The princes were assured that they would not be put to any financial hardship. The formula that was worked out for them, after intensive consultations with various government departments, was a lump sum equal to ten years' privy purse, without tax, for each ruler. They would also be allowed to keep one palace, fly their own flags and have red number plates, on which they were very keen. It appeared to me that they were more interested in the frills than the substance of what was being offered to them.

To my great surprise, pressure was also put on me by three Cabinet Ministers to persuade my mother-in-law to leave the concord. Sardar Swaran Singh, Information and Broadcasting Minister K.K. Shah and Minister of State I.K. Gujral individually asked me to do so. I was very upset. I went to the Parliament House to meet her. She was in the Lok Sabha. I sent her a note saying that I wished to see her urgently. She came out of the House right away. 'What's bothering you, Natwar?' I said I was in her office as a member of the Indian Foreign Service and not as the son-in-law of the Maharaja of Patiala. I never discussed politics or official matters with my mother-in-law. I gave her the names of the three ministers. In the next couple of days, she called each of the ministers separately and told them to keep 'Natwar out of it. He works for me and under my instructions'. It was for these reasons that she received total loyalty from all. I cannot think of another Prime Minister taking such prompt action at the complaint of a middle-level official.

The Bill for Abolition of Privy Purses of Princes was passed in the Lok Sabha, but was defeated in the Rajya Sabha by one vote. This defeat was a challenge to the government. The same night, a notification was sent to the President de-recognizing the princes, which the President approved.

The concord took the matter to the Supreme Court, which upheld the government's decision. In 1971, the 26th Amendment to the Constitution was passed, which terminated the privy purses and privileges of all the rulers. The princes, by their thoughtlessness, did themselves irreparable harm. They were now ordinary citizens of India and would be paid no lump sum in lieu of their privy purses, nor retain any of their privileges.

In the end, however, the government agreed to give each of them one year's privy purse and the princely order became history.

◆

Prime Minister Indira Gandhi decided to attend the twenty-fifth session of the UN General Assembly in October 1970, which a large number of Heads of State and Heads of Government also attended. She left by a special Air India plane on Tuesday, 20 October and arrived in New York at 4.00 p.m. on the same day. She was accompanied by the Minister of State, Nandini Satpati, her Principal Secretary P.N. Haksar, Sharada Prasad, her Information Adviser, her doctor K.P. Mathur and me. At New York she had a reception to which came a large number of leaders from various countries. She was always keen to meet intellectuals on her foreign trips. Here, too, several authors, musicians and academicians were invited. She addressed the UN General Assembly on 23 October.

> I have come here to reiterate my country's deep commitment to the principles and purposes of the Charter. Ever since India became sovereign, the United Nations has occupied a pivotal position in her foreign policy. In his very first policy statement after India attained freedom, Jawaharlal Nehru declared:
>
> The world, in spite of its rivalries and hatred and inner conflicts, moves inevitably towards closer co-operation and the building of a world commonwealth. It is for this One World that free India will work, a world in which there is free co-operation of free peoples and no class or group exploits another. [...]
>
> [...] We have always affirmed that the way of the world should not be power but peace, not confrontation but co-operation. The world is not for destruction, it is for development.
>
> The irony of mankind is that we have the means, and we have the vision, but we lack the will and the trust to

take the one big step forward. As the Maitreyi Upanishad says, 'The mind is the source of all bondage, and also the source of liberation; It is by breaking through the cages of constrains that man can go forward.'

In the years to come, let the United Nations strive to think about an era of international transformation by consent, a new era of justice and peace.

◆

The Indian Ambassador to the US, L.K. Jha, requested Mrs Gandhi to leave New York on 25 October after attending President Nixon's dinner in Washington on the 24 October. She did not agree, so he requested her to write a letter to President Nixon, explaining why she could not attend the dinner. The Prime Minister asked me to draft a letter. Knowing her dislike for Richard Nixon, I wrote something diplomatically correct, but lacking in warmth. When Jha read it, he was very disappointed. He asked me to persuade the Prime Minister to make her letter more cordial. I told Jha that he knew her well; she had written the letter after much consideration and was not likely to make any changes. I thought it extraordinary that President Nixon did not realize that Indira Gandhi was unlikely to join a jamboree.

On the return journey, the PM stopped in Cairo and met President Anwar Sadat at the Tahira Palace.

In her opening remarks, she said that she, the government and the people of India had been shocked to hear the news of the death of Egyptian President Nasser. For her, the sadness was personal as the friendship between her father and President Nasser had been deep.

The Prime Minister told the President that India was deeply concerned about the future of the United Arab Republic (UAR), particularly in the Asian region, which was strategically important. She was confident that President Sadat would continue the policies of President Nasser. India supported the legitimate rights of the people of Palestine and the UAR's efforts for a negotiated peace. The PM also gave the President a brief resumé of the situation in India. She said that we were facing a complex situation as economic power was concentrated in the hands of the very wealthy and agriculture was confined to irrigated areas. The most pressing problem in India was of poverty. The people wanted change—economic equality combined with social justice. The policy of the government was being attacked both by the right and the left wings. The USSR was helping India but we wished to diversify our imports and not be dependent on one source only. Pakistan was creating problems for India. The economic condition in East Pakistan was bad. She also referred to India's relations with China.

She requested the President to give his assessment of the latest situation in West Asia. Saddat said that after the revolutions in Sudan in June 1969 and Libya, it had become clear that there was some activity which would be hostile to the UAR. The UAR had hoped that the United States would consider the situation in West Asia, but they continued to help Israel in every way.

When the US representative Mr Richardson came to President Nasser's funeral, he had asked him how it was possible for a small country like Israel to drop bombs worth one million pounds on UAR territory every day. On account of this, the UAR had sought help from the Soviet Union. If the Americans stopped aiding Israel, the UAR would not get any arms from the USSR. The President informed Mrs Gandhi that President Yahya Khan of Pakistan had visited Cairo and had taken the American line with regard to West Asia. The people of Egypt would never forget Jawaharlal Nehru's speech in the Indian Parliament in 1956 at the time of the Suez crisis. The talks lasted for two hours. Indira Gandhi also invited the President to visit India.

Before leaving Cairo, she and the Indian delegation paid homage to President Nasser at his grave. Indira Gandhi also met the widow and son of the late President.

◆

Having completed five years in the Prime Minister's Secretariat, I was keen to get back to External Affairs. She kindly agreed and I was posted to Poland. Even before my leaving, on 25 March 1971, the armed forces of Pakistan commenced their brutal suppression of the people of East Pakistan. I left Delhi on 2 April for Warsaw to assume charge as Ambassador of Poland. By the time I presented my credentials to the Polish President, the horrific events in East Pakistan were making news even in that faraway country. The Polish government adopted a cautious stance and issued no statement. The Ministry of External Affairs kept me informed of the unfolding tragedy.

Romuald Spasowski, the Polish Deputy Foreign Minister in charge of the Indian subcontinent, had been Ambassador to India. I got to know him well and had arranged for him to meet the Prime Minister more than once. Spasowski was an outstanding diplomat. From time to time, I used to meet him in the Polish Foreign Office and brief him on the events in East Pakistan. The world was gradually becoming aware of the atrocities being committed in that region which were arousing great indignation everywhere. The burden on India was immense; ten million refugees from East Pakistan poured into India.

In the last week of October, the Pakistani Ambassador to Poland, a Bengali, asked to see me. Unlike most West Pakistanis, he was a low-key individual and a likeable person. During our meeting, he broke down when narrating that his people were facing a ruthless onslaught by the Pakistani Army, which was 85 per cent Punjabi. It had become impossible for him to serve a government which was destroying East Pakistan and killing its people. I told him that we fully sympathized with his people and were discreetly doing what we could to help.

The Ambassador had recently attended a meeting of Pakistani Ambassadors held in Geneva. The main topics of discussion were the events in East Pakistan and India's role therein. Ambassador Bashir handed me a large envelope. 'This is the record of the Geneva meeting. Please send it to your Prime Minister. She knows you well. Ask her to save my people.' I was speechless. This was an extraordinary event. Here was the Ambassador of Pakistan handing over a top-secret document to the Ambassador of India. One only reads about such occurrences in spy stories. I assured the Ambassador that the report would reach the Prime Minister by the end of the week. I deliberately sent the package to the Prime Minister and not the Ministry of External Affairs, where it would only have been shunted from one desk to another.

A few days later, there was a dramatic sequel. The Ambassador met me late at night at my residence. I could see how distraught he was. Without wasting any time, he said, 'Here is the cipher code which Pakistani Ambassadors use.' I was flabbergasted. For an Ambassador, the cipher code is of the highest importance, as it is the key for conveying top secret information to the Ministry. Only two people in an Embassy are privy to this code: the Head of Mission and the Cipher Assistant. I personally took the Pakistani cipher code to Delhi and handed it over to the RAW Chief, Rameshwar Nath Kao. An accomplished intelligence agent, few had heard of Kao; fewer still knew his face.

By the time I returned to Warsaw, the Ambassador had resigned from the Foreign Service of Pakistan. He had informed the Polish Foreign Office of this. So far he had not been declared persona non grata, but his diplomatic immunity had been withdrawn. He faced an intolerable situation; if his government asked him to vacate the official residence, he would have nowhere to go. Secondly, if his official car was withdrawn, he would be immobile. The saving grace, however, was that he was not short of money as he had withdrawn all his official and personal funds from the bank. Since he was no longer an Ambassador, he could not see anyone in the Polish Foreign Office. I faced a dilemma—should I intercede on his behalf or not? Beyond a point, I could not help my Bengali friend. I did unofficially talk to the Deputy Foreign Minister to request him to let the Ambassador stay on at his official residence. This he ensured. Not a word appeared about the Ambassador in the Polish media. The Pakistani government was facing a desperate situation and had no time to worry about an Ambassador in Warsaw.

On 16 December 1971 Indira Gandhi made the following speech in Parliament:

> I have an announcement to make. The West Pakistan forces have unconditionally surrendered in Bangladesh. The instrument of surrender was signed in Dacca at 16.31 hours I.S.T. today by Lieutenant-General A.A.K. Niazi on behalf of the Pakistan Eastern Command. Lieutenant-General Jagjit Singh Aurora, G.O.C.-in-C. of the Indian and Bangladesh forces in the Eastern Theatre accepted the surrender. Dacca is now the free capital of a free country.
>
> This House and the entire nation rejoice in this historic event. We hail the people of Bangladesh in their hour of triumph. We hail the brave young men and boys of the Mukti Bahini for their valour and dedication. We are proud of our own Army, Navy, Air Force and the Border Security

Force, who have so magnificently demonstrated their quality and capacity. Their discipline and devotion to duty are well known. India will remember with gratitude the sacrifices of those who have laid down their lives, and our thoughts are with their families.

Our Armed Forces are under strict orders to treat Pakistani prisoners of war in accordance with the Geneva Convention and to deal with all sections of the population of Bangladesh in a humane manner. The Commanders of the Mukti Bahini have issued similar orders to their forces. Although the Government of Bangladesh have not yet been given an opportunity to sign the Geneva Convention, they also have declared that they will fully abide by it. It will be the responsibility of the Government of Bangladesh, the Mukti Bahini and the Indian Armed Forces to prevent any reprisals.

Our objectives were limited—to assist the gallant people of Bangladesh and their Mukti Bahini to liberate their country from a reign of terror and to resist aggression on our own land. Indian Armed Forces will not remain in Bangladesh any longer than is necessary.

The millions who were driven out of their homes across our borders have already begun trekking back. The rehabilitation of this war-torn land calls for dedicated team work by its Government and people.

We hope and trust that the father of this new nation, Sheikh Mujibur Rahman, will take his rightful place among his own people and lead Bangladesh to peace, progress and prosperity. The time has come when they can together look forward to a meaningful future in their Shonar Bangla.*

---

*A golden Bengal

They have our good wishes.

The triumph is not theirs alone. All nations who value the human spirit will recognize it as a significant milestone in man's quest for liberty.

◆

1974 brought a tragic note into my life. I was then the Deputy Commissioner in our Embassy in London. On 17 June, I was sitting in my office, reading some letters that had arrived by the diplomatic bag. My secretary came in around 12.30 p.m. and told me that my father-in-law, Maharaja Yadavindra Singh of Patiala, was on Line One. At the time, the Maharaja was the Indian Ambassador to Holland. He was a healthy, active and energetic person. In the seven years that I had known him since my marriage, he had never been ill.

We had a routine conversation, inquiring about each other's health and affairs. However, the conversation ended with his asking us (Hem, the children and I) to look after ourselves. This was unusual. I felt slightly uneasy.

I had a lunch appointment at Lancaster House that day. When I returned to India House around 2.30 p.m., my secretary followed me to my room. Noticing his woebegone face, I asked, 'What is the matter with you? Why are you so downcast?'

Hesitatingly he replied, 'Maharaja Saheb has passed away.'

I told him not to talk nonsense, reminding him that I had spoken to my father-in-law only two hours earlier. 'Sir, I know, but your father-in-law had a massive heart attack and died twenty minutes back. His private secretary telephoned from The Hague. There was no way of contacting you.'

For me, this was no ordinary bereavement. Its suddenness stunned me. He was only sixty-one. For several minutes, I sat with my head in my hands.

After calming myself down, I left for our house on 84 Park Street. On the way, my only thought was how to break the news to my wife. I found her in the drawing room arranging flowers. Before I could utter a word, she said, 'Papa...'

'Yes,' I said. 'Who told you?'

Her reply was, 'No one, but I knew as soon as you walked into the room.'

We caught the first flight to Amsterdam and drove to the hospital. The Maharaja's body was lying on a large table. His turban had been taken off and his kingly face appeared untroubled, tranquil and at peace. Hem kissed her father's forehead and I touched his feet. She then broke down.

On 21 June 1974, Maharaja Yadavindra Singh was consigned to the flames in the family samadhi before sunset. The funeral procession was witnessed by a quarter of a million people. The newspapers had articles about him on the front page for a week. Tributes kept pouring in.

Before returning to London, Hem and I met Indira Gandhi, who took us to the garden behind her house on 1, Safdarjung Road. Mrs Gandhi had known the Maharaja of Patiala for over thirty years and used to be on friendly terms with the Maharani. Following the death of her husband Feroze Gandhi, Mrs Gandhi had spent several weeks with my mother-in-law in Chail, the summer resort of the Patialas. They were intimate friends.

◆

Hem had been imploring her father to write his autobiography for some time before his death and the Maharaja had written a few pages. The first paragraph on the first page read:

To sin by silence when one should protest makes cowards out of men. Let him who dares, speak and speak again, to right the wrongs of men. They say what they say, let them say.

This could be his epitaph.

10

EMERGENCY

Speaking at one of the debates of the Constituent Assembly, Dr B.R. Ambedkar said, 'Democracy in India is only a top dressing on Indian soil, which is essentially undemocratic.' There is considerable truth in this assertion, but the reality is that Indian democracy withstood the brutal assault made on it on 26 June 1975 by Indira Gandhi.

The most authoritative and objective book on the subject is P.N. Dhar's *Indira Gandhi, the 'Emergency', and Indian Democracy*. He writes,

> I argue that if by 'emergency' is meant an abridgement of the rule of law which is the governing principle of a democracy, then in India the democratic substance started deviating from the long form long before 26 June 1975. The process was so gradual that it went unnoticed until the dramatic turn of events on 26 June 1975 forced it on the Indian consciousness.*

---

*P.N. Dhar, *Indira Gandhi, the 'Emergency', and Indian Democracy*, New Delhi, Oxford University Press, 2001

The literature on the Emergency is vast. I am confining myself to the impact of the Emergency in England only.

By any standard, Indira Gandhi was a powerful, dynamic and charismatic leader. After the 1971 war with Pakistan, her reputation took an upward trajectory and she could do no wrong. This euphoria was short-lived, though, and in the next three years, things started to go haywire on both the economic and political fronts. In 1974, Jayaprakash Narayan's Lok Satta Movement, which exhorted citizens to non-violently transform the nation, caught the imagination of the people.

Indira Gandhi attended the Commonwealth Summit in early June 1975 at Kingston, Jamaica. She cut short her visit on hearing the news of the death of Padmaja Naidu. On 12 June, Justice Jagmohanlal Sinha of the Allahabad High Court delivered the judgement on Raj Narain's petition against the Prime Minister. Justice Sinha not only set aside her election from Raebareli in 1971 but also debarred her from elective office for six years. Her initial reaction was to step down but Siddhartha Shankar Ray and Sanjay Gandhi persuaded her not to resign. She hit back on 26 June. The President, Fakhruddin Ali Ahmed, issued an order declaring a state of National Emergency:

> In exercise of the powers conferred by Clause (1) of Article 352 of the Constitution, I, Fakhruddin Ali Ahmed, President of India, by this Proclamation declare that a grave emergency exists whereby the security of India is threatened by internal disturbance.

The Cabinet was informed that the decision had been taken. Sardar Swaran Singh asked a question or two as to why it was necessary to declare Emergency. He did not last long.

Indira Gandhi's principal advisers were what the rest of us called the 'triumvirate'—D.K. Barooah, Siddhartha Shankar

Ray and Rajni Patel. According to Inder Malhotra in his book *Indira Gandhi*, '[Patel] had a brief moment of glory but was soon discarded along with his colleagues.'

By early morning of 26 June, hundreds of leaders from different political parties were arrested, including Jayaprakash Narayan (he had accused Indira Gandhi of the 'rape of democracy'), Morarji Desai, Atal Bihari Vajpayee, L.K. Advani, Charan Singh, Ashok Mehta, M. Karunanidhi, and the Rajmatas of Gwalior and Jaipur. Strict press censorship was imposed, electricity of critical newspapers was cut, sterilizations were arbitrarily undertaken, and the structures around Turkman Gate were demolished, allegedly under Sanjay Gandhi's orders.

The initial British reaction to the Allahabad High Court verdict was to give Indira Gandhi the benefit of doubt. One of my closest British friends, the well-known author and columnist John Grigg, wrote an article in the *New Statesman*, making light of Justice Sinha's 12 June verdict.

From 26 June onwards, however, the British media took a 180-degree turn. A full-page advertisement appeared in *The Times*, carrying the names of hundreds of eminent and distinguished people, the most prominent being Fenner Brockway, Mrs Laski, Lady Cripps and Dame Sybil Thorndike, all friends of India, all condemning the Emergency and the arrest of hundreds of prominent national and regional leaders, in particular Jayaprakash Narayan. By the middle of July, the British media was gunning for Sanjay, who was apparently influencing and guiding his mother.

Amnesty International was pushing B.K. Nehru and me; Socialist International was pressing for the release of George Fernandes, who had instigated a railway strike. He was then a member of the group, well known among the English and continental Socialists. British Foreign Minister James Callaghan spoke to Indian External Affairs Minister Y.B. Chavan about Fernandes's incarceration.

Three months after the declaration of Emergency, I wrote a personal letter to Indira Gandhi. While supporting the Emergency, I said that it was my hope that it would be short-lived. Uncharacteristically, the Prime Minister did not reply. At a Buckingham Palace reception hosted by the Queen, Lord Mountbatten said to B.K. Nehru and me, 'You have locked up all my friends.' He was referring to the Rajmatas of Gwalior and Jaipur, and Bhawani Singh, the Maharaja of Jaipur. We kept silent, but everyone heard what Mountbatten said.

The most vocal critic of the Emergency was Fenner Brockway. He was an important Labour Member of Parliament and had known Gandhiji and Jawaharlal Nehru in the 1920s and 1930s. He had also met Indira Gandhi several times. Brockway had supported India's freedom movement. Hence, he could not be ignored. I sought an appointment with him. Brockway spoke with fury against the Emergency and the arrest of Jayaprakash Narayan: 'You were probably not born when I first met Jayaprakash. Gandhi introduced him to me. Four years ago you sent him to London to put across India's view about the brutal suppression of the people of East Pakistan by Pakistan. I arranged a meeting of Conservative and Labour Members of Parliament here to meet him. Jayaprakash Narayan spoke with feeling and sincerity. His presentation of India's case was convincing and his speech made a very favourable impression on the Members of Parliament. Now you want me to believe that he is a traitor?'

It would have been counter-productive for me to get into an argument with him. I ventured to suggest that he might consider writing to the Prime Minister on the lines of what he had said to me and assured him that the letter would be forwarded to her by diplomatic bag. After a few days, his letter arrived and

I sent it to the Prime Minister. I also, rather daringly, wrote to her, 'I know what to say to our critics, but I do not know what to say to our friends.' She did not reply. Brockway also wrote to Jayaprakash Narayan, but that letter failed to reach him.

The Indian community in England was a house divided. Roughly 30 per cent supported the Emergency, the rest did not. Several demonstrations were held in front of India House, asking for the release of JP and other leaders. India House is located in one of the most prominent parts of London. The demonstrators had specially chosen this venue, being sure that it would get maximum media coverage. During one of the demonstrations, the High Commissioner had to use the back door to avoid being accosted by the demonstrators. All our efforts to contain the hostility of the media failed, particularly after the BBC office in India was asked to close down.

Unexpected side effects of the Emergency ensued. I used to regularly review books for the *New Statesman*, a Left-wing weekly wielding considerable influence. The editor, Anthony Howard, removed my name from the list of reviewers soon after Emergency was declared.

I have refrained from mentioning the socio-economic consequences of the Emergency. These were undoubtedly considerable, but no one in the UK looked at them. Politics took precedence.

During the first few months, I did endorse the Emergency, although I did not propagate it. Looking back on those melancholy and debilitating weeks, months and years, I now realize that my professional conduct did me no credit.

In November 1975, Congress President D.K. Barooah came to London and attended a dinner on 14 November, arranged by the well-known Indian businessman, Lord Swraj Paul. The guests included Michael Foot, Reginald Maudling, Shridath 'Sonny'

Ramphal and James Cameron. The Congress President made an appalling speech in which he justified the Emergency. His delivery was so poor that the guests made no attempt to hide their boredom.

I personally liked D.K. Barooah. He was affable, amusing and a voracious reader. But he was unacquainted with British norms and mores. Post-dinner speeches in England are brief and witty. My own speech to some extent made up for the damage done by Barooah.

I include here a brief extract of my speech:

> Two days ago, some of us were discussing the arrangements for this dinner. To my horror I discovered that Mr Michael Foot would speak earlier than myself. My heart sank. Some years ago at the United Nations, his elder brother Hugh and I sat in the same committee on opposite sides of the fence. It was hard enough dealing with the right Foot but there is no keeping up with the left Foot.
>
> Mr Eldon Griffiths, MP and our Chairman tonight, being the shrewd person he is, must have observed the look of agony on my face and asked me: 'Is it absolutely necessary for you to speak?' Now, Eldon, that is the kind of question a diplomat like me would love to ask a politician like you...
>
> Had this been a purely British function, I would have followed Mr Griffith's suggestion. Since it is a happy Indo-British occasion, I shall make a compromise. It is well known that functions connected with India in this country never start on time and having once started never seem to finish. Mr Griffiths's ensured that this function began punctually. It is now left to me to ensure that it does not end punctually.
>
> The British are slaves to petty punctuality. No offence meant. We in India suffer from no such handicaps. But when it suits the British they do not particularly care to look at the

clock. For nearly forty years, Mahatma Gandhi and Pandit Nehru in a polite non-violent way kept on reminding the British that it was time for them to go home, but our British friends totally ignored the clock of Indian independence. You will, therefore, forgive me this evening if I take an extra minute or two of your time.

The dinner was completely ignored by the media.

In December, I was asked by the Ministry of External Affairs to reach Delhi for consultations. I briefed the Prime Minister on the difficult time we were facing in justifying the Emergency. She was dismissive and curt. She said, 'Your High Commission is not functioning well.' I was unable to fathom how she had managed to arrive at this worrying conclusion. I couldn't say much in reply; only that those of us who were in London could merely do damage control. It was virtually impossible to 'sell' the Emergency in London which, in many ways, was an extension of India.

I did at a later date tell her of Cabinet ministers, Members of Parliament and other 'do-gooders' descending on India House, asking the High Commissioner to arrange for them meetings with leaders of the Labour and Conservative parties and other senior people. No one in the British establishment wished to meet these misguided people. It was impossible to sell the Emergency in England. The reaction in America was similar. Even Dorothy Norman, a well-known New York celebrity and close friend of Jawaharlal Nehru and Indira Gandhi, opposed the Emergency.

In December I came to India. During my stay, I got the distinct impression that the Prime Minister was under the sway of people like Bansi Lal, the Defence Minister, and Sanjay Gandhi, who kept telling her that the Emergency was necessary and had mass support. I was told that trains were running on time, and that officials had discovered the virtues of punctuality. Discipline was being enforced. Even Acharya Vinoba Bhave called the Emergency an 'Anushasan Parva'—the Time for Discipline.

A few days later, the Prime Minister asked me to join her for lunch. If I remember correctly, Rajiv Gandhi, Sonia Gandhi and Farooq Abdullah were also present. Controversial subjects were avoided, although I got the impression that Rajiv disapproved of his brother's activities and how helpless he was in the matters related to the Emergency.

B.K. Nehru wrote about that time:

> But I did discuss Sanjay's doings with Rajiv. He was as discontented, disgusted and depressed with what was happening as was everybody not belonging to the small clique of Sanjay's buddies and supporters. I asked Rajiv why his mother allowed all this to happen; he said that the fact was that she had abdicated in favour of her son. She exercised none of the powers of the Prime Minister, they had all been delegated to Sanjay. From what I myself had seen it seemed that she was operating as if she were the President and the Foreign Minister. It seemed that she did not know what was happening inside the country. Fori Nehru, not as circumspect as myself…had no hesitation in telling her [Indira Gandhi] of what she had heard in Chandigarh about the compulsory sterilisation of young boys and old men and of the discontent this was causing. To this, Indira's answer was to take her head in her hands and say, 'What am I to do? What am I to do? They tell me nothing.'

The next day, I accompanied the Prime Minister on her tour of South India. She attracted huge crowds. The south had, by and large, escaped the oppression of the Emergency. I met several of my colleagues in the IAS. Some were overtly cautious, others openly critical of the Emergency. In their judgement, it was not just an administrative undertaking, it was a moral issue as well. One of them said that the Prime Minister was damaging the ethical underpinning of our polity. I really had no convincing answer. In normal times, I would have reported this to the Prime Minister but those were not normal times. She would have asked me for their names. Those I could not give—it would amount to breach of trust.

On my return to New Delhi, I met Foreign Secretary Kewal Singh, a mild-mannered man and a member of the ICS. He was competent and hard-working but lacked courage and imagination. Aware of my ready access to the Prime Minister, he declared that I was doing an exceptionally good job at a very difficult time. I thanked him. He was a man who, soon after the declaration of the Emergency, had sent an almost unreadable circular to all Indian missions. I found it preposterous. Let me quote the paragraphs which highlight its absurdities:

> If officers have any serious reservations regarding Government policies already on the anvil or hesitations in implementing them, these doubts should be set aside or in the alternative they should report their inhibition and seek to retire immediately rather than show a half-hearted commitment to political policies and considered decisions.

Not only that, he talked of a 'Constitutional Emergency'!

> We expect Heads of Mission and all officers under them to observe the well-established ethics that a loyal civil servant must identify himself in implementing Government policies with unreserved dedication. Government have [sic] a right to expect such a commitment. Serious note will be taken if any further reports are received of critical comments

or lukewarm support of Government policies by our own officers. While this is a personal letter to the HOMs, we expect you to be vigilant and effective in ensuring the same discipline from all your subordinates.

In the middle of 1976, an English arms dealer came to see me. He said that India was going to revise her defence policy and would no longer be buying military equipment from the Soviet Union. He said that he had been to Delhi and had met the Defence Minister, who had conveyed this information to him. I was astounded. As the High Commissioner was away, I immediately sent a top secret telegram to the Foreign Secretary. This telegram was shown to Sanjay, who, in any case, was seeing files from most ministries and summoning ministers.

By the end of 1976, Indira Gandhi began to feel uneasy at the state of affairs. Some of her advisers had proposed that the term of the Lok Sabha be extended to six years and that the Emergency be continued. To her credit, it must be said that she followed her instinct and her democratic side asserted itself. She announced elections to the Lok Sabha which were then held in early 1977. During her election campaign, she faced an unusual situation. Her meetings were poorly attended and, in some cases, the people who turned up waved black flags in protest. One or two meetings were even disrupted. Meanwhile, Jayaprakash Narayan had succeeded in putting together leaders from various political parties who jointly contested the Lok Sabha election. When the results were announced, Indira Gandhi and her son lost their Lok Sabha seats from Amethi and Raebareli. The Congress won only one seat in all of North India even though it fared slightly better in the south.

The Emergency was lifted on 21 March 1977. Immediately after, Babu Jagjivan Ram, former Uttar Pradesh Chief Minister

H.N. Bahuguna and Nandini Satpati from Orissa resigned from the Congress and joined hands with the JP group. After the ensuing elections, a coalition government of the Janata Party under the leadership of Morarji Desai was sworn in on 22 March 1977. To us in the High Commission, the degree to which the Congress had been wiped out came as a surprise. We had had our doubts, but were wholly unprepared for the rout.

Even after four decades, the memory of the Emergency survives. All those above the age of fifty remember those turbulent months with trepidation. The Emergency made a permanent dent on Indira Gandhi's reputation. And while I know that she regretted it, she had no one to blame but herself. She had once even claimed that the reason for declaring the Emergency was a conspiracy to overthrow the government. To this date, no proof has come up of any such conspiracy.

While it is the duty of a diplomat to justify the policies of his government, there are times when a great strain is put on him to do so. What we had, in fact, been doing was justifying the unjustifiable, selling the unsaleable, promoting the unpromotable and legitimizing the unlegitimizable. And, in the process, I was disregarding my conscience. It is one period of my life which I do not look upon with pride.

11

MY YEARS IN ZAMBIA

It was not until 1977, after Morarji Desai had become Prime Minister, that his not-so-benign shadow crossed my professional path. At the time I was Deputy High Commissioner in London. A top-secret telegram arrived on 24 March 1977 telling the High Commissioner, B.K. Nehru, that I should immediately be asked to proceed on leave and hand over charge. This entailed considerable upheaval for my wife and our two little children.

In June, the Commonwealth Summit was held in London and Morarji Desai decided to attend. He stayed with Indira Gandhi's cousin, B.K. Nehru, at 9 Kensington Palace Gardens, one of the most elegant addresses in London. This surprised me. B.K. Nehru, like me, had defended the Emergency. I learnt that as soon as Morarji Desai took over as PM, Fori Nehru, B.K. Nehru's wife, had written him ingratiating letters. Mrs Gandhi was livid when she learnt that her second cousin was playing host to her principal political opponent. As I was on compulsory leave, I kept out of the way of the Prime Minister. One evening, I got a telephone call from B.K. Nehru telling me that the Prime Minister wished to see the High Commissioner's 'Discretionary

Grant' register. Important diplomatic posts have such funds at their disposal and I, as Deputy High Commissioner, had charge of the Discretionary Grant. B.K. Nehru asked me how much of the grant we had utilized in the past one year and how much was sanctioned by the government. I told him to send for the grant register and show it to Morarji Desai. The amount sanctioned was five thousand pounds, of which five hundred pounds had been utilized. The rest had been surrendered.

I was later told that the Prime Minister was quite beside himself on hearing this and accused me of hiding facts. He had apparently been told by some of his admirers in London that Mrs Gandhi was in direct touch with me and vast amounts of foreign currency were sent by diplomatic bag to me. In retrospect, this sounds farcical and fanciful. It was not so pleasant at the time.

Obviously Morarji Desai had not the vaguest idea of what a diplomatic bag contained. Diplomatic bags are not used to smuggle currency. Category A diplomatic bags are used to send secret dispatches, confidential records and the like, while Category B and C bags carry newspapers and other unimportant items. No cash can be included in these bags. The bags are opened under the supervision of a First Secretary. Since Morarji Desai could not prove his claim, he calmed down.

A day or two later, B.K. Nehru called again. 'Natwar, the PM tells me that on 26 June [the day the Emergency was declared] you threw a champagne party at the High Commission.' This was preposterous. I reminded Nehru that on the 26th, he and I were together at the High Commission throughout the day, answering queries mainly from the media. I could not resist telling him, 'Bijju Bhai, are you sure you did not give a champagne party at 9 K.P.G?' B.K. Nehru had a sense of humour and enjoyed the joke.

◆

Some weeks after Morarji Desai was sworn in as Prime Minister, I was posted as High Commissioner to Zambia. In the Janata establishment, all African countries were considered punishment postings—Kala Pani. Had Morarji Desai been aware that I knew President Kenneth Kaunda rather well since 1962, he would have posted me elsewhere. I got to know Mr Kaunda when he appeared as petitioner before the Decolonization Committee in New York and I was the rapporteur of the committee.

We left London on 10 August 1977, arriving in Lusaka the next morning after a ten-hour flight. I had been to Lusaka twice, with the UN Committee on Decolonization, but this was my wife's first exposure to the African continent. Our two children, Jagat and Ritu, were nine and seven years old then. We sent them both to boarding schools in India.

Lusaka was a leisurely place, with an amazing climate. Zambia at the time was the frontline state against the apartheid regime in South Africa and the Ian Smith government in Southern Rhodesia. It was a hospitable destination for exiled Southern African freedom fighters. The leaders of the African National Congress (ANC) of South Africa, the Zimbabwe African People's Union (ZAPU), and the South West Africa People's Organization (SWAPO) spent most of the time in Lusaka. I got to know and admire them. They were fighting against heavy odds. The Western democracies were supporting the racist South Africa and the Ian Smith regimes. He proclaimed that not in a thousand years would Southern Rhodesia have elections on the principle of one man, one vote. In fact, it was all over for Ian Smith by April 1980. South Africa had to wait for another ten years to put an end to Apartheid. Nelson Mandela was released on 10 February 1990. That day Africa changed.

I was also accredited to Botswana, led by President Seretse Khama. In 1950, Sir Seretse Khama married an English girl while at Oxford, and this became a cause célèbre. The British government opposed this marriage, and his uncle, the Chief of Botswana, disowned him. Sir Seretse Khama did not bend or bow. After ten years, he made a triumphant return to Gaborone, the capital of Botswana.

President Kaunda of Zambia was deeply religious, happily married and hero-worshipped Mahatma Gandhi. He was a genuine friend of India. He and Indira Gandhi had a close relationship. When Indira Gandhi lost the 1977 elections, President Kaunda said to me, 'Natwar, Indira has lost the elections. She has not lost my friendship. Tell her so in whatever way you can.' Kaunda had an Indian 'guru', Ranganathan, who had come to Zambia as a teacher. Ranganathan had a remarkable facility; he could describe future events with astonishing accuracy and Kaunda consulted him before taking decisions of vital national interest. Thanks to Ranganathan, I was the best informed diplomat in Zambia and could also meet the President at short notice. No other Head of Mission had this privilege.

Joshua Nkomo was a well-recognized leader of Southern Rhodesia. He had come as a petitioner to the UN in 1962. India fully backed him in the Committee on Decolonization. I was the Indian representative on the committee and got to know him well. From 1964 to 1974, he was imprisoned by the Ian Smith regime. As soon as I got to Lusaka, I established contact with him. The first news he gave me was of his abortive meeting with Morarji Desai in London, a few months earlier, at the Commonwealth Summit. The Prime Minister had called him a terrorist. One of the leading freedom fighters of Southern Africa, Joshua Nkomo, had been deeply offended and had terminated the meeting. I got to know him well in Lusaka. He enjoyed Indian food. We had long and lively political discussions. He improved my knowledge of the situation in all colonial countries in Southern Africa.

Morarji Desai had no notion of what was happening in South Africa, Southern Rhodesia and Namibia; neither did he personally know the leading luminaries of Africa, south of the Sahara. He made no effort to get to know them either. Jawaharlal Nehru, Indira Gandhi and Rajiv Gandhi, on the other hand, knew many of them personally. African leaders looked up to India and held Gandhiji, Jawaharlal Nehru and Indira Gandhi in high esteem.

A few months after my arrival, I wrote to the Ministry of External Affairs that Joshua Nkomo wished to visit India. He would be accompanied by three senior leaders of ZAPU. He asked for first-class air tickets from Lusaka to Nairobi and to New Delhi. I assured him that his wishes would be respected. Such invitations do not involve any policy decisions. We were spending millions on humanitarian assistance to almost all freedom movements in Africa; four first-class air passages would be no burden on the ministry's budget. The response from the ministry was as unexpected as it was wooden-headed. The government would sanction first-class air travel only for Joshua Nkomo; his colleagues would be given economy-class air tickets. I sent a coded telegram to the head of the Africa division in the ministry, conveying my views on treating a popular and courageous leader in this demeaning manner. I also injected a bon mot as a teaser: 'Having swallowed camels we are now straining at gnats.' My telegram was shown to Prime Minister Morarji Desai by the Foreign Secretary. The Prime Minister, who probably did not understand the phrase, remarked that I was being impertinent and disobedient.

I told Nkomo that the present time was not suitable for the Indian government to receive him. Perhaps later, mutually convenient dates could be worked out. What else could I tell him? He was too seasoned a man not to see through my diplomatese.

In February 1978, I came home on leave for two months. I naturally met Mrs Gandhi and gave her President Kaunda's and Nkomo's greetings. I was shadowed by the IB when I went to meet her at her new residence at Willingdon Crescent.

During my absence from Lusaka, Prime Minister Mainza Chona of Zambia wrote a long letter to *The Times* of London about the ill-treatment of Mrs Gandhi by the Morarji Desai government. The matter was taken up in Parliament. Although I had nothing whatsoever to do with the Zambian PM's letter. Prime Minister Morarji Desai linked my name with the Zambian Prime Minister's letter. The clamour soon died down, however.

On my return from leave, an unpleasant 'gift' from Morarji Desai awaited me. During my leave, President Kaunda had written to Prime Minister Desai regarding the crisis that was unfolding in Southern Africa, with particular reference to Southern Rhodesia. He concluded his letter with an exceptionally generous reference to me:

> Finally and on a different subject may I say, as a mark of sincere appreciation, your new envoy to Zambia—His Excellency High Commissioner Kunwar Natwar Singh—is settling down very well. I am very pleased with his rare political insight and the fast speed at which he is clearly grasping the complexities of the current Southern African crises.
>
> I must say I was somewhat apprehensive when I heard you were taking out your previous High Commissioner, a man I had found to be very wise and capable. I did not, of course, know the replacement you were going to send us. To my great satisfaction you have just sent us the right man.
>
> As it happens, I have known His Excellency Mr Kunwar Natwar Singh since the days of Zambia's struggle for independence. While he was at the UN he was extremely

helpful to me when I had to present Zambia's case for independence to the United Nations in 1962.

You could certainly not have picked […] a better person as your envoy in this region at this time of complicated liberation issues in Rhodesia, Namibia and South Africa.

Prime Minister Desai, in his reply, had this to say:

> I have read with interest your views regarding our new High Commissioner. I hope that Natwar Singh comes up to your expectations. He has been keeping us informed of the developments in Southern Africa.

I felt that the Prime Minister had let his High Commissioner down. On 15 May 1978, I wrote to him:

> Dear Prime Minister,
>
> On my return to Lusaka, I saw your reply to President Kaunda's letter of 18.12.1977. The President referred to my work in generous terms. Normally government should have welcomed this. The extreme austerity of your reply must make my task in Lusaka infinitely more difficult. I am sure it was not your intention to belittle or undermine the position of your High Commissioner in Zambia, but such an inference can be drawn and is being drawn. This is not a personal matter.
>
> Having been called a 'distinguished and trusted citizen of India' in my letters of credence, I continue to hope that I have your fullest trust and confidence, without which no diplomatic agent can discharge his duties and responsibilities.

The Prime Minister replied on 23 May 1978:

Dear Natwar Singh,

Please refer to your letter no. H.C/3/78 of May 15th 1978. I am surprised that you should attach so much importance to certificates from foreign dignitaries. They are entitled to their opinion as we are entitled to ours and they cannot expect us always to endorse their opinions without any reservation. I do not see why anything that I wrote in my reply to President Kaunda's letter should embarrass you in the discharge of your duties. You are needlessly sensitive about this matter and I am wondering how this sensitiveness fits in with the discharge of your duties as High Commissioner. There can be no question of lack of trust and confidence in representatives in a foreign country. If there were any such lack of confidence or trust, they would not be there.

Yours sincerely,
Morarji Desai

I had some friends in the ministry who kept me informed of the sordid state of affairs. Those who had crawled before Indira Gandhi when she was PM were now abusing her and prostrating before Morarji Desai. I also learnt that my telegrams and letters to the PM were taken as acts of wilful insubordination, which they indeed were. My reply to Morarji Desai's letter on 1 June 1978 was sufficiently insolent to annoy him.

Dear Prime Minister,

I am most grateful to you for your prompt reply to my letter of May 15. Parts of your letter do grave injustice to me. Constituted as I am I cannot but respond. I do so with the utmost humility and respect.

I completed twenty-five years in the Indian Foreign Service on 14.4.1978. Five of these were spent on the staff of a great Prime Minister (It is for this that I have been singled out for special treatment. But I cannot and will not deny my past). During these two-and-a-half decades, I have never needed nor sought certificates from any one. I would consider such activity contemptible and degrading. However, when the distinguished Head of State of a friendly country speaks well of your representative in his capital, the least we can do is to thank him for it. You will, Sir, agree with me that President Kaunda is not just any 'foreign dignitary'. He has presided over the destiny of his country and people for fourteen years. A somewhat longer tenure at the helm compared to some other Heads of Government.

In your letter you say that I am being 'needlessly sensitive'. Sensitivity is an attribute of refinement of character.

Finally, Prime Minister, I am comforted to learn that I do have the confidence and trust of the government over which you preside.

With respects

I received no reply. I did not expect one. The only result was denial of promotion.

◆

The Commonwealth Summit was scheduled to be held in Lusaka in July 1979. By then I had completed two years in the Zambian capital. The economy had deteriorated; the national currency, Kwacha, was on a downward slide. Earlier in the year,

Southern Rhodesian troops had attacked ANC cells in Zambia and had burnt down Joshua Nkomo's bungalow in the centre of Lusaka without being challenged by Zambian troops. Regardless, Kenneth Kaunda's authority and popularity was unchallenged. One item on the Commonwealth Summit agenda was the election of the Secretary General of the Commonwealth. Shridath 'Sonny' Ramphal's five-year term was ending in 1980. He was seeking a second term and had informed President Kaunda about his intention. I knew Ramphal well. He had been an excellent Secretary General and was well liked. I took it for granted that he would be unanimously re-elected.

In early June, the British High Commissioner casually said to me, 'So, Jagat Mehta is your candidate for the Secretary General's post. You must have been asked to sound out the Zambians. What was their response?'

I was astonished. The ministry had not informed me of this. I immediately sent a telegram to the Foreign Secretary. He did not reply.

President Kaunda, as host, was to preside over the summit. He sent for me and asked why India was opposing the re-election of Sonny Ramphal. It was news to me, I told President Kaunda, adding that there must be some communication gap or misunderstanding. Dr Kaunda asked me to check with Delhi and report back to him.

As luck would have it, Moni Malhoutra, Special Assistant to Secretary General Ramphal, was due in Lusaka in a couple of days. We had been colleagues for five years in Indira Gandhi's office. Moni Malhoutra confirmed that India was opposing Sonny Ramphal's re-election. 'Who is India's candidate?' I asked.

'The Foreign Secretary, Jagat Mehta,' he replied.

'Had New Delhi not informed you?'

'No.'

We both shook our heads in disgust, if not despair. Lusaka was the nerve centre for the Commonwealth Summit, and the Indian High Commissioner was being kept in the dark.

A circular reached me on 17 June, stating that Jagat Mehta would be India's candidate. The letter also said that all Commonwealth countries had been informed except Guyana, Ramphal's homeland. In league with Kaunda, I followed the Indira Gandhi line to give Ramphal a second term.

Through my sources, I got some notion of the administrative chaos in South Block. My telegrams were not being circulated. Worse still, Indian missions in all Commonwealth countries were asked not to send any communication to Lusaka. Even Prime Minister Morarji Desai was being kept in the dark. As a matter of fact, he was being informed that I was working against India's interests. Despicable sophistries were being concocted to convince Morarji Desai that I was sabotaging Mehta's candidature. The Prime Minister was being further misled by the Foreign Secretary that his own candidature had majority support.

The advance party of the Indian delegation arrived in Lusaka a few days before the leaders. The officials had been handpicked by Jagat Mehta and given suitable instructions.

By now, President Kaunda and Sonny Ramphal had the latest tally. Ramphal had near-unanimous support.

Prime Minister Morarji Desai was to lead the Indian delegation. I can't say I was enthusiastic about this development. Morarji Desai's eating and drinking peculiarities were well known. His diet requirements were conveyed to me before his arrival. These certainly did not indicate a poor man's fare, nor that of an ascetic. Indian sweets (prepared from cow's milk) such as sandesh, peda, chamcham, gajar halwa formed part of it. Some 'Gandhian' diet!

Political events in India took a dramatic turn in the meantime.

A week before the summit, Morarji Desai lost his job. That came as a great relief to the Zambians, the Commonwealth Secretariat and me.

After the resignation of Morarji Desai, Chaudhary Charan Singh became Prime Minister. He had minimal knowledge of diplomacy or foreign policy and was wise enough to recognize his limitations in these fields. However, he made a serious error in appointing Shyam Nandan Mishra as External Affairs Minister.

S.N. Mishra arrived in Lusaka on 1 August 1979. The same evening President Kaunda met him. He informed S.N. Mishra of the latest position regarding the election of the Secretary General.

The Foreign Secretary, Jagat Mehta, arrived a day before the conference began. I frankly told him that he was not likely to make it. He would have none of it.

The Heads of State met in a restricted session the next day. The first item on the agenda was the election of the Secretary General. President Kaunda informed the heads that a consensus had been reached in favour of Sonny Ramphal, who would hold the post for the next five years. That should have ended the matter, but what followed was appalling. At Commonwealth summits, Foreign Ministers are seen but not heard. Mishra asked to speak. To my horror, he claimed the procedure followed for the election of the Secretary General was not proper. Mishra, thus, not only cast aspersions on the Chairman but also questioned the wisdom of Presidents and Prime Ministers.

President Julius Nyerere of Tanzania, the senior-most among the Commonwealth leaders, was so put out that he asked Mishra how many summits the Indian minister had attended. None. He told Mishra in curt terms that Ramphal had been unanimously re-elected. The procedure had the approval of 'all of us'. Next to speak was Margaret Thatcher. She was dismissive of

Mishra's intervention. The conference had more serious issues to deliberate, the most important being Southern Rhodesia. A momentous decision was taken on Southern Rhodesia, that it should become a sovereign state in which all citizens would enjoy equal rights. This was a major breakthrough. Within eight months, Rhodesia-Zimbabwe would be independent.

S.N. Mishra, however, did not give up. The day after the summit, he wrote Kaunda a letter in which he elaborated his reservations. He had been Foreign Minister for seventy-two hours. The sensible thing would have been to keep quiet and accept with grace the almost unanimous decision of the Heads of State.

President Kaunda's reply was scathing and a firm put-down.

Soon the role of the Minister and Foreign Secretary was exposed. The Indian press was more than critical of the Lusaka fiasco. Nemesis overtook Desai, Mishra and Mehta. They entered a territory called oblivion. No tears were shed.

◆

Morarji Desai was an astute politician, but he was obdurate, self-righteous, and lacked warmth and a sense of humour. He probably had not read a word of anything John Maynard Keynes wrote. As Prime Minister, he was pedantic and unimaginative. Today, he is a forgotten man merely thirty-five years after his death.

Morarji Desai was Deputy Prime Minister when I served in Indira Gandhi's Secretariat from 1966 to 1971. The two of them had different visions of India. Indira Gandhi was the future, Morarjibhai the past. While Mrs Gandhi always treated him with due regard and he, too, was correct in his own way, privately, he was unsparingly critical of her. He had convinced himself that the Kamaraj Plan, which suggested that senior Cabinet ministers and chief ministers should resign ministerial berths to devote more time to the organization, was directed against him by Jawaharlal Nehru.

Towards the end of 1978, when I was in Lusaka as High Commissioner to Zambia, President Kaunda decided to send his Prime Minister, Daniel Lisulo, to India with a large delegation. The Zambian PM had studied at Delhi University. The standard practice was for Heads of Mission to either accompany the delegation or arrive in New Delhi a day or two earlier to brief the Prime Minister and the Foreign Minister. I heard nothing from the ministry till the last day so I decided to accompany the Zambian Prime Minister's delegation.

When we reached New Delhi airport the next morning, there was surprise all around. I later learnt that a deliberate decision had been taken not to ask me to come to India. It seemed to have occurred to no one that Africans are excessively protocol conscious. The Zambian Prime Minister and President Kaunda would have considered the absence of the Indian High Commissioner a public slight.

My unexpected arrival was immediately reported to Prime Minister Morarji Desai. The next day I was told that the Prime Minister would see me at 8 a.m. My wife and I were staying at her mother's farmhouse in Chattarpur. It was bitterly cold. My wife drove me to 1 Safdarjung Road. Memories flooded my mind. For five years, I had come to this house almost every day. The elegance and the style of those days were gone. I was conducted to Morarji Desai's room which looked empty and bare.

Morarji Desai's opening words were: 'Aap bagair bulaye aagaye [You came without being summoned]?'

I said I had been told that he wanted to see me, therefore I had arrived.

'I am talking about your coming to India without permission.

You should have asked,' he countered.

I explained to him the reasons for my accompanying the Zambian dignitaries. He insisted that I should have taken the Ministry's permission.

There was an awkward pause, followed by the outrageous question: 'Why are you encouraging that terrorist, Nkomo?' He was referring to Joshua Nkomo, the freedom fighter.

'He is not a terrorist,' I replied. 'He is a courageous freedom fighter. We have been helping him and his ZAPU in every way we can.'

Morarji Desai was adamant. 'No, I do not want our diplomats encouraging terrorists.' This was said half to me and half to himself. After a pause, he told me that my reports from Zambia were too 'pro-Zambian'. I explained that I was in Zambia to strengthen bilateral relations, and that Zambia was a friendly country. Why should my reports be anti-Zambia? Kaunda was a committed Gandhian.

Morarji Desai's response was: 'Gandhian! He is financing terrorists.'

He had no feel for Africa and was trying to browbeat me. What amazed me was his untruthful claim that he had read my reports from Lusaka. I told him that he was the only person reading my reports; nobody else did. As I made to leave, he asked me where my wife was. When I told him that she was waiting outside in the car, he wished to see her. I refused. As politely as I could, I told him that while he could order me about on official matters, he could not do so on personal matters.

My mother-in-law was, at the time, a Janata Party member of the Rajya Sabha and was close to Morarji Desai. When she returned from Parliament in the evening, she told me that Morarji Desai had said, 'Your son-in-law is a badtameez [rude].'

Morarji Desai had behaved as he always did and I had behaved as I always did. Purely from the point of view of my career, it was not perhaps the best way to deal with the Prime Minister.

In December 1979 I took a short holiday in London. The main purpose of my visit was to give the manuscript of my book *Maharaja Suraj Mal* to my publishers Allen & Unwin.

The colonial office in London was fully preoccupied with the fast-developing events in Southern Rhodesia following the decision at the Lusaka Summit. It was decided that Southern Rhodesia would become independent on 20 April 1980 and the name would be changed to Zimbabwe. Robert Mugabe would be sworn in as President.

Indira Gandhi had become Prime Minister for the second time on 24 January 1980. Soon after taking over she telephoned me in Lusaka and asked when I would be coming to India. I said I would come as soon as she desired. I paid a brief visit to Delhi. My wife told me she had seen the Prime Minister who had asked about my next posting. She answered, 'Pakistan'. The speculation in the ministry had been that I would be posted to London as High Commissioner. But Hem and I preferred Pakistan.

Soon after returning to Lusaka I flew to Harare to meet Robert Mugabe. I met him at midnight at the place where he was staying, one known to very few people. I asked him about the programme being arranged for Zimbabwe's Independence Day celebrations. He said that was being arranged by the Governor, Sir Christopher Soames. I said to Mugabe that his country was the last to attain independence from Britain. If the arrangements were left to the British, the ceremony celebrations would be brief and not worth remembering. I also asked him if I could convey his invitation to Indira Gandhi to attend the Independence Day celebrations. I made sure that All India Radio broadcast this news. The result was that more than eighty Presidents and Prime

Ministers attended the celebrations in Harare on the 20th.

In Harare many Heads of State and Government called on Mrs Gandhi including President Zia-ul-Haq. Mrs Gandhi told me that she would like to call on the Pakistan President. Zia-ul-Haq insisted on calling on her. He was nervous during the meeting and she made it clear that his policy towards India needed correction. The meeting was not memorable. Before leaving, Zia presented the Prime Minister with a photo album on Pakistan. After he left I opened the album and found that the whole of Kashmir had been shown as part of Pakistan. The Prime Minister was not amused and asked me to return it to Zia. I sat on it till I arrived in Islamabad two months later.

12

IN PAKISTAN

Indo-Pak relations have been, and are, accident-prone. The future lies in the past. Kashmir is the ultimate hurdle. We have to deal with Pakistan in a pragmatic manner if we are not to make a mess of the relationship.

◆

I arrived in Islamabad on 20 May 1980 with my wife Hem. On landing, I looked out of the aircraft window. The media was on the tarmac in full force. I was pleasantly surprised—the Government of Pakistan had obviously taken a policy decision to give the Indian Ambassador a red-carpet welcome. But, as I descended the ladder, not a camera clicked and the TV-wallahs took no notice. Who were they waiting for? It was only when the passenger following me came to the door of the plane that the media got going. The object of their lenses was the diminutive Foreign Minister of the Maldives.

Senior officers of the Embassy, led by my deputy-to-be, Satti Lambah, received me. I was eager to get started at my job without delay. I was somewhat apprehensive. Islamabad was the most challenging posting the ministry could offer.

Before leaving for Islamabad, I had called upon the Pakistani Ambassador to India, Abdus Sattar. We had first met in London in July 1954 during a four-week course at the Foreign and Commonwealth Office in London. We exchanged pleasantries and he wished me luck and success. Finally, I said to Sattar, 'I have, like you, been long in the diplomatic arena. I know what to say to our friends across the border. Tell me what I should not say.' His candid answer was one which I have not forgotten to this day: 'Never say that we are the same people. We are not. If we were, then why did we part company in 1947?' Throughout my stay in Pakistan, I kept his advice in mind.

I also read up extensively on Indo-Pak interactions. Many people take a black-and-white view of Pakistan. That is a simplistic and superficial way to look at this devilishly complex phenomenon. Pakistan has geography, but no history. Efforts to invent a five-thousand-year-old history could not and did not succeed. The most serious problem in the country is the unsuccessful search for 'identity' which still remains unresolved. The most traumatic event came in December 1971 when the people of East Pakistan revolted. They deeply resented being treated as second-class citizens who were never considered to be at par with the swaggering Punjabi Mussalman, the trigger-happy Pathan, or the Baluchi tribal lord or the Sindhi Wadera.

In order to create an identity, people need an idea of nationhood which transcends religion. Pakistanis to this day have not been able to answer that profound question: who are we?

For an Indian, Islamabad is a difficult posting. It was like living in a fish bowl. The same cannot be said of Pakistani diplomats in New Delhi; they greatly look forward to a New Delhi posting.

They do not feel as isolated in New Delhi as Indian diplomats do in Islamabad.

An Ambassador has to perform multiple duties. The most seminal is to get to know where power lies. In Pakistan, it was easy. Power was neither diffused nor shared. President Zia-ul-Haq had no equals. He was Chief of the Armed Forces as well as Chief Martial Law Administrator and President. He was not answerable to any legislature. The media, though not censored, did not have unlimited licence to write or say anything remotely critical of the President and his army.

I presented my credentials to President Zia-ul-Haq on 28 May 1980. The credentials ceremony in Islamabad is not quite as spectacular, colourful and impressive as the one in New Delhi. Nevertheless, it is still an event to remember. Before leaving for Islamabad, Indira Gandhi had asked me to take up with the President the plight of Indian prisoners in Kot Lakhpat Jail in Lahore. This I did. President Zia feigned ignorance, but said he would immediately inquire and let me know.

The President had power, but not personality. There was something misshapen about it. He was subjected to nationwide derision in the early years of his dictatorship. The President was aware of what was being said about him behind his back and took it in his stride. His lack of charisma was made up for by a stunning display of tahzeeb, tahammul and sharafat (politeness, patience and civility). Like Chou En-lai, he was a master at public relations. Zia-ul-Haq went on to become the longest-serving Pakistan Head of State; his tenure lasted eleven years.

After the coup in 1977, as a result of which he wrested power from the ruling Pakistan People's Party, President Zia-ul-Haq had assumed extra-constitutional powers and was answerable to no one. While he publicly announced that he would hold early elections in Pakistan, his declaration did not carry conviction.

The Pakistan People's Party, too, after the execution of Zulfikar Ali Bhutto, was a spent force and the party itself was deeply divided. The occupation of Afghanistan by the Soviet Union turned out to be a blessing for Zia-ul-Haq. His political isolation, following Bhutto's execution, ended the day the Soviet Union marched into Kabul. Muslim countries which had boycotted him so far now embraced him and he became Chairman of the Organisation of Islamic Countries. He faced no serious challenge. None would be tolerated. Although there was discontent in Balochistan and Sindh, nothing appeared in the press regarding these two provinces. The political process was at a standstill.

Zia-ul-Haq was proud of being a Stephanian and sharing an alma mater with the General helped me. While the General had not distinguished himself at college, he made up for the educational shortcomings by his military ascendancy. Another factor in my favour was my easy access to Indira Gandhi; Zia-ul-Haq knew that I carried weight in South Block.

Within a short time, Zia-ul-Haq and I established a comfortable working relationship. He was cordial and polite, I was correct and respectful. As the months rolled by, he became increasingly candid. While there was no fraternization, there was a degree of easy access.

In his personal life, Zia was a puritan. He did not smoke and loathed those who consumed alcohol. He prayed five times a day. Many Pakistanis enjoyed their whisky, but during Zia's eleven-year rule, never in public. His passion for austerity did not impress the upper-class Punjabis and the Karachi elite. They were hedonists, flamboyant and unabashedly feudal. Their lifestyle was both lavish and ostentatious.

Josh Malihabadi, the great Urdu poet, once opened up his heart to me. He deeply regretted migrating to Pakistan, ignoring Nehru's advice. And while Josh-sahib was not an alcoholic, the bottle and he were no strangers. Whisky inspired him to write brilliant poetry. A total misfit in Zia-ul-Haq's Pakistan, Josh-sahib drank daily but clandestinely. I did not. On Muslim festivals I sent him appropriate gifts.

Saideen, the M.F. Husain of Pakistan, was a less discreet consumer of alcohol. He told me of his encounter with President Zia at the Lahore museum. Saideen was thin as a stick. The President asked him, 'Kuch khate peete nahin, itne duble ho gaye ho.[Don't you eat or drink anything? You've become so thin]'. His response was, 'Janab Sadr sahib, khane ka to pata nahin, magar peeta zaroor hun [Mr President, I can't say about eating enough, but I certainly drink]'.

By the time I arrived in Pakistan, it had become a fanatically Islamic country. In Zia-ul-Haq's Nizam-e-Mustafa, the Ahmedias and Shias became second-class citizens. Within two weeks of my arrival in Islamabad, I sent my preliminary assessment of the situation in Pakistan and how it affected Indo-Pak relations. I did so because I wanted to give my views before I fell into a rut or acquired any prejudices. India was, of course, enemy number one. A wholly distorted picture of India was being projected in the country by the Urdu press. The Urdu media in Pakistan is very influential. The owners and editors of newspapers and news channels are, by and large, rabidly anti-Indian. I remember extremely vicious articles being written about Indira Gandhi and her family. One paper wrote that the Indian Prime Minister was suffering from a nervous breakdown and had asked a hundred astrologers and pandits to pray for her. Another absurd story was that of Maneka Gandhi being placed under house arrest. Our secularism was derided, our democracy depicted as being phoney, our economic and industrial progress was doubted, and our treatment of Muslims deplored. I wrote to the Prime Minister that I welcomed the challenges I would face.

'I quite like my job,' I wrote, quoting Ogden Nash. 'I sit in my office at Islamabad Avenue/ And say to myself, you have a responsible job, havenue?'

What were the challenges? First and foremost was Kashmir. The second was to understand Pakistan's serious identity problem which had affected every aspect of life in the Islamic Republic. The third was to keep a sharp eye on the ISI, which at that time was believed to be funding the Khalistan movement. Fourth was getting to the owners and editors of the leading Urdu papers, in particular the *Nawa-i-waqt*. The fifth was to deal with the residual problems of Partition.

Kashmir has poisoned relations between the two countries for the past sixty-six years and there is no mutually acceptable solution in sight. The status quo continues, as does infiltration by hardliners from Pakistan.

Kashmir was the principal issue on the agenda of the Pakistani government and it kept me busy throughout my stay in the country. Pakistan, was then, as it is today, obsessed with the Kashmir issue and raised it at most international fora, be it the Non-Aligned Movement, the Commonwealth summits, or at the United Nations. India, while not willing to concede even an inch, was not as wholly taken up by the issue. The Pakistani Army, the most powerful institution in Pakistan, was completely and openly opposed to any compromise or concession. Obsession and diplomacy do not go together.

The economic situation in Pakistan at the time was unsatisfactory. Inflation was high, prices were rising, industrial production was low and so was national morale. Balochistan and Sindh were restive. No worthwhile land reforms had been undertaken and Pakistan remained a largely feudal state. The bureaucratic-military establishment was all powerful. While Pakistan is not a failed state, it is a fragile one.

However, on the question of bilateral trade, which could have improved the economic health of the country, it was the Pakistan government which backtracked all the time and India's proposals for increasing trade were ignored without any compunction. The defence budget of Pakistan, too, was very high.

The quality of Pakistani diplomats cannot be questioned. They are a formidable group, and their best are as good as our best. For some Pakistani diplomats, the foreign service was both a cause and a career and, for a handful, it was a crusade. I developed a healthy respect for the diplomatic sophistication and subtlety of Sahabzada Yaqub Ali Khan, Agha Shahi, Abdus Sattar, to name a few. Keeping the Kashmir question alive on the international agenda for so long needed determination and skill. Even greater was their achievement in maintaining excellent relations with China and the US, at India's expense. That, too, when Americans were dead opposed to Mao's China between 1962 to 1971. Pakistan's relations with the United States were close and multi-faceted—the Americans supported Pakistan's stand on Kashmir. This trend was reflected in the Pakistani media, particularly the Urdu press. They reportedly financed Zia and gave him arms and ammunition. They created, trained and armed the mujahideen who later re-emerged as the Taliban. It was the US which sowed the seeds of Islamic terror and was later forced to reap the fruits of it.

For a military man, Zia-ul-Haq proved to be a shrewd politician. He used four instrumentalities to retain control over the country. Firstly, as Supreme Commander, he had full support of the armed forces; secondly, he assiduously cultivated religious leaders and orthodox religious parties; thirdly, he received considerable funds from Saudi Arabia and Kuwait to open a large number of madrasas; and, finally, he fully exploited the Soviet occupation of Afghanistan, which he projected as an attack on Islam.

Zia-ul-Haq's India policy was many-layered, and one of the most important aspects related to visiting Indians. He received everyone, regardless of rank, status or importance. Upon being posted to the country, I found that my predecessor did not attend the meetings Zia-ul-Haq held with Indians. I reversed the process. It was a change which was not welcome to the President or to Pakistan's foreign office. For the Indian Ambassador to be absent from such meetings I found unacceptable.

President Zia-ul-Haq was such a puritan in his personal outlook that he did not allow any cultural exchanges with India. He once told me that the scantily dressed young girls who would present dance performances during these cultural exchanges bothered him. Even Indian musicians were discouraged from visiting Pakistan—we, however, did not discourage their singers and musicians from coming to India. I was able to make one exception to Zia-ul-Haq's rule. For the Republic Day in January 1981, I invited Ustad Amjad Ali Khan to give a sarod recital at my residence, to which I invited a large number of Pakistani musicians and officials. The event was a great success.

◆

Karachi is to Pakistan what Bombay is to India. Cosmopolitan, hedonistic, business-minded, suspicious of Delhi/Islamabad officialdom, wealthy and anthropologically interesting. Both cities served dinner past midnight. Both boasted hostesses who added nazakat (finesse) to hospitality unsurpassed anywhere. Sindhi Waderas led luxurious lives. Pathans all but controlled the truck business. Baluch tribesmen looked fierce with their garments and guns—murder was common, recourse to courts rare. The tribe killed, the tribe provided justice. The Mujahirs kept alive the language of Lucknow. The Sabri brothers excelled

(*above*): Indira Gandhi, K. Natwar Singh, Queen Elizabeth II, New Delhi, 1983

(*below*): Having a word with Indira Gandhi, Palam, 1967

(*right*): The Zambian Prime Minister, Morarji Desai, and Atal Bihari Vajpayee; K. Natwar Singh behind Morarji Desai, New Delhi, 1983

(*above*): With Atal Bihari Vajpayee, Nairobi, 1977

(*right*): Shridath (Sonny) Ramphal, K. Natwar Singh and Julius Nyerere, 1982

(*top*): Hem and K. Natwar Singh with Lata Mangeshkar, 1975

(*bottom*): K. Natwar Singh with Emperor Haile Selassie I's lion, Addis Ababa, 1962

K. Natwar Singh with President Zia-ul-Haq, after presenting his credentials, 1980

(above):
Indira Gandhi, Fidel Castro
and K. Natwar Singh,
Non-Aligned Summit, 1983

(right):
K. Natwar Singh, Gabriel Garcia
Marquez and Fidel Castro,
Havana, 1987

Being awarded the Padma Bhushan by President Giani Zail Singh, 1984

Hem in a pensive mood, London, 1974

(*above*): After being sworn in as Minister of State, awaiting his turn to meet President Zail Singh, 1984

(*below*): With officials of the Ministry of External Affairs, Paris, 1988

in that exceptional art form, the qawwali. And Ahmed Ali was the epitome of Delhi's rich culture, immortalized by him in *Twilight in Delhi*.

I first met Ahmed Ali in Peking in July 1956. He had come with Prime Minister Huseyn Shaheed Suhrawardy. When we met in London in 1976, he had no recollection of that forgettable occasion. When I was Ambassador to Pakistan, we met often. The 'rebel' had become an establishment figure. I used to pull his leg about this. He died in Karachi at the age of eighty-four.

Karachi's prominent citizens in my time included Begum Liaquat Ali Khan, a Christian who converted to Islam after she married Nawabzada Liaquat Ali Khan. She was sent as Ambassador to several countries, where she entertained in the style and scale of Vijaya Lakshmi Pandit, flouting most budgetary considerations. She was an aging prima donna who had to be kept in good humour. Professor I.M. Qureshi, a great pre-1947 protagonist of Pakistan, was no longer mobile. I saw him once in the Naval Hospital in Karachi. A staunch supporter of Jinnah, he was not remembered by many Pakistanis. But Zia-ul-Haq kept in touch with him. Qureshi had taught Zia at St. Stephen's.

There was Sherbaz Khan Mazari—a sophisticated tribal lord, handsome, an epicure, a voracious reader and a gentleman politician who deserved to go far but did not. The Hafiz Pirzadas made a stunningly good-looking couple, and provided excellent conversation and delicious quail. It was difficult not to fall for the lady's charm and beauty. The Jatois, the Haroons, the Daulatanas maintained princely establishments and belonged to the twenty-two families who once possessed almost 30 per cent wealth of Pakistan. Their lifestyles made a mockery of the French and Russian revolutions. They only ate cake; bread was for the lesser breeds. All were in politics, in and out of provincial and national cabinets.

From 1981 onwards, Zia followed a two-track policy towards India. He launched a peace offensive towards India, the aim of which was to convince not only the Islamic world but other countries as well that Pakistan was making genuine efforts to maintain good neighbourly relations. On the other hand, he did everything he could to erode our influence, and continually accused us of exercising hegemony over the entire SAARC region. While we had no choice but to deal with the man in authority, I felt at that time that it was important that we avoid giving the people of Pakistan the impression that we were accepting the Zia setup. I believed that our aim should be to speak more about the people of Pakistan rather than about the government. I now accept that my perception was wholly wrong. The citizens almost always support their country's foreign policy.

During my tenure, Indo-Pak relations were correct but not cordial and, from time to time, they became strained. I had several meetings with General Zia when the US gifted F-16 planes to Pakistan. He told me with unusual asperity, 'Kunwar Sahib, you are getting much more from the Soviet Union.' Without being disrespectful, I asked why Pakistan needed such a large army and an excessively bloated defence budget. After the birth of Bangladesh, both the army and the budget should have been reduced. His answer was along expected lines: 'Our problem is India. Half of your army is facing our border.' Without entering into an argument, I reminded him that India faced military hostility from Pakistan and China, hence the large army.

Zia and I frequently assaulted each other with good manners. He was an expert at dissimulation, which he combined with a natural courtesy. And when it came to the question of Kashmir, he was implacable. He once said to me, 'Kunwar Sahib, Kashmir is in my blood.'

'Sir, Kashmir is in my bone marrow,' I replied.

It was a mutually fruitless play of words.

On the surface, the President always showed great regard for me and emphasized his desire to maintain good neighbourly relations with India, but I knew through our own intelligence agencies what Pakistan was doing to needle India. One evening, a banner headline was broadcast in a cinema hall stating that a member of the Indian Embassy had been killed in a motor accident. Two or three families from our Embassy were present in the hall. They rushed out as soon as they saw this horrifying news item but found that there was no truth to it and every member of our staff was safe.

At times, even more ridiculous situations developed. One day, my deputy, S.K. Lambah, was called to the foreign office and informed that two diplomatic officials of the Embassy were being declared persona non grata as they were involved in unlawful activities, harmful to the state of Pakistan. Their names were Santosh Kumar, the First Secretary and Major V.H. Rao, our Medical Officer. Lambah and I were both amused because neither of them had anything whatsoever to do with intelligence work. We, of course, felt concerned about our colleagues because their life would be disrupted. For Major Rao, it was a tragedy; he would never get another foreign posting.

There was yet another incident which caused great furore in India, both in Parliament and in the press. I had sought permission from the foreign office to visit Wali Khan, the son of Khan Abdul Ghaffar Khan. Not only was Wali Khan well known in India, he had many friends in the country, too. He lived in his family village Charsadda, not far from Peshawar. Permission was refused to me. Someone in my office informed the BBC representative in

Islamabad and the news was broadcast all over the region.

India reacted strongly to the refusal of permission. Pakistan had not expected this and, after few weeks, I was able to meet Wali Khan. The Pakistan government had put him in prison several times, but he hadn't agreed to any of the compromises offered to him and had maintained his almost complete control over the Pashtuns. During the three hours I spent with him, he gave me a detailed assessment of the current situation in Pakistan. He told me that President Zia-ul-Haq had asked the Governor of the Frontier province to meet Wali and offer him the Prime Ministership of Pakistan. Wali refused because one of his conditions—that the army be sent back to the barracks—was denied. He had a commanding personality and a sense of humour. I got to know him fairly intimately. He enquired about Indira Gandhi, whom he had known well before Partition. He gave me a handwritten letter for her which I passed on. I was grateful to have his overview of Zia's government and his policies.

Zia-ul-Haq was keen that Pakistan become a West Asian country, but the Arabs, though friendly, were not willing to include the country in the grouping. His relations with Saudi Arabia were extremely close and several regiments of the armed forces of Pakistan were serving in Saudi Arabia. Zia-ul-Haq himself had been there at one time. Wali said that both India and Pakistan carried a lot of baggage, which did not allow either a free role to follow a consistent policy. The residual problems of Partition remained—one brother was buried in India, the other in Pakistan; one daughter of a family was married to an Indian, and an Indian to a Pakistani. Many holy places of the Sikhs were in Pakistan, including Nankana Sahib and Panja Sahib. For the Pakistanis, Nizamuddin Dargah and Ajmer Sharif in India were places of pilgrimage. While it was impossible for any Sikh, or indeed any Indian, to get lost in Pakistan, it was very easy for Pakistani pilgrims to disappear in India. Wali Khan was a worthy son of a worthy father: fearless, courageous, defiant and charismatic with an engaging personality. I returned more than satisfied with my visit to Chardasa and greatly valued my meeting with a man of such distinction.

I met President Zia more frequently than any other Ambassador, with the exception of the ones from Saudi Arabia and the US. In one meeting, he was in a very relaxed mood and I ventured to ask him if he had any doubts about Pakistan being an Islamic state as he frequently emphasized that he was Muslim and Pakistan was an Islamic country. I was a Hindu, but I did not find it necessary to flaunt my religion. He responded in mock horror. 'Kunwar Sahib, how can you say such a thing? I am a Sunni Muslim and my Musalmaniat should not be questioned. I want to introduce Islam in Pakistan in the true sense. Our present political edifice is based on the system of the West which has no place in Islam. This country was created in the name of Islam. In Islam, there is no provision for Western-type elections.'

I was walking on my terrace one day when my servant came and told me, 'The President is on the line.' When I took the call, President Zia, after inquiring about my health, asked me if I was free to have dinner with him that night. I agreed. He said, 'Could you also give me a list of names of your friends?' I replied, 'Sir, your intelligence agency already has the names of my friends. As for the one or two who aren't on the list, I would like you to spare them!'

It is interesting to contrast Zia-ul-Haq's position with the one stated by Mohammad Ali Jinnah who, on 11 August 1947, spoke to the Constituent Assembly of Pakistan:

> We should begin to work in that spirit and in course of time all these angularities of the majority and minority

communities, the Hindu community and the Muslim community, because even as regards Muslims you have Pathans, Punjabis, Shias, Sunnis and so on, and among the Hindus you have Brahmins, Vaishnavas, Khatris; also Bengalis, Madrasis and so on, will vanish. Indeed, if you ask me, this has been the biggest hindrance in the way of India to attain the freedom and independence and but for this we would have been free people long, long ago. No power can hold another nation, and specially a nation of 400 million souls in subjection... Therefore, we must learn a lesson from this. You are free; you are free to go to your temples, you are free to go to your mosques or to any other place or worship in this State of Pakistan. You may belong to any religion or caste or creed, that has nothing to do with the business of the State... We are starting with this fundamental principle that we are all citizens and equal citizens of one State. The people of England in course of time had to face the realities of the situation and had to discharge the responsibilities and burdens placed upon them by the government of their country and they went through that fire step by step. Today, you might say with justice that Roman Catholics and Protestants do not exist; what exists now is that every man is a citizen, an equal citizen of Great Britain and they are all members of the Nation.

Zia's desire was to see Pakistan become the most important Islamic country on account of its size and population. He did not succeed in having that desire fulfilled. His first hurdle was Iran, which was a Shia country. Secondly, neither Saudi Arabia nor Egypt would countenance Pakistan's claim to be the number one Muslim country.

President Zia-ul-Haq would mention time and again that he was unable to tell why Indira Gandhi was hostile to him. After all, he had had very good relations with Morarji Desai. On 10 January 1981, I had a long and tedious meeting with the President at his residence in Rawalpindi. I had gone to deliver Indira Gandhi's letter to him, in which she strongly urged the normalization of relations between the two countries to build an atmosphere of peace, trust and stability, particularly in the context of the situation in Afghanistan.

He read it and felt that the letter demonstrated a degree of hesitation, suspicion and misunderstanding. He said that he was surprised that the Prime Minister had been unhappy with his references to Kashmir. According to the President, the Simla Agreement, signed between Mrs Gandhi and Zulfikar Ali Bhutto in 1972, did not prevent him from referring to Kashmir at international conferences. It clearly stated that the ultimate solution of the Kashmir problem would be negotiations between the two countries. He implied that there was an unwritten understanding between Zulfikar Ali Bhutto and Mrs Gandhi, which was not reflected in the Simla Agreement. Pakistan, he asserted, was fully committed to the Simla Agreement.

I reminded the President that he had connected the Kashmir question with Palestine in his speech at the United Nations. This was contrary to the letter and spirit of paragraph six of the Simla Agreement:

> Both Governments agree that their respective Heads will meet again at a mutually convenient time in the future and that, in the meanwhile, the representatives of the two sides will meet to discuss further the modalities and arrangements for the establishment of durable peace and normalization of relations, including the questions of repatriation of prisoners

of war and civilian internees, a final settlement of Jammu and Kashmir and the resumption of diplomatic relations.*

This point continues to harm Indo-Pak relations to this day.

I felt at that time that Zia-ul-Haq was simply playing with words and using the Simla Agreement as an excuse to make his anti-India pronouncements. In public he spoke in favour of the Agreement but, for all purposes, he did not think much of it because it had been signed by Zulfikar Ali Bhutto. For example, he said that he was willing to accept India as a bigger state and that Pakistan was not in competition with India and wanted to live in peace with us. At the same time, he said that he did not want to live under the umbrella of Indian security. From my talks with him, it became clear that his concept of non-alignment was basically different from ours.

While he accepted that India had taken important steps like increasing bilateral visits and setting up a Consulate General's Office in Karachi, he added, 'We cannot forget what happened in Bangladesh. We have also fears of motives of the Soviets through Afghanistan.' His country wanted to live in peace with India, but he felt that the Indian leadership did not appreciate this.

The fragile peace missive, however, produced one or two positive results. Pakistan agreed to release sailors and fishing craft which had strayed into Pakistani waters and which the country had detained. For the first time, he allowed me as the Indian Ambassador to speak on Pakistan TV on 26 January 1981. I had to, of course, submit the text of my broadcast to the foreign office. I spoke in Urdu and was later told that the broadcast was widely seen throughout Pakistan.

---

*http://mea.gov.in/in-focus-article.htm?19005/Simla+Agreement+July+2+1972, accessed 11 July 2014.

IN PAKISTAN

♦

President Zia-ul-Haq was invited to deliver a speech at the United Nations in his capacity as Chairman of the Organization of Islamic Countries in 1980. I was asked by the Ministry of External Affairs to be present in New York during Zia's visit. Both in New Delhi and Islamabad, we had cautioned that an unbridled statement on Kashmir by the President during his UN speech would have the most adverse impact on Indo-Pak relations. We were assured in New Delhi, Islamabad as well as in New York that the President was aware of our sensitivities and would keep them in mind.

I arrived in New York on 28 September. I was coming to the UN after five years. Not much had changed. The External Affairs Minister, P.V. Narasimha Rao, had already arrived and so had the permanent Indian representative, Brajesh Mishra: a clear-headed, cool, self-assured, occasionally aggressive man who would go on to become India's National Security Advisor.

As expected, we received news that the Pakistanis had gone back on their word. President Zia would be saying much more on Kashmir than what we had been told. We acquired an advance copy of the President's speech and found that parts of it were utterly unacceptable. Brajesh and I advised Narasimha Rao to not be present in the General Assembly hall when the Pakistani President spoke.

On 1 October, when Zia-ul-Haq entered the hall, it was less than half full but representatives of all the Muslim countries were present. After he had been greeted by the President of the General Assembly, he walked to the podium where he stood in silence. A moment later, we heard the recorded voices of a maulvi intoning verses from the Koran! Such an act in the General Assembly was without precedence. The President delivered a speech that was ridden with clichés and was unimpressive, but he spoke for eighty-five minutes. He shrewdly dove-tailed the Kashmir issue with platitudes on Palestine.

> We are conscious of the circumstances which have prevented it from enforcing its decisions in respect of the right of the people of Palestine to establish a sovereign State of their own in their homeland, or redeeming its promise to the people of the state of Jammu and Kashmir to enable them to decide their future in accordance with its relevant Resolutions.
>
> Since the reference to the State of Jammu and Kashmir touches upon Pakistan's relationship with India, I would like to say that, in conformity with our established policy, we have continued our efforts for further normalization of relations with India on the basis of the principles of the Simla Agreement of 1972.

For Zia-ul-Haq, it was a moment to cherish. A year ago, he was a person who was not welcome even in Muslim countries following the execution of Zulfikar Ali Bhutto. Now he was legal tender. He returned to Pakistan brimming with confidence and self-assurance. His performance at the UN and Washington enhanced his eminence and stature in Pakistan. That he could be away from Islamabad for over two weeks speaks for itself. He was safe at home and acceptable abroad.

The big event in the middle of that year was the visit made by the Indian External Affairs Minister Narasimha Rao. He was not keen on visiting Pakistan, but I requested the Prime Minister to ask him to do so. Narasimha Rao emphasized India's genuine desire to maintain good relations with Pakistan. The discussions between representatives of the two countries were conducted in a very courteous manner and Narasimha Rao's visit produced a fair amount of goodwill.

IN PAKISTAN

In June of that year, I was in Delhi for consultations when the Pakistan Ambassador to India met the Foreign Secretary. I was also present at the meeting. The Ambassador referred to an 'invisible Indian veto on Pakistan's re-entry' into the Commonwealth. Both the Foreign Secretary and I said the Government of India had not even applied its mind to the problem as the problem had not arisen. Now that the Pakistan Ambassador had made known his country's intentions, we would think about the matter.

I was clear that Pakistan should not be re-admitted to the Commonwealth. This was not a simple problem, because a number of Commonwealth countries, including UK, Australia, Canada, New Zealand and some Islamic nations, were canvassing for Pakistan. My reasons for disallowing Pakistan's entry were that when the country had left the Commonwealth, it was functioning as a diluted democracy. (Zulfikar Ali Bhutto had walked out of the Commonwealth in 1972 following the 1971 Bangladesh war.) However, at the moment, it was under a military dictatorship, the head of which had abrogated the Constitution, rendered the judiciary ineffective, and had publicly gone back on his word about holding national elections more than half a dozen times. Besides, Pakistan would raise the Kashmir issue at the Commonwealth summits. The Prime Minister agreed with this approach.

In September 1981, the Commonwealth Heads of State met in Melbourne and one of the key items on the agenda was the re-entry of Pakistan. India was a key player as far as the decision of the re-entry was concerned. I kept in close touch with the Secretary General of the Commonwealth, Sonny Ramphal, and Moni Malhoutra, his political adviser, to keep an eye on Pakistani activities in this regard. Without India's agreement, it would not be possible for Pakistan to rejoin the Commonwealth. At Melbourne, this issue did not come up for discussion in the plenary session, although it was informally discussed among some countries favourably inclined towards Pakistan. The Pakistan government was naturally unhappy with the outcome of the Melbourne conference. It was only in 1989 that Pakistan was re-admitted in the Commonwealth in Kuala Lumpur.

On 29 September 1981, an Indian Airlines flight travelling from Delhi to Srinagar was hijacked by members of the Dal Khalsa, who were in direct contact with Pakistani intelligence agencies. At the time, the Prime Minister was attending the Commonwealth Summit. I spent twenty-four hours at the Lahore airport and kept the Foreign Minister and Prime Minister informed about the situation. All at once, one of the hijackers was produced before me. He stuck his hand out and I shook it, not knowing who he was, after which I was told that he was the leader of the hijackers. I was worried that if the photograph appeared in the Indian press, all hell would break loose and was greatly relieved when the photograph was not published. I repeatedly asked President Zia for the hijackers to be extradited to India. He promised several times to do so, but did not.

◆

Every year, a large contingent of Sikh pilgrims from India visited Nankana Sahib, the birthplace of Guru Nanak. Towards the end of 1981, about 3,500 Sikh pilgrims came for a week from 21 to 28 November. Their leader was Sardar Atma Singh, a former Akali minister. The ladies' contingent of five hundred was led by Dr Rajender Kaur, a Member of the Rajya Sabha. They were accompanied by an official from the Ministry of External Affairs.

My wife and I drove to Nankana Sahib from Lahore on 22 November and spent several hours there. She was, of course, greeted by a large number of Sikh pilgrims, being the daughter of the Maharaja of Patiala. The arrangements that were made by the Pakistan authorities were first rate. All the buildings had been whitewashed and the lawns and the gardens looked well manicured. It was obvious to me and our intelligence staff that quite a few of the pilgrims had close links with the ISI. Another distressing feature was that a lot of illegal transactions were conducted between the pilgrims and the Pakistanis. Shawls and silverware had been brought from India and sold in Pakistan.

The pilgrims were received by President Zia-ul-Haq on 26 November. They also came to Islamabad and several senior Sikh delegates called on the President. In 1981, the External Affairs official who was accompanying the Sikh pilgrims was a woman, Lakshmi Puri. I informed the Pakistani foreign office that I would be present at the meeting and that I would be bringing Lakshmi Puri with me. She had accompanied Narasimha Rao during his visit to Pakistan, but had had a rough time. At that time, there was nothing I could do because the Foreign Minister accepted the Pakistani point of view but, as Ambassador, I wanted to make sure that Lakshmi Puri should be treated as an officer of the Indian Foreign Service and not merely as a woman. I asked Lakshmi to accompany me regardless of what the Pakistan Foreign Ministry had said. When Zia-ul-Haq saw Lakshmi, he was visibly put out and for the first and last time, he addressed me as Mr Ambassador.

The President was to meet the Sikh delegation in the lawns of his residence. When I arrived, the pilgrims were already seated. I sat down on a chair allotted to me and I invited Lakshmi to sit opposite me. President Zia did not take any notice of her. Soon I saw one of the ADCs of the President coming up to her. I thought that she would be asked to leave and immediately decided to leave with her. But then Begum Zia appeared on the other end of the lawn—Lakshmi Puri was being invited to have tea with her. I had scored my point and the President had scored his.

The Pakistani media and the government made much of the Sikh pilgrims. They were lavishly welcomed and their visit was extensively covered in the media. This was a very calculated ploy on the part of the President.

After the Sikh delegation had left, I spent about twenty minutes with the President. I presented him with an album of stamps commemorating the Hijri which we had brought out and also gave him a copy of an anti-Hindu pamphlet published from Lahore, which was being widely circulated. The President said that he knew the man who had brought out the pamphlet and was surprised that he had written such a thing. I said that incidents like this came in the way of improving relations between our two countries. He promised to look into the matter, but nothing was done to withdraw the pamphlet. The third point I took up was in connection with the celebrations of the two-hundredth birth anniversary of Maharaja Ranjit Singh. The Pakistan government had refused to allow Sikh visitors from India into the country. For the first time, I found the President somewhat preoccupied and subdued.

I discussed the activities of some of the Khalistanis, including Ganga Singh Dhillon, Jagjit Singh and their colleagues, who had been allowed to indulge in political activities harmful to India during their visit to Nankana Sahib. I cautioned the President about the perils of allowing the setting up of a Khalistani government in exile. The President laughed and said, 'You can rest assured that we will not allow Sikh yatris to indulge in any activities that would embarrass India. They would only be permitted to confine themselves to religious activity.' He further reported that while he had met Ganga Singh Dhillon thrice, Dhillon had never mentioned Khalistan to him.

I then took up the question of the handing over of the hijackers of the Indian Airlines plane. The President promised that the men would be given to us once inquiries were completed. I drew the attention of the President to what the Pakistan Ambassador had said to a senior member of the Ministry of External Affairs—that in the absence of an extradition treaty between India and Pakistan, it would not be easy for his government to hand over the hijackers to India. This was in contradiction to what the President had just told me. The President replied that while he had not heard from the Ambassador, I could take it that the hijackers would be returned and that the signing of an extradition treaty between the two countries would not come in the way of such a handover. The two issues should not be linked. Pakistan would very much like to sign such a treaty with India, at any time and any place that India wanted.

Having said that, Zia hoped that the goodwill shown by Pakistan with regard to return of the hijackers would be reciprocated when any member of the Al-Zulfikar group used Indian soil to attack him and his regime. On my part, I assured the President that such a thing would certainly not be allowed to happen. Finally, I told the President about the highly objectionable stories appearing in the Pakistani press about Prime Minister Indira Gandhi and her family. The President expressed regret and said that censorship in the country was applied to four or five items, that is, Islamization, the Head of State, Defence, Islamic countries and the Ideology of Pakistan. On other matters, the papers could write what they wished.

Soon after, I left for a brief visit to India. On my return to Islamabad, I met President Zia-ul-Haq and gave him a list of unauthorized intrusions into Indian territory made by the Pakistani Air Force between 14 and 22 December 1981. He read these carefully, picked up the telephone and asked his Military Secretary to get Air Chief Marshal Anwar Shamim on the phone.

He read out the list I had given him to the Air Chief Marshal and asked him to immediately report to him. Zia jokingly said to me, 'I give full marks to the Indian authorities for spotting an intrusion which was only four nautical miles in Indian territory and lasted two-and-a-half minutes.'

Next, I broached the subject of the hijackers yet again and the President reiterated that the results of the inquiry were not yet available. Quite unexpectedly, he began referring to the elections that were soon to be held. Under the Constitution, he would have to allow a ninety-day election campaign and, during that period, total chaos would prevail in Pakistan. The President rued the fact that the political immaturity of the leaders would poison the campaigning process and commended India for having leaders with generations of experience behind them. I responded with the observation that our institutions were working well and had been strengthened by Prime Minister Indira Gandhi.

A few months later, a group of students from St. Stephen's College, accompanied by the principal and two teachers, one of whom was Professor E.R. Kapadia, visited Pakistan. I requested the President to spare a few minutes to receive the team from St. Stephen's. His response was overwhelming. At the Wagah border, the President spoke to Professor Kapadia over telephone; the professor was quite overcome.

I accompanied the Stephanians to the dinner hosted for them by the President. The young students were extremely excited, as was Principal Rajpal. While I had expected a small, informal dinner, when we arrived at State House, we were conducted to a large drawing room. Apart from the President, those present included three Cabinet Ministers and four Chancellors, among others. Even I was surprised. The boys, of course, were awe-struck. Principal Rajpal brought out an old photograph taken in 1944, in which Zia-ul-Haq was also present. Accepting the photograph, the President touched it to his forehead and said that he would treasure it. He did not have a copy of the photograph because he could not afford to buy one in his college days. During dinner he asked Principal Rajpal which places he and his students were proposing to visit in Pakistan. He was told that they were going to Mohenjo-daro and Karachi by train. The President offered to fly them in his personal plane instead. The entire team was thrilled. Once they returned to their hotel, they found yet another surprise in store. In each room, gifts had been placed, some of them rather expensive. The professors were given a carpet each. Had a group of Pakistani students visited India, they would not have been received even by a Minister of State, let alone the President.

1981 was also the centenary year of St. Stephen's College. President Zia was keen to come to India and attend the centenary celebrations, but Indira Gandhi had her reservations. So instead, I asked the President if he was willing to write an article for the centenary issue of the college magazine, *The Stephanian*. He did so, and I presented him with a copy of the magazine for his perusal. While reading the magazine, he came across an article by Augustine Paul, who used to be his roommate while he was studying at St. Stephen's. The President asked me to find out Paul's whereabouts, so that he could write to Paul and send his autographed photograph along with the letter. With some difficulty I managed to trace Paul. He was working with the Indian Embassy in Bangkok. The President wrote to him, but did not receive a reply even after six or seven weeks. He asked me to enquire. I did so and like a good civil servant Paul reported that he had indeed received the letter and photograph. That changed his life. Since the news got out, the Indian Intelligence Bureau hounded him regarding his connection to the Pakistan President. They made his life hell. It finally took my intervention to get Paul off the hook. All for a friendship forged at college! This shows how fragile India-Pakistan relations were at the time.

◆

Soon after I was posted to Pakistan, I discovered that the Indian Embassy in Islamabad had no contact with the Bhutto family. During Morarji Desai's regime, our Ambassador in Pakistan, the able and affable Shankar Bajpai, had been instructed to keep away from the Bhutto family. This I found extraordinary. During my next visit to New Delhi in June, an opportunity presented itself when Nusrat Bhutto sent a condolence message to Indira Gandhi on the death of her son, Sanjay. I sought Mrs Gandhi's permission to get in touch with Begum Nusrat Bhutto. She immediately agreed.

The Bhutto family lived in Karachi. Mrs Bhutto was confined to her house on Clifton Road which was always surrounded by the Pakistani Army and intelligence agents. The Consul General Mani Shankar Aiyar could not help because he, too, was forbidden to have anything to do with Mrs Bhutto. S.K. Lambah, my energetic and well-informed deputy, was discreetly in touch with a small number of non-establishment Pakistanis, among them Dr Niazi, Zulfikar Ali Bhutto's dentist. He was also a member of the Pakistan People's Party and had been jailed several times. I fixed an appointment with Dr Niazi under the pretext of having my tooth checked. When I got to his clinic, I told him that I wanted his help in getting in touch with Mrs Bhutto. Dr Niazi himself was under surveillance. He told me that it would not be easy, but he would try his best to arrange a meeting. After several weeks, he informed me that Mrs Bhutto would be glad to see me at her house in Karachi on 21 August. Within a few days, I flew to Karachi. Accompanied by Consul

General Mani Shankar Aiyar, I drove to Mrs Bhutto's house in Clifton. It was one of the most painful encounters of my diplomatic life.

Zulfikar Ali Bhutto was born with a silver spoon in his mouth. His father, Sir Shah Nawaz Bhutto, was a man of some consequence. Bhutto was educated at Stanford University and Oxford. An accomplished diplomat, he successfully cultivated China at our expense and, in July 1972, he got the better of Indira Gandhi during the Simla Agreement negotiations. She let him off the hook on P.N. Haksar's advice. He was taking a long view of Indo-Pak relations. Bhutto could not survive a day if he returned empty handed. An unstable Pakistan was not in India's interests. The Cabinet Ministers, Swaran Singh, Y.B. Chavan and Fakhruddin Ali Ahmed, kept silent. Haksar carried the day. The Simla Agreement, signed on 2 July 1972, continues to haunt us.

Zia-ul-Haq was Bhutto's protégé. When the post of the Chief of the Army Staff fell vacant, Bhutto superseded several generals senior to Zia to give him the post. Bhutto assumed that a mild and submissive officer like Zia-ul-Haq would not cause him any trouble and paid with his life for reposing his trust in the man.

The house had a gloomy air about it. I found Mrs Bhutto with her younger daughter, Sanam—her elder daughter, Benazir, was then in prison in Larkana. When I thanked her for receiving me, she said that she was not sure that I would turn up as she had received confusing signals. I assured her that nothing would have prevented me from meeting her because I had brought a letter from Prime Minister Indira Gandhi. In Bhutto's time, the house would have been full of activity. Now it looked like a well-kept graveyard. It was quite obvious that Mrs Bhutto was suffering from severe depression. Not only did she have no contact with Benazir, she could not meet anyone else either. As a well-wisher, I asked her to recount the true circumstances under which her husband had been hanged. According to Mrs Bhutto, her husband had been killed several hours before he was hanged. The Jail Superintendent had informed them that the hanging would take place at 4.30 a.m. and had allowed the family one hour between 8 and 9 p.m. the previous night for one final meeting. Then, the time of his hanging was changed to 2 a.m. A senior General of the Pakistani Army, accompanied by one or two other officers, had come to Bhutto's cell an hour before his hanging and asked him to sign a document which would exonerate the Pakistani Army for their actions in East Pakistan. Bhutto caught the General by the collar. A scuffle followed during which Bhutto fell and cracked his skull. The Pakistani Army, according to Mrs Bhutto, hanged a man who was already dead.

As soon as I returned to the hotel, I received a telephone call from President Zia-ul-Haq asking me how I was and how was I spending my time in Karachi. This was to tell me that he knew what I had been up to.

My next lengthy meeting with Mrs Bhutto took place at her home in Karachi in the winter of 1981. Mrs Bhutto was all alone then, quite unwell and coughing up blood. The Pakistan government would not allow her to go abroad for treatment and no one in Pakistan was willing to plead her case with the President. I suggested that she could get the government to depute half a dozen senior doctors to examine her and submit a report to the President. If the report confirmed that she must be sent abroad for treatment, Mrs Gandhi could make a public appeal to President Zia-ul-Haq purely on humanitarian grounds.

A few days later, as per my advice, a panel of eminent doctors examined Mrs Bhutto and declared that she needed immediate treatment abroad. I sent a message to Mrs Gandhi and was asked to come to Delhi to brief her. She decided to write to the President of Pakistan to allow Mrs Bhutto to go abroad for treatment, purely on humanitarian grounds. I was to personally deliver the letter to the President. When I gave the letter to President Zia-ul-Haq, he was not amused, and considered our plea on behalf of Mrs Bhutto interference in the internal affairs of his country. I respectfully said to him that Mrs Gandhi had made her appeal after mature consideration and no politics was involved. It was, of course, up to the President to turn down her appeal. This I knew he could not do. Having hanged Bhutto, the last thing he wanted was the death of his widow on his hands. Mrs Bhutto left for London to be medically treated and Benazir became the leader of the Pakistan People's Party in her place.

Several times I mentioned to the President that our two countries would profit if the trade route from India to Islamabad was kept open. The goods that Pakistan was getting from America and Japan were available in India at much lower prices and that would also favourably impinge on the political situation. But the business lobby and the all-powerful army were against it. Although my job was challenging and interesting, at times I felt frustrated, particularly when I realized that for my Pakistani counterpart in Delhi all doors were open.

A few months before my departure from Pakistan the Secretary General gave me a document which contained the offer of an Indo-Pak no-war pact. No mention of it had been made three months earlier when P.V. was in Pakistan. The timing, I later discovered, was to impress the American Congress which was about to vote on aid for Pakistan.

Unfortunately, we in India did not respond to the Pakistan offer for nearly two months. This was doing us no good. The impression going around was that we were dragging our feet. Finally the Foreign Secretary, R.B. Sathe, and I succeeded in persuading the Prime Minister to respond. P.V. was in no hurry.

He was stuck on the 1949 offer of a no-war pact by India. I told him not to insist because that offer included arbitration and determining the vision of the people of Kashmir. Eventually India offered a treaty of friendship. By the time I left Islamabad on 1 May we hadn't received Pakistan's reply.

I am an ardent supporter for India and Pakistan to have close, cordial and good neighbourly relations. The main hurdle is the Kashmir issue. If one goes to South India, this issue is seldom mentioned. In Pakistan wherever one may go, the Kashmir issue is always raised.

Having been intimately connected with this matter for many decades, I do believe that no government in India and no government in Pakistan would agree to concede an inch of territory. Any government doing so would fall the next day. The Pakistan Army and the ISI would never allow any Pakistan President or Prime Minister to make any concession on Kashmir.

13

THE TWO SUMMITS

At the Commonwealth Summit held in Melbourne in October 1981, it was decided that the next Commonwealth Heads of Government Meeting (CHOGM) would be hosted by India. While not doubting our ability to efficiently organize a summit, Mrs Gandhi had some doubts about our surpassing the Australians. Within a few days of her return from Melbourne, she began to look for a chief coordinator for CHOGM 1983. I often came to New Delhi for consultations and, on one of my rounds of South Block, I gathered that my name too was doing the rounds. A day before I left for Islamabad, I received a phone call asking me to see the Prime Minister. At the meeting, the Prime Minister came straight to the point. 'You better pack your bags in Islamabad. You will be in charge of CHOGM 1983.' I was not entirely surprised.

I thanked her for placing so much confidence in me. It was a great honour. Out came the platitudes drip by drip. 'Madam, I have never organized even a Foreign Minister-level meeting. My only exposure to summitry was when I accompanied you to the Lusaka NAM Summit in 1970 and the Commonwealth Summit in Kingston, Jamaica, in 1975. I have been in Pakistan only two years. I like the job and have reason to believe that I was not making a hash of it.' She heard me out as she continued to sign her files. After I finished, she said without raising her eyes, 'Go and see Alexander.' End of the meeting.

I left Islamabad with regret, giving up perhaps the most exciting and responsible job the Ministry of External Affairs could offer. I was returning to South Block after serving eleven years in Warsaw, London, Lusaka and Islamabad. A new post was created for me as Chief Coordinator, CHOGM 1983. No one had the faintest idea how to run a summit which would bring forty-five Heads of State, including Queen Elizabeth, to New Delhi.

Just as I was beginning to come to grips with planning for the CHOGM, an entirely unexpected situation arose. I had accompanied the Prime Minister to Washington in July 1982. On the return journey, we stopped for twenty-four hours in Tokyo. G. Parthasarathi and P.C. Alexander were the senior mandarins on the trip. While G. Parthasarathi was unflappable, Alexander was immovable. From these two peas in the prime ministerial pod, I learned that the Seventh NAM Summit could not be held in Baghdad on account of the Iraq-Iran war. President Fidel Castro, the NAM Chairman at the time, had asked Indira Gandhi if India would agree to hold the summit in New Delhi in March 1983. My reaction was 'thanks, but no thanks'. NAM Summits needed three years to plan and prepare. Vigyan Bhavan was not even adequate for CHOGM, let alone a NAM Summit. On our return to New Delhi, serious deliberations were held to consider Fidel Castro's proposal, and it was finally accepted. The Indian Prime Minister would have the unique distinction of presiding over two summits in the same year.

The priority now was the NAM Summit. Unlike CHOGM, NAM Summits have a Secretary General provided by the host

THE TWO SUMMITS

country. Once again the Prime Minister selected me, disregarding the advice of her senior advisers. The general view was that I would not be up to the job and that the Prime Minister's faith in my organizational abilities was misplaced. But luck was on my side and I paid no heed to the naysayers. The Prime Minister had selected me and no one else mattered. I picked my own team from the Ministry of External Affairs, each one efficient, hard-working, enthusiastic and entirely dependable. Together, they worked as a homogenous group and laboured beyond the call of duty. Occasionally, minor hitches occurred but were resolved in no time, thanks to our team spirit.

Then, a meteor struck. The Prime Minister sent for me and asked why leaders and their delegations could not be put up in the Asiad Village. Not only would that save money, ensuring security would not be a problem either. I was dumbfounded. I thoughtlessly said, 'Madam, you can't be serious.' It was too late to retract. I had neatly shot myself in the foot. The Prime Minister put aside the papers, took off her spectacles, fixed her eyes on me and said, 'Dear Mr Natwar Singh, I am very serious.' Pause. 'Where do you think the money is coming from? Why can't we do this in an austere way?'

Having known her for decades, I knew it was perilous to say anything when she was worked up. I kept quiet. She again turned to her files. After a while I asked if I could have my say. She nodded. I told her of my visits to Baghdad, Belgrade and Havana to look at the arrangements these countries had made for the NAM Summit. We could not do worse than them. 'My accommodation in Lusaka was nothing to write home about,' she told me.

'Madam, New Delhi is not Lusaka. The Zambians did the best they could. You were given a villa, as were the other Heads of State. I was with you in Lusaka. All delegates were put up in five star hotels, not university hostels.'

However, there was a point beyond which one could not argue with the Prime Minister. She was not convinced. She decided that a large group including Rajiv Gandhi; G. Parthasarathi; P.C. Alexander; Jagmohan, the Lt Governor of Delhi; and I should visit the Asiad Village. On arrival, I observed G. Parthasarathi and P.C. Alexander waiting for Rajiv's comments. Rajiv first had a look at the dining room which resembled a college canteen—no benches to sit on, and long tables without tablecloths. Rajiv said nothing and we proceeded to look at the flats for the athletes. There were three small bedrooms with a common bathroom and no telephone. Parthasarathi said that perhaps these could be allotted to foreign ministers. By then I had had enough. I emphatically told Rajiv that not even first secretaries would be happy with these hostel facilities. How could we expect NAM foreign ministers to share bathrooms? Rajiv saw my point and the absurd idea was dropped. It was probably one of his inexperienced friends who had proposed this silly idea and had then convinced Mrs Gandhi.

We were losing precious time. My neck was on the line, not Parthasarathi's or Alexander's. To my horror, no decision was taken about the Asiad. But, at this critical stage, fate intervened. The Ambassadors of the NAM countries got wind of the Asiad proposal and told my deputy, S.K. Lambah, that if the rumour about the Asiad was true, then their Presidents and Prime Ministers would not attend the summit. I conveyed this to Rajiv and the Prime Minister and, to my relief, status quo was restored.

A high-powered Cuban team arrived in early February 1983 to discuss security matters with our people. The team was led by the Vice President of Cuba, Carlos Rafael Rodriguez. Rodriguez was an intellectual, urbane and wise; a man of refined temperament and with a subtle sense of humour. It was a pleasure

THE TWO SUMMITS

to get to know him. At the end of the session, he said to me, 'My dear friend, we are fully satisfied with the progress of the arrangements you have made. And you have done so in record time. Nevertheless, I am concerned about security. I say this as a friend. Nine attempts have been made to assassinate Fidel. All failed. We never let our guard down.'

I replied rather complacently, 'We have no serious concern about security. Nothing untoward is likely to happen. Relax.' I told him that the Prime Minister travelled in a car which was followed by a security vehicle. I could observe his scepticism, but he was too sensitive a person to get into an argument. We left it that. Nineteen months later, Indira Gandhi was assassinated.

In three months, we had achieved an organizational miracle. Thousands of people had worked long hours without complaining—esprit de corps can do wonders. Recurring administrative creases were ironed out without hurting egos, and mistakes were sorted out without the media getting wind of them. Some bloodletting was unavoidable, though.

It had been decided that all Heads of State and Government were to enter the plenary hall in Vigyan Bhavan, through the ornamental gate facing Maulana Azad Road. They would be received by the Prime Minister at the gate.

A few days before 7 March, I learnt that there would be only one entrance for all, including Heads of State and Government. I called the Prime Minister and requested her to visit Vigyan Bhavan to see for herself the implications of the new decision. She sent for me within a few minutes. 'What's bothering you now, Natwar?' I told her what had been conveyed to me and continued: 'Madam, have you ever been frisked? Have you ever stood in a queue at NAM Summits? For the 10 a.m. opening ceremony, we have asked foreign ministers and delegates to arrive at 7 a.m. The Heads arrive between 9.15 and 9.55 a.m.

The security outfits will never agree to their Kings, Presidents, Vice Presidents and Prime Ministers standing in a queue with other delegates. Please come to Vigyan Bhavan and see the security arrangements for yourself.'

The Prime Minister took one look at the security equipment installed at the entrance and asked sharply, 'Who has changed the security arrangements?' I pointed to the man responsible for the fiasco who was standing next to P.C. Alexander. Alexander did not dare to overrule him. She gave him a bit of her mind and then decided. 'Heads will come via Maulana Azad Road, through the ceremonial gate.' If I did not have ready access to the Prime Minister, the summit would have begun in chaos and ended in discord.

Lighter moments eased my burdens. The Deputy Foreign Minister of North Korea arrived with a large delegation to oversee the arrangements for his Great Leader's stay in New Delhi. Their demands: Kim Il-Sung would require an entire hotel for himself and his delegation. No one else should stay there; the road from the hotel to the conference venue should be closed twenty-four hours before the inauguration; the Great Leader's delegation would require eight seats in the Plenary Hall.

Here I stopped His Tiresome Excellency and told him that his leader, for whom we had the utmost respect, would be treated like all the other Heads of State. No exception would be made. To our great relief, the Great Leader decided not to come.

President Saddam Hussein of Iraq threatened to arrive with a hundred-member delegation on a Boeing 747. His bulletproof cars and commandos were to fly in another 747. He did not come, but his Vice President did, along with the commandos and was put up in Hotel Taj Mansingh. The Iraqi commandos tried to throw their weight around but our commandos soon sorted them out.

THE TWO SUMMITS

There were other issues. The Iranians had serious reservations about sitting next to the Iraqis. The Jordanian Foreign Minister asked if His Majesty could be given a seat away from Iraq and Iran. His Majesty, the King of Nepal, discovered slights where none existed. His courtiers were a bigger nuisance. President Zia-ul-Haq of Pakistan offered namaz five times a day and a special prayer room had to be allotted for this purpose.

On 7 March, President Castro inaugurated the Seventh Non-Aligned Summit. Never had so many Heads of State and Government assembled in New Delhi. On that morning, there were no delays, no logistical headaches, no security hassles. As I stood on the dais with Indira Gandhi and Fidel Castro, I felt my spirit soar. How happy my parents would have been! The next day, newspapers round the world had the picture of the three of us on their front pages.

It was too good to last. Trouble descended on me the same afternoon. It was Satti Lambah who dropped the diplomatic bomb: 'Sir, we have a hell of a problem on our hands. Mr Arafat has just informed us that he was insulted in the morning session by being asked to address the plenary session after the King of Jordan. He intends to leave Delhi at the earliest.' I immediately informed the Prime Minister. Fidel Castro would be handing over to her at the beginning of the afternoon session and it was she who would have to handle the mess. She said she would come to Vigyan Bhavan right away and asked Fidel Castro to join her. Castro called Yasser Arafat and asked him to come to Vigyan Bhavan as well. To watch the Cuban leader handle the temperamental Arafat was both a treat and an education. The PLO leader was a prima donna but Fidel Castro knew Arafat well and his tantrums did not intimidate him. He asked the recalcitrant Arafat if he considered himself a friend of Indira Gandhi. The response was: 'Friend! She is my elder sister. I will do anything for her.' The Castro coup de grace was then deftly delivered. 'Then behave like a younger brother and attend this afternoon's session.' It was over in two minutes.

Apart from Indira Gandhi, it was Castro who was the star of the summit. Castro had included Nobel Laureate Gabriel Garcia Marquez in his delegation. H.Y. Sharada Prasad and I took him to the Prime Minister. She was delighted and he was thrilled.

After the Summit in India, the Non-Aligned Movement emerged stronger and more united than ever. The Iran-Iraq and Kampuchean disputes which were going on at that time were, after vigorous behind-the-scene confabulations, not permitted to explode. The Summit itself concluded on a high note and was by all standards a huge success. I was given some credit for that. No civil servant had received such exposure. While my organizational capacities received accolades from unexpected quarters, the one that I valued most was a letter the Prime Minister wrote to me on 18 March 1983.

Dear Natwar,

I write to express my appreciation of your work for the Non-Aligned Meeting. Now that it is over, we can safely say that our fears and apprehensions regarding the shortness of time and a myriad other difficulties were unfounded, or perhaps provided motivation to redouble our efforts. That the meeting was an unqualified success is confirmed by all. Please also convey our appreciation to all members of your team. You shouldered a heavy responsibility and bore it cheerfully. But this is the beginning, and the next three years will be full of problems and difficulties. We must maintain the team spirit and start planning for the successful 'Delhi Declaration'.

THE TWO SUMMITS

Unwinding after the NAM Summit was out of question, for CHOGM was a few months ahead. However, Commonwealth Summits are more manageable. The membership is below fifty and the deliberations are conducted in English, unlike at NAM Summits. The Commonwealth has an elected Secretary General for a five-year term and a permanent office in London. The NAM does not. There is another difference—the retreat. During the weekend, Commonwealth leaders meet informally and without aides. That year, the Prime Minister selected Goa for the retreat. At the retreat, the heads of government met informally and had a great time. There were some indiscretions committed too. Goa had been completely transformed; the wonderful churches were painted and roads remade.

That year, Sonny Ramphal from Guyana made a model Secretary General. He had been elected for the second term, which was to end in 1985. I told the Prime Minister that at the next summit, it was unlikely that Sonny would be re-elected. If she agreed, we could clinch the 1985 election in 1983. She directed me to consult Presidents Kaunda, Nyerere and Burnham and Prime Minister Lee Kuan Yew. This I did. We were a step ahead of Margaret Thatcher, who did not hold the Secretary General in high esteem. She quietly got to know that Ramphal had Indira Gandhi's full support and was not pleased. The Iron Lady could be intimidating but she respected Indira Gandhi and was nervous in her presence. I once asked Mrs Gandhi what she thought of Thatcher. She said, 'What Iron Lady? I saw a nervous woman sitting on the edge of the sofa.'

On the second day of the summit, the Prime Minister asked me to quietly enquire from Rashtrapati Bhavan if the Queen was holding an 'investiture' for Mother Teresa, who was to receive the Order of the Merit, there. The Military Secretary confirmed this news. Not only had the venue been decided, invitations to the event had been sent out on Buckingham Palace stationery.

I conveyed this to the Prime Minister who wasn't pleased. Meanwhile, Hemvati Nandan Bahuguna, member of the Lok Sabha, had written to the Prime Minister saying that the Queen could not hold an 'investiture' at Rashtrapati Bhavan—only the President could. He added that the matter would be raised in the Lok Sabha. Bahuguna was right. The British had perhaps erred in good faith but the error had to be rectified. It fell to my lot to sort out this unprecedented breach in protocol. Mrs Gandhi asked me to get in touch with Mrs Thatcher and get back to her. I asked Robert Wade-Gery, the British High Commissioner, to convey to Mrs Thatcher that the venue for the 'investiture' must be changed. I added that while we held Her Majesty the Queen in high esteem, and Mother Teresa was a very special person, we ought to have been consulted on the matter. I also gently reminded him that Her Majesty was not the Queen of India.

Within a couple of hours, he rang back to say that Mrs Thatcher felt it was too late for a change of venue. Not only would the Queen be inconvenienced, the UK media was also aware of the event.

Here was high-grade protocol dynamite. The dramatis personae consisted of four world-famous ladies: two Prime Ministers, one Queen and the fourth, more than a saint. What if the Indian media got scent of this story!

I conveyed Mrs Thatcher's answer to the Prime Minister and could discern a fleeting irritation. After a moment's pause came a masterly googly. 'Natwar, go back to Mrs Thatcher and tell her from me that while the Queen can hold the "investiture", the matter will be raised in Parliament the next day. Critical references will be made and the Queen's name will be dragged in. It is only fair that the Queen be made aware of this.'

THE TWO SUMMITS

No 'investiture' was held at Rashtrapati Bhavan. The Queen invited Mother Teresa to tea in the Mughal Gardens where she handed the Order of Merit to the Nobel Laureate, who was blissfully unaware of the upheaval she had caused.

At the end of CHOGM, Mrs Gandhi wrote to me, praising my work during the summits in Delhi and at the retreat in Goa.

I replied:

> When the Russian novelist Pasternack received news of the reward of the Nobel Prize, he sent a telegram to Anders Osterling, Permanent Secretary of the Nobel Prize Committee, 'Infinitely grateful, touched, proud, surprised, overwhelmed.' I felt exactly the same when I received your letter of the 14th of December. It is you who needs to be congratulated by the entire nation.
>
> With best wishes for 1984.

At the end of CHOGM, I sent my recommendations for the Padma Awards: those without whose hard work and dedication the two summits would not have been such resounding successes. My list included half a dozen names. The officials and non-officials who had organized the 1982 Asian Games had been generously given Padma Bhushans and Padma Shris. But the Prime Minister, to my great surprise, said that there was no need to give any awards to those who had worked at the NAM and CHOGM summits. She made it worse by adding that 'these were routine conferences'. I was quite put out and my response verged on impertinence, 'Madam, most respectfully, I beg to differ. Meetings at such high levels cannot be called routine. The next summit will not be held in Delhi for the next twenty-five or more years. Secondly, the generous doling out of rewards to the Asian Games people makes me wonder if a rather novel criteria is being applied for NAM and CHOGM. Don't give me any award, but surely the others need some recognition.'

Finally, two awards were announced on 26 January 1984. Hamid Ansari, now the Vice President of India, and I received the Padma Shri and Padma Bhushan respectively. At the awards ceremony at Rashtrapati Bhavan on 31 March, while congratulating me, the Prime Minister continued, 'Don't let it go to your head.'

It is on this day that I finally met Thakazhi Sivasankara Pillai, among the best novelists in Malayalam, though not too well known in North India. He too was being conferred the Padma Bhushan. Thakazhi came into my life when I reviewed his superb novel *Chemmeen* for the *New York Times Book Review* in the summer of 1962. Three years later, when I was putting together a collection of modern Indian short stories for Macmillan New York, I requested him to permit me to use one of his stories. He obliged.

Pillai was born in 1914 in a village called Thakazhi. His father was a farmer, but their home was steeped in the rich traditions of Sanskrit culture and the indigenous arts of Kerala. He began by reading Marx and Freud, but soon abandoned them. His political inclinations were left of centre. In a letter to me in 1964, he wrote, 'I am a farmer by birth, a lawyer by profession and a writer by choice. Flaubert, Balzac, de Maupassant, Hugo, Gogol, Dostoevsky, Tolstoy influenced me. No Indian writer was directly responsible for my writing... Even Tagore was not responsible for the development of Malayalam fiction.'

14

NINETEEN EIGHTY-FOUR

Throughout my years of service, the possibility of me joining politics one day had always been at the back of my mind. During my stay in Pakistan, the urge became a not-so-mild obsession.

In 1983 I successfully organized two hugely successful, back-to-back summits, and that gave me a national profile. This was most unusual for a civil servant.

For some days after the conclusion of the second summit, I deliberated with myself to resolve the dilemma that confronted me. Should I continue in the IFS or try my luck in politics? I was risking giving up a steady career—at that point I had over five years until retirement. But though I looked back at my thirty years in service with pride, I knew only too well the fate of the retired officers—the doers of yesteryears become the drifters of today. I would find such a life unbearable. If my desire to take up a new career was rewarded, I would be plunging into unknown waters. At the conclusion of the Commonwealth Summit, I had asked the PM for a few minutes of her time. I had told her that while I had got to the top rung of the bureaucratic ladder,

I did not look forward to another five years in the IFS. I was keen to join politics and had Rajya Sabha in mind. She raised her eyebrows and uttered five words which left me in limbo: 'I will think about it.' Later, I took R.K. Dhawan into confidence. He said he would help.

Had I been unwise, impetuous? Was I a victim of cheerful fatalism or had I been foolhardy? Had I leaped before looking? I consoled myself by taking comfort in the debilitating dictum, 'Nothing venture, nothing gain'.

For the next few weeks I was restless and though cheering news came on the eve of Republic Day, I was like a cat on a hot tin roof. Relief came when P.C. Alexander sent for me and said I could make it to the Rajya Sabha. The news leaked, as most 'confidential' matters do in our set-up. I heard from my grapevine that the boy scouts around Rajiv Gandhi were hell-bent against my induction into the Rajya Sabha. Taking advantage of Rajiv's innocence, they had got to him, telling him that I should be asked to contest for a Lok Sabha seat.

Indira Gandhi, too, was made to change her mind. Their reasoning was that if this suggestion was to come from the PM I would give up my political ambitions. Little did they know me.

The PM sent for me and said, very calmly, 'Natwar, why don't you go to the Lok Sabha?' I was not wholly unprepared for this and replied, 'Madam, I leave it to you. Whatever you decide I will gladly accept. I will resign right away.' This was not one of life's minor detours. It was a momentous decision, the likes of which I had not taken since my marriage.

Hem was fully supportive—we had both had enough of packing our bags every three years. I gave the obligatory notice to the Ministry of External Affairs, seeking premature retirement. I felt no regret, but could not put aside the memories and experiences of the last thirty years. I bid goodbye to South Block and friends with a lump in my throat.

By then, I was in my mid-fifties. There was no guarantee that I would get elected to the Lok Sabha. One thing was in my favour: I would not have to look for a constituency. My hometown Bharatpur would be my constituency. My family was well-known there. I visited Bharatpur a few times to test the waters and found the response quite encouraging.

◆

On 6 June 1984, a politically seismic event occurred. The government of India decided to flush out Khalistani terrorists from the holy shrine of the Sikhs, the Golden Temple. The reaction to this outrage was fierce not only among the Sikhs but among other communities too.

At the time P.V. Narasimha Rao and I were in Jakarta, Indonesia, for a meeting of the Heads of Mission with the Indonesian leaders. On 5 June, we saw on television that the situation back home, in Punjab in general and Amritsar in particular, was full of tension and becoming more and more sinister by the hour. Jarnail Singh Bindranwale and his supporters had locked themselves up inside the Golden Temple and they were fully armed. The army had been deputed to keep a watch on the activities in and around the Golden Temple. By late evening, the situation had become alarming. The PM got minute-by-minute information on the crisis. She was told that there was no way out except to enter the Golden Temple and disarm Bindranwale and his followers. Her instructions were that on no account should the Golden Temple be fired upon. These were ignored. The Akal Takht was severely damaged. The next day, the Indian Army, under the command of Lt Gen. Krishnaswamy Sundarji, launched a full-scale attack on the Golden Temple

Complex. Tanks were used to break open the large doors, and intense firing took place. The firing from both sides went on for a long time. Eventually, the army was able to control the entire compound. Bhindranwale was dead and so were all his followers, including Maj. Gen. Shahbeg Singh, a defector from the Indian Army who had joined the Khalistanis. I remember telling Narasimha Rao, 'This is a great tragedy. It could have been avoided. The Sikhs will neither forget nor forgive.' Deep in thought, Narasimha Rao's silence was eloquent enough.

A few regiments of the army revolted; the Sikh community was deeply hurt within India and abroad. President Zail Singh was in dismay. Apparently, he had not been taken into confidence. My brother-in-law, Captain Amarinder Singh, who was a Congress member of the Lok Sabha, resigned not only from the Lok Sabha but from the Congress Party as well.

It was a different Delhi to which we returned. The tension was palpable. When the full extent of the tragedy became known, the PM concluded that her life was in great danger. She used to tell her close confidantes that she did not mind what happened to her, but could not take it if anything happened to her son and grandchildren. The national mood and political climate changed, and the ensuing months were depressing and full of anxiety. Indira Gandhi was aware that she was living on borrowed time. The situation was extremely tense not only in Amritsar but throughout North India. President Giani Zail Singh had been put in a very awkward situation. As a Sikh, he considered the army action a desecration of the most Sikhs' holy place.

I had to be admitted to hospital as my slipped disc was playing up and I was in considerable pain. On 8 August, I received a commiserating note from her in hospital. In October, I met her three times, including a couple of days before her assassination. She had returned from a trip to Srinagar and was still wearing

NINETEEN EIGHTY-FOUR

Kashmiri clothes. I told her I was leaving for Bharatpur to start politicking. My first priority would be to acquire a new wardrobe—the Congress livery. Her reaction was: 'Now that you are coming into politics, a thicker skin would be more useful.' Two days later, she was in Bhubaneswar and returned late in the night on 30 October. The next morning, the unimaginable took place.

Indira Gandhi's assassination on 31 October 1984 shook the nation. That morning, I was getting ready to leave for Bharatpur. Around 9.15 a.m. my RAX telephone rang. H.Y. Sharada Prasad was calling to say that a terrible thing had happened—the PM had been shot. Sharada was the least excitable man I have ever known, always in control of his emotions. On this occasion, his voice was trembling. I, too, was overwhelmed. She had done so much for me.

When I got to 1 Akbar Road, Sharada took me to the spot where the PM had been shot by her two Sikh security guards. On the glass river donated by the Czech government were lying her spectacles, her chappals and her bag. The blood had not yet dried. Sharada narrated what had happened. The PM had agreed to give an interview to the well-known film actor and producer, Peter Ustinov, that was to be held at 1 Akbar Road, which was in the compound of 1 Safdarjung Road. Sharada was talking to Peter Ustinov when Indira Gandhi was sprayed with bullets at point-blank range. The gunshots were recorded by Ustinov's technicians and Sharada and I pleaded with Ustinov to not use the recording of the gunshots. He kept his word till his dying day.

Sonia Gandhi and R.K. Dhawan put her blood-soaked body in a car and headed for the All India Institute of Medical Sciences (AIIMS) where she was rushed immediately into the operation theatre. But the PM had died on the spot.

Nothing seemed to go right. Rajiv Gandhi was away on tour in West Bengal while President Giani Zail Singh was in Yemen. The Principal Secretary to the Prime Minister was also out of Delhi, as was the Cabinet Secretary. The news was officially announced at 5 p.m. after the President's return. Huge crowds gathered at AIIMS. Cabinet ministers, Congress workers, the media, all rushed to the hospital. Attacks on the Sikh community commenced.

Rajiv Gandhi could not be sworn in as Prime Minister until the President's return. Sonia was totally opposed to her husband succeeding his mother—she feared that he, too, would be killed. Rajiv's reply to her was that he would be killed in any case. It was first decided that Rajiv Gandhi would be the only person to be sworn in. But as this would have sent out the wrong signal, half a dozen senior ministers were inducted into the new Cabinet.

Even as political events went on apace, with each passing hour, the atrocities against the Sikh community increased. At the end of three days, nearly 3,000 had been brutally murdered. Property was destroyed and homes set on fire. There was restlessness in the army and one or two Sikh battalions rebelled and were discarded. This information was kept secret.

At the time of her death, Indira Gandhi was one of the outstanding leaders of her time and had an international constituency. The world's who's who turned up for her funeral. Apart from Fidel Castro, Margaret Thatcher, J.R. Jayewardene, Zia-ul-Haq and Kenneth Kaunda, many other Heads of State and Government attended, such as the Deputy Prime Minister of the USSR, the Prime Minister of Iran, the President of Syria and the American Vice President George Bush Sr.

After all the leaders had departed, Rajiv Gandhi asked me to join him for dinner at 1 Akbar Road. Only rice and dal without salt was served. Those present included M.L. Fotedar and Arun Singh. In the middle of the meal, Rajiv asked me to follow him to the lawn. He told me that the situation in the city was very alarming. He planned to remove the Lieutenant Governor at once and had decided that he would appoint me in his stead. This was the last thing that I had expected. I told him that having been a career diplomat for thirty-one years, I had no administrative experience to assume this office. After all, I had resigned from the Foreign Service because his mother had decided that I should contest the Lok Sabha elections. Second, I told him that I must consult my wife.

Hem was totally opposed to Rajiv's proposal. She was a Sikh and the community was being butchered. What kind of message would Rajiv send out by appointing the son-in-law of the Maharaja of Patiala as Lieutenant Governor?

I told Rajiv that, in these circumstances, it would not be advisable for me to take up the job. In my absence, Arun Singh and Fotedar had again persuaded Rajiv that I was the only person who could handle the Delhi situation. P.V. Narasimha Rao, the Home Minister, was to arrange my swearing-in ceremony the next day at 11.00 a.m. Arun Singh warned that I could not disobey the Prime Minister. However, at this juncture, Fotedar changed his mind and supported me. After that, Rajiv did not insist.

This idea of me becoming the Lieutenant Governor was the brainchild of Gopi Arora, Arun Nehru and Arun Singh to prevent me from contesting the Lok Sabha elections. When their scheme failed, they thought of an alternative. Arun Nehru called me to say that the Prime Minister wished me to go to London as High Commissioner. I met the Prime Minister, telling him that I was mystified by Arun Nehru's call as I had already left the Foreign Service. I was also aware of the machinations of his inner circle to deny me the Lok Sabha ticket, now that Indira Gandhi was dead. Rajiv reassured me that no change would be made and I would be the Congress candidate from Bharatpur. What distressed and annoyed me was that some of his closest advisers were misguiding a decent and trusting man at such an ominous time.

15

THE RAJIV GANDHI YEARS

In the December 1984 Lok Sabha elections, the Congress Party won by an astounding margin. No one, not even the most optimistic Congressman, had expected the final tally to be 413 out of 543 seats. Rajiv had achieved what his grandfather and mother had not. The Bharatiya Janata Party (BJP) managed only two seats in that election, won by Atal Bihari Vajpayee and Lal Krishna Advani.

Euphoria was not confined to the Congress; the nation, too, rejoiced. A young leader had led from the front. He came as a breath of fresh air and offered an audacious vision. He made the nation conscious of the twenty-first century, which was just sixteen years away. The atmosphere radiated a mood of confidence and exultation. It may not have been a new dawn, but the darkness had receded. Indira Gandhi's posthumous contribution to Rajiv's unprecedented triumph was only too manifest. Her name was on every lip. The sympathy wave had had a powerful impact on the hearts and minds of the voters.

I, too, had won from my constituency, Bharatpur, by a big margin. As a first-term Member of Parliament, I did not think

I would be included in the Council of Ministers. While I was having lunch at the Ashoka Hotel in Delhi with Sunil Dutt, a close friend and also a first-time MP, the hotel manager came up to me and said, 'Sir, the Prime Minister wishes to speak to you.' I was surprised as I had met him only the previous evening. What could have happened since then?

'What are you doing at 5 p.m.?' asked the PM.

'Nothing,' I replied.

'Be at Rashtrapati Bhavan at 5 p.m. sharp.'

'I will, but what are you giving me?'

'You will know when you get there.' He hung up. I told Sunil Bhai about the call and he was delighted. He was certain that I would get a ministerial berth.

Hem and I arrived at the Ashok Hall in Rashtrapati Bhavan a few minutes before 5 p.m. I was escorted to the chairs reserved for those who were to be sworn in. I was to be a Minister of State. President Zail Singh administered the oath of secrecy and my pulse quickened as I signed the register. But the mystery of my portfolio remained.

At the high tea after the swearing-in, I learnt that I was to be Minister of State for Steel. I had, for obvious reasons, ruled out External Affairs. I had hoped to be Minister of State in the Home, Information and Broadcasting, or Defence ministries.

The next morning, the Prime Minister met the Ministers of State in the conference room in South Block. He spoke in general terms. All eyes were on Arun Nehru and Arun Singh, Rajiv Gandhi's close confidants. Both had come from the corporate sector. They wielded much power, exceeded their authority and used their influence with thoughtless rigour, without care or caution. Both controlled access to the Prime Minister. Their administrative experience was nil; they were purblind to the complexities and intricacies of governance.

I gradually became familiar with the production and politics of steel. I visited all the steel plants in India, getting to know an aspect of the country about which I had no previous knowledge. It did not take long for me to learn that the production of steel depended on the politics of steel. Each plant had several powerful trade unions—the CPI ran one group, the Congress another, the CPI (M) yet another. Discipline was abysmal; punctuality was a casualty. The steel mafia was more than a nuisance. One exception was the Tata Plant at Jamshedpur. There, Russi Mody allowed no trade union activity. That made all the difference.

At that time, our annual steel production was far below that of South Korea, China, the US, the UK, Russia and Japan. Each steel plant cost thousands of crores to set up and employed hundreds, including top-class engineers. What was missing was work ethic. The mafia and union leaders were constantly in touch with Chief Ministers who indulged them as they needed their votes.

The Chief Minister of Andhra Pradesh, N.T. Rama Rao, kept a keen eye on the steel plant at Vizag (Visakhapatnam). A film actor turned politician, his following was in millions. A spell-binding orator in Telugu with a booming voice, he was a formidable person. The Congress Party had denied him a Rajya Sabha seat. Rama Rao had then launched the Telugu Desam Party which swept the Assembly polls.

He once invited me to lunch at his Hyderabad home. His appetite was gargantuan; I counted fourteen food items on my thali. My chief purpose at the lunch was to discuss the problems of the Vizag plant. The Chief Minister was well briefed and assured me that certain local difficulties in the plant would be remedied. His concern was larger. He asked that the people of Andhra be given preference over non-Andhraites for employment as the plant was located in Andhra. I reminded him that the plant had been entirely funded by the central government. Employment was open to all Indians—but appointments would be on merit. In deserving cases, preference could be given to Andhraites, but only as an exception. I dug in my heels. He relented with an actor's grace.

The Chief Minister was a natural showman. He gave me a grand tour of his sprawling residence. It was a combination of a film studio and a well-stocked museum. We parted on a friendly note.

As a minister, I had a personal monthly quota of one million tons of steel, which I could allot to whom I pleased. This I surrendered. If I remember right, I set up a committee for disbursing it. With this I went up in the esteem of the officials. The ubiquitous lobby of steel magnates, too, concluded that I was no pushover.

The first three months gave some indication of the functioning of the Rajiv Gandhi government. V.P. Singh as Finance Minister was the favourite. In Cabinet meetings, he sat to the right of the Prime Minister, while P.V. Narasimha Rao sat on his left. Ministers of State were at a loose end. Their Cabinet Ministers kept them at arm's length and sent no important files to them. The Cabinet Minister for steel, Vasant Sathe, was a decent man. He was not narrow-minded or a stickler for rules and regulations. He gave me a free hand.

My heart, however, was not in steel; it was in the Ministry of External Affairs. I was delighted when, on 11 March 1985, Rajiv Gandhi asked me to accompany him to Moscow for the funeral of Konstantin Ustinovich Chernenko, General Secretary of the Communist Party of the Soviet Union and Chairman of the Presidium of the USSR. The Prime Minister's delegation included P.V. Narasimha Rao; P. Shiv Shankar, who was the head of the foreign affairs department of the All India Congress Committee;

the venerable G. Parthasarathi; and Romesh Bhandari. We flew in a Boeing 747 plane, the interior of which had been remodelled to provide the PM with a bedroom, a bathroom and a conference room.

The same evening, the Indian delegation paid respects to Chernenko, whose flower-bedecked body lay in state. Next morning, all delegations stood in the Red Square to the right of Lenin's tomb. It was bitterly cold. Chernenko's coffin was brought out of the Kremlin. He was buried under the Kremlin wall. Then there was a reception given by the newly elected General Secretary, Mikhail Gorbachev.

The great hall in the Kremlin, where the reception was held, is the last word in grandeur and splendour. The tsars had been forgotten, but not their wonderful buildings, palaces, churches and monasteries. The PM introduced us to the new General Secretary, with whom he had a brief meeting. He also met Margaret Thatcher, Zia-ul-Haq, several European and Asian leaders. This was his maiden foreign trip as Prime Minister. Sonia was a model of sophistication, good taste and debonair civility.

On our return to Delhi, I resumed my desultory duties. I was getting no job satisfaction. In the middle of the year, I was appointed Minister of State for Fertilizers. If steel was a bore, fertilizers were even worse. The wags made merry: 'Natwar is now minister for cow dung!' One time, I was shown a bag full of a white substance which I thought was sugar. The secretary of the department looked at me with a mixture of dismay and mild disdain. It was a bag full of fertilizer.

Rescue, unknown to me, was waiting in the wings. This was one of those windfalls which ought to be always remembered. The Ministry of Fertilizers is as far from the Ministry of Foreign Affairs as chalk is from cheese. Yet, Rajiv Gandhi told me that he would include me in his delegation to the Commonwealth

Summit to be held in October at Nassau, the capital of the Bahamas. He asked me to immediately proceed to Nassau to see if we could help the tiny Caribbean island in any way.

I first stopped in New York. I asked our Permanent Representative to the United Nations to get in touch with the Ambassador of the Bahamas and ask him to arrange my meeting with their Prime Minister, Sir Lynden Oscar Pindling. I waited for a couple of days but the Bahamas delegation did not respond. I left for Washington to try my luck there. We did not have an Embassy in the Bahamas. The Ambassador in Washington, Pratap Kaul, contacted his counterpart in the Bahamas Embassy, requesting him to arrange my meeting with his Prime Minister. In Washington, too, I fared no better. It became clear that the diplomats from the Bahamas were a hard-to-find tribe. After three wasted days, I decided to return to New York. Just then, the Ambassador informed me that the holy man Chandraswamy wished to speak to me. How in the name of heaven did the swami get to know of my presence in Washington DC? When I took the call, the swami was chuckling. 'Kunwar Sahib, Pindling se meeting nahi ho rahi hai aap ki (Kunwar Sahib, are you not able to meet Pindling)?'

'How do you know?' I asked, a little irritated.

He ignored my question. 'Maine aap ki meeting ka intezam kar dia hai. Pindling aap se kal milenge (I have arranged your meeting. Pindling will meet you tomorrow).'

Where diplomats had failed, the swami had succeeded.

The next day, I was received by Sir Lynden. He was short, dark and a smile never deserted him. From what he said, I concluded that he was quite clearly being helped by the British for the arrangements. In my two days in Nassau, I noticed that pleasure, not politics, was a national passion. Nassau was for fun and frolic. These were taken seriously, not Commonwealth summits.

THE RAJIV GANDHI YEARS

We left for Nassau in October 1985. Rajiv Gandhi made a brief halt in London to meet Prime Minister Margaret Thatcher at 10 Downing Street. The main topic discussed was the South African apartheid regime. The British PM was rigid and self-righteous on the matter of apartheid. British policy was to have the cake and eat it too. While they mildly criticized the apartheid regime in public, they maintained the closest trade relations with them. India's policy on South Africa was clear-cut. Apartheid was an abomination and we had severed all contacts with Cape Town in 1954. Rajiv strongly argued with the British PM on this issue and it was finally decided that a group of seven senior former Commonwealth leaders would visit South Africa and give a report at the next UN summit.

Nassau was a tourist's paradise. The climate, the sun, the sand and the sea combined to make their holidays memorable. Inhibitions were shed; sensuality and sex took over.

On the opening day at the Nassau conference, Rajiv was the second speaker after Margaret Thatcher. It was not an easy act to follow because she was an accomplished speaker. I was sitting behind Rajiv. When he put aside the written text I was apprehensive. He spoke so well that several Heads walked up to him to congratulate him. This was rarely done. However, this speech was not a patch on the one he made to the joint session of the US Congress in June. That was a stunning performance. He mesmerized his audience—the senators and Congressmen, hard-boiled professionals to whom such occasions were routine. Rajiv made it an occasion to remember.

◆

In 1985, Rajiv Gandhi was both Prime Minister of India and President of the Congress Party. In December of that year, he was at the peak of his popularity. Rajiv considered it essential to revitalize and even reinvent the Congress Party, as Mahatma Gandhi had done years ago. The centenary session of the Congress was held in Bombay that year.

The Congress is among the world's oldest democratic parties, having been founded on 29 December 1885 by an Englishman, A.O. Hume. Until the arrival of Mahatma Gandhi on the Indian political scene, it was an upper-middle-class organization. The opening and closing sessions began with prayers for the long life of Queen Victoria, King Edward VII and King George V. Gandhi took over the Congress in 1920 and, within a very short time, turned it into a mass movement. He rewrote the party's Constitution, established a Working Committee and the All India Congress Committee and brought about a political revolution without shedding blood. He asked people to stand up and walk with their heads held high. At one time he mobilized forty million people to participate in the freedom movement. Above all, he awakened the masses.

The security arrangements at Brabourne Stadium, where the centenary session was being held, were very tight. At the entrance, I saw the police pushing away several senior Congress leaders. I managed to squeeze in with the help of Sunil Dutt. I was asked to look after the large number of foreign delegations who had been invited to join the celebrations. The most prominent guest was Khan Abdul Ghaffar Khan.

When Rajiv Gandhi got up to speak, he got a standing ovation. It was a very emotional moment. His great-grandfather, grandfather and mother had all been Presidents of the Congress. Rajiv spoke like a visionary. He was dismissive of some of the policies the Congress had been following. He particularly targeted the power-brokers, whose thinking was behind the times, whose dedication was questionable and, worst of all, who had no vision. For them, money took precedence over morality.

Rajiv's speech made a tremendous impact. It was well drafted and he spoke a new language. Tradition was not to be jettisoned but innovation would be on top of the agenda. He was preparing the Congress and the country for the twenty-first century.

We all returned from Bombay surcharged. However, as the weeks went by, I could see that the old guard of the Congress had not taken kindly to the speech. These were the real power-brokers of the party and, in the long run, it was they who succeeded in skilfully out-manoeuvring Rajiv. In front of him, they praised him for the great speech but behind his back, they sabotaged him and his programme. At this time, Rajiv was guided chiefly by his close friends, who were very bright, full of vigour, and genuinely wanted to see him succeed. But their inexperience was all too visible and their grasp of the complexities he faced was limited. They were not familiar with the history of the Congress, or with the freedom movement. They suggested change without realizing that change had to be managed, guided, monitored and, eventually, change had to change. The memory of Rajiv's speech and the Congress centenary faded away all too soon.

◆

In October 1986, the PM shifted me to the Ministry of External Affairs. A month earlier, on 1 September 1986, Rajiv participated in the Eighth Non-Aligned Summit in Harare, Zimbabwe, to which I accompanied him. At the time he was still the Chairman of the summit and was to hand over the responsibility to Zimbabwe Prime Minister Robert Mugabe that afternoon. At the morning session, Yasser Arafat, Chairman of the Palestine Liberation Organization, launched a blistering attack on Iran. During the lunch break, we heard that the leader of the Iranian delegation,

Ayatollah Khomeini, would exercise his right of reply. I told Rajiv that in that case, the summit would begin on a confrontational note. I suggested that he ask to see the Ayatollah. Rajiv asked me to arrange a meeting with him. I told the Ayatollah that the Indian Prime Minister wished to see him at his convenience. He readily agreed. Rajiv and I went to see the great man. Rajiv said that he had come to the Ayatollah not as a Prime Minister, but as a friend and well-wisher of Iran and its people. There was a centuries' old relationship between the two countries. Rajiv then said, 'I have come to ask you for a favour.'

'Please let us know what you want us to do,' the Ayatollah replied.

Rajiv said, 'We have heard of your intention to exercise your right of reply to Arafat.'

The Ayatollah again enquired what the Indian PM wished him to do. Rajiv requested him to not exercise the right of reply. After fifteen seconds the Ayatollah said, 'If the Prime Minister of India, as a friend, asks me to do so, I will oblige him.' It was a triumph of Rajiv Gandhi's diplomacy.

◆

Rajiv Gandhi took Indo-Soviet relations to new heights. He had first met Mikhail Gorbachev, the leader of the Soviet Union, very briefly during the funeral of the General Secretary of the Communist Party of the Soviet Union, Konstantin Ustinovich Chernenko, in March 1985, as mentioned earlier. Two months later, Rajiv and Sonia paid a week-long official visit to the USSR in May 1985. Apart from visiting several parts of the Soviet Union, Rajiv Gandhi and Gorbachev had prolonged discussions about Indo-Soviet relations. They discussed the progress that two countries had made in political, economic, cultural and military cooperation as well as the problems of modernization and radical reform. Several agreements were signed on the development of trade, as well as economic, scientific and technological cooperation. They also discussed the possibility of joint ventures for building various industrial lands in India. Gorbachev supported the initiative launched by Argentina, India, Greece, Mexico, Tanzania and Sweden calling for a worldwide moratorium on nuclear testing and the production and development of nuclear weapons and delivery systems. There was commonality of views on the situation in the Asia Pacific region, which was of vital interest to both countries. They had common views on the West Asian conflict and the role of non-aligned countries.

Gorbachev took a personal interest in Rajiv's programme and held lengthy talks with him. Both were modern-minded leaders—innovative, forward-looking and open to new ideas. Both the Soviet Union and India at the time faced problems of modernization, renewal and radical reform. In the final communiqué, the two countries declared that they opposed any infringement of the right of every state and nation to its own independent and peaceful development and opposed any form of imperialism, colonialism or neo-colonialism, domination and hegemony.

Within a very short period after becoming General Secretary of the Communist Party of the Soviet Union, Gorbachev had abandoned the fundamentals of the Soviet Union's relations with the rest of the world. Internally, his aim was to overhaul the entire Soviet system which, for the past several decades, had stagnated. Gorbachev was dedicated to the transformation of Russian society through accelerated social and economic reforms. In other words, he wanted his country to embark on the democratization of society and the state. This reform was called 'Perestroika'. At the same time, he launched a programme for drastic economic development, termed 'Glasnost'. The whole world watched the revolutionary changes that Gorbachev had initiated with eager interest. But he got his priorities wrong. He put Perestroika before Glasnost. The Chinese were more realistic—Glasnost took precedence over Perestroika.

On his return, Rajiv briefed some of his ministers and said that he was much impressed by what Gorbachev was doing. There was considerable opposition to Gorbachev's reforms in USSR, particularly by the older members of the Central Committee and Politburo. But Rajiv was confident that Gorbachev would overcome these hurdles and take the reforms forward.

Gorbachev was scheduled to visit India in 1986. After the SAARC Summit in Bangalore ended, preparations for the all-important visit started in earnest. He and his wife got a tremendous welcome on their arrival in Delhi on 25 November 1986. It reminded me of the popular welcome Khrushchev and Bulganin had received in 1955. Rajiv had a one-on-one meeting with Gorbachev at the Rashtrapati Bhavan. No one else from the Indian side was present, although a Soviet interpreter was allowed to take notes. This was unfortunate, as we had nobody to do so. While we were preparing for Gorbachev's visit, P.N. Haksar had repeatedly told me to take down everything that transpired during the meetings of the two leaders as the Soviets would record every word. In the plenary on the afternoon of 27 November, I saw Gorbachev dominate the meeting. The achievement of Gorbachev's visit was the signing of the Delhi Declaration by the two leaders on 27 November 1986. The Delhi Declaration was a product of the 'new thinking' of both leaders. Its immediate impact was intense. The declaration said:

> In the nuclear age, mankind must develop a new political thinking in a new concept of the world, which provides

sound guarantees for the survival of mankind.

The world we have inherited belongs to the present and future generations alike. Hence he must give priority to the universal human values.

Human life must be acknowledged [as] the supreme value. Non-violence must become the basis of human co-existence and the rights of every state. Political and economic independence must be acknowledged and respected. The balance of sphere must be balanced by a global system of international security.

That a Soviet leader had agreed to sign an agreement that made a reference to non-violence showed that the Soviet Union had come a long way from the Stalinist era. The two countries also proposed an international convention that would ban the use or the threat of the use of nuclear weapons. This was remarkable and unprecedented.

The officials of two countries had spent many hours in preparing the declaration. I, too, participated in the discussions and witnessed the change in the working style of the Soviet official team. They were no longer parroting standard clichés. It was quite obvious that Perestroika was working.

Gorbachev's wife, Raisa Maksimovna, and Sonia Gandhi spent many hours together. Rajiv and Sonia, however, did not warm up to Mrs Gorbachev, who was fastidious and somewhat demanding, and excessively preoccupied with her clothes.

Gorbachev came to India again in November 1988 to participate in the closing ceremony of the Indo-Soviet festival, which had been launched a year earlier. It was a friendly occasion. The trust between the two leaders was visible to all in their body language. They had established a cordial personal rapport. Gorbachev, in his talk with the Indian Prime Minister, gave first-hand information about the changes taking place within the Soviet Union. He also said that he was worried about separatist movements and ethnic conflicts. Rajiv, in turn, mentioned his own concern about the increasing aggressiveness of some Sikh leaders. On his return, Gorbachev wrote a long letter to Rajiv Gandhi, requesting him to convey in writing details of how India dealt with internal crises. Rajiv Gandhi sent him a detailed thirty-page note on the matter.

Rajiv and Sonia Gandhi visited the Soviet Union in February 1991 after Rajiv had resigned and Chandra Shekhar had taken over as Prime Minister. Not only was the visit not properly organized, we did not have any set agenda. Rajiv Gandhi decided not to inform Prime Minister Chandra Shekhar about the visit. When we arrived in Moscow, there was no senior Soviet official to receive Rajiv Gandhi, Sonia and the members of the delegation, which included Romesh Bhandari, Mani Shankar Aiyar and Rajiv Shukla, at the time a journalist on the rise.

We were put up in two guest houses not too far from the Kremlin. Rajiv asked to meet Gorbachev and Gorbachev changed the timing of his meeting three times and, when it happened, nothing substantial was discussed. In the evening, he invited Rajiv and Sonia, other members of the delegation and me to see a performance at the Bolshoi Theatre. We were a bit surprised that the Soviet leader, who had publicly recognized the role Rajiv Gandhi was playing to strengthen Indo-Soviet relations and had been full of praise for the former Prime Minister, did not attach much importance to Rajiv's February visit. The next morning, we left for Tehran and Rajiv was received by the President Rafsanjani. He surprised Rajiv by telling him that Gorbachev had told him that he would be coming to Tehran. Current Vice President Hamid Ansari was the Ambassador to Iran. He made us feel at home, giving a masterly analysis of Indo-Iranian relations.

However, in his *Memoirs*, Mikhail Gorbachev wrote with great emotion:

> When last time we met, Rajiv Gandhi had already resigned as Prime Minister to become leader of the Indian Opposition. I could understand the way he must have felt, and Raisa Maksimovna and I did everything we could to show our sympathy and support. However, the moment we met our Indian friends, we realized that they had already swallowed the bitter pill. Rajiv made a sound analysis of the reasons for his party['s] defeat and criticised both the policy of the Congress Party and his own political errors, particularly concerning the pace of reforms. Like a mature statesman, he weighed up the pros and cons of his new situation— he had become an experienced, tough politician. Then I later learned about his successful election campaign, I felt sincerely glad for my Indian friend and I was deeply shocked on hearing the untimely tragic death of this outstanding man.*

---

*Mikhail Gorbachev, *Memoirs*, New York: Doubleday, 1996

16

THE TRAGEDY OF SRI LANKA

In November 1986, the SAARC Summit was to be held in Bangalore.

Rajiv Gandhi and Sri Lankan President J.R. Jayewardene were the most sought after leaders at the summit. The unwritten rule followed at summits is that bilateral issues are not raised. At the opening session, all Heads of State speak and controversy is avoided. We managed to get hold of a copy of Jayewardene's speech, which was a severe indictment of our Sri Lanka policy. We conveyed our misgivings to him and he assured us that he would delete the portions which we found objectionable.

On the podium, President Jayewardene announced that he was so moved by the welcome he had received in the land of Gandhi and Nehru that he would speak from the heart. He then proceeded to attack India's 'support' to Tamil terrorists in Sri Lanka and invoked the Panchsheel Treaty agreement signed between Nehru and Chou En-lai, which spoke of non-interference in the internal affairs of other countries. Rajiv wisely decided not to respond. At the end of the first day, he instructed P. Chidambaram and me to meet the Tamil Nadu

Chief Minister M.G. Ramachandran, who had brought with him Velupillai Prabhakaran, the founder and leader of the Liberation Tigers of Tamil Eelam (LTTE). M.G. Ramachandran, who was not comfortable with English, brought with him one of his ministers to act as interpreter, also named Ramachandran. Prabhakaran, too, did not speak English. He had brought with him Anton Balasingham as his interpreter. Balasingham was a crypto communist, the sort of man one could neither ignore nor trust.

My first impression of Prabhakaran was not favourable. He was short, strongly built and stubborn with a one-track mind. He was committed to the idea of Eelam and would not let go of it. I told him that India was fully acquainted with the just demands of the Sri Lankan Tamils. The Prime Minister had spoken to President Jayewardene candidly of the grievances of the Tamils. India was opposed to Eelam and supported Sri Lanka's sovereignty and territorial integrity.

Talking to Prabhakaran was an exhausting experience. I told him that there could come a time when he would have to face the combined might of the Indian and the Sri Lankan armies. He was obdurate. His response to my scarcely veiled threat was: 'I shall never give up Eelam even if I am to die for it.' Frankly, at that time, I underestimated the depth of his fanatical determination. We had kept Prabhakaran's presence in Bangalore a secret but somehow, President Jayewardene got to know. 'Rajiv, hand him over to me. I shall hang him in Jaffna, where he shot dead the Mayor who was a Tamilian,' he threatened.

The Prime Minister held several meetings with Jayewardene. For some reason, Rajiv was in a great hurry to find a solution for the ethnic problems in Sri Lanka. Perhaps it was his successful handling of the Punjab and Assam crises which had given him confidence. However, Rajiv Gandhi was not familiar with the history of the ethnic problems in Sri Lanka. It is my firm belief that Presidents and Prime Ministers should not get involved in the nitty-gritties of negotiations. They neither have the time nor the expertise for it. As the weeks went by, I got the impression that Jayewardene was getting the better of Rajiv Gandhi.

In the next few months after the summit, Minister of State P. Chidambaram and I made several trips to Sri Lanka. On the way, we made it a point to visit M.G. Ramachandran, a former film star who, apart from being head of the government, had a huge personal following in the state. It was widely alleged that he covertly supported and financed the LTTE and their cadres were being given military training in Tamil Nadu. He also considered Jaffna an extension of Tamil Nadu. Prime Minister Rajiv Gandhi realized that we had to keep MGR on board and he was right in doing so, because to bypass so formidable a Chief Minister would only add to our problems.

The most important trip that Chidambaram and I made was on 19 December 1986. Chidambaram was much more knowledgeable about Sri Lanka than I was. Apart from meeting the Sri Lankan President, we held detailed and extensive discussions with ministers Lalith Athulathmudali and Gamini Dissanayake. They were the upcoming men of Sri Lanka. Lalith Athulathmudali was in charge of National Security and he was also in close contact with the Americans. He did not trust India. Our High Commissioner in Sri Lanka, J.N. Dixit, said that he would keep an eye on Lalith Athulathmudali. Gamini was a man after my heart and we took to each other from our very first meeting. While Chidambaram and I were in conference with the two ministers, news came that a Srilankan Airlines plane had been attacked just as it was about to take-off. Sixteen people were dead and over forty seriously injured. Lalith Athulathmudali implied that the blast had been carried out at the behest of RAW to put pressure on Sri Lanka. I gently cautioned him that no useful purpose would be served by taking India's name every time things went wrong in his country; he should be spending more time in resolving internal problems. This was also the first time that I had worked with Chidambaram. I witnessed first-hand his subtlety of mind and his mastery over details. He had one other important asset—he never got into a flap.

We also paid our respects to Mrs Sirimavo Bandaranaike, the former Prime Minister, in an attempt to reduce her hostility to India's efforts to find a solution. She heard us out but did not hide her intense dislike for Jayewardene, who had treated her rather indelicately. She blamed Rajiv Gandhi for interfering in the internal affairs of Sri Lanka.

The Prime Minister, Ranasinghe Premadasa, did not participate in the meetings called by his President during our stay in Colombo. Not only that, he refused to meet us. During our visit, the 'December 19th Proposals' were accepted by both sides and became a point of reference for future negotiations. On our return to Delhi, we told the Prime Minister that the Sri Lankan leadership was a house divided. Prime Minister Premadasa and Security Minister Lalith Athulathmudali were on one side and Minister of Lands, Lands Development and Mahaweli Development Gamini Dissanayake and Minister D'Silva were with the President. My assessment of Jayewardene was, on the whole, favourable. He spoke well and was never in a hurry. A devout Buddhist, he never raised his voice and was always calm. But there was a negative side—he was clever and shifty, and it was difficult to pin him down.

The December 19th Proposals were conveyed to M.G. Ramachandran. Our intelligence agencies were keeping track of Prabhakaran and his henchmen. 1986 ended with uncertainties and the dim prospect of a conflict-free Sri Lanka. The Sri Lankan economy was haemorrhaging on account of the conflict between the government and the LTTE.

Chidambaram and I made a couple more visits to Colombo. We also met Prabhakaran in Chennai, in the office of the Chief Minister, when we went to convey the December 19th Proposals to M.G. Ramachandran. MGR, without informing us, had gifted 40 million rupees to the LTTE. All rules and regulations had been flouted but Rajiv Gandhi was unable to do anything about this. MGR's vision was confined to Tamil Nadu. To make matters worse, our intelligence agencies were at sixes and sevens. Pakistan, Saudi Arabia, China and Israel were fishing in the turbulent waters of Sri Lanka. The Israelis were training Sri Lankan commandos; at the same time, they were also training our commandos. Only they could achieve this. The Commonwealth Secretary General suggested that some Commonwealth countries could mediate to bring about a solution. We discouraged him as we did not wish to internationalize the Sri Lankan situation.

In May 1987, a crisis developed. Jayewardene was persuaded by Lalith Athulathmudali that the time was ripe for operation 'liberation'. Jaffna was cordoned off and even essential supplies were prevented from getting to the city. To make matters worse, on 27 May, Jayewardene announced, 'This time, the fight is a fight to the finish.' Rajiv Gandhi was troubled at this outburst and conveyed his displeasure through our High Commission. On 28 May, the Prime Minister warned Sri Lanka that India would intervene to safeguard the welfare of Sri Lankan Tamils. This was ignored. Meanwhile, the situation in Jaffna was deteriorating and essential commodities were running short. The Jaffna peninsula was on the verge of a humanitarian tragedy. Rajiv decided to send essential food and medical supplies by sea on 2 June 1987. P.V. Narasimha Rao and I were asked to draft a statement conveying India's intention to the Sri Lankan authorities. The

THE TRAGEDY OF SRI LANKA

glaring fact was that Sri Lanka had not asked for humanitarian aid and not only were we forcing their hand, we would also be violating the maritime boundaries of a friendly country.

The flotilla arrived in Jaffna waters on the given date. The Sri Lankan navy stopped the Indian boats and asked them to return, which they did. We had instructed the commander of the flotilla to avoid a confrontation. The Prime Minister did not take kindly to this and decided to take stern action. A meeting was called at 7 Race Course Road. I was also asked to attend. I arrived a few minutes late and the meeting had already begun. It was being attended by senior Cabinet Ministers, Defence Chiefs, the Principal Secretary to the Prime Minister, the Cabinet Secretary, RAW officials and the Foreign Secretary. After listening to the proceedings for about ten minutes, I began to feel uneasy. I realized that something extraordinary was being discussed. I asked the PM, 'What action do we have in mind?' His reply increased my disquiet—he had decided to airdrop humanitarian aid over Jaffna. I enquired if we had informed the Sri Lankan government. A member of the Cabinet almost shouted at me, 'Natwarji, what are you saying? Why should we inform the Sri Lankans?'

'Because Sri Lanka is an independent sovereign nation and a member of the United Nations, the NAM and the Commonwealth. It is also our close and friendly neighbour. It is not a hostile country. If we were to send planes to drop humanitarian supplies into Jaffna, we would be violating Sri Lanka's air space,' I replied. I asked if we had informed our Permanent Representative at the UN, Chinmaya Gharekhan, about this decision. This had not been done either. I said that it was imperative for us to do so to make sure that the Security Council did not meet to discuss Sri Lanka. (Sri Lanka at that time was a member of the Security Council.) I had no doubt that most of the Security Council members would sympathize with Sri Lanka. The Prime Minister agreed that I must speak to Chinmaya, a mature and level-headed diplomat. I told him what we had in mind. He was appalled. I told him that no meeting of the Security Council should be held to discuss this. He delivered; no meeting was called. I asked the Prime Minister if we had informed the Sri Lankan High Commissioner in New Delhi, Bernard Tilakaratne. The Prime Minister said that I should ask him to see me at South Block at noon.

Bernard was, as usual, his ebullient self. When I broke the news to him, he slumped in his chair. He asked me when the airdrop would take place. I told him that it would be sometime between 2.30 and 3.30 p.m. I asked him to speak to his President. He said he could not get through in time. 'Use my phone,' I said. He spoke to his President in Sinhalese. I could not follow what was being said, but I heard the President's voice loud and clear. He sounded enraged about not being informed earlier.

I informed J.N. Dixit in Colombo and gave him the time of the airdrop. Two planes were to fly in, one carrying aid and the other representatives of the media. I made sure that the aid items were loaded into the first plane in the presence of the media, who might otherwise report that India was dropping arms meant for the LTTE.

The airdrop was eventually completed on 4 June 1987 by cargo aircraft escorted by fighter airplanes. The Sri Lankan reaction to this demonstration of military might was one of shock, anger and outrage. We had violated an independent nation's airspace. The government of Sri Lanka had not asked for aid.

The Sri Lankan Army continued their onslaught on the LTTE and Prabhakaran soon realized that he was cornered. He instructed one of his representatives in Singapore to contact N. Ram, the editor of *The Hindu*, to tell him that the LTTE

K. Natwar Singh, B.R. Bhagat, Margaret Thatcher, Rajiv Gandhi and P.C. Alexander,
at 10 Downing Street, London, 1985

(*above*): With President Ronald Reagan at the White House, 1986

(*below*): With Deng Xiaoping, as P.V. Narasimha Rao and Dinesh Singh look on, Beijing, 1988

(*above*): (left to right) Rajiv Gandhi, K.R. Narayanan, K. Natwar Singh and H.Y. Sharda Prasad

(*left*): Fidel Castro receives Rajiv Gandhi, Sonia Gandhi and K. Natwar Singh, Havana

(*right*): Yasser Arafat with K. Natwar Singh and Rajiv Gandhi

K. Natwar Singh, Rajiv Gandhi and Fidel Castro, Havana

(right): K. Natwar Singh, Rajiv Gandhi and Nelson Mandela, Namibia, 1990

(left): P.V. Narasimha Rao, Rajiv Gandhi and K. Natwar Singh, 1989

(above): G. Parthasarathi, P. Shiv Shankar, P.V. Narasimha Rao, Rajiv Gandhi, K. Natwar Singh and Romesh Bhandari, 1985

(right): With Rajiv Gandhi, Moscow, 1985

(*above*): K. Natwar Singh, Kenneth Kaunda, P.V. Narasimha Rao, New Delhi, 1996

(*below*): Taking salute at the Guard of Honour in Warsaw, 1971

(*above*): Rajiv Gandhi and Sri Lankan President, J.R. Jayewardene, sign the Sri Lankan Accord K. Natwar Singh and P.V. Narasimha Rao look on, Colombo, 1987

(*below*): Rajiv Gandhi smiles as K. Natwar Singh speaks. Seated behind them is V.P. Singh, 1984

The last meeting. K. Natwar Singh with Rajiv Gandhi, Bharatpur, 17 May 1991

would accept a political compromise, provided the Sri Lankan government agreed to the proposals that he would make. N. Ram passed the news on to Gamini Dissanayake, with whom he had cordial relations. The LTTE's proposals were (i) military operations by the Sri Lankan government should cease and Sri Lankan troops should be confined to their barracks in Jaffna; (ii) the Northern and the Eastern Precincts should be merged; (iii) power should be devolved on the basis of the December 19th Proposals; (iv) Tamil should be recognized as the official language at par with Sinhalese and (v) a Tamilian should be the Vice President of the country. Gamini passed these to Dixit. On perceiving that the Sri Lankan government reacted positively to Prabhakaran's proposals, Rajiv had a change of heart. He said that we could take these proposals further and come to an agreement with the Sri Lankan government. This U-turn was wholly unexpected.

The next few days witnessed frantic activity in Colombo and New Delhi. A draft agreement was being prepared by Dixit and Gamini, called a 'non-paper'. A team which, including others, comprised K.P.S. Menon Jr.; Kuldip Sahadev; Ronen Sen, Director, RAW; and senior representatives of the Ministry of Defence met under my leadership every day to fine-tune the draft agreement which would then be approved by the Prime Minister.

The only fly in the India-Sri Lanka ointment was P.V. Narasimha Rao. He had reservations about the draft, but was unwilling to take them up with the Prime Minister. While there was merit in Narasimha Rao's doubts, it was too late to change anything. A climate of conflict was giving way to an atmosphere of conciliation.

President Jayewardene asked Gamini Dissanayake to contact Prabhakaran to inform him about the agreement, which was broadly along the lines of what he had said to N. Ram.

While hope had appeared on the horizon in the Sri Lankan conflict, on the Indian side, there was great confusion. Too many agencies and departments of the Government of India had their fingers in the Sri Lankan pie. The Prime Minister changed his Indian interlocutors every few months. Soon, officials in the Prime Minister's Office were directly in touch with Dixit in Colombo but I was completely bypassed. It was a strange way to function! I later discovered that, at one stage, Dixit was asked to contact Prabhakaran and persuade him to come to Delhi. The person who eventually contacted Prabhakaran was a first secretary in the High Commission.

As the final touches were being given to the text of the agreement, around 25 July, I was asked to attend one of the meetings held at 7 Race Course Road. It seemed that while India wanted the agreement to be signed in Colombo on 26 July, Colombo felt that the date was too early. They wanted the Prime Minister to agree to move the event to 29 July. I also learned then that Prabhakaran was staying at Ashoka Hotel—he later claimed that we had kept him under house arrest. The Prime Minister had apparently met him and he was being difficult. Rajiv Gandhi asked MGR to come to Delhi to knock some sense into Prabhakaran and MGR had succeeded.

My view was that the Prime Minister should not have met Prabhakaran. Later, when I asked if the PM had got anything in writing from the LTTE chief, he got irritated and said, 'He has given me his word.' I said that Prabhakaran's word meant nothing. He should have been asked to give his consent in writing. He would double-cross us when it suited him. This, Prabhakaran did more than once.

It was mutually agreed that the agreement would be signed in Colombo on 29 July. I suggested to the Prime Minister that in his delegation, he should include two senior Cabinet

Ministers, preferably P.V. Narasimha Rao and N.D. Tiwari. Only P.V. Narasimha Rao came, along with a large number of Tamil Nadu's MPs. We landed at Colombo Airport at 10 a.m. on 29 July 1987. The Prime Minister was informed by the minister who received him that he could not proceed to Colombo by road. The highway was blocked by several thousand Sri Lankans who were opposed to the Indo-Sri Lanka Agreement. Helicopters took us to Colombo city. It resembled a ghost town. There had been violence and widespread arson. Even the property of the President had been set on fire. Rajiv, usually a crowd-puller, was met with silence and unconcealed hostility. Senior members of the Sri Lankan government boycotted the arrival ceremony, as they later did the signing of the agreement at the Presidential palace. This included Prime Minister Premadasa, Lalith Athulathmudali and Mrs Sirimavo Bandaranaike.

The President's lunch, too, was poorly attended and the guests talked in subdued tones. The agreement was signed at 3 p.m. following which the President held a reception. P.V. Narasimha Rao and I were speaking to some of the Sri Lankan politicians who had been invited to the reception, when we noticed that Rajiv, President Jayewardene and several officials were having a serious discussion. P.V. asked me to find out what was happening. When I asked the Prime Minister what was being discussed, his answer only added to my apprehensions. Jayewardene had told him that he feared that unless India immediately sent troops to Sri Lanka to contain the deteriorating law and order situation, a coup could take place that very night. I told the PM to take a decision on so grave a matter only after consulting his senior Cabinet colleagues on his return to Delhi. To my utter surprise, he said that he had already given orders for the immediate dispatch of Indian troops by air to Colombo. P.V. was very disturbed when I informed him of the Prime Minister's decision but, as usual, he was unwilling to confront the PM. The reality on the ground was that India was being sucked into the Sri Lankan ethnic conflict at a scorching pace.

30 July 1987 was a dark day. As Rajiv Gandhi commenced inspecting the Guard of Honour, Vijitha Rohana Wijemuni, a sailor, struck Rajiv Gandhi with the butt of his rifle. While the PM's reflexes saved him from serious injury, he still received a nasty blow. The simmering discontent had found expression, and was a dark indicator of things to come.

The next few months brought no respite. The IPKF arrived in August. The expectation was that we would be able to eliminate the LTTE sooner than later. The Chief of Army Staff boasted that he could take care of the LTTE and Prabhakaran in two weeks. It was a foolish boast. The IPKF went in without clear briefings or objectives. Neither were the troops told about the geography of the Jaffna peninsula nor about the LTTE's hideouts.

As the number of casualties mounted, so did the criticism of the government in Parliament. J.N. Dixit wrote: 'Rajiv Gandhi was given inaccurate advice about the political, military and intelligence factors... He decided to go ahead with the agreement on wrong predictions, which led to hurdles which the agreement ultimately faced.'* The fact is that Dixit was Rajiv Gandhi's advisor. I myself was often kept in the dark. But it was I who was asked to defend the agreement in the Parliament.

Verma, the RAW Chief, got Rajiv Gandhi to agree that RAW would deal directly with Jayewardene without the knowledge of the Ministry of External Affairs or Ministry of Defence. However, RAW's back-channel diplomacy proved disastrous. Jayewardene sarcastically told Dixit, 'How many policies does the Government of India have regarding the Sri Lankan situation?' There was

---

*J.N. Dixit, *Assignment Colombo*, New Delhi: Konark Publishers, 1997.

no cohesive policy and no coordination at the operational level. The senior army officers—majors and lieutenant generals—did not get along amongst themselves. One of them had serious differences with the High Commissioner.

There was no way in which Jayewardene could avoid the affairs of the IPKF and the LTTE which were causing problems for him and the government in one form or another, and at the most unexpected moments. There had always been a suspicion that a reluctant LTTE had been cajoled into accepting the Indo-Sri Lanka Agreement in late July-early August 1987 through some secret deal. In April 1988, it was revealed that the Indian government had agreed to provide the LTTE with a substantial amount of money in return for their support for the agreement. An enterprising Indian journalist broke the news through the London *Observer*. The source of the leak was traced back to the Indian High Commission in Colombo, and to Dixit himself. The timing had a great deal to do with a new peace initiative with the LTTE, in which RAW took the lead. The leak was seen as an attempt to muddy the waters.

An embarrassed Indian government felt compelled to make an official statement on this in the Parliament. As the Minister of State for External Affairs, I told the Parliament:

> In order to help LTTE make the difficult transaction from military to peaceful democratic policies, it was agreed to extend some interim financial relief to LTTE on the understanding that such relief would only cover the period till the rehabilitation of its cadres...I would like to categorically refute the misleading newspaper reports that this payment was to persuade Shri Prabhakaran to accept the Indo-Sri Lankan Agreement. This kind of aspersion is beyond contempt. As I have said, Prabhakaran had already

accepted the agreement. But he had explained certain practical problems in respect of his cadres during the transition. The financial assistance was intended to help LTTE overcome these problems.

The fact is that the LTTE had extracted a monetary payment from the Indian government before they expressed their willingness to accept the Indo-Sri Lanka Agreement as political reality. Eventually only the first installment was paid, but that was because within three months of agreement signing the accord, the IPKF was at war with the LTTE in Jaffna.

As the months rolled by, the agreement began falling apart. Jayewardene retired in late 1988. Premadasa took over and gradually dismantled Jayewardene's policies. He and Rajiv were like chalk and cheese.

In 1989, Rajiv Gandhi lost the Lok Sabha elections. V.P. Singh succeeded him as Prime Minister. V.P. Singh and President Premadasa of Sri Lanka agreed that the IPKF should be withdrawn from Sri Lanka. From the very beginning, the Sri Lanka ethnic issue was mishandled and ended as a complete failure.

17

THE CHINA BREAKTHROUGH

One of my minor achievements as a diplomat was my involvement in the breakthrough in Sino-Indian relations in December 1988. Three weeks after taking over as External Affairs Minister, I had a meeting with the Prime Minister. At that time, our relations with the US, China and Pakistan were highly unsatisfactory. We had warred thrice with Pakistan and once with China. Soon after taking over in 1986, I had a long discussion with the Prime Minister. I put it candidly to him. 'What is your foreign policy vision? What are your priorities?' He countered, 'What are yours, Natwar?' This gave me the opening I was looking for. 'I have one paramount priority—to improve relations with China.' I told him that I began my diplomatic career in China. I was the first IFS officer to opt for Chinese as my language. I had been the liaison officer to Chou En-lai when he came for his final discussions with his grandfather in April 1960. We had then missed a great opportunity to resolve the border problem. We now had three options: (1) Not to disturb the status quo; (2) War; (3) Negotiations. Status quo suited China. War was not a realistic option. Negotiation was the only practical policy.

And negotiations had to be held at the highest level. Even in November 1962, Nehru had told the Parliament that ultimately the dispute had to be resolved through negotiations.*

At that time, we had an influential anti-China lobby in the Ministry of External Affairs, consisting of P.V. Narasimha Rao, G. Parthasarathi and S. Gopal. All three were still bitter over the 1962 war and one of them remarked that it was Chou En-lai who had killed Nehru. These three had immobilized Indira Gandhi's foreign policy. I told Rajiv that foreign policy could not be based on sentimentality and emotion. I further said, 'You have 413 members in the Lok Sabha, you are Jawaharlal Nehru's grandson and Indira Gandhi's son. No one in his right mind would ever accuse you of any foreign policy sell-out. A Prime Minister's visit to China is long overdue.'

Rajiv agreed to my suggestion and asked that the groundwork to his China visit be laid. However, the actual work on his China initiative had to wait for nearly eighteen months, because the Bofors question took up a lot of his time and so did the Sri Lankan problem. Serious preparations could begin only after January 1988. First, it was absolutely necessary to prepare the country for a drastic change in our approach to relations with China. I was deputed to meet Atal Bihari Vajpayee of the BJP, E.M.S. Namboodiripad and Rajeshwar Rao of the CPI as well as Jyoti Basu, Chief Minister of West Bengal. They all supported Rajiv's China visit. Jyoti Basu cautioned me that the visit must be very carefully prepared. The Chinese, he said, while not recognizing the McMahon Line, shared our view that some progress on the border question should happen. Jyoti Basu, on a previous visit, had asked his Chinese hosts why they did not recognize Sikkim as part of India. They had told him that this was a mere

---

*K. Natwar Singh, *My China Diary: 1956-88*, New Delhi: Rupa Publications India, 2009

formality which could easily be corrected. Rajiv found Basu's inputs very useful.

To make sure that China indeed was keen to welcome Rajiv Gandhi, Rajiv secretly sent P.N. Haksar to Beijing a few months before his visit. Haksar held extensive talks with Chinese leaders and, on his return, told Rajiv that there was genuine interest in his visit to China.

On 18 December 1988, Rajiv Gandhi left for China. His delegation included P.V. Narasimha Rao, Dinesh Singh, B. Shankaranand and me. A team of officials, headed by Foreign Secretary K.P.S. Menon also accompanied him.

In Peking, Rajiv Gandhi was received by the Minister of Metallurgy, Qi Uanjim, and Indian Ambassador C.V. Ranganathan. At 10 a.m. there was a ceremonial welcome by Prime Minister Li Peng in the Great Hall of the People. This was followed by delegation-level talks. The PM held three meetings with his counterpart. All aspects of Sino-Indian relations were discussed at length and in considerable detail. Li Peng told Rajiv that his visit marked a new direction in Sino-Indian relations. He said that his government had decided to take concrete steps to resolve the boundary issues. Both agreed to revitalize and restructure bilateral relations and the importance and relevance of the Panchsheel Agreement initiated by Chou En-lai and Jawaharlal Nehru in 1954. Neither avoided reference to 1962, but agreed that they should look to the future. Li Peng accepted Rajiv's proposal to establish three working groups. The first was to deal with the boundary question, the second with economic issues and the third with trade, science and technology.

Rajiv later told me that it had not been smooth sailing. He had also found Li Peng somewhat pedantic and uninspiring. Chinese diplomacy is subtle, surefooted; conceptual thinking goes hand-in-hand with strategy and tactics. It is nuanced and not hurried. The Chinese do not believe in quick fixes. Chinese diplomacy takes a long view of international affairs. Its traditions are centuries old. Chinese diplomats are 'slow burns'. China let the British hold on to Hong Kong till 1997. They could have walked in anytime after 1949.

The Chinese are shrewd practitioners of realpolitik. Patience and deep study inform their foreign policy and diplomacy. Their military thinking and philosophy of warfare are off-shoots of Sun Tzu's treatise *The Art of War*. In the twentieth century, Mao Tse Tung, Ho Chi Minh and General Nguyen employed Sun Tzu's principles of indirect attack. In foreign policy they do not take a white and black attitude; they pay more attention to grey areas. Henry Kissinger in his book *On China* writes, 'Chinese statesmanship exhibits a tendency to view the entire strategic landscape as part of a single whole. Strategy and statecraft [foreign policy] become means of "combative co-existence" with opponents. The goal is to manoeuvre them into weakness while building one's own strategic position.'* We delude ourselves by expecting an early solution to the border problem. China takes a long view of history. Like the ancient Mayans, the Chinese take a long-duration position on statecraft, while we take a short-duration view.

The two leaders had discussed international matters, too. The most significant development for China was the end of their border dispute with Russia and the end of the Vietnam War. Rajiv also gave Li Peng the gist of his discussions with USSR President Mikhail Gorbachev during his recent visit to India. Li Peng informed Rajiv that China's relations with the US were good; in fact, the US was China's second largest trading partner after Japan.

---

*Henry Kissinger, *On China*, New York: Penguin Group US, 2011

THE CHINA BREAKTHROUGH

Rajiv was so decent a leader that he would not shy away from having erred. He had not taken along K.P.S. Menon, the Foreign Secretary, for his meeting with Li Peng and asked me how he could assuage Menon's feelings. I told him that he should send for K.P.S. and tell him that he had erred. Rajiv did so and further added, 'You will now join me in all meetings.' Not many Prime Ministers show such grace.

In the next two days, Rajiv had meetings with President Yang Shangkun, who had been in jail for thirteen years during the Cultural Revolution, which he had called a frightful disaster. Yang was keen to get a clear indication of our policy on Tibet. Rajiv told him that India recognized Tibet as an autonomous region of China. The Prime Minister told me that the Chinese leadership was concerned about the situation in Tibet. He also had long talks with Communist Party General Secretary Zhao Ziyang.

However, the outcome of Rajiv's visit depended entirely on his meeting with Deng Xiaoping. The all-important meeting was fixed at 10.30 a.m. on 21 December in the Great Hall of the People. The venerable, all-powerful Deng's opening words to Rajiv were, 'I welcome you, my young friend. This is your first Chinese visit.' Their handshake lasted almost forty-five seconds. It signalled that Deng wanted the visit to succeed. Symbolic gestures are more important in China than in any other country. Had the handshake been a perfunctory one, the visit would have collapsed then and there. Deng told Rajiv, 'I met your grandfather and your mother when they visited China in 1964. I was then General Secretary of our party.'

The Chinese and the Indian media present were hanging on to every word and noticing every gesture. Each word the Chinese leader uttered was pre-mediated and carefully delivered. The handshake had already produced an electrifying effect. Decades of sterile unfriendliness seemed to melt away in a few minutes.

Rajiv had achieved what Nehru and Indira Gandhi had failed to do. For those present, it was a moment of history.

Deng and Rajiv agreed that both countries should forget the unpleasantness of the past and now look to the future. Deng's tour d'horizon was of immense significance. He said that global equilibrium could be helped by India and China coming together. He also placed great importance on the economic development of both countries in the coming decades. Deng wanted development not only for China and India, but for humankind as a whole. He summed up his policy with the words, 'Oppose hegemonism and maintain world peace.'

In Deng's view, humanity was facing two vital questions—peace and development. China's relations with the United States had improved. Deng spoke of his conversation with Reagan, whom he had asked to abandon the policy of 'four unsinkable submarines'—Taiwan, South Korea, South Africa and Israel. There had been changes in varying degrees in the US policy on all four. Relations were now normal with the US.

He said that one-fifth of the world was doing very well but was not willing to share wealth with the rest. One of the things he mentioned to Rajiv was that before talking about the twenty-first century, he wanted China to arrive in the twentieth century. In the Chinese leader's view, the world was changing and the thinking of people would also change. He then made a startling observation. China had made mistakes and wasted twenty years. Since the fall of the Gang of Four in 1976, China had changed. It had substituted class struggle with the pursuit of modernization. China was opening up to the world. There were changes in every field and PM Rajiv Gandhi would see that for himself when he travelled outside the Chinese capital. Deng again emphasized that the Asia Pacific century would not become a reality without development in China and India. Deng then referred to the five principles of peaceful coexistence, or Panchsheel, approved by Chou En-lai and Nehru in 1954, which could be the basis for taking forward the international dialogue. He also confided that the Soviet Union was in favour of the five principles.

Rajiv took Deng into confidence about developments in India. Old barriers and roadblocks were being knocked down, paving the way towards modernization. This reflected in the performance of our economy.

In the evening I asked Rajiv how his meeting with Deng had gone. 'We have moved forward; 1962 is now behind us,' he told me. He told me that the more he spoke to the Chinese leader, the more he saw similarity in their views.

The Deng-Rajiv meeting created a stir, not only in China and India but around the globe.

Later, Rajiv held talks with Premier Li Peng as well. In their discussion, they stressed that the five principles of mutual respect for sovereignty and territorial integrity, mutual non-aggression, non-interference in each other's internal affairs, equality and mutual benefit, and peaceful coexistence, which were jointly initiated by India and China and had proved full of vitality through the test of history, constitute the basic guiding principles for good relations between the two states. These principles also constitute the basic guidelines for the establishment of a new international political order and the new international economic order. Both sides agreed that their common desire was to restore, improve and develop India-China neighbourly and friendly relations on the basis of these principles. This not only conformed to the fundamental interests of the two countries, but would actively contribute to peace and stability in Asia and the world as a whole. The two sides reaffirmed that they would make efforts to further their friendly relations.

The leaders of the two countries held earnest, in-depth

discussions on the India-China boundary question and agreed to settle this question through peaceful and friendly consultations. They also agreed to develop their relations actively in other fields and work hard to create a favourable climate and conditions for a fair and reasonable settlement of the boundary question, while seeking a mutually acceptable solution to this question. In this context, concrete steps would be taken, such as establishing a joint working group on the boundary question and a joint group on economic relations and trade, and science and technology.

The Chinese side expressed concern over anti-China activities by some Tibetan elements in India. The Indian side reiterated the long-standing and consistent policy of the Government of India that Tibet was an autonomous region of China and that anti-China political activities by Tibetan elements were not permitted on Indian soil.

The trail-blazing visit was Rajiv Gandhi's outstanding foreign policy triumph. The fact that the Sino-Indian border has been tranquil for twenty-five years is his gift. It was for me a momentous event, one in which I had played a modest role.

18

THE DECLINE OF THE CONGRESS

The Congress's landslide victory of 1984 was a tribute to Indira Gandhi. It had nothing whatsoever to do with sound policies and programmes. By 1989, voters were disenchanted with the Congress and showed it the door. Lack of cohesion in government, the loss of morals in the party, anger in the Parliament and the country over the Bofors scandal were some of the causes for the debacle.

1986-87 were very trying years for the Prime Minister. He was losing his grip over his government. Cohesion was lacking. A directionless drift was all too visible. He had to deal with the agitation in the Darjeeling hills led by the Gorkha National Liberation Front, the fallout of the Shah Bano case and the Ram Janmabhoomi issue. He mishandled all three.

The people of Darjeeling had been demanding a separate state, Gorkhaland, since 1907. By 1986, the Gorkhaland was restive. Under the leadership of Subash Ghisingh, the Gorkhaland National Liberation Front mounted a violent protest which led to the loss of many lives and almost shut down the state. The agitation went on for two years until 1988, when Darjeeling was granted semi-autonomous status.

Shah Bano was a Muslim divorcee who had gone to the Supreme Court seeking a monthly maintenance of five hundred rupees from her husband. In 1985, the Supreme Court ruled in her favour while maintaining that the ruling was consistent with Shariat law. Fundamental Muslim clerics were incensed at the Supreme Court's decision. Regardless, Rajiv decided that Arif Mohammad Khan, a junior minister in his government, should defend the ruling. While Arif made a brilliant case for the government, the reaction of the Muslim Personal Law Board to Arif's speech was hostile. They put pressure on the Prime Minister, who was advised that a large part of the Muslim community would be alienated if his support for Shah Bano continued. The Prime Minister changed his mind. Arif Mohammad rightly resigned because he could not accept the Prime Minister's volte face. The countrywide reaction was that the Prime Minister had not handled the issue well.

In 1986, the Babri Masjid-Ram Janmabhoomi issue surfaced. After simmering for a number of years, the crisis came to a boil after the locks placed on the sites were taken away, and worship begun, allegedly at the behest of Arun Nehru, one of the Ministers of State closest to Rajiv Gandhi. The Prime Minister's judgement was questioned and the political temperature rose dramatically. The issue culminated in the rath yatra undertaken by L.K. Advani in 1990 and the demolition of the mosque on 6 December 1992, following which there were communal riots in many parts of the country.

On 24 March 1986, a 285-million-dollar contract was signed between the government and the Swedish armaments company, Bofors, for the supply of 410 155-mm Howitzer guns. About a year later, on 16 April 1987, Swedish radio alleged that Bofors had paid kickbacks to a number of Indian politicians and key defence officials for this deal. The opposition parties went for the kill and targeted Rajiv Gandhi for his alleged involvement in bribe-taking. I felt then, and still do, that the Prime Minister could have handled the matter in a more nuanced manner. All that Gandhi had to do was to appoint a committee of senior officials under the chairmanship of the Cabinet Secretary to deal with the Bofors issue. Inevitably, this would not have satisfied the Opposition, but could have saved him from venomous attacks on his integrity. He could have exercised nuanced restraint. This he did not do. Instead, he plunged into the Bofors mud. Some of it stuck.

By 1987, the Rajiv Gandhi government had run out of steam.

Rajiv Gandhi was a man in a hurry. What he achieved during his five-year term was quite remarkable. He succeeded in changing the mindset of a large number of Indians and prepared the country for the twenty-first century. Impetuous at times, he believed that intricate problems could be solved by verbalization, which inevitably led to unforeseen consequences.

Between 1984 and 1989, he made over two dozen reshuffles in his Council of Ministers. The only minister who completed five years in his Cabinet was Railway Minister Madhavrao Scindia. The Ministry of External Affairs saw four Cabinet ministers and six Ministers of State during his prime ministership. In short, the ministers were not able to settle down in their jobs or offer any long-term policy proposals. For the first eighteen months of his prime ministership, Rajiv Gandhi depended almost wholly on a team of ignoramuses with inflated egos. They were bright but brash. One claimed to be a socialist while one was an inept political wheeler-dealer. A third was a meddling nuisance. Collectively, they were an irresponsible group that showed little regard for senior Cabinet ministers and government rules and regulations. They dented Rajiv Gandhi's prestige and his image.

In January 1986, President Najibullah of Afghanistan was expected in New Delhi. Rajiv called me up on the RAX and asked me to join him. He was about to leave for Palam airport to receive the President. On the way to Palam, to my utter surprise, Rajiv said, 'Natwar, are we about to go to war with Pakistan?' 'Operation Brasstacks' had become a problem. Several versions of Operation Brasstacks exist. I will give mine for what it's worth.

The Indian Army, commanded by Chief of Army Staff General Krishnaswamy Sundarji, had planned extensive military exercises on the Indo-Pak border codenamed 'Brasstacks'. Details were cleared by Arun Singh, then Minister of State for Defence. Given the massive scale of these exercises, fears had arisen in Pakistan that these exercises were a cover for cross-border intervention. Reports appeared in the Indian press that Pakistan was mobilizing its troops into battle positions.

I told Rajiv Gandhi, in my capacity as Minister of State for External Affairs, that the Ministry of External Affairs knew nothing about this. The Prime Minister said that neither did he. I was appalled. Apparently, Arun Singh and Gen Krishnaswamy Sundarji had acted without his approval.

The Prime Minister asked me and N.D. Tiwari, the External Affairs Minister, to call the US and Soviet Ambassadors and request them for detailed information on Pakistan troop movements, based on their satellite surveillance. The US and Soviet envoys soon reported that there was nothing to suggest that the Pakistan Army had assumed offensive positions on the border. The PM called a meeting to discuss the outcome of our discussion with the embassies in which N.D. Tiwari, Arun Singh, M.L. Fotedar, Lt Gen. Hazari and I were present. I placed the information given by the Ambassadors before the PM. Arun Singh questioned the efficiency of the American and Russian satellites. This was laughable. Rajiv accepted what Tiwari and I said.

After the meeting, he asked Tiwariji and me to stay back. Turning to Tiwariji, he said, 'What do I do with my Minister of State for Defence?'

The External Affairs Minister looked at me and kept silent. Rajiv Gandhi then sought my view. I told him that he should sack the minister. 'Arun Singh is a friend,' was his response. With some firmness I said, 'Sir, you are not the President of the Old Boys' Association of Doon School. You are the Prime Minister of India. Prime Ministers have no friends.'

When we were leaving the Prime Minister's Office, Tiwari said, 'Natwar Singhji, you were very frank.' I told him that it was our duty to place the facts before the Prime Minister and give him our advice. It was for him to accept or reject it. A few days later, Arun Singh was transferred to the Ministry of Finance. He opposed the move, but his resistance was short-lived. By this time, Rajiv Gandhi had come to know of some of his junior minister's decisions. He dropped him from the Council of Ministers and also asked him to resign from the Rajya Sabha.

We in the Ministry of External Affairs worked overtime to defuse the 'Brasstacks' crisis. The PM asked me to invite the Pakistan Foreign Secretary, Abdus Sattar, for delegation-level talks on disengagement and de-escalation. An agreement was signed with Pakistan to withdraw troops in the Kashmir area. Later, another agreement was signed to withdraw further troops. President Zia-ul-Haq also spoke to the Prime Minister when he visited India in February 1987 to watch a cricket match. What alarmed me was the cavalier manner in which the Minister of State and the Army Chief had acted on such a sensitive and important matter.

♦

From 1986 onwards, Rajiv Gandhi's relations with President Giani Zail Singh deteriorated by the week. A stage was reached when public accusations were made by one against the other. The President's grievance was that the PM did not see him every week (as was the custom), nor did he care to brief him on important matters facing the country. Battle lines were drawn. Zail Singh said he would dismiss Rajiv who, in turn, threatened to impeach the President. The crisis only ended when Zail Singh's five-year term ended in 1987.

◆

The public dismissal of Foreign Secretary A.P. Venkateswaran by the Prime Minister also caused a furore. It did colossal, even irreparable harm. The entire bureaucracy was agitated and hurt. Venkateswaran took over as Foreign Secretary in the middle of 1985. I had known him for a long time. He was a year senior to me. His service record was without blemish. He had a fine brain. His sense of humour sometimes went astray but this was harmless on most occasions. At times, it degenerated into irreverence. As Foreign Secretary, he was expected to be discreet and responsible. His ability had never been questioned. It was his judgement that finally got him into trouble. I had once or twice cautioned him to be careful and not rub the PM the wrong way.

When I joined the Ministry of External Affairs in October 1986 as Minister of State, I, to my great dismay, saw that the link between the Prime Minister's Office and the Ministry of External Affairs was not at all satisfactory. Both sides were to blame. Venkateswaran did not take kindly to the constant interference by the PMO in the Ministry of External Affairs. Soon after taking over, I discerned the Prime Minister's coolness towards his Foreign Secretary. I also noticed that the Foreign

Secretary was treating the Prime Minister in a somewhat light-hearted manner. Venkateswaran was also openly and unwisely critical of the abilities and functioning of the Prime Minister. Inevitably, his views reached Rajiv Gandhi.

On a visit to Pakistan, Venkateswaran, in his discussions with his Pakistani counterpart, volunteered the information that the Prime Minister was keen to visit Islamabad. He had no authority to do so. We were all surprised and the Prime Minister was visibly annoyed. The Foreign Secretary had placed the government in an awkward position. Immediate damage control was necessary and all efforts were made to check the media excitement.

On 21 January 1987, the Prime Minister held a press conference. His special assistant, the self-effacing Ronen Sen, told him that Venkateswaran would be present at the conference. A question was put to the PM about the Foreign Secretary's pronouncement about his visit to Pakistan. The Prime Minister's incredible answer was, 'You will soon have a new Foreign Secretary.' At the time, the Foreign Secretary was sitting in the front row facing the Prime Minister. Venkateswaran resigned that very day.

A public dismissal of the Foreign Secretary of the Prime Minister was unprecedented. I was in Moscow at the time and heard the news on the radio. I immediately decided to return to Delhi.

As soon as I arrived in Delhi, I proceeded to the PM's residence at 7 Race Course Road. N.D. Tiwari was also present. I told the PM that the manner in which he had sacked Venkateswaran had invited the wrath of the civil service. Senior civil servants like L.P. Singh and P.N. Haksar were severely critical. I later learnt that even Sonia had upbraided him. He innocently said, 'I did not know he was sitting in the front row.'

◆

Post Rajiv's loss in the 1989 Lok Sabha elections, six PMs occupied 7 Race Course Road in the nineties. A new coalition government was formed in 1989 by the National Front, headed by Rajiv's erstwhile Finance, then Defence Minister Vishwanath Pratap Singh. He had resigned from the Congress and the Lok Sabha in 1987 after being dismissed from the Cabinet. Arun Nehru and Arif Mohammad Khan also joined the National Front.

♦

On 10 February 1990, Nelson Mandela was released from prison. The eyes of the world were fixed on him. The V.P. Singh government at the Centre decided to send an Additional Secretary of the Ministry of External Affairs to convey their greetings to Mandela. It was a thoughtless decision. I suggested to Rajiv Gandhi that a high-powered Congress Party delegation should be sent to felicitate Nelson Mandela, to which he agreed. P.V. Narasimha Rao, Anand Sharma and I met Mandela and Mrs Mandela in a village about 100 miles west of Tanzania's capital, Dar es Salaam. Mandela was deeply appreciative of this gesture. He said that Mahatma Gandhi and Pandit Nehru had been an inspiration to him. He was grateful for the assistance that was given to the African National Congress by India during his twenty-seven years in prison.

His dignity, poise and self-assurance were extraordinary. I noticed that he spoke little. His serenity was exceptional. We were in the presence of a person of the highest integrity, courage and vision.

On 21 March 1990, Namibia was to celebrate its independence. I mentioned to Rajiv that this was an occasion which he should be present at. Rajiv said he had received no invitation. I telephoned President Kaunda at Lusaka about this and the invitation arrived within twenty-four hours. The only means to reach the Namibian capital, Windhoek, was via South Africa. Rajiv refused to go that way. The Zambian President invited Rajiv to travel in his private plane.

On the 18th, we arrived in Bombay to catch a flight to Lusaka on Zambian Airways. Rajiv had decided to travel economy class. As soon as the plane took off, passengers rushed to get his autograph. The commotion was such that the cabin steward implored him to move to first class, otherwise, it would be impossible to serve dinner. Rajiv said that he alone could not shift to the first class cabin; I, too, should be upgraded. This was agreed to and the crew was more than relieved.

Although Rajiv was not holding any office at that time, Kaunda treated him as if he was still the Prime Minister. We were put up in State House, which was the President's residence. Kaunda hosted a dinner the day we arrived for several delegates going to Windhoek for the independence day celebrations. Among them was the Foreign Minister of the Soviet Union, Eduard Shevardnadze. He hardly noticed Rajiv. When Rajiv was Prime Minister, Shevardnadze had missed no opportunity to get near him. Rajiv did not react, but I thought poorly of this behaviour.

Early next morning, we left for the Namibian capital in the President's plane. At Windhoek, President Kaunda and Rajiv were received by the Prime Minister designate, Hage Geingob. The atmosphere was festive and people danced and sang. On the 21st it rained, which made it difficult to get to the stadium where the celebrations were to be held. Somehow we managed to reach in time to witness the lowering of the South African flag and the hoisting of the Namibian flag. Rajiv and I were seated along with the foreign ministers of other countries. The name of each leader was announced. When Rajiv's name was called, there was clapping. Before him, the name of Prime Minister V.P. Singh had been called, but there was no response. The Prime Minister had failed to arrive in time to witness the birth of an independent Namibia. Most African Heads of State had journeyed to Namibia for the great event. Mandela sat in the front row. Also present was the South African President, F.W. de Klerk. The Secretary General of the United Nations, Javier Pérez de Cuéllar, handed over the reins of state power to President Sam Nujoma at the swearing-in ceremony. It was a historic and deeply moving moment, all the more special for me because I had played a modest role by vigorously supporting Namibia's independence in the UN Committee on decolonization.

The following day, Rajiv decided to have dinner at a restaurant. When he arrived, there was spontaneous clapping. Half the restaurant was filled by whites, who were not particularly happy at the end of white rule in Namibia. Nevertheless, they honoured Rajiv. Rajiv asked me, 'How do they know me?'

I replied jocularly, 'Because your name is not Natwar Singh.'

Early morning the next day, we proceeded to meet Nelson Mandela who was staying outside the city. Rajiv's opening words were, 'When my daughter learnt that I would be meeting you, she said that when I shake hands with Mr Mandela, I should be thinking of her. This I am doing now.' Rajiv spoke about the Indian scene, the problems that beset us and the efforts that were being made to rectify them. He spoke as an Indian, not as a Congress leader. Mandela gave an overview of what was happening in South Africa in particular and southern Africa in general. He foresaw complex and prolonged discussions with the South African President, which would lead to the black majority assuming the reins of power in an independent democratic South Africa. The road would be long and full of hurdles. The white community at the moment was not reconciled to giving up their supremacy. The most difficult issue would be that of land, three-fourths of which was owned by the whites. This, Mandela felt, would be among the toughest problems he would face.

Mandela said that he looked forward to having close relations with India. He also asked for some financial assistance for the African National Congress which Rajiv promised to give.

Also present at Windhoek was Tiny Rowland, an Englishman who had a vast business empire in southern Africa. I had known him in Lusaka. He was an amazing character; jovial, calculating, and a genius when it came to trade. I told him that we were finding it difficult to get a flight to London as all seats were booked. Rowland said that he had a private plane and would be only too glad if Rajiv and I would fly with him to London.

Before leaving for the airport, Rajiv, an avid photographer, walked into a camera shop to buy some film. The shop owner was a white Afrikaner. He would accept no payment.

We flew the whole night in Rowland's deluxe private plane, arriving in London the next morning. Rowland was an entertaining host and his knowledge of southern Africa was vast.

Before catching the flight to Delhi, Rajiv asked me to contact Margaret Thatcher and the Labour Leader Neil Kinnock. We got through to Mrs Thatcher's office but her staff was unhelpful. Kinnock was delighted to say hello to Rajiv. Mrs Thatcher later complained to the Commonwealth Secretary General, Sonny Ramphal, that Rajiv had spoken to Kinnock, but not to her. Sonny passed this on to us and I wrote to her to give the facts. Her office conceded that an error had been committed.

I had never before been alone with Rajiv. He was always surrounded by crowds. On this trip, he was condemned to spend five days in my company. He was the most natural, charming and least pompous man I had met. No sides, no angularities, no pretence; a great sense of humour and no airs. He made me feel comfortable. He did not like to be alone. He was a technology buff. He had brought a small radio with a contraption that looked like an aerial. He soon fixed it and then we heard the BBC news.

While we were in Lusaka, the Indian High Commissioner, S.P. Singh, invited us for dinner with five or six Indian expatriates. They were overawed, momentarily speechless, but in no time, Rajiv put them at ease, speaking to them as if they were old friends. He treated them as his equals. Only a man of self-confidence and poise could do that. From prime ministership to becoming a mere MP is like falling from a cliff. Rajiv, however, did not fall. A leader's real test is his conduct in adversity.

◆

Turbulence in the early nineties started with the publication of the Mandal Report—that advocated 27 per cent reservation in a certain portion of government and university jobs for OBCs—by V.P. Singh. A party that espoused Hindutva ideology, the Bharatiya Janata Party, emerged and began to make a mark. This led to disturbances in New Delhi, culminating in a student immolating himself in protest against the Mandal Report.

V.P.'s Deputy Prime Minister, Devi Lal, fell out with the PM, whose ouster he sought. V.P. resigned in November 1990 and was succeeded by Chandra Shekhar, the one-time leader of the Young Turks in the Congress. Rajiv Gandhi, who was the Leader of the Opposition, decided to support him. Chandra Shekhar had only forty-four MPs. The Rajiv-Chandra Shekhar partnership was short-lived, though. Serious differences surfaced between them over the Gulf War, following Saddam Hussein's invasion of Kuwait. Chandra Shekhar permitted American military aircraft to refuel in Bombay and Chennai on their way to the Gulf and Rajiv took exception to this, terming it the 'mollycoddling of the Americans'. Rajiv also made several attempts to speak to President George Bush, Sr, but he did not take the calls. Ultimately, President Bush sent a curt oral reply through the US Embassy in New Delhi to Rajiv Gandhi's letter of 7 February. It was blunt:

> We have no plans to use nuclear weapons in the conflict. Your recent comments reported in the press suggesting that India should implement its potential to make nuclear weapons are very alarming. Such a course of action would reverse India's firm stand against doing so, and could seriously destabilize South Asia.
>
> I am also concerned that you have opposed India's decision to refuel our military supply flights to the Gulf. These flights are very important, and we hope that they can soon be resumed. Your use of them as a political issue can only damage a bilateral relationship you did so much to build up.

Rajiv Gandhi had decided to topple the Chandra Shekhar government. PM Chandra Shekhar sent Ronen Sen, at one time Rajiv's Foreign Affairs' aide, to show him the file in which Rajiv had approved landing facilities to US military aircraft at Madras and Bombay. It made no difference. Chandra Shekhar had to go. Rajiv met President R. Venkataraman, informing him of his decision to withdraw support to the government. Chandra Shekhar acted with alacrity, resigning on 21 June 1991, before he could be defeated on the floor of the Lok Sabha.

◆

Lok Sabha elections were to be held again, and the Congress started campaigning with full force to regain its former glory. On 17 May 1991, Rajiv Gandhi came to my Lok Sabha constituency, Bharatpur, to address a public meeting for the elections. The meeting concluded at 3.30 a.m. and we reached Bharatpur at 4. Rajiv Gandhi, his close friend Suman Dubey, who had accompanied him, and I spent the early morning at the Forest Lodge. Unlike me, Rajiv needed only three to four hours of sleep. He was up at 7 a.m. After breakfast, we left for Agra, where I said goodbye to him and wished him all the best for the remaining part of the election campaign. That was the last time I saw him.

On 21 May, I was campaigning thirty-five miles away from Bharatpur. It was a dark night, and soon there was an unseasonal rainstorm. No meetings could be held in such weather, so I returned to Bharatpur. There, I was told that Rajiv Gandhi had been killed in a bomb blast by a suicide bomber. I could scarcely believe it. To make sure, I telephoned the Chief Election Commissioner T.N. Seshan. By a miracle I got him on the line. Seshan confirmed that Rajiv Gandhi had been assassinated at 11 p.m. at Sriperumbudur in Tamil Nadu. My wife and I immediately left for Delhi in the pouring rain. Throughout the drive, we talked about the horrific tragedy. Rajiv was only forty-six at the time of his death. Our hearts went out to Sonia, Rahul and Priyanka.

Although the distance between Bharatpur and Delhi is only about 86 miles, that night it seemed as if we would never reach Delhi. I dropped my wife off at our Vasant Vihar home and drove to Palam airport. I saw President R. Venkataraman waiting to receive the body. Also at the airport were V. George, M.L. Fotedar and a few others. The plane landed at about 5.45 a.m. Sonia and Priyanka Gandhi had also travelled by the same plane. No words are adequate to express Sonia's grief.

After coming out of the plane dressed in white, Sonia put her head on the President's shoulder and broke down. Those present could not restrain their tears. My world too had disintegrated. Priyanka came out a few minutes later and then Rajiv's body was placed into a vehicle. He was covered in a white sheet. Sonia and Priyanka drove with the President.

The body was taken to the All India Institute of Medical Sciences for a post-mortem. After that, it was taken to 10 Janpath and then to Teen Murti House. A state funeral was held for him on 24 May. The funeral procession took more than three hours. Hundreds of thousands of people had lined the route. A large number of foreign dignitaries also arrived to pay homage. Although at the time of his death, Rajiv was not even a Member of Parliament, yet his funeral was attended by Vice President Dan Quayle of the United States, Prince Charles accompanied by two former Prime Ministers of England, Benazir Bhutto and Nawaz Sharif of Pakistan, Yasser Arafat, the Deputy Prime Ministers of China and the Soviet Union, the King of Bhutan and the foreign ministers of many other countries.

Before leaving Delhi, most of the VIPs called on Sonia Gandhi at 10 Janpath. I was present at all the meetings. I distinctly remember Benazir Bhutto telling Sonia that she should keep away from politics and look after her son and daughter after such a tragedy. Sonia sat in silent sorrow. I told Benazir that she had not followed what she was preaching: 'You have stepped into the shoes of your father. The Gandhis have a tradition and legacy of serving India. They could not abandon their heritage.' Benazir said that these were seductive words. I did not wish to bandy words with her on so sombre an occasion.

The day after the cremation, Rajiv's ashes were taken to Allahabad in a special train, accompanied by forty senior members of the Congress. Throughout the night, thousands of people waited at every station to pay their homage to their beloved leader. At the Triveni Sangam, where Rajiv's ashes were immersed, the crowd could not have been less than half a million. After the immersion, we spent a few hours at Anand Bhavan before catching the special train back to Delhi. None of us could sleep and we spent our time recalling our close associations with him.

Jawaharlal Nehru had died peacefully in bed. Sanjay Gandhi, at the age of thirty-three, was killed in an air crash on 22 June 1980. Indira Gandhi was assassinated on 31 October 1984 and now Rajiv Gandhi, on 21 May 1991. I could not help thinking that the Nehru-Gandhi family attracted lightning and thunder. Some sinister fate pursued them.

Two days after Rajiv's death, I wrote in an article, 'The country weeps. The world mourns. I feel a terrible emptiness within and there is no drowning this sorrow. At the moment our consolations are few, our torments many. When the tears have dried, the anger subsided, the horror diminished, the scar will remain. So will the heartache.'

◆

After the funeral, there was intense political activity. The aspirants to the post of Congress President included Arjun Singh, N.D. Tiwari, Sharad Pawar and Madhavrao Scindia. Sonia Gandhi herself refused to be the President when it was suggested to her. I told her that the time had come for her to indicate her preference for the role; whoever she chose would naturally become PM. For so momentous a decision, I suggested she ask P.N. Haksar for advice. She said she would let me know. Meanwhile, she consulted several people, including M.L. Fotedar.

THE DECLINE OF THE CONGRESS

The next day, she asked me to bring Haksar to 10 Janpath. Haksar's advice was to offer the post to Vice President Shankar Dayal Sharma. He suggested that Aruna Asaf Ali and I should sound out the VP. Aruna Asaf Ali's standing in the country was very high. She had played a heroic role during the Quit India Movement in 1942. She knew Shankar Dayal Sharma well. I had also seen much of Shankar Dayalji for decades. I had first met him when he was Chief Minister of Bhopal. A common link between us was Cambridge University.

Aruna Asaf Ali conveyed Sonia's message to the VP. He gave us a patient hearing. He said he was touched and honoured by Soniaji's placing so much trust in him. What followed staggered Arunaji and me. The VP continued, 'The prime ministership of India is a full-time job. My age and health would not let me to do justice to the most important office in the country. Kindly convey to Soniaji the reasons for my inability to take on so awesome a responsibility.'

After hearing of the VP's refusal, I asked Sonia to once again send for P.N. Haksar, who advised her to call P.V. Narasimha Rao. Thereafter, the Congress Working Committee met and unanimously elected P.V. as Congress President. I was in touch with P.V. at the time. For the first few days, he was reluctant to show his hand, but he was holding wide-ranging discussions with senior Congress leaders and with P.C. Alexander, then Governor of Tamil Nadu and his close friend.

The problem lay in pacifying Sharad Pawar and Arjun Singh. If my memory serves, a solution was found by which Sharad Pawar withdrew his candidature. Arjun Singh also withdrew from the prime ministerial election as he was led to expect that he would become Congress President. P.V. Narasimha Rao agreed to this, but once he became Prime Minister, he decided that he would hold on to the post of Congress President as well.

Thus the seeds for further differences between P.V. and Arjun Singh were sown.

◆

P.V. Narasimha Rao came from a humble home. His intellectual centre was India; his roots were deep in its spiritual and religious soil. His knowledge of Sanskrit was profound. He was a man of learning, a scholar, a linguist and a thinker of the first order. Although a picture of serene calmness, he was no saint—his private life inclined towards passion and sensuality. Very few were privy to this aspect of his life. He was astute, crafty and patient, but also capable of radioactive sarcasm. He smiled without a smile.

In early 1990, he had decided to retire from politics when Rajiv Gandhi denied him a Rajya Sabha seat. This saddened him as he was a very senior Congress leader. Being a reticent person, he did not create a ruckus but made arrangements to go back to Hyderabad, when Rajiv was tragically assassinated.

I had first met P.V. in 1976 at a havan organized by the guru Chandraswamy in a house in Panchsheel Park. In the middle of May 1980, P.V. became the External Affairs Minister. Indira Gandhi's choice took everyone by surprise as P.V. then had no experience whatsoever of diplomacy and foreign policy. He began by keeping a very low profile and was for a long time unable to take any kind of initiative. He was very slow at taking decisions and would often change his mind. He was a loner and avoided familiarity. He was a man transformed after becoming Prime Minister.

◆

When P.V. became PM, the country faced a very serious balance-of-payments crisis. For the first time, India had to deposit forty-seven tons of gold with the Bank of England to tide over the immediate crisis. The most important issue at the time was the selection of the Finance Minister. The first choice was I.G. Patel, who had had a very distinguished career and was one of the eminent economists of the country. I.G. was unable to accept on account of his health and also because he lived in Baroda and did not wish to shift to Delhi. Manmohan Singh was then invited. He had, for the past three years, been heading the South-South Commission and had functioned from Geneva. After his tenure as Secretary General of the South-South Commission ended, Manmohan was without a job and was for a short time economic adviser to Prime Minister Chandra Shekhar. He had also been selected to head the Union Public Service Commission. To begin with, Manmohan Singh was not keen to become Finance Minister, but was persuaded to do so and proved to be an outstanding one.

India sought relief for its financial crisis from the IMF, which insisted that economic reforms be introduced before a loan of 1.4 billion dollars was approved. Thus, economic reforms were launched to open up the economy to foreign investment and business competition. Senior Congress Party members were unhappy at P.V. abandoning Nehru's socialist economic policies and ending the state-controlled mode of functioning. They favoured a mixed economy. To begin with, even the corporate tsars were critical of the reforms. They had earned vast amounts during the Licence Raj and wished it to continue. However, they embraced Manmohan Singh and his policies within six months.

◆

P.V. Narasimha Rao faced the most serious crisis of his tenure on 6 December 1992—the Babri Masjid in Ayodhya was demolished by unruly Hindu karsevaks. The UP and the central governments looked helplessly on and the world saw the demolition live on television. After the demolition, riots broke out in Aligarh, Agra, Varanasi and many other cities. Bombay saw the worst rioting. Six days of lawlessness left 222 dead and 600 injured; almost everyone who died was Muslim. The seeds for Hindutva had been sown. P.V. had lost his nerve and came out of the whole sad episode with his fingers burnt. His indecisiveness, at such a time, did him no credit.

When I met the Prime Minister in the Parliament after the demolition, he was in a daze. I asked if the Ministry of External Affairs had been instructed to send telegrams to all Indian missions to explain the reasons for bringing down the mosque as they would be inundated with queries by the respective governments and the international media. This was finally done.

◆

I had many differences with P.V.'s style of functioning and openly spoke against him, along with a group of Congress leaders, including Arjun Singh, N.D. Tiwari, Shiela Dikshit, Shiv Charan Mathur, M.L. Fotedar, P. Shiv Shankar and the late K.N. Singh. This crusade was masterminded by Arjun Singh. The attack on Narasimha Rao was two-pronged. First, he had gone back on the assurance given that after becoming Prime Minister he would give up the post of Congress President and second, the economic reforms introduced by him were contrary to the policies of the Congress Party. We broke away from the main Congress and formed a new party, the Tiwari Congress.

The climax of our stand-off was reached at the AICC meeting

in Surajkund, Haryana, in March 1993. By then, the Tiwari Congress had been formed and the fourteen of us sat in protest. Around this time, Arjun Singh resigned as Minister for Human Development. M.L. Fotedar had done so earlier. Narasimha Rao was not a confrontationist and wanted to reach a compromise. A meeting was arranged by Madhavrao Scindia between me, K.N. Singh, Sheila Dikshit, M.L. Fotedar and the Prime Minister at his residence. Fotedar refused to join us because he was allergic to having to do anything with Rao. Our meeting did not go well. I asked him what his objection was to giving up the presidentship of the Congress Party. His response came as a surprise to me—he said that the Prime Minister of India could not be seen carrying files to the Congress President. I told him that if Jawaharlal Nehru as PM could go to Congress President U.N. Dhebar, why could he not? He made things worse by hinting at governorships for us.

◆

For almost two years P.V. did not appoint an External Affairs Minister. In early 1993, he appointed the highly respected Pranab Mukherjee, the senior-most Congressman.

In 1993, India and China signed an agreement on Maintaining Peace and Tranquillity on the Line of Actual Control and Reducing Military Forces on the Border Areas, pending a final decision. This was an extension of the statement issued during Rajiv Gandhi's memorable visit to China in December 1988. As a China-watcher, I made every effort to keep pace with the fast-moving consolidation of Sino-Indian relations. These were further strengthened in 1996, during the visit of Jiang Zemin, the first Chinese Head of State to come to India. He and P.V. Narasimha Rao signed an important agreement on 29 November, 'On Confidence-building Measures in the Military Field along the Line of Control in the India-China Border'. In diplomacy, even modest progress is worthy of respect.

P.V. backed out from conducting nuclear tests in 1995. His advisers and experts had convinced him that India was in a position to do so and he had agreed. But the American satellites picked up the activities around Pokhran. The satellite photographs were brought to India by the American Ambassador, who showed them to the PM. President Clinton also spoke to him in strong terms, and P.V. changed his mind.

◆

Our concerted effort to remove P.V. did not succeed because he was far cleverer than all of us. But he did not have the support of Sonia Gandhi either. An impression was created by one or two senior members of the CWC that Sonia Gandhi was not happy with the reform process and that Narasimha Rao was ignoring her. The attempt was to weaken the hands of Narasimha Rao. Almost all the senior members of the Congress Party were aware of Sonia Gandhi giving him the cold shoulder.

In the months to come, a stage was reached when communication between 7 Race Course Road and 10 Janpath almost ceased. This was good neither for the party nor for the government.

◆

In the 1996 Lok Sabha elections, every candidate of the Tiwari Congress other than Sis Ram Ola lost the elections. Some senior members had hoped that the party had or would have the support of Sonia Gandhi. But Ms Gandhi did not oblige and remained aloof from all political activities. I remember Arjun Singh telling me, 'This is the reward for loyalty.'

The Congress also lost the 1996 Lok Sabha elections and P.V. sat on the Opposition benches. He made one or two brilliantly argued interventions in Parliament, but the loss of power also meant loss of influence and patronage. Soon, a concentrated attack was mounted against him and he ceased being President of the party. Thereafter, he disappeared into oblivion. The well-heeled treasurer of the Congress Party, Sitaram Kesri, succeeded him.

As PM, P.V. had shown uncommon political skill. Heading a minority government, he was able to complete five years by keeping his allies with him throughout.

Between 1996 and 1998, India was in deep political crisis. To everyone's surprise, the non-Congress parties selected H.D. Deve Gowda as Prime Minister in 1996. He was a major political figure in Karnataka but was hardly known in North India. He spoke no Hindi, lacked charisma, and was not a leader who inspired confidence.

As an individual, Deve Gowda is likeable if not lovable. A fine and charming man, even his idiosyncrasies are endearing. He always addresses me as 'senior leader' and refers to himself as a 'poor farmer'. In his short tenure, his only remarkable act was to speak of 'maximum autonomy' for Kashmir. His government fell in April 1997 and he was replaced by Inder Kumar Gujral. Like Deve Gowda, Gujral belonged to the United Front and became PM with the Congress's support. I had known him when he was Minister of State in Indira Gandhi's government and he was among the very few ministers who stood up to Sanjay Gandhi. He had vision, and his sophistication was not elitist. He had been a card-carrying member of the Communist Party before the Partition. His 'Gujral Doctrine' was an imaginative contribution to India's foreign policy. His tenure, like that of

Gowda, was short-lived: April 1997 to March 1998.

The Congress Party with Sitaram Kesri as President was not an effective or assertive outfit. It had lost its bearings. After the 1996 elections, it was reduced to 112 members. Sonia asked me how she should proceed. 'Reinvent the party,' I advised, a counsel that was easier offered than implemented. Would she be up to the job? What would her priorities be? These questions were being asked in clandestine, disgruntled group meetings. It was abundantly clear that without Sonia at the helm, the future of the Congress looked bleak.

Kesri did not last long. A coup did him in, even though he had the support of several senior members of the CWC. Sonia was unanimously elected to succeed him. Immediately after Sonia's election as Congress President, the Tiwari Congress dissolved itself and returned to the parent party. But it was not all smooth going. The well-entrenched old turkeys worked behind the scenes to block the Tiwari Congress's return. Sonia saw through their unseemly designs, though, and overruled them.

In 1997, India celebrated the fiftieth anniversary of her independence. Indian democracy, our humane pluralism, our secularism, had not only survived, but had taken root. How did this happen? Primarily, it was thanks to the innate wisdom of our people. As a nation, we are good at crisis management, and also at reconciling contradictions. It was appropriate that in this year India elected a Dalit as its President. Gandhiji's dream came true when, on 25 July 1997, K.R. Narayanan was elected President of India. The remarkable fact was that Narayanan had not even been canvassing to secure his elevation. The demand to put him in the Rashtrapati Bhavan was unanimous.

◆

In 1998, Sonia's most challenging task was to ensure that the Congress did well in the Lok Sabha elections to be held in early May. She came to my constituency where I had ensured a large audience. I won comfortably even though the Congress fared very badly over all. The National Democratic Alliance, led by Atal Bihari Vajpayee, formed the government at the centre.

On 11 and 13 May, the NDA government tested five nuclear devices at Pokhran, Rajasthan. The worldwide reaction was without exception hostile, and sanctions were placed against India. Within the country too, there were sharp divisions. The Congress Party faced a dilemma—should it welcome the tests or not? Hair-splitting was resorted to—the party congratulated the scientists for the achievement but not the government. I met P.N. Haksar for advice and he was categorical that the Congress must welcome the five tests. It would damage the party if it condemned them.

Under normal circumstances, the Prime Minister should have taken into confidence the Leader of Opposition before going ahead with the tests, but this Vajpayee did not do because he feared that somebody would leak the news. In the debate in the Lok Sabha on the nuclear issue on the 28th, I was the first speaker from the Congress Party. I spoke at length and, as I continued, I sensed the mood in the House changing and, gradually, the government was put on the spot. The PM, instead of writing to the Heads of State of the Permanent Members of the United Nations Security Council, should have immediately called a special session of the Lok Sabha. This, too, he did not do.

I was in the lobby of the Lok Sabha when L.K. Advani told me that Pakistan had also conducted five nuclear tests in response to ours on 28 May. The security situation in the Indian subcontinent changed dramatically. For all the past decades, India had military superiority over Pakistan in conventional weapons. This advantage disappeared when both countries became nuclear powers. The Americans had tried very hard to persuade Pakistan Prime Minister Nawaz Sharif not to respond to India's tests. The Pakistani Prime Minister was called to Washington and spoken to sternly by President Clinton. Nawaz, who was in a panic, responded that if Pakistan did not respond to India's tests, not only would his government fall, there would be widespread disturbances throughout the country.

The ramifications of the nuclear tests were worldwide. While there was tremendous excitement and approval in the Muslim community about what was foolishly hailed as the 'Islamic Bomb', the US and other Western countries, as well as countries like China, Japan and Australia condemned the tests and imposed stern sanctions on both countries which, predictably, did not last long.

After the tests, the Non-Proliferation and Comprehensive Nuclear-Test-Ban Treaties once again surfaced. We refused to sign these treaties because they had one standard for the Permanent Members of the Security Council and another for the rest of the UN member countries.

However, in order to mend the strained relations between India and Pakistan following the nuclear tests, both countries signed the Lahore Declaration on 21 February 1999. The agreement contained several measures to prevent the outbreak of a nuclear conflict between the two countries, and emphasized a joint commitment to resolve the Kashmir situation. Prime Minister Vajpayee put in place several measures towards peace at the time, including the inauguration of a Delhi-Lahore bus service.

It was later discovered that around the same time, Pakistan was covertly sending some of its troops to cross the Line of Control and infiltrate parts of Kashmir, around a town called

THE DECLINE OF THE CONGRESS

Kargil. By May 1999, the conflict had intensified as certain sectors, including the Batalik and Akhnoor sectors and parts of the Siachen Glacier, were occupied by Pakistani forces. Indian forces launched an offensive, 'Operation Vijay', to recapture these points. After international pressure, which included a phone call from US President Bill Clinton to Pakistan Prime Minister Nawaz Sharif, and post India's recapturing of key peaks, Pakistan withdrew its troops from the area. On 26 July 1999, the Kargil war came to an end with the removal of all Pakistani intruders.

In the aftermath of the war, elections were held in 1999 after the AIADMK withdrew its support to the government. The NDA won by a huge margin, securing a majority. Vajpayee was once again sworn in as PM.

In December 1999, another cross-border crisis occurred, as an Indian Airlines plane, IC-814 from Kathmandu to New Delhi, was hijacked by terrorists en route and flown to Kandahar in Afghanistan. Under extreme pressure, the NDA government had to succumb to the demands of the terrorists, which included the release of three hardcore terrorists. External Affairs Minister Jaswant Singh personally flew to Kandahar to exchange the terrorists with the passengers. The Kandahar visit of Jaswant Singh was widely deplored.

◆

Personally, the nineties were a mix of good and bad. The birth of my grandsons brought indescribable joy to my family. Hanut was born on 21 November 1995 and Himmat on 7 January 1997.

1998 ended on a not-so-good note. On 6 November 1998, I woke up early in the morning feeling extremely weak, tired and breathless, with a nagging discomfort in the chest. I immediately telephoned my friend, Dr Ravi Kasliwal, an outstanding cardiologist at the Escorts Heart Institute. An angiography followed, which showed that two of my main arteries were 85 per cent blocked and the third, 60 per cent. In plain language, I was a walking heart attack. I felt as if a horse had kicked me in my stomach.

Unlike most Indians, I was careful about my health. I used to go for medical check-ups twice a year—usually, my ECG, echo and blood pressure tests would all be normal. Till the age of sixty, I played reasonably good tennis. I was and am a teetotaller, neither did I smoke. I was not overweight. I slept for seven hours each night. I was happy with my job. I kept a twelve-hour schedule and had even successfully contested a Lok Sabha election earlier in 1998. Foolishly, though, I paid no need to the fleeting heart palpitations I experienced from time to time, thinking them to be due to my hernia.

It was decided that I would undergo heart bypass surgery. At this time I had second thoughts—I would go to London for the operation. But Dr Kasliwal and Dr Naresh Trehan, my heart surgeon, informed me that it would be risky. Following their advice, we immediately decided to have the operation on 14 November at the Escorts Heart Institute in Delhi.

How does one react to or handle such a grim situation? To claim that I was not apprehensive and nervous would be dishonest. However, I did not panic. And while I do not believe in mysticism, mediums or the occult, I do believe in spirituality. Something totally inexplicable happened to me the night before the operation. I clearly heard a voice telling me, 'Have no fear, go to the operation theatre with confidence, your operation will be successful.' I slept soundly and went into the theatre without any qualms. When I regained consciousness at the end of six hours, the doctors told me that my positive attitude, self-confidence and will to live had contributed to the success of the operation. Not only this, unlike most patients, I did not go into a post-surgical depression. Some benign shakti saw me through my ordeal. The agents of this shakti were doctors Trehan and Kasliwal, who gave me a new lease of life.

After my operation, K.R. Narayanan, a 'bypasser' himself, called. He said, 'Welcome to the club, Natwar.' I replied, with due apologies to Karl Marx, 'Bypassers of the world unite, you have nothing to lose but your blockages.'

19

THE DEMISE OF THE USSR

Nikita Khrushchev by 1955 had eased out all his rivals in the Politburo and the Central Committee—G.M. Malenkov and V.M. Molotov, a man who had held the senior-most party posts and had been Foreign Minister for over a decade. L.M. Kaganovich, too, received similar treatment.

By 1956, Nikita Khrushchev had no equals. He was General Secretary of the Communist Party and the senior-most member of the Politburo. On the night of 24-25 February 1956, he addressed a secret meeting at the twentieth Congress of the Communist Party. His criticism of Joseph Stalin shook the communist world from Peking to Prague. The speech gradually leaked out. He said, 'It is clear that here, Stalin showed in a whole series of cases, his intolerance, his brutality and his abuse of power.' The first nail in the coffin of Communism had been hammered. China was an exception. Publicly, Mao Tse Tung supported Nikita Khrushchev but in private he condemned him and his unbridled denunciation of Stalin. In 1964, Khrushchev was the victim of a coup led by L.I. Brezhnev, who assumed the mantle of the General Secretary of the Party. The rot had set in. The US was bleeding the USSR in insidious and clandestine ways. The USSR in those years was spending 25 per cent of its budget on the military—navy, air force and the nuclear programme.

An earth-shattering event occurred in October 1991. This was the break-up of the Union of Soviet Socialist Republics, a nation with which India had shared close relations for decades.

Thirty years ago, the communist world extended from Peking to Prague. Vietnam and Cuba were also communist states. Between 1917 and 1989, millions around the world became Marxists. The Soviet Union was looked upon as a champion fighting against class injustice and economic disparities. In other words, Marxists were destined to change the world.

In 1956, I was in Peking and came under the spell of Mao Tse Tung and other first-generation leaders of the Communist Party of the Republic of China. It was during my stay in China that the Hungarian Revolution occurred in the autumn of 1956. The Soviet Union considered this a serious challenge. The revolution was crushed by the military might of the Soviet Union. Hundreds of thousands of communists resigned from parties in various parts of the world as a protest against the Soviet atrocities in Hungary.

India's attitude to this event was ambiguous. Krishna Menon, contrary to advice from Delhi, abstained in the Security Council resolution condemning the Soviet invasion of Hungary. Later, the Prime Minister did deplore the Soviet invasion. By then the damage had been done. He was accused of double standards, one for the Suez crisis and the other for Hungary.

In November 1957, the fortieth anniversary of the founding of the USSR was celebrated in Moscow. Mao led a high-powered Chinese delegation, including Deng Xiaoping, there. I was among the many to see him off at the airport. Mao was given the place of honour at every function he attended. Khrushchev still believed that the Soviet Union was the true leader of the communist world. Mao Tse Tung did not accept Khruschev as the leader of the communist world. His record as a revolutionary was far superior to that of any living communist leader.

By the early 1960s, the differences between the two countries increased at a rapid pace. Tens of thousands of Soviet engineers, scientists, university professors and doctors were asked to leave China. In those years, China was solely dependent on the Soviet Union for aid in many crucial areas and only a handful of countries recognized the People's Republic.

Hungary was the rebel in November 1956, followed by Czechoslovakia in 1968. Soviet troops brutally crushed the Czech revolt and large numbers of Czechs were killed. The Prague Spring was over. India did not condemn the Soviet invasion. For this, P.N. Haksar was responsible. He convinced Indira Gandhi that condemnation of the Soviet Union was not in India's interest. I was, frankly, uneasy at our decision.

In 1970 fell Lenin's birth centenary and with it, the differences between the Communist Party of Russia and Communist Party of China came out in the open. The Sino-Soviet border looked like a war zone. The communist world was divided and so was the Communist Party of India. The Soviet Union, from 1975 onwards, was ruled by a bunch of geriatrics. Only three or four members of the Politburo took the decision to invade Afghanistan in December 1979. Afghanistan proved to be the Vietnam of the Soviets. I remember Indira Gandhi telling USSR's President Brezhnev that India, on account of her close relations with the Soviet Union, had refrained from publicly deploring their invasion of Afghanistan, but feelings in India were very strong. The sooner the Soviets pulled out of Afghanistan the better.

In 1985, Gorbachev became the General Secretary of the Communist Party of the USSR. He was a new type of Marxist leader, intelligent and in a hurry to reform and restructure a stagnant, over-stretched Soviet Union with a weak economic base and rampant social decay. It was his belief that what the USSR needed was reform and restructuring. The world watched and analysed every speech of his. American think tanks worked overtime to read between the lines to find out what this new, dynamic General Secretary was up to. Gorbachev visited India twice, in 1986 and 1988. When delivering speeches he spoke rapidly without referring to notes or briefs.

On the surface, the Soviet Union seemed to be sailing in calm waters. But beneath this deceptive tranquility storms were gathering, which Gorbachev did not foresee. When the strong winds burst on the political shores of Mother Russia, Gorbachev was overwhelmed.

By the late eighties, the end appeared inevitable. Events started moving at a fast pace in the Soviet Union. In August 1991, Gorbachev and his family were holidaying at Foros, the official summer residence of the President in Crimea. He was obviously out of touch with what was happening within the highest echelons of the Communist Party. The KGB was divided, half were with Gorbachev and half with Boris Yeltsin. While Gorbachev was on holiday, a plot was hatched in Moscow to get rid of him. Three senior party leaders arrived at Foros without any invitation from him. He dealt with them with a firm hand and asked them to go back to Moscow. Nevertheless, from 18 to 21 August, he and his family were kept under house arrest. All telephones were dead. Electricity had been switched off and no newspapers were delivered. Gorbachev finally returned to Moscow on 22 August. By then, events had overtaken him. Gorbachev's two schemes, Perestroika and Glasnost, had failed, as also his attempt for political liberalization. It had by now become abundantly clear that the Soviet Union was in terminal crisis.

The USSR collapsed in October 1991. One of the great nuclear superpowers had fallen off the map. An alternative point of view had disappeared, leaving America the sole superpower in the world. Another consequence of the collapse of the Soviet Union was that China became the second superpower. In one of my articles I called Gorbachev the pallbearer of the coffin of the USSR.

The disappearance of the Soviet Union had very serious consequences for India. Indo-Soviet friendship had been a vital part of our foreign policy. Bilateral relations were as close as they could be. These were further strengthened by the signing of the Indo-Soviet Friendship Treaty in 1971. Mutual respect and confidence were the twin pillars of the relationship. The Soviet Union had stood by India when we were isolated in the Security Council on Kashmir and Goa. The two countries worked closely at the United Nations. Both had identical views on decolonization and racialism. The Indo-Soviet Defence Cooperation was of great importance to India. We paid the Soviet Union in rupees, thus saving much-needed foreign exchange.

Gorbachev's successor Boris Yeltsin headed the Russian government for almost nine years. He was in the hands of the US and his personal behaviour was boorish. Indo-Russian relations took a turn for the better after the arrival of Vladimir Putin at the helm. The UPA II neglected Russia and Barack Obama neglects India.

20

SONIA GANDHI

'Natwar, before you hear it from someone else, let me tell you that Rajiv is getting married,' Indira Gandhi said to me one day in late 1967.

'Who is the lucky girl?' I enquired.

'She is an Italian. They met at Cambridge.'

'When is the marriage?'

'In February,' Mrs Gandhi announced.

This was news indeed. Rajiv was the most eligible bachelor in the country; handsome, and with an immensely engaging personality. Sonia, two years younger, was not only marrying a member of the most well-known political family in the country, she was marrying into an institution, the Nehru-Gandhis. There had been many outrageous rumours about Rajiv earlier, which were silenced only after the news of Rajiv's marriage to Edvige Antonia Albina Màino broke.

The wedding took place on 25 February 1968. The day after, Mrs Gandhi held a reception for Rajiv and Sonia in Hyderabad House. All eyes were on the bride. I remember how nervous she was. From Turin to New Delhi was quite a leap. The daughter of a staunchly Roman Catholic family, she found herself in a totally alien environment. The cultural shock would have been unnerving. She had no friends in India, no knowledge and understanding of Indian languages, culture, customs, mores, heritage, history and religion. All that mattered was her love for Rajiv and his love for her. She once told me that there had never been any other man in her life. Both she and Rajiv would have defied the world to get married. They made a striking couple—the handsome Rajiv and Sonia, with her debonair civility.

Sonia's life can be divided into four phases. The first phase was an era of matrimonial bliss, love, enjoyment and apprenticeship under a world-famous mother-in-law. Sonia walked demurely in the light of fortune. That ended on 31 October 1984, the day Indira Gandhi was assassinated. Sonia and R.K. Dhawan took her bullet-ridden bleeding body to All India Institute of Medical Sciences.

The second phase lasted a short seven years. The Congress Working Committee passed a resolution electing Rajiv to succeed his mother. Sonia fought like a tigress to prevent him from becoming Prime Minister—she feared that he, too, would be killed. But Rajiv had a duty to perform; personal considerations were irrelevant. Sonia's carefree days had ended. She became the First Lady, accompanying her husband on his official visits the world over. No longer could Rajiv and Sonia see life from afar; they were the centre of the turbulent drama of politics. Sonia at the time appeared aloof, but was deeply involved. In the earlier days, she was ill at ease with strangers and said little. One seldom witnessed her having an animated conversation with any Head of State.

This phase was too good to last. Implacable fate felled Rajiv Gandhi. On 21 May 1991, the scenery collapsed when Rajiv was killed at Sriperumbudur in Tamil Nadu. The spring went out of Sonia's life.

Phase three lasted from 1991 to 1998. Sonia lived in seclusion, keeping the memory of Rajiv alive. Attempts to persuade her to join politics were rejected. The most public appeal to her was at an AICC meeting in Talkatora Gardens. When Sonia entered, everyone stood up and a deafening chant began—'Sonia, Sonia'—imploring her to sit on the dais. The clapping did not die down for ten minutes. One member of the Working Committee walked over to request her to step on the dais. Sonia, in no uncertain terms, told him that she would leave if the demonstration was not stopped.

During that time, Sonia established the Rajiv Gandhi Foundation and published two handsome volumes on Rajiv, which kept her busy for the better part of three years. She also succeeded Rajiv as chairperson of the Nehru Memorial Fund and the Indira Gandhi Memorial Trust and organized six international conferences in Delhi, to which we invited eminent scholars, artists and politicians. I suggested that Sonia hold similar conferences in different parts of the country. In each city, the response of the media, the intelligentsia and the universities was heartwarming. Sonia was naturally the main attraction. The more she kept away from the media, the more it pursued her. At the conferences, she only read her speech and let me run the events.

Sonia had made P.V. Narasimha Rao Prime Minister. But she wasn't very fond of him. I, too, had fallen out with him and joined the Tiwari Congress, but we later made up.

In December 1994, when my relations with him had been repaired, he asked me to see him at his house, 5 Race Course Road. He seemed uncharacteristically agitated and restless. He said, 'I can take on Sonia Gandhi. But I do not want to do so. Some of her advisers have been filling her ears against me. I don't take them seriously. Sonia's case is different. Her attitude towards me is affecting my health. If she wants me to go, she only has to say so. I have done my best to meet all her desires and requirements promptly. You worked closely with her and must know and should know why Sonia is so hostile to me.'

As Vice Chairman of the Indira Gandhi Memorial Trust and Secretary of the Nehru Memorial Fund, my meetings with Sonia Gandhi were mostly confined to the activities of the two institutions. I seldom discussed politics with her and told him so. One thing I did know was that she was upset that the trial of Rajiv Gandhi's assassins was moving at a very slow pace. P.V.'s reply was that he had sent P. Chidambaram to her with the necessary papers. He had also sent Home Minister S.B. Chavan to brief her on the latest position of the case. Finally, he said, that he himself had gone with the necessary files and explained to Ms Gandhi the legal difficulties in hastening the trial. According to him, she had listened and said nothing.

He continued his tale of woe. 'You know, I go out of my way to be polite to her. We do whatever she wishes. She never telephones me. One day, after the meeting of the Nehru Fund Trustees, I suggested to her that I would have a RAX phone installed at No. 10 so that she could call me whenever she wished to. She agreed. An hour later, she sent a message that she did not want the RAX. It was like a slap on my face.'

I suggested that he contact Mohammad Yunus, who was constantly in touch with Sonia. Yunus had been an intimate friend of the Nehru family for decades. He was Khan Abdul Ghaffar Khan's nephew. He was the only member of his Pathan family who did not migrate to Pakistan. He was forthright, faithful and exhilarating company. A few days later, P.V. arrived at Yunus's house after 9 p.m. without any fanfare or police escort. It was a clandestine rendezvous at which I was also present. That P.V. agreed to such a meeting was in itself a clear indication of how keen he was for a patch-up with Sonia. But it did not happen. It is possible that Yunus's intervention irked Sonia.

I vividly remember the Trivandrum conference in September 1995. The night before her arrival, the head of security informed me that the Babbar Khalsa group would make an attempt on her life. I, in turn, informed A.K. Antony, the Chief Minister of Kerala. Ever since I have known him, I have called him St Anthony. He is a low-key, unassuming, courteously candid, soft-spoken person. Like me, he was most disturbed. He came to my hotel and asked me what we should do. I suggested calling Prime Minister P.V. Narasimha Rao. We proceeded to Antony's house. He had no police escort, no personal security officer. At the gate of the house, I saw no sentry or guard. I asked him where his private secretary was. The answer astounded me: 'It is past 6 p.m. and my staff has left.' 'Do you have the Prime Minister's telephone number?' I enquired next. He did not. I succeeded in getting through to the PM, who had already heard the alarming news. 'Natwar, you tell her from me that for security reasons, she must not travel to Trivandrum,' he said.

'Why don't you tell her?' I asked.

'It's better for you to convey my message to her,' was the reply.

I knew P.V. well, but this, I thought, was a bit much even for him. Here was an extremely dangerous threat to Sonia from terrorists and he was not willing to speak to her. I called Sonia. The answer was, 'I am arriving in Trivandrum by the morning flight. If I do not do so, I shall never be able to stir out of 10 Janpath.' Sonia was taking a serious risk. Antony and I looked at each other. There was nothing further to do.

Meanwhile, P.V. Narasimha Rao acted with alacrity. Overnight, commandos were flown into Trivandrum. Raj Bhavan, where Sonia was staying, became a mini fortress. The conference venue received the same security treatment.

The fourth phase of Sonia's life began on 14 March 1998, when she formally took over as Congress President at a specially called meeting of the AICC at Siri Fort, New Delhi. She was neither a communicator nor an orator; both indispensable skills for any frontline politician. Preparing her maiden speech took several agonizing hours. She arrived at Siri Fort accompanied by Priyanka, then sent for me and asked me to sit next to her. Jairam Ramesh too was sent for, to fine-tune the speech. But Sonia successfully crossed the first hurdle in spite of her nervousness.

I remember how each of Sonia's speeches was an exercise that would take six to eight hours. Sometimes, these agonizing 'speech sessions' lasted till midnight. There were occasions when she and I would be alone, working on them. She would read the speech aloud, I would time it. It would then be translated into Hindi. The Hindi version would then be transliterated into English and printed out in bold letters. This situation did not last long.

Her English is near perfect; Hindi is the problem—she cannot speak the language without a written script in front of her. To my suggestion to her that she learn by heart a chaupai or two of Tulsidas's or Kabir's dohas and use them in her speeches, she threw her hands up. 'I go blank even with a written text. You want me to say something extempore? Forget it.'

Many senior Congressmen sent suggestions and drafts for her speeches; seldom were these used. Jairam Ramesh became a regular presence at the marathon 'speech sessions'. Being a wizard with the computer, he was useful. He is good company. His brain is razor sharp but his wit occasionally got him into trouble. At times I was the target of his wit. Sonia used to enjoy my discomfiture.

By now I was meeting Sonia frequently. I reminded her that

her family had an international constituency which had been neglected since Rajiv's death. She must revive it. She asked how I would achieve this. I told her that with the assistance of my erstwhile colleagues in the Ministry of External Affairs, I would ensure that visiting Foreign Ministers and Prime Ministers called on her. After all, as head of the Congress Party, she was the de facto Leader of Opposition.

I sounded out my friend Brajesh Mishra on this. He was not dismissive, but made no commitment. After some months, the MEA began to include a call on the Congress President in the programme of visiting ministers and Prime Ministers.

To begin with, Sonia did not look forward to these meetings. 'What do I say to them?' she would ask. My advice was, 'Listen. You will gather much information.' I used to be present at most of the meetings between 1999 and 2005, arriving at 10 Janpath a few minutes before the visiting dignitary. Initially, Sonia would turn towards me with embarrassing regularity. This did not go unnoticed. I asked her to try not to do so. As time went by, the media's interest in Sonia's exchanges with these visitors increased.

On 14 November 1998, I had bypass surgery at the Escorts Heart Institute. Throughout my stay in hospital, Sonia telephoned Dr Trehan, my heart surgeon, inquiring about my medical condition. She visited the hospital twice. Her genuine concern meant much to Hem and me. On several occasions, she would telephone late at night to ask if I was watching a particular TV programme. My wife, too, received such calls.

9 May 2002 was the darkest day in my family's life. Our beautiful daughter, Ritu, passed away. The family was shattered. The moment I informed Sonia, she came immediately to our house. She spent many hours with Hem, Jagat and me. She shared our grief. That we shall never forget.

Sonia used to worry a lot about the security of her

grandchildren, as well as Priyanka's safety. I promised to speak to Brajesh Mishra and did sound him out later. He promised to do the needful discreetly, as Sonia had wished.

My growing proximity to Sonia could not go unnoticed. I was at 10 Janpath almost every day. I was seen as one of her closest confidants and some 'well-wishers' pumped me, saying, 'You are the best troubleshooter she has.'

My reply was: 'Nonsense.'

The political discussions between Sonia and I were exclusive, serious and to the point. Our informal chat sessions, though, were a delight. On returning from one of my trips abroad, 'I missed you,' were her opening words.

Sonia was becoming less diffident in public, but still had a long way to go. In a male-dominated society, she could never relax. Even in the Working Committee meetings, she was taut, and spoke very little.

Jairam once invited Sonia's wrath for an indiscretion. She refused to see him. Banishment from the darbar was the ultimate manifestation of her displeasure. Jairam could not take it beyond a week. He came to see me, distraught and anguished. 'Sir, if she does not see me, I don't know what I will do,' he declared. I told him, 'Ramesh, whatever you wish to do, please don't do it in this room.' I asked him to calm down, assuring him that I would speak to Sonia. I did, telling her about Jairam's agitation. Sonia eventually relented and Jairam lived happily ever after.

The second incident that I know of which invited Sonia's wrath involved Arjun Singh, who was the mystery man of the Congress. Every negative adjective was used for him—wily, silent, schemer, etcetera. At the time, he was down in the mouth. At a function where several senior CWC members were present, in his speech, he hinted that Sonia was surrounded by people who denied access to lifelong Congressmen. Sonia was told that

Arjun Singh had spoken of her being surrounded by a 'coterie'. She refused to see him. He was not only a member of the CWC, but had been a Governor, Chief Minister, Vice President of the party and a Cabinet minister. All his attempts to meet Sonia were spurned. After these snubs, he came to my house and narrated his tale of woe. I conveyed to her Arjun Singh's misery, and also clarified that he had not used the word 'coterie'. She let Arjun Singh swing in the air for a few days and finally gave him an audience. He drove straight to my house from 10 Janpath and thanked me profusely, adding, 'Natwar Singhji, at this level in politics, no one makes the intervention you made on my behalf.' It was a compliment I deeply appreciated.

◆

1997 witnessed a happy event in the Gandhi family—the marriage of Sonia's daughter, Priyanka. She reminds people of Indira Gandhi, both in looks and grit. She fell in love with a Christian, Robert Vadra, who had his limitations, and her choice surprised one and all. The date of the marriage was announced—18 February 1997. The invitation list was a matter of conjecture and hopefuls kept telephoning 10 Janpath. Finally, elegantly printed invitation cards were sent out to a handful of people who were not members of the extended Gandhi family. Amitabh Bachchan and his son, Suman Dubey, Sunita Kohli, Satish Sharma, Sheila Dikshit, my wife and I were on the guest list. The wedding was elegant, in the Kashmiri tradition, and was followed by dinner. Priyanka looked stunning. The media was kept out.

◆

On 15 August 1997, during the occasion of fifty years of India's independence, the Indira Gandhi Memorial Trust organized an international conference to which former Zambian president, Kenneth Kaunda, was invited. In previous years, all participants had been put up in Lalit Suri's hotel on Barakhamba Road.

For the 1997 conference, Sonia decided that all invitees would stay in the Oberoi Hotel. Kaunda arrived a day late and, like in previous years, he drove from the airport to Suri's hotel. I informed Sonia of his arrival, and that he was staying at Lalit's hotel. She was incensed and asked me to meet Kaunda and request him to shift to the Oberoi. It was a manifestly unreasonable demand. I had known Kaunda for many years but my errand was a painful one. When I told him about this, he said he had settled down and, after a long flight, needed rest.

I conveyed Kaunda's message to her. That should have ended the matter; it did not. Arrogance took over. She asked me to go back to Kaunda and ask him to shift to the Oberoi. I attempted to dissuade her but she did not relent. I told her she was being irrational.

Kaunda was one of Africa's most admired and respected leaders. He was twenty-two years older than Sonia. Indira Gandhi and Rajiv would never have behaved in such an insensitive manner. On hearing her second message, Kaunda said that this would put him in an embarrassing position. 'What do I tell Suri?' he asked. Kaunda could observe my discomfiture. I told him there had been a falling out. Kaunda agreed to shift after apologizing to Suri.

Sonia was deliberately capricious. It was unbecoming of her. The Kaunda incident left a bad taste in the mouth.

◆

In 1998, Sonia decided that the time had come for her to be

in the Lok Sabha. She was elected with a huge majority from Amethi, the family borough. She naturally became President of the Congress Parliamentary Party. However, in the Lok Sabha, she did not speak even once in her first term. After becoming Congress President, Sonia made two mistakes.

I was confined to bed with viral fever when I received a call from Gopalkrishna Gandhi, the level-headed secretary to President K.R. Narayanan. He asked me to meet Sonia to request her to support Jyoti Basu as Prime Minister of a secular government. It was a sensible suggestion. I went to 10 Janpath to convey this to her. On entering her study-cum-conference room, I saw that Pranab Mukherjee, Arjun Singh and M.L. Fotedar were with her. After I said my piece, I found all three of them were opposed to Jyoti Basu—and Sonia was tending towards their point of view—whereas I felt that Jyoti Basu would be an improvement on his two predecessors. The problem was finally solved by his party as the politburo of the CPM did not permit him to seek prime ministership. They later regretted this blunder.

The second misjudgement occurred in the last week of April 1999. Hectic political activity was taking place as Atal Bihari Vajpayee, the leader of the National Democratic Alliance, was unable to form a government. The Congress, with the support of other opposition parties, staked its claim to form the government. Sonia met President Narayanan at the behest of Arjun Singh and others, telling him that she had the support of 272 MPs. Narayanan gave her two days to prove her majority. Mulayam Singh Yadav, who had earlier offered support, pulled the rug out from under the Congress's feet by doing an about turn.* The Lok Sabha was dissolved on 26 April 1999. Sonia was more

---

*Aditi Phadnis, 'Mulayam Singh Yadav: The King of U-turns', Rediff.com, 26 June 2012

than embarrassed. She was a novice at the time, yet to discover that politics was a blood sport. Any other Congress leader would have been shown the door for such a gaffe.

◆

Between 2000 and 2003, Sonia travelled to the US, where she met dignitaries such as Vice President Dick Cheney and Secretary of State Condoleezza Rice. She also visited Oxford and Hong Kong. I accompanied her on these trips. She was a different person abroad, relaxed, amusing, less demanding and more considerate.

In New York there occurred an incident worth recounting. Sonia and her delegation—Manmohan Singh, Murli Deora, Jairam Ramesh and I—stayed in the Carlyle Hotel, where we arrived late in the evening. To my horror, I discovered that the New York authorities had not provided any security for Sonia. Anyone could walk into her suite. Sonia made light of it, but I immediately telephoned Prime Minister Vajpayee. It was nearly midnight in Delhi. I told the PM that it was too risky to leave Sonia without any security. The large-hearted Vajpayee said he would get back to me. Half an hour later, Lalit Mansingh, our Ambassador in Washington, was on the line. He said that the PM had just called him and asked him to ensure immediately that Sonia Gandhi was given a security detail. He was as good as his word.

In 2004, the NDA, led by Atal Bihari Vajpeyee, lost the Lok Sabha elections. They could not manage to sell the 'India Shining' mantra to the voting public. Sonia and the leaders of several non-NDA parties put together the United Progressive Alliance with Sonia as chairperson. The expectation was that Sonia would occupy 7 Race Course Road as Prime Minister.

The Gandhi family, however, was a house divided. Rahul was vehemently opposed to his mother becoming Prime Minister, fearing that she would lose her life, much like his grandmother and his father. Matters reached a climax after Rahul said that he was prepared to take any possible step to prevent his mother from taking up the prime ministership. Rahul is a strong-willed person; this was no ordinary threat. He gave Sonia twenty-four hours to decide. Manmohan Singh, Suman Dubey, Priyanka and I were present at that moment.

Sonia was visibly agonized and in tears. As a mother, it was impossible for her to ignore Rahul. He had his way. That was the reason for her not becoming Prime Minister.

Only Manmohan Singh and I were aware of Sonia's decision. Later, she called a meeting in which she announced that she was offering the post of PM to Manmohan Singh.

Once, I pulled Sonia's leg on this, telling her that only two people in history had refused the crown, both Italians by birth. 'Who is the other?' she asked. 'Julius Caesar,' I replied.

◆

A few days before the new government was sworn in, Sonia hosted a dinner on the lawns of 10 Janpath. Amar Singh came along with Harkishan Singh Surjeet. At the dinner, Manmohan informally told me that I was getting External Affairs and Arjun Singh, the Ministry of Human Resource Development. After dinner, Sonia asked me to come with her. She told me that she was under great pressure from various quarters, including the Americans, to not appoint me as External Affairs Minister. Would I consider taking another ministry? With some heat, I turned down her suggestion. I had been her principal foreign affairs adviser for several years. None in the party had the expertise or the experience

I did. Did she feel I was not up to the job? 'For heaven's sake, Natwar, I am not an idiot,' she replied with some asperity.

Rahul's arrival, followed by a cute puppy, eased the tension. I asked him which of the books I had lent him he had read. He reads quite a lot and Sonia, too, is a voracious reader. He told me he had finished the autobiography of Shimon Peres and Anthony Sampson's biography of Nelson Mandela. He had found the autobiography disappointing. He had yet to read Roosevelt's biography by Conrad Black. Sonia asked Rahul which of my books the puppy had chewed. He did not remember the name. I gave him the title, *Against All Enemies*, a book analysing America's war on terror by former US Chief Counter-Terrorism Adviser, Richard A. Clarke.

♦

Once the UPA came to power, it was widely known that Sonia very discreetly monitored the functioning of the most important ministries in the government, displaying a Machiavellian side to her character. Even mine was not spared. There was a mole on my staff feeding false information to 10 Janpath. Little men can, without realizing, do much harm to institutions. While they are mere chaff, they destroy the wheat.

On 22 February 2005, I drove to 10 Janpath to accompany Sonia to her meeting with Afghanistan's President, Hamid Karzai. The moment I entered the meeting room, she said, 'I shall not be taken for granted. There will come a time when I will do something unpredictable.' Then followed the outrageous remark, 'You are getting involved in defence deals.'

This was verbal terrorism. Something snapped inside me. I said, 'You are making a serious allegation and questioning my integrity, honour and honesty. You must provide evidence of these allegations. I am not enamoured of a ministership—I will resign, but questioning my integrity is unacceptable.'

There followed another preposterous insinuation: 'There is a delegation from Africa and you have passed a file on some defence deals to Pranab Mukherjee.'

I said I had only spoken to him. 'Do my signatures appear on the file?' I enquired. She had no answer, and never referred to the matter again. Obviously, the mole was at work. It seems that she had access to confidential information.

She then asked, 'Did you take M.J. Akbar with you on your special plane?'

I told Sonia he had not travelled on my special plane. Besides, we had no control over journalists' travel to cover international visits of important ministers. The external publicity division sends a circular to TV channels and newspapers to send names of journalists to it, out of which selections are made. Akbar had not approached the division; he had directly applied to the Pakistan High Commission for a visa. We could not prevent him from flying to Islamabad. Sonia asked, 'Why did you meet him?' I told her I had not. He had merely been present at my largely attended press conference.

◆

Later in the summer of 2005, Sonia and I flew to Moscow by special plane for a convention. After the meeting, Sonia and I flew to a little town called Vladimir by helicopter. I was mystified, wondering why she had chosen this town which I had never heard of. Located in the middle of a forest, Vladimir offered peace and tranquillity. Sonia walked towards one of the larger buildings, which had been converted into a small museum. We entered an octagonal room, the walls of which were covered with little handwritten pieces of paper. She was intently looking at these chits. Turning to me, she said, 'Natwar, my father, during the Second World War, was a prisoner of war in this room. He escaped and walked all the way to Italy.' We then roamed around the village. It was a beautiful summer day. The pace of life in Vladimir was unhurried. Ladies smiled and waved to Sonia but their curiosity was not intrusive. Vladimir was an ideal place to read, relax and retire.

◆

Sonia's behaviour during my implication in the Volcker Report was vicious and venomous, and caused me great pain. I was in Frankfurt when the allegations surfaced. Before I left for New Delhi, Foreign Secretary Shyam Saran showed me an email which stated that Ambika Soni of the Congress Party had said in an official statement that the party was clean and Natwar Singh should take care of himself. I was outraged. This statement had obviously been issued with the approval of the Congress President.

After returning to Delhi, I did not contact Sonia and she did not contact me.

On 8 November 2005, a fortnight after the report was made public, Prime Minister Manmohan Singh told me that it had been decided by the Congress President and himself that I should give up the External Affairs portfolio and be a minister without portfolio. I resigned on 6 December. Manmohan Singh is a decent though spineless man, who never stands up for his colleagues. He asked me to meet Sonia. I refused. Where honour was involved, no compromise was possible.

On 15 November, Sonia Gandhi gave a keynote address during the Hindustan Times Summit at the Maurya Sheraton

(*left*): Being sworn in as Minister of External Affairs, 2004

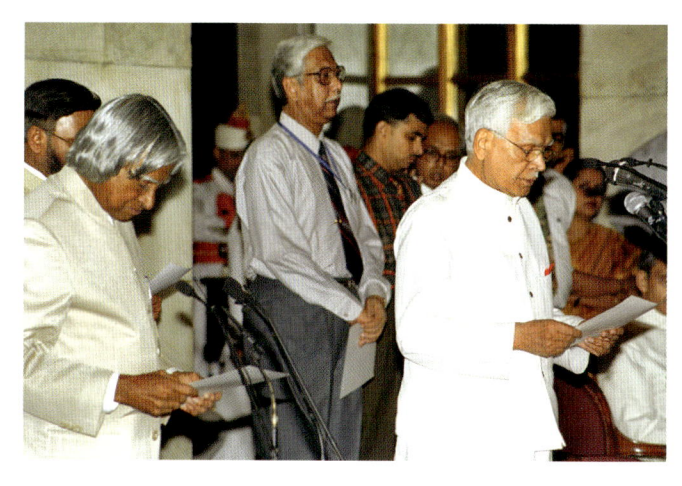

(*above left*): With Hillary Clinton, 2005
(*above right*): With Condoleezza Rice, US Secretary of State, New Delhi, 2005

(*right*): With the Chinese President, Hu Jintao, 2005

(*above left*): With George Bush Sr., Washington, 1986; (*above right*): (left to right) K. Natwar Singh, Gursharan Kaur, Laura Bush, Manmohan Singh, George Bush Jr., Washington, 2005

(*left*): K. Natwar Singh with the Foreign Minister of Spain and US Secretary of State on his right and Foreign Ministers of Pakistan, Japan and Russia on his left

(*above left*): With Pervez Musharraf, Islamabad, 2004
(*above right*): With King Gyanendra Shah, Kathmandu, Nepal, 2004

Sonia Gandhi and K. Natwar Singh, 10 Janpath

(*above*): With Sonia Gandhi and Vladimir Putin, St Petersburg, June 2005

(*below*): Archbishop Trevor Huddleston being awarded the Indira Gandhi International Prize, 1995. Seen in picture, (left to right): Sonia Gandhi, Archbishop Trevor Huddleston, Nelson Mandela, President Dr Shankar Dayal Sharma, Vice President K.R. Narayanan, Prime Minister P.V. Narasimha Rao and K. Natwar Singh

(*above*): With Benazir Bhutto and Sonia Gandhi, New Delhi, 2002

(*below*): With Sonia Gandhi and Colin Powell, US Secretary of State, New Delhi, 2003

With Manmohan Singh and Pervez Musharraf, New York, 2004

K. Natwar Singh and son Jagat meet PM designate Narendra Modi in Ahmedabad, February, 2014

Photograph by Lord Snowdon

At ease at home

hotel. At the end of her speech, the anchor, Vir Sanghvi, asked her what she thought of me after the allegations made in the Volcker Report. Sonia replied that she was 'very angry and hurt' with me. She further said, 'I had a...working relationship [with Natwar Singh].'*

Almost a year later, in an interview that was telecast in October 2006, again with Vir Sanghvi, Sonia replied to a question about the Volcker controversy saying that I had 'misused the name of the party and I felt extremely betrayed. [...] He was a colleague in whom I had placed trust and I felt very terribly betrayed.'**

My wife and I, when watching both interviews on TV, were amazed.

While I was still a minister without portfolio, the President hosted a dinner for the Czech President, in which I was seated next to Sonia. She did not say a word to me throughout the dinner. Strangely, she did not say a word to the chief guest, who was sitting on the other side, either!

♦

Sonia's public image is not flattering. To an extent, she has herself to blame for it. She never lets her guard down, never gives away what is in her mind. Obsessively secretive and suspicious, she evokes awe, not admiration.

Her remarkable life reminds one of a Greek tragedy enacted on a vast Indian stage. She is every biographer's dream. And while several have taken a shot at telling her tale, their efforts

---

*'Guilty Will Be Punished: Sonia', *Hindustan Times*, 15 November 2005, from http://www.hindustantimes.com/news/specials/leadership2005/coverage_story8.shtml
**Vir Sanghvi, 'I Had Doubts on SEZ Policy: Sonia', *Hindustan Times*, 26 October 2006, from http://www.hindustantimes.com/news-feed/nm18/i-had-doubts-on-sez-policy-sonia/article1-165637.aspx

have been found lacking. In their books, substance and style are absent, as are analysis and understanding.

From the day she set foot on Indian soil she has been treated like royalty; she has behaved like a prima donna. Over the years she has evolved from being a diffident, nervous, shy woman to an ambitious, authoritarian and stern leader. Her displeasure strikes fear among Congressmen. No one has been Congress President for fifteen years. Her hold on the Congress Party is total; firmer and more durable than even that of Jawaharlal Nehru. Under her, dissent is smothered, free discussion fenced in. Silence is used as a weapon and every subtle gesture is a message, an icy stare a warning. Even opposition parties handle her with kid gloves (this is now rapidly changing). She is never blamed or criticized for failures and defeats of the party. 'Soniaji can do no wrong,' chant the battalions of cacophonous sycophants. From her privileged perch, she reigns and rules.

Favours are granted piecemeal, lèse-majesté is given short shrift. Beneath all that posturing an ordinary and insecure person emerges. Her capriciousness is lauded. A fine-tuned personality cult is promoted. Politics has coarsened her.

21

THE MILLENNIUM YEARS

K.R. Narayanan's term as President ended in 2002 and presidential elections came up once more. Sonia Gandhi had asked Dr Manmohan Singh and me to keep an eye on the fast-moving developments related to the election. We met President Narayanan, who said that he was not sure if he would seek a second term. A little while later, he changed his mind and said that he would contest if the National Democratic Alliance (NDA) put forward P.C. Alexander as their candidate. While his lack of clarity was disconcerting, he nevertheless had the full backing of the Congress President.

It was Alexander who was the frontrunner. A good man and an outstanding civil servant, he was also ambitious. In his autobiography, *Through the Corridors of Power*, Alexander writes that he did not seek the presidency but was invited by the NDA to take up the job. This, to say the least, was disingenuous. Actually, in his pursuit of the presidential chair, Alexander displayed an extraordinary lack of political judgement. He became the NDA's candidate and took the Congress's support for granted.

Two issues need clarification—why the NDA was opposed to

Narayanan and why the Congress did not support Alexander. I was in close touch with Brajesh Mishra who, at the time, was Principal Private Secretary to the Prime Minister and National Security Adviser. He gave several reasons why the NDA did not support Narayanan, chief among which was Narayanan's poor health. In addition, Narayanan had refused to go on a state visit to the Philippines but had had no objection going to Sweden where his daughter was the Ambassador. He also refused to meet Indonesian President Megawati Sukarnoputri on 2 April 2002. These incidents, Brajesh claimed, were a dereliction of duty.

Sonia had nothing personal against Alexander—after all, he had served under her mother-in-law for over three years. The objection was political: how could the Congress support the NDA candidate? The second reason was that both President Narayanan and Alexander hailed from Kerala. One Keralite President could not succeed another. Other states, too, had to be considered.

Events were moving fast. The Congress President met Prime Minister Vajpayee at 7 Race Course Road on 19 May. She confirmed that the Congress supported Narayanan. The Prime Minister told her that the NDA was unable to agree to a second term for Narayanan. President Narayanan returned to Delhi on 22 May after undergoing Ayurvedic treatment at Ooty. On 28 May, the Congress President called on him to renew her support for a second term. Two days later, Prime Minister Vajpayee met the President and told him that the NDA was not in favour of his continuing for another five years.

In his autobiography, Alexander holds me responsible for denying him the presidential chair. He also takes several swipes at Brajesh. He writes, 'At this stage a totally unforeseen development took place, which contained all the ingredients of a palace plot—the sudden projection of Vice President Krishan

Kant as a candidate for the presidential election. The principal characters behind this new move were Natwar Singh and, most unexpectedly, Brajesh Mishra, Principal Secretary to the Prime Minister.'*

It did not behove a man of Alexander's experience and stature to make such a preposterous observation. It was no secret that Chandrababu Naidu was supporting Krishan Kant. Krishan Kant had been Governor of Andhra Pradesh and was on intimate terms with Naidu.

Alexander further stated in his book that Brajesh and I colluded to keep him out without the knowledge of our political leaders. Throughout his narrative, he relentlessly hammered out on this theme—'Natwar and Brajesh' were hell-bent on eliminating him from the race. But we were only following instructions.

Alexander even quoted *India Today*, which had carried a story that the following deal had been made—'Krishan Kant for President and Natwar Singh for Vice President'. No one bought that story because it was pure fiction.

To suggest that both of us were working on our own against Alexander is too outlandish. This was out of character; normally he conducted himself with dignified restraint. We all have our bad days. At a crucial time in his life, Alexander was not fortune's favourite.

President Narayanan's dithering did not help matters. Finally he was persuaded to opt out. A three-line statement was issued from Rashtrapati Bhavan: 'There have been recent media reports suggesting that President K.R. Narayanan may be the candidate for the Presidential election of 2002. This is to clarify that he is

---

*P.C. Alexander, *Through the Corridors of Power: An Insider's Story*, New Delhi: HarperCollins India, 2004

not a candidate.' It took much time to draft these three lines. The draftsmen were distinguished political pundits from the right and the left.

The Congress declared support for Vice President Krishan Kant. It was now evident that Alexander's chances had receded.

The crucial day was 8 June 2002. Brajesh telephoned me in the forenoon, asking me to meet him in his office in South Block. He informed me that the NDA also supported Vice President Krishan Kant. In my presence, he telephoned Vajypayeeji: 'Natwar is here and [has] confirmed the Congress's support for Krishan Kantji.' Brajesh told me that the NDA's official decision to support the Vice President would be taken at a lunch that was being hosted by the Prime Minister. The others attending the lunch would be L.K. Advani, Jaswant Singh, George Fernandes and Pramod Mahajan. In the evening, the Prime Minister and the Congress President would meet the Vice President to convey their decision.

I informed Sonia Gandhi. Krishan Kant was already aware of this decision through Chandrababu Naidu. At about 3 p.m., Brajesh asked me to see him urgently. When I met him, he said that the Prime Minister had not succeeded in convincing his lunch guests to opt for the Vice President. P.C. Alexander was back in the reckoning. I told Brajesh that I would immediately convey what he had told me to the Congress President, but I was certain that she would not change her mind about Alexander.

When Krishan Kant learnt that the NDA had abandoned him, he was devastated. Unfortunately, he died of a heart attack. Within a few minutes of his death, Sonia and I arrived at his residence. The saddest sight was his 104-year-old mother sitting with her son's head on her lap. There is no greater tragedy in life than for parents to cremate their children.

Then suddenly, A.P.J. Abdul Kalam's name began doing the

rounds. Kalam, who was not even considered a dark horse, finally made it to Rashtrapati Bhavan. He did not seek the office; the office sought him. Before A.P.J. Abdul Kalam took his oath as President, Pramod Mahajan, Minister for Parliamentary Affairs, called on him. He requested Dr Kalam to get one or two closed-collar suits and modify his hairstyle. Dr Kalam agreed to the coats, but the hairstyle was non-negotiable.

◆

In 2003, the Americans invaded Iraq, bypassing the Security Council. A secular socialist non-aligned country was destroyed. The excuse for the invasion was that Saddam Hussein had weapons of mass destruction hidden away. But no such weapons were found. The NDA government seriously considered sending Indian troops to Iraq. The Congress vigorously opposed doing so, unless Indian troops were to function under the UN. The troops were finally not sent. There were debates in the Lok Sabha and Rajya Sabha regarding India's stand on the invasion and a joint resolution of both houses was passed, reflecting the view of the Parliament on the war, which was critical. I spoke in the Rajya Sabha, deploring the invasion of Iraq by the USA and their moth-eaten coalition.

◆

In the 2004 Lok Sabha elections, the NDA lost and the Congress, along with several other parties, formed the United Progressive Alliance (UPA) to stake claim to the majority and form the government. Everyone expected Sonia Gandhi to become the Prime Minister. When the anticipated announcement was not made, rumours started doing the rounds and television channels started announcing that Sonia was not becoming Prime Minister.

A meeting of the Congress leaders was called. If my memory serves me right, those present were Manmohan Singh, Pranab Mukherjee, Arjun Singh, Shivraj Patil, Ghulam Nabi Azad, M.L. Fotedar and I. None except Manmohan and I knew why the meeting was called. Sonia softly announced that she had asked Manmohan Singh to become Prime Minister. Manmohan's immediate response was, 'Madam, I do not have the mandate.'

No one spoke. I was asked to speak. I told Manmohan that the person who had the mandate was passing it on to him. He had no choice but to head the UPA government.

Sonia choosing Manmohan as Prime Minister did not go down well with the senior Congress leaders. Most members of the Congress Working Committee (CWC) were senior to him. This was a bitter pill to swallow. The members were also resentful of having been kept in the dark.

Our next big problem was to get the UPA partners to accept Sonia's decision. Senior CWC members were deputed to meet the alliance leaders to plead with them to accept what Sonia had decided. M.L. Fotedar and I were asked to meet V.P. Singh, Lalu Prasad Yadav and Ram Vilas Paswan. Lalu and Paswan were both furious. Lalu gave us a tongue-lashing in chaste Bihari, demanding to know why he had not been consulted and why he had had to hear the news on television. Ram Vilas Paswan delivered the same message in less colourful language. It was a colossal mess and I found my diplomatic skills being stretched to breaking point.

Sonia Gandhi called a meeting of the alliance partners at 10 Janpath the same afternoon. The heavyweights arrived, fuming—Harkishan Singh Surjeet, M. Karunanidhi, A.B. Bardhan, Sharad Pawar, Lalu Prasad Yadav, Ram Vilas Paswan, Farooq Abdullah and E. Ahamed, among others. They had, in good faith, elected Sonia Gandhi as UPA Chairman, not Manmohan Singh. Why had they been kept in the dark? It took more than an hour to bring them around. Sonia was exhausted by the end of it but her inner strength pulled her through.

On 19 May, Sonia, Manmohan and I informally discussed names for the posts of Principal Secretary to the Prime Minister and National Security Adviser (NSA). Manmohan's choice for Principal Secretary was T.K.A. Nair, whom he knew well. Manmohan asked my advice on the appointment of the NSA. I told him I was not in favour of the post. After all, we had done without one for five decades and the post had been created only in 1999 at the behest of Brajesh Mishra. Manmohan eventually selected J.N. Dixit as NSA.

Manmohan Singh was inundated with requests from job hunters, including the upwardly immobile. The most important Cabinet ministries were Finance, Home, Defence and External Affairs. The Prime Minister was the Chairman of the Committee on Security. The other members were Pranab Mukherjee for Defence, Shivraj Patil for Home, P. Chidambaram for Finance and I for External Affairs.

Sis Ram Ola told me that Harkishan Singh Surjeet had spoken to Manmohan and Sonia to put me in the Ministry of External Affairs. Surjeet was worried that the American lobby would work against my getting MEA. I had, over the years, acquired a reputation of being anti-American. I was opposed to several aspects of American foreign policy.

The Manmohan Singh government was sworn in on 22 May. I took my oath as External Affairs Minister. My wife Hem and Jagat, my son, were present in the Ashoka Hall. For all three of us, it was a day never to be forgotten.

In the evening, I met Manmohan Singh. He had fought hard for me to get the MEA and, till the last moment, the

American lobby had allegedly tried to derail my appointment. Manmohan was apprehensive and mentioned how powerful the Americans were and that perhaps they could go to any extent to destabilize certain countries, including India. I appreciated Manmohan cautioning me but reminded him that our foreign policy was made in New Delhi, not in Washington, D.C. While I would do my best to further strengthen Indo-US relations, bowing before them was out of the question.

♦

In June 2004, I represented India at President Reagan's funeral in Washington. After the funeral I had a meeting with Secretary of State, Colin Powell, followed by a joint press conference. To a question about India sending troops to Iraq, I said that the Security Council was seized of the matter and that we would take a look at the outcome. The Press Trust of India correspondent filed a report saying that Natwar Singh had declared that India would send troops to Iraq. All hell broke loose in the Parliament. I was being criticized by the very people from the NDA whom we had stopped from sending troops.

♦

In July 2004, I accompanied Prime Minister Manmohan Singh on a state visit to Thailand. In Bangkok, we met the Prime Minister and the Foreign Minister of Thailand. The Prime Minister called on His Majesty the King of Thailand, Bhumibol Adulyadej.

On 31 July, Manmohan Singh asked me to see him, if I was free. I was, so I went up to his sixteenth-floor suite at the hotel. He said he was a very lonely man. He seemed to suggest that the present arrangement to have a dyarchy was unsatisfactory.

We discussed state matters, after which I told him that he was the best man for the job and he had Sonia's full confidence. 'We are all with you,' I assured him.

In September 2004, I accompanied the Prime Minister for the annual session of the UN General Assembly. We had meetings with a large number of Heads of State and Foreign Ministers. Of particular interest were meetings with the leaders of the five permanent members and the Heads of Non-Aligned States. The Prime Minister and I called on Secretary General Kofi Annan. I remember that the Prime Minister had an hour's meeting with Paul Volcker, alone.

My next trip was to Indonesia. An urgent meeting of about thirty countries had been set up in Jakarta with the aim of providing relief funds for the tsunami-hit Indonesia. All delegations were led by Heads of State. I was the only Foreign Minister, as the Prime Minister could not go. I was visiting Jakarta after thirty-five years, having first gone there in 1969 with Indira Gandhi.

◆

Our economy was booming and there was a flood of foreign dignitaries coming to India. Most of the Afro-Asian countries wanted India to help them and the dignitaries from Europe and America wanted to invest in India. In the summer of 2004, I went to Pakistan, and held discussions with my counterpart, Khurshid Mahmud Kasuri, on all aspects of Indo-Pak relations, including Kashmir. There was no common ground on Kashmir. I also spent forty-five minutes with the President, General Musharraf, whose personality and self-confidence impressed me. He was both candid and cordial. He was the man who mattered in Pakistan. The media, with the exception of a couple of Urdu papers, welcomed my visit and I got a particularly warm welcome in Lahore. By the end of 2004, it was abundantly clear to the world that India was gradually emerging as a country to be reckoned with. We were no longer living at the mercy of others. In the modern world, economic policy takes precedence over foreign policy. This is a fundamental change in the way the world is moving today.

2005 was when the UN celebrated the sixtieth anniversary of its founding. The widespread feeling in the UN was that the UN Charter needed to be revised to make it more relevant to the present world. This was particularly applicable to the functioning of the Security Council.

The permanent membership had not been increased. I, along with the Foreign Ministers of Japan, Brazil and Germany, visited several countries to emphasize the importance of the revision of the UN Charter. The sixtieth anniversary was a good occasion to do so. It was obvious that no single country could be made a permanent member. It had to be a package: India, Japan and Indonesia from Asia; Nigeria and South Africa from Africa; Brazil and Argentina from Latin America. Even this package could not go through because China would oppose Japan; Russia would deny Germany a permanent seat and so on. The five permanent members continued to exercise their rights to veto and prevented any revision of the Charter.

However, the existing permanent members were not willing to give the new members a veto. My view was that India would not accept second-class permanent membership. In New York during the General Assembly, the President of Brazil, the Prime Minister of Japan, the Foreign Minister of Germany and Dr Manmohan Singh were present to hear an account of their Foreign Ministers' efforts for the revisions of the Charter. These had not met with success. The permanent five were totally opposed to increasing the number of permanent members. A miniscule minority was holding the majority to ransom.

At the founding of the UN in October 1945, Cordell Hull, Secretary of State for the US had declared:

> The veto provision was an absolute condition for US participation in the United Nations. The super powers would not be subject to any collective coercion. The veto ensured that the General Assembly or the Security Council could not act against any of the permanent five.

In other words, the vital national interests of the P5 (five permanent members) could not and would not be submitted to UN jurisdiction.

No wonder the Mexican delegate at San Francisco said in October 1945 that under the UN Charter 'The mice would be disciplined but the lions would be free.'

Mannmohan Singh met Volcker again in September 2005. No one knows what they talked about.

♦

On the midnight of 14-15 June 2005, Sonia Gandhi and I left for Moscow by special plane. She had been invited by Vladimir Yakunin, convenor of the World Public Forum, to discuss 'The Dialogue of Civilizations'.

Soon after arrival, Sonia addressed the forum. In the afternoon, after the meeting, Sonia and I flew to the town of Vladimir by helicopter.

The next morning, we flew to St Petersburg. Founded by Peter the Great, who called it his window to the West, this dazzling city is, along with Rome, one of the most sublime creations of man. Pushkin lived and died in the city. So did Dostoyevsky and Anna Akhmatova.

President Putin and Sonia Gandhi spent three-and-a-half hours in a meeting. Putin has an engaging personality and it seems he has jettisoned his KGB past. His regard for Sonia was quite evident. Bilateral, regional and global issues were discussed. On the expansion of the Security Council, Putin said that it was in the interest of Russia to see India as a permanent member of the Security Council. But the expansion of the Security Council would be a complicated matter as no single country could become a permanent member.

The talks were followed by lunch. Mr Putin was accompanied by one of his senior advisers, who also acted as interpreter. Though Putin spoke English fluently, on formal occasions, he spoke Russian. This was not a formal lunch by any means, but Putin stuck to Russian. After lunch, the President took leave of Sonia.

Our programme included a boat trip in the Gulf of Finland. When we arrived at the exclusive pier, we saw President Putin standing next to the boat. I whispered to Sonia that this was a very special gesture. He was treating her as a Head of State. Not only that, the President announced that he would accompany us on the boat trip. I reminisced about the visit of Nikita Khrushchev to India in 1955. During his two-day stay in Srinagar, he had announced that Kashmir was a part of India. This made Khrushchev very popular in India. I also put in a favourable word about Vladimir Yakunin, the Deputy Minister of the Russian Railways, who had accompanied us to the town of Vladimir and had given us an interesting overview of the Russian political scene.

The boat excursion took forty-five minutes. At the Peterhof pier, the President saw Yakunin. He walked up to him and said, 'What fairy tales have you been telling the Foreign Minister?' Yakunin's jaw dropped. The President then said goodbye to Sonia and me.

Later, Yakunin escorted us to the State Hermitage Museum. It had been destroyed during World War II, but rebuilt exactly as it had been before the war. I had heard much about it, yet I was not prepared for what I saw. Sonia is very knowledgeable about art. She pointed out to me some of the most famous paintings by Edgar Degas, Paul Gauguin, Leonardo da Vinci, Claude Monet, Henri Matisse, Raphael, Renoir, Michelangelo, Rembrandt, Van Gogh and Titian. The only other place where one could see such treasures was the Louvre in Paris. Sonia, like her mother-in-law, walks very fast. I could not keep up with her, especially on that very warm day. Noticing this, Sonia told me to go back to the guest house as she wanted to spend some more time at the Hermitage.

After dinner, Yakunin insisted that we attend an opera. Neither Sonia nor I enjoyed it. It had been a long day and we were both tired. But Yakunin was a persistent host and pleaded that Sonia and I watch the White Nights festival. As soon as we entered the gulf, we saw a most wonderful sight. At midnight, it was bright as day. In all my globe-trotting, I had not seen such a unique phenomenon.

A few minutes later, Yakunin came and sat next to me. He asked, 'Mr Minister, what did you say to the President about me?'

I replied, 'I told the President that you were a so-and-so.'

'Please don't joke,' he said. 'You must be a very powerful man, because the President has just appointed me the Railway Minister of Russia.'

◆

Winston Churchill, when summing up Lord Curzon's life, wrote 'The morning was gold, the afternoon was silver, the evening lead.' Dr Manmohan Singh's tenure as Prime Minister could be similarly described.

He forgets no slight but is an expert at camouflaging his emotions.

In a press conference on 3 January 2014, he flagged the nuclear deal as his greatest achievement. For almost a decade, I have not said anything on it or my role in it. Let me make amends now.

No one hears of the nuclear deal anymore. It is, for all purposes, dead. Nevertheless, it was a major event in Indo-US relations. The negotiations were intense and prolonged. I give a brief account here.

The Indo-US Civil Nuclear Agreement was the logical though somewhat unexpected culmination of the Next Steps in Strategic Partnership (NSSP) which India and the US had committed themselves to during the earlier NDA government and President Bush's first term. The NSSP opened the door to a resumption of Indo-US bilateral cooperation in the fields of nuclear energy, space and defence (especially Ballistic Missile Defence), though within very limited parameters. In return for the US lifting some of the technology denial measures imposed on it, India agreed to align its export controls on sensitive materials and technology with those laid down by the Nuclear Suppliers' Group (NSG) and the Missile Technology Control Regime (MTCR). India also agreed to adopt legislation that would provide a comprehensive legal regime for export controls over sensitive materials and technology.

The UPA government continued this engagement with the US. The US was deeply concerned over the rise of China and its implications for US presence, particularly in Asia. A strategic partnership with India offered a significant means of confronting this challenge. India's rapidly growing economy and its obvious strengths in key areas of science and technology, its emergence as a credible maritime power and its strong democratic credentials, convinced President Bush and his key advisers, including Condoleezza Rice, Secretary of State, that the US must establish a strong, long-term strategic partnership with India. A state visit by PM Manmohan Singh was planned in mid-2005. This would be the occasion to formalize and announce the partnership.

The negotiations were led by the Foreign Secretary Shyam Saran on our side and Nicholas Burns, the Undersecretary, US Department of State, on the other. They began to hammer out an agreed formulation on civil nuclear energy cooperation, to be incorporated in the Indo-US Joint Statement, to be issued during the Prime Minister's state visit to Washington. On 18 July 2005, the Joint Statement drafted by them was the culmination of what proved to be extremely difficult and complex negotiations and went down to the wire. The final text was only agreed on minutes before President Bush and PM Manmohan Singh concluded their meeting in the forenoon of 18 July.

Later that evening the entire delegation accompanying the PM, including Department of Atomic Energy Secretary Dr Anil Kakodkar, met to discuss the proposed Joint Statement. There was fierce opposition from some key members of the delegation to the proposed nuclear deal. The main burden of criticism was that the proposed deal could limit India's autonomy in pursuing its strategic nuclear programme, that the separation of civil and military components of our programme would be difficult and even costly, and that gains to India were problematical. Counter arguments were put forward forcefully and I argued that this was an opportunity that should not be lost. However, the PM reluctantly agreed to drop the more detailed formulation from the Joint Statement and settle for a bland and in-principle commitment to pursuing civil nuclear energy cooperation with the US in the future. The Foreign Secretary was asked to convey this to his US counterpart that same night.

Condoleezza Rice, who was the Secretary of State in the administration of President George Bush, has written about the deal in her autobiography, *No Higher Honour: A Memoir of My Years in Washington*. I start by quoting some lines from it:

> I met the day before my Indian counterpart Natwar Singh in his suite at the Willard Hotel. Frankly, there was so much buzz around the State Department that we wanted to work in a location away from the press and where the atmosphere was more informal. [...] Natwar was adamant. He wanted the deal, but the Prime Minister wasn't sure if he could sell it in New Delhi. I was a bit surprised, perhaps having misread Natwar's determination as an indicator that he had the authority to speak for his government...*

After our meeting, Condoleezza had called the President, telling him that Manmohan Singh couldn't make the deal happen. She wanted to meet Manmohan but he refused to see her. She then called me and asked me why he was being recalcitrant. I told her that he didn't want to say no to her. I had done my best to convince him, but he said that he wouldn't be able to sell the nuclear deal in Delhi. Condoleezza pleaded with me to arrange a meeting and I finally managed to do so.

The Secretary of State arrived for breakfast the next day. She had brought the revised text of the agreement for Prime Minister Manmohan Singh's approval. I, too, was present. When Manmohan had reservations about one or two points in the text, I asked Foreign Secretary Shyam Saran and Anil Kakodkar to come up with fresh text including the points raised by the Prime Minister. With the new text, she left for the

---

*Condoleezza Rice. *No Higher Honour: A Memoir of My Year in Washington* London: Simon & Schuster, 2011

THE MILLENNIUM YEARS

White House to show the draft to the President. It was already past 9.30 a.m. and the George Bush-Manmohan Singh meeting had been scheduled for 9. I arrived before the Prime Minister and sat next to Condoleezza. We finally got a go-ahead on the negotiations.

On my return to Delhi, I saw Sonia Gandhi, who was far from approving. 'Natwar, how could *you* of all people agree to this?' she asked. 'You know there is an undercurrent in the country regarding America's policy.' Yet six months later, she changed her mind.

The Nuclear Bill came up before the Lok Sabha in 2008. It was passed with a very small majority, and only because the Samajwadi Party supported the deal. However, in 2013, Mulayam Singh Yadav, leader of the SP, admitted that they had 'made a blunder of a lifetime' by supporting the nuclear deal. On the nuclear deal the Parliament, the scientific community and the country, all were divided. Incidentally, what has become of the much tom-tommed nuclear deal?

◆

As far as Manmohan Singh's foreign policy was concerned, he didn't have one. The Ministry of External Affairs was demoralized because it was run from the Prime Minister's Office. Matters were made worse when the Prime Minister sent a former Cabinet minister to Japan as a special envoy, even though we had a senior Ambassador in Tokyo.

There was a broad national consensus on foreign policy till Manmohan became Prime Minister. He leaned backwards to accommodate the US, even when they displayed indifference. India did not utter a word against the US's spying over a large number of countries, including India. What else could one expect from a Prime Minister who once told President George Bush, 'Mr President, the people of India dearly love you.' Which Indians did he have in mind?

As long as Manmohan Singh was in office, it seemed that India was almost absent from US President Barack Obama's foreign policy radar. During the Prime Minister's visit to Washington in 2013, he was, according to reliable sources, given a lukewarm reception and nothing substantial was achieved.

Even with our neighbours, our relations were not what they should have been. When the Prime Minister was going on a visit to Bangladesh in 2011, he was snubbed by Mamata Banerjee, the Chief Minister of West Bengal. The AIADMK in Tamil Nadu too had no time for the Prime Minister's Sri Lanka policy.

As far as Pakistan was concerned, Manmohan's first blunder took place in 2006 when, in Sharm el-Sheikh, he issued a joint statement with Pakistani President Yousaf Raza Gillani in which he seemed to substantiate Pakistan's allegations of Indian interference in the Balochistan strife. He was severely criticized for this on his return to India.

After Manmohan's meeting with Prime Minister Nawaz Sharif of Pakistan in New Delhi in 2013, the latter remarked that it was no use to talking to him. Pakistan would talk to the next Prime Minister.

In his 3 January press conference, the Prime Minister said that he hoped to go to Pakistan before the general elections in May 2014. This was a surprising announcement. For the past ten years, he had been trying to go to Pakistan and had not succeeded because the Pakistanis had repeatedly acted against our interests. Each time Manmohan Singh wanted to visit Pakistan, an anti-Indian incident took place.

Traditionally, India has had good relations with the Arab countries but during his tenure, we seemed to be absent from the West Asian radar, too. Similarly, in Afghanistan, where we have vital national interests, we had been pushed around by the Americans and the Pakistanis. As far as China was concerned, we were constantly needled by incursions into Indian territory.

In the last decade, when the Prime Minister was in power, he visited dozens of countries but no meaningful follow-up happened. Similarly, a large number of foreign leaders visited India, but nothing substantial happened insofar as our bilateral relations were concerned. And we were absentees even in Southeast Asia, our own neighbourhood. With Russia, our relations deteriorated, in spite of President Putin's desire to strengthen and extend existing historical bonds.

There are nearly 140 foreign missions in New Delhi. Each day, they sent reports to their governments about the domestic disarray in India which consistently weakened our foreign policy and diplomacy. It was generally agreed that the Manmohan Singh government hobbled on crutches for quite some time.

On 16 May 2014 the Congress suffered its worst defeat ever in the 2014 Lok Sabha Election because of the failure of the party and the UPA government to respond to the demands of the people.

In the press conference of 3 January, the Prime Minister waxed eloquent about his economic policies. He is rightly considered an eminent economist, having obtained a PhD in the subject and he has even written a book, *India's Export Trends and Prospects for Self-Sustained Growth*. But the hard truth is that our GDP rate went down to 4.5 per cent during his tenure.

The Hindu, in its editorial, had this to say about the Prime Minister's press conference:

> However, glaringly evident was the Prime Minister's refusal to acknowledge the UPA's singular moral culpability for the

mega-scandals involving spectrum allocation and coal block allotments. He went on to make the indefensible argument that being elected a second time absolved the UPA from its responsibility to face the corruption charges. Dr Singh's complacent recounting of the UPA's achievements wore thin in the face of the clear dodging of accountability in this regard. The political costs of the UPA's continuing state of denial are bound to be high.*

What will be history's verdict on Dr Manmohan Singh's prime ministership? It will either be benignly indifferent or reduce it to a mere footnote. What will be Manmohan Singh's legacy? Sadly, there will be none.

---

*'Dr. Singh Clears the Decks', *The Hindu*, 4 January 2014

22

THE VOLCKER CONSPIRACY

On 2 August 1990, Saddam Hussein, the President of Iraq, invaded Kuwait, starting what became known as the Gulf War. The move was widely condemned and sanctions were imposed on Iraq almost immediately by the UN Security Council. Allied forces from thirty-four nations sent their forces into Kuwait to drive out Iraq, managing to do so on 24 February 1991. Even after that, the Security Council did not lift the sanctions against Iraq. In 1996, the Security Council established the Oil-for-Food Programme to help the people of Iraq. Under this, the government of Iraq could sell oil under the supervision of the UN and buy food and medical supplies for its people in return. These transactions had to be routed through the UN.

On 20 March 2003, US forces invaded Iraq looking for 'weapons of mass destruction'. Saddam Hussein was ousted (and finally executed on 30 December 2006) and the sixty-billion-dollar Oil-for-Food Programme came to an abrupt end. Documents then surfaced revealing discrepancies in the functioning of the programme. It was found that surcharges or bribes were being added to the oil price, which were being pocketed by Saddam Hussein.

The United States Senate asked for an inquiry into the manner in which the programme was being conducted. The Volcker Committee, then called the Independent Inquiry Committee, was set up by UN Secretary General Kofi Annan some years later to investigate the allegations. It was chaired by Paul Volcker, former chairman of the United States Federal Reserve. The principal allegations which Volcker had to examine were related to the activities of Annan and his son, Kojo. The committee took eighteen months to finish the report and submitted it on 27 October 2005. In its enclosures, the Volcker Report listed the names of companies and individuals who had profited from the Oil-for-Food Programme.

◆

On 26 October 2005, I visited Moscow to hold bilateral talks with the Russian Foreign Minister, Sergey Lavrov. Before the meeting, I was informed that President Putin would himself be present at the afternoon session. I was greatly surprised, because Heads of State do not participate in discussions between Foreign Ministers. President Putin arrived on time and sat on the table facing me. His Foreign Minister was sitting on the right. The meeting lasted over ninety minutes. I kept asking myself why Mr Putin was bestowing this honour on me. I concluded that it was because Putin had seen me in June when I accompanied Sonia Gandhi on her visit to Russia and must have observed that Sonia and I were very friendly throughout the trip, particularly when he saw us on the boat that was taking us to the Hermitage. My last meeting with him was to be on the afternoon of 28 October. The afternoon session concluded at 5 p.m. and, two hours later, I took a flight to Frankfurt, where I was to spend the night.

The next day at 5 a.m., the Director of my office came rushing to say that the Permanent Representative of India at the United Nations, Nirupam Sen, wished to speak to me urgently. I asked Nirupam why he had woken me up so early in the morning. I was astounded when he told me that the Volcker Report had been presented to the UN Secretary General and it carried my name, that of the Congress Party and several corporate houses as non-contractual beneficiaries. According to the report, the Congress had been in the oil business with Iraq since 1997. At around 6.30 a.m., I also received an email carrying a front-page report from *The Hindu*, which highlighted this fact.

At no time did Volcker inform the Congress Party or me before including our names. He should have done so.

This was truly a bolt from the blue. When I was in New York with Prime Minister Manmohan Singh in late September 2005, I had heard that the Volcker Report would be submitted to the Secretary General sometime in October. Manmohan Singh had also met Paul Volcker in September 2004. I was a bit surprised at why he needed to spend so much time with the man. On my return from New York I also remember mentioning to Sonia Gandhi that Kofi Annan would lose his job if he was named in the Volcker Report.

After I had spoken to Nirupam Sen, I sat down to reflect on what I had been told. I had two options before me: one, to proceed to New York, meet Paul Volcker and ask him for an explanation; two, to submit my resignation to the Prime Minister. But my conscience was clear, why should I resign? I decided to go to Delhi and meet the Prime Minister and the Congress President.

I had a very restless day. I sent a telegram to the PM telling him that I would explain my position as soon as I reached Delhi. Before I left, I was shown the statement of the Congress

General Secretary, Ambika Soni, in which she said—clearly referring to me—that 'as far as individuals were concerned, they were competent to defend themselves'.* I was outraged. I had spent my whole life in the foreign service and in politics and I knew that such a statement could not have been issued without the approval of the Congress President. My relations with the Gandhi-Nehru family had begun in July 1944; at least I should have been given the benefit of doubt by the party chief.

I landed at Palam Airport at 10.30 p.m. and noticed a group of media persons waiting for me. I ignored them and arrived home at about 11.30 p.m. To my amazement, I saw that my house had been surrounded by more than a dozen TV vans and a large number of photographers and reporters. With some difficulty, I managed to get into the house.

Next morning, I discovered that the PM was out of town. I did not contact Sonia because I was still very upset by the official statement of the party and I had expected her to send for me, bearing in mind that she was aware of what was going on and why. In the next few days, life became intolerable. The media had already decided that I was guilty. This line had been fed to them by a group of senior Cabinet ministers.

The messages from our Permanent Mission to the UN categorically stated that the names of several important personalities had been mentioned in the report as having benefited from the Oil-for-Food Programme, including Heads of State and prominent politicians. The complete list provided to the Volcker Committee by the global policy forum had two names from India: Bhim Singh of the Panther Party of Kashmir and the Congress Party.

---

*'Volcker Report Allegations Baseless: Natwar', Rediff.com, 29 October 2005, accessed on 6 June 2014

A discussion on the report was held by the Subcommittee on Oversight and Investigations of the US House of Representatives on 9 February 2005. The list of 270 beneficiaries at the time did not include my name. At the meeting, as is documented,* a Dr Nimrod Raphaeli of MEMRI presented the list. But in a list presented at a meeting on 9 March, my name was inserted. All the countries named, other than India, rejected the report.

The matter came up in the Indian Parliament after my return. I made a statement in the Rajya Sabha explaining my position. In both the Houses of Parliament, the government categorically stated that I had committed no financial impropriety and that Volcker had not contacted the Indian Mission in New York or me or the Government of India. I was greatly relieved, but not for long.

Within a day or two, a tsunami hit me. Aniel Mathrani, a junior functionary of the Congress and the Indian Ambassador to Croatia, gave an interview to *India Today* saying that the Congress Party and I had asked for vouchers for oil barrels to be allocated to me during a visit to Iraq in 2001. Mathrani had worked under me in the Foreign Affairs department of the All India Congress Committee. In his interview, he said, 'Of course, he [Natwar Singh] knew all these things from the beginning but preferred to keep quiet. [...] That Natwar and the Congress never knew is hogwash.'**

In January 2001, the Congress Party had sent a fraternal delegation to Baghdad on the invitation of the Deputy Prime Minister of Iraq, Tariq Aziz, whom I had known for a number of years. The delegation was led by me. Its other members

---

*http://commdocs.house.gov/committees/intlrel/hfa98601.000/hfa98601_0f.html
**'Natwar Received Oil Allotment from Saddam: Mathrani', *Outlook*, 2 December 2005 http://www.outlookindia.com/news/article/Natwar-received-oil-allotment-from-Saddam-Mathrani/339046

were A.R. Antulay, former Chief Minister of Maharashtra; P. Shiv Shankar; Cabinet Minister Shri Eduardo Faleiro; and Aniel Mathrani, then Secretary of the Congress's Foreign Affairs department. I had carried a letter from the Congress President for President Saddam Hussain, which I delivered to Tariq Aziz. Before leaving for Iraq, I had a long and detailed discussion with Sonia Gandhi on my itinerary there and the likely agenda with the Iraqi government. My son, Jagat Singh, who was a General Secretary of the Youth Congress, had accompanied me on the trip because I needed assistance after my bypass surgery. As a Youth Congress member, he had also been officially invited to Iraq by Non-Aligned Students' Youth Organization (NASYO) member Subodh Kant Sahay to attend the NASYO conference. He went to Iraq a second time as well for this purpose. Sahay, too, I think was with us on this flight.

Andaleeb Sehgal, a friend of Jagat's, and a businessman with Iraqi links, happened to be in Baghdad during our delegation's stay. He was also apparently friendly with Robert Vadra. He regularly visited Baghdad.

The Mathrani interview was taken up by the Opposition in Parliament, a growing number of Congress ministers, and the media. Over a period of two to three days, the atmosphere became very hostile. People who used to hang around me, asking me to put in a favourable word on their behalf to Sonia Gandhi, suddenly viciously turned against me. The most outlandish stories about me were planted in the media. For weeks, I was on the front pages of newspapers throughout the country and pilloried on television. It was all too obvious that the campaign had been well-orchestrated against me by the powers that be. Nowhere was it mentioned that the Volcker Report had named the Congress Party as one of the non-contractual beneficiaries too. However, there were people all over the country who wrote and spoke in my favour—former Prime Minister Chandra Shekhar was among them. At a press conference, Leader of Opposition L.K. Advani asked whether I was being made a scapegoat because the Congress wanted to put a lid on its own involvement.*

My temperament is such that I do not get into a flap, neither do I panic. Regardless of the relentless slander, I did not wilt.

I got to know that on 28 January 2004, three years after my Iraq visit, the Indian Ambassador to Baghdad had written a letter to the Foreign Secretary, Shyam Saran, saying that he had seen two articles, one on the website of the Pakistan daily, *Jung*, and the other in the Iraqi Arab daily, *Al-Naida*, which had mentioned that Saddam Hussein had given away oil to foreign individuals and institutions in return for political favours. In the list of recipients, the Congress Party and Bhim Singh's names had been mentioned. Both were alleged to have received one million barrels each sometime after June 1997. This letter was seen by the secretary in the Ministry of External Affairs and the NDA Foreign Minister Yashwant Sinha, but no action had been taken on it.

I had a long meeting with Manmohan Singh on 8 November. It was not a pleasant meeting and I was so agitated that I spoke in a tone which he must have found offensive. It had been decided by the Congress President and the Prime Minster that I should, in view of this controversy, give up the External Affairs portfolio and take up the post of minister without portfolio. A team of accomplished intriguers holding high posts in government and the party had decided to target me. Nothing happens in the Congress without the knowledge and the nod of Sonia Gandhi. This is power without responsibility and backseat driving with impunity. I soon found myself completely isolated and the trial by the media put more pressure on me and my family. On 6

---

*'Why is Sonia Gandhi Silent on Volcker Issue, Asks Advani', *The Hindu*, 11 April 2006

December, I resigned from the Cabinet.

On 7 November 2005, Virendra Dayal, former Undersecretary-general of the UN, was appointed by the Indian government as Special Envoy to liaise with the Volcker Committee. He left for New York on 17 November, accompanied by the Enforcement Director, to collect all the relevant documents from the UN regarding the involvement of the Indians named in the report. On 24 November, Dayal came back with thousands of documents which he submitted to the Enforcement Directorate (ED).

The government constituted the Justice R.S. Pathak Inquiry Committee under the Commission of Inquiry Act to look into the allegations on 11 November 2005. However, after looking at the way in which it was constituted, it became apparent that the proceedings were likely to be one-sided. I give below some of the clauses:

> 4.1 By another notification No. S.O. 1593(E) of the same date, the Central government acting under section 11 of the Commissions of Inquiry Act, 1952 declared that certain specified provisions of that Act would be applicable to the said Authority. They were sub-section (4) of Section 3, Section 4, Sub-sections (2), (3), (4) and (5) of Section 5, Section 5A, Section 6, Section 9, Section 10 and Section 10A. Notable among the provisions not included are Section 8B and Section 8C. Section 8B entitles a person in whose conduct the Commission considers it necessary to inquire or whose reputation is likely to be prejudiciously affected by the Inquiry, a reasonable opportunity of being heard in the Inquiry and to produce evidence in his defence. Section 8C entitles a person whose evidence is recorded by the Commission to cross examine a witness other than the witness produced by it or him, to address the Commission

and to be represented before the Commission by legal practitioner or by any other person.

4.2 The Commissions of Inquiry Act, 1952 embodies a code of provisions considered necessary for an inquiry conducted by a Commission under that Act. An Authority set up under an order of the Government for the purpose of making an inquiry into a definite matter of public importance may be directed to apply only such of the provisions of the Act as are made applicable to that Authority. When the Government selects only some of the provisions of the Commissions of inquiry Act, 1952 and not others for application to the said Authority, it is clear that the Government does not intend that those other provisions should be applied to the said Authority. When it was open to the Government to apply Section 8B and Section 8C of the Act and it does not do so when selecting the provisions which it considered should constitute the envelope of power of the said Authority, it may be taken to have deliberately excluded Section 8B and Section 8C of the Act from application to the Inquiry before the Authority. Where a provision in the notification setting up the Authority empowers it to adopt such procedure as it considers appropriate during the Inquiry, the Authority must ensure that the contours of such procedure conform to the limitations so imposed on it. In this view of the matter, it is clear that this Inquiry Authority does not enjoy the power to permit the cross-examination of a witness or representation by legal practitioner or by any other person.

I had known Justice Pathak for a long time. I also knew his father, G.S. Pathak, when I was serving in Prime Minister Indira Gandhi's Secretariat. Soon after his retirement in 1987, G.S. Pathak had approached me to support his candidature as a judge of the International Court of Justice at The Hague. I was then Minister of State for External Affairs. The Ministry of External Affairs had worked very hard to get him selected. He had been extremely friendly whenever I had met him thereafter.

I had submitted my affidavit to the committee in a sealed envelope on 24 March 2006. Yet portions from it were quoted in newspapers in early April. I wrote to Justice Pathak about the leak, but did not receive any reply.

On 31 May 2006, I was asked to present myself before the Pathak Inquiry Committee. Apart from Justice Pathak, there were senior legal consultants present to assist him, each one handpicked by the concerned ministries. Within five minutes it became clear that the committee was extremely biased. They had been instructed to absolve the Congress of all charges.

Justice Pathak formally handed his report to the PM on 7 August 2006. In his conclusions, he totally exonerated the Congress Party. About me, he said, 'There is no material to show that Natwar Singh derived any financial or other personal benefit from the contracts.' Regardless of this, my son and I were chargesheeted by the ED of the Finance Ministry. Justice Pathak once confided in me that he had been under extreme pressure. He also told me that he had not been able to find any evidence of financial misdeeds by me.

In February 2006, I met P. Chidambaram at my friend and Rajya Sabha member Shobhana Bhartia's house. She is the daughter of the late K.K. Birla. Chidambaram asked me if I had any objections to visiting the office of the ED, as the government wished to close the case in two weeks. I agreed. He assured me that no publicity would be given to my visits to ED.

I had two meetings with the ED. The news of both meetings appeared in the media the very next day. I telephoned the Finance Minister about my ED meeting appearing in the media.

His answer was, 'Natwar, we are a democracy.'

My son was also called twice, although his name did not even appear in the Volcker report. His passport was impounded and he was chargesheeted.

I got to know that the documents obtained by Virendra Dayal were never shown to the Pathak Committee. When I asked Justice Pathak about the whereabouts of the Virendra Dayal documents, his reply was, 'What can I say, that is a long story.' Till this day, their contents are a mystery. We had approached the Delhi High Court asking to be shown the documents, but our appeal was turned down on the grounds that the court did not have any jurisdiction over the ED.

In 2006, a Bangalore-based lawyer, Arun Kumar Agarwal, filed an RTI application asking for the documents to be presented before the Central Information Commission (CIC). Then Chief Information Commissioner Wajahat Habibullah upheld Agarwal's petition and asked for the documents to be produced. At first, various ministries in the government kept passing the buck to each other, claiming that the file had been transferred. After much reluctance, it was revealed that the file lay with the ED. The ED, in return, filed pleas with the High Court and the Supreme Court seeking exemption from producing the documents, which were turned down. Finally, in May 2013, the CIC turned down Agarwal's appeal, saying that the disclosure of the documents may 'adversely affect the friendly relations of India with the foreign countries under reference'.*

Why was the UPA government reluctant to reveal the content of these documents? The conclusion is obvious: there are uncomfortable truths in them that they are trying to hide.

---

*Details of the step-by-step processing of the appeal can be found at http://www.rtiindia.org/forum/7170-where-virendra-dayal-report-oil-food-scam.html.

Some of the activities of the ED and other intelligence agencies were also farcical. A team was sent to Jaipur to prove that I owned a house in Beni Park. The team located a house on the gate of which was written Natwar Singh. They rang the bell. A servant came out. He was asked, 'Where is Natwar Singh?' 'He has gone for a walk and should be back soon,' the servant replied. At that moment, Natwar Singh's son appeared. He did not resemble Jagat Singh, my son, who was an MLA from Laxmangarh and was well known. He asked the team what they were looking for and who they were. He was told that they were from Delhi and wanted to meet Natwar Singh. 'What is his profession?' the team asked. The son said that his father had worked in a tea estate in Assam for thirty-one years. His full name was Natwar Singh Shekhawat. He did not use his surname. I later mentioned this to Bhairon Singh Shekhawat, who was very amused.

The team was subsequently sent to London, Geneva, Cyprus, Amman, Baghdad and New York. They looked for a numbered account in Geneva. It did not exist. In London, they looked in vain for a property I was supposed to own. No such property existed. Since I had known several officers in the department, they told me in the strictest confidence that I had committed no impropriety nor had I any property or bank accounts in foreign countries. They were decent enough to say that they were helpless.

I received a number of strange visitors, including a 'lecturer from Delhi University', a 'farmer from Bhiwani', a 'Supreme Court lawyer', and a 'sadhu' and 'sadhvi', all under various pretexts. They did not come on their own, they were sent by intelligence agencies. It was bizarre. My family's telephones were tapped and our mail tampered with. Contrary to accepted practice, our bank accounts were examined and our house was bugged.

At a largely attended meeting in Jaipur on 26 February

THE VOLCKER CONSPIRACY

2008, on the occasion of the centenary of Maharaja Suraj Mal, I resigned from the Congress Party and the Rajya Sabha.

◆

The appointment of Paul Volcker as the head of the inquiry committee raised several questions. The inquiry should have been headed by a neutral party, and Volcker definitely was not one. There was a conflict of interest as he was friendly with Kofi Annan. He was also a Director of the United Nations Association of the US and associated with several UN committees. It is hard to see how a team of investigators handpicked by the UN Secretary General who, along with his son, was himself being investigated, can be considered independent.

Volcker confessed to a reporter from *Los Angeles Times* that his report had the potential to expose the UN and remove Annan from his post, but when it came to the moment, he said, 'I felt uncomfortable.'* According to the report, hours before the publication of the Volcker Report, the Secretary General and his lawyer asked Volcker to 'change the language about the business dealings of Kojo Annan'. When asked whether he knew about the UN Secretary General's son using the connections of his father to profit by the Oil-for-Food Programme, Volcker said, 'To this day, I still don't know.'**

◆

The ED has still not concluded my case, which has been hanging

---

*Maggie Farley, 'U.N. Oil-for-Food Inquiry Findings Surprised Volcker', *Los Angeles Times*, 28 October 2005.
**Ibid.

for almost seven years. The ED has only given one hearing to my lawyer in all these years. There are still some apparently cooked-up income tax cases against us. The media crucifixion continued till 2010. But there are many who believe in my innocence. Arun K. Agarwal, in *Reliance: The Real Natwar* says, '...the inclusion of the Congress in the Volcker report was deliberately exploited to create panic by the power brokers and fund collectors of the Congress party itself [...] to justify a devious conspiracy to hang Natwar Singh in the main square...'* He also says clearly that I was 'set up' as the 'fall guy'.

The Asian Age in 2005 reported that a US think tank stated that my ouster 'signals India's intent to make relations with the United States as warm as naan bread straight out of a tandoori oven' and that it 'conspicuously parallel[s] US interests'.**

Politics is a blood sport where there are no friends at the top. The harassment, the innuendoes and the character assassination ceased only a year ago. I was isolated and slandered. It was a trying time, not just for me but for my family, too. But we all have strong nerves and a sense of honour. Being gritty, we survived.

---

*Arun K. Agarwal, *Reliance: The Real Natwar*, Delhi: Manas Publications, 2008
**Ramesh Ramachandran, 'US Think Tank Glad Natwar Out', *The Asian Age*, 12 November 2005

THE VOLCKER CONSPIRACY

Memorandum of Action Taken on the Report of the Justice R.S. Pathak Inquiry Authority
August 7, 2006

By Government of India notification No. 8/35/2005-E.S. dated November 11, 2005, the Government of India constituted the Justice R.S. Pathak Inquiry Authority with the following terms of reference:

(1) To inquire into the sources of information, materials and documents that were available with the Independent Inquiry Committee (appointed by the Secretary General of the United Nations to investigate the administration of the UN Oil-For-Food Programme) with reference to the Report (including the Tables) of the said Committee pertaining to contracts bearing number M/9/54 and number M/10/57 and to give its opinion on the authenticity and reliability of the said sources, materials and documents, and whether, in its opinion, the purported transactions in oil are genuine or not.

(2) To inquire into the aforesaid information, materials and documents, and any other material or evidence that may be obtained by the Inquiry Authority, and to give its opinion whether the references to Indian entities and individuals pertaining to contracts bearing number M/9/54 and number M/10/57 are justified or not.

(3) To inquire into the question whether any Indian entity or individual received any money or other consideration from, or paid any money or other consideration to, any Government, agency, company, firm or individual in connection with the purported transactions in oil under the United Nations Oil-For-Food Programme pertaining to contracts bearing

numbers M/9/54 and number M/10/57.

(4) To inquiry [sic] into any other aspect or matter relevant to the Inquiry pertaining to contracts bearing number M/9/54 and number M/10/57.

(5) To make any recommendations or suggestions that the Inquiry Authority may consider necessary or proper.

2. The Inquiry Authority submitted its report to the government on August 3, 2006. The Inquiry Authority has reached the following conclusions on the terms of reference:

(1) The documents available with the Independent Inquiry Committee (the Volcker Committee) were authentic and reliable. The documents were genuine and full reliance could be placed upon them by the Inquiry Authority. The transactions in oil covered by the two Contracts were genuine.

(2) The Inquiry Authority has absolutely no evidence whatsoever to link the Congress party to the transactions discussed in this Report and except for the fact that Shri K. Natwar Singh and Shri K. Jagat Singh belonged to the Indian Congress party there is not a shred of evidence to link the Congress party to the said transactions. The Inquiry Authority believes upon examination of all the documents and material which exist before it that no wrong doing can be attributed to the Congress Party.

Shri Natwar Singh mentioned as a non-contractual beneficiary with respect to Contract No. M/09/54, was a beneficiary in so far that the role played by him in influencing and facilitating the procurement of the Contracts had fructified. There is no material to show that Shri Natwar Singh derived any financial or other personal benefit from the contracts. As regards the Indian Congress Party, it has been shown as a non-contractual beneficiary with respect to

Contract No. M/10/57. The Inquiry Authority has found no evidence that the Congress Party was involved in the Contract and that it derived any benefit at all from the Contract. Indeed, there is nothing to show that the Indian Congress Party had anything to do with the Contracts M/09/54 and M/10/57.

Consequently, the reference to Shri Natwar Singh with respect to Contract No. M/09/54 is justified in the sense explained earlier, while the reference to the Indian Congress Party with respect to Contract No. M/10/57 is not justified at all.

(3) Shri Aditya Khanna, Shri Andaleeb Sehgal, Sehgal Consultants and Hamdaan Exports.
(4) No answer.
(5) No answer.

3. The Government have examined the Report and have accepted the conclusions contained in the Report.

4. Having regard to the observations made by the Inquiry Authority in paragraphs 4.3 and 4.4 of the Report, the Government have decided to forward the Report in its entirety to the following authorities to be treated as information and for such action as may appear to them warranted under law:
    (i) The Directorate of Enforcement;
    (ii) The Central Board of Direct Taxes;
    (iii) The Central Board of Excise & Customs.

5. The Report is placed before the Houses of Parliament as required under Sub-section (4) of Section 3 of the Commissions of Inquiry Act, 1952.

Covering Letter and Articles Related to the Volcker Report

AMBASSADOR OF INDIA
BAGHDAD

28 January 2004

From: B. B. Tyagi, Ambassador of India, Baghdad

To: Foreign Secretary, New Delhi

My dear Foreign Secretary,

We have seen two articles today, one on the website of Pakistani daily "Jung" and the other in Iraqi Arabic daily "Al Neda". They mention that Saddam Hussein gave away oil to foreign individuals and institutions in return for political favour. In the list of recipients of such oil, Indian Congress Party and Mr Bheem Singh's name has been mentioned. Both are alleged to have received one million barrels each some time after June 1997. (Mr Bheem Singh has written a book on Saddam Hussain.)

Jung news item and the translation of Al Neda item are enclosed.

With best regards

Yours Sincerely

(B. B. Tyagi)

THE VOLCKER CONSPIRACY

Article Published in *Al-Meda*, 28 January 2004

Al-Meda obtained special tables with company names and persons "amounts of crude oil have been allocated to them during the stages of MOU" as mentioned in the documents of SOMO (a general company attached to the ministry of Oil) with tables including names of persons, companies, parties, groups and organizations in which the previous regime allocated amounts and quantities mentioned in details all through the phases of the MOU. The allocation as mentioned in the documents started from the third phase of the MOU because in the first and second phases it was for companies that own refineries (end users) meaning that the following published information are for groups with no refineries (non end users) or for mediating companies.

Under this interesting title we see names that are not related to oil companies, nor distributing reserving or selling oil or having any concern with oil companies, such as the Russian Orthodox Church and the Russian Communist Party.

As for individuals, the issue is more exciting and questionable. Do we understand that the Algerian journalist Mrs. Hameede Na'na who defended the previous regime wants to maintain her independent enterprise through an oil deal? It is strange to see the name of the son of late Jammal Abdul Nassir (Khalid), the name of the Jordanian MP Mrs. Tojan AlFaisal, the present Indonesian president, the name of the Syrian defense minister's son Mr. Firas Mustafa Tlas or the name of the president of Lebanon's son!

From the moment in which Saddam approved to the MOU, or what is know as Oil for Food, he changed this memorandum into a vile commercial and political game by financing secret arm purchases, expensive construction materials to build his palaces and mosques, luxurious items for lavishness and recklessness in addition to shifting it as the largest contemporary historical known operation by buying consciences, pens and squandering the wealth of the nation.

Since that time rumors spread about the coupons signed by Saddam to some Arabs and foreigners to supply them with crude oil in exchange for their support in breaking his international isolation, financing a campaign to lift the economic sanctions imposed upon him and brighten his picture.

But the regime exploited the human and moral substance of the international campaign to lift the unjust sanctions that did not target him but the poor and middle classed- people, and we see that whenever the campaign was about reach its aim the regime would again, through his behavior and arrogance, return it back to a dark tunnel again, and in correspondence switched our country to an open and rich table needing nothing but ostentation and excellent caters and devoted servants.

What was so distinguished about the fascist regime was that it had no courtesy and was in constant need to use others so that it can feel superior and from this it demoralized even those with good wills and noble intentions in defending the people of Iraq to lift the sanctions. The regime knew nothing but (opening the wound) and that is why he gathered around him only those whom he wanted them to beg in order to satisfy the sense of superiority over them.

If a person had the chance of knowing Ba'thists who do not fear, because of their rustic nature, to boast he would have heard from them little or a lot about the visitors of Iraq who had increased in the lately years, he would have also known that the visitors who came to defend the case of Iraq came also to collect the price. We can confirm this information; who spread the rumors about the Arab and foreign visitors are the Ba'thists themselves in a moment of countryside gossips.

THE VOLCKER CONSPIRACY

It passed from mouth to mouth some names mentioned in this list, amongst them Mr. George Gallaway, member of the labour party.

His condition is completely tragic the man who defended the Arab cases, came out corrupt once he approached the Iraqi issue. Mr. Gallaway, who was dismissed from the party for this reason and not only defended himself very strongly but attacked the British policy and Mr. Tony and Mr. Bush, I don't think he can deny the convicting documents.

Al-Meda got six requests forwarded by the executive director of SOMO to the minister of Oil to "ratify the crude oil contracts" all under the name of Mr. Gallaway not as the holder of the contract but an indication that it belongs to him. Mr. Gallaway is hiding behind a company not a personality, or behind a nationality other than his nationality.

The way these contracts are conducted sheds a light on the mechanism in which these coupons were paid out and the grand wish of the president of the republic. From this we would like to forward them especially that some names were mentioned singularly like "Sameer" and it is not known whether it is the name of a person or a company?

The article carries a list of large number of individuals and institutions from various contries. The entries from India are as follows:

India:
Bheem Singh– one million barrels (in the newspaper spelt as Behm Singh, the way it is pronounced in Arabic)
Indian Congress Party– one million barrels

Article Published in the *Daily Jung*, 28 January 2004

BAGHDAD: Iraq plans to investgate allegations that dozens of officials and businessmen worldwide illegally received oil in exchange for supporting former leader Saddam Hussein, officials said on Tuesday. Their statements came after al-Mada, an independent Baghdad newspaper, published a list it said was based on oil ministry documents showing 46 individuals, companies and organisations from inside and outside Iraq who were given millions of barrels of oil. "I think the list is true. I will demand an investigation. These people must be prosecuted," Naseer Chaderji, a Governing Council member, told Reuters. The list includes members of Arab ruling families, politicians and political parties from Egypt, Jordan, Syria, the United Arab Emirates, Turkey, Sudan, China, Austria, France and other countries. Organisations named include the Russian Orthodox Church and the Russian Communist Party, India's Congress Party and the Palestinian Liberation Organisation.

Prime Minister

New Delhi
May 8, 2006

Dear Natwar Singh ji,

    I have received your letter of May 3, 2006 and noted your concerns. The Finance Minister has been keeping track of the investigations being carried out by the Enforcement Directorate and the Justice Pathak Authority. Recently some extension of time had to be given to the Inquiry Authority as all the necessary documents had not been received by it from the various sources. I hope it will now be able to complete its assignment within the extended period and I would request the Finance Minister to convey this appropriately to the Authority.

    With regards,

Yours sincerely,

(Manmohan Singh)

Shri Natwar Singh, MP
19, Teen Murti Lane
New Delhi – 110 011

ONE LIFE IS NOT ENOUGH

My Letter to Prime Minister Manmohan Singh

31st August 2006

Dear Prime Minister Sahib,

You are aware of the impact of the Volcker Report on my personal and political life. Thereafter at the instance of the Government, the Enforcement Directorate carried out some investigation both in India and abroad. They found nothing. The Pathak Authority was asked to probe these allegations. The Pathak Authority has categorically stated that "There is no material to show that Shri Natwar Singh derived any financial or other personal benefit from the contracts". I was asked to file an Affidavit which I did. I was summoned by the Pathak Authority and asked questions which I truthfully answered on the 31st of May 2006. Some days later, the statement was shown to me and after making a few corrections I put my signature on the document after hearing the recording.

I expected that my affidavit and my sworn statement will find substantial mention in Mr. Pathak's final report. I must say that I was surprised that there is hardly any significant reference to these two documents. Facts are being suppressed from Parliament and the people.

I need a copy of my statement because I must pursue my remedy if not in a Court of law but at least in the Court of the People of India.

My reputation has been blemished by un-verified insinuations totally negatived by the available evidence.

The statement is a public document. I am entitled to it as a matter of law.

The use that I propose to make of it is extremely laudable and legitimate.

I hope I don't have to become an applicant under the Freedom of Information Act.

I hope the copy will be supplied to me without any avoidable delay.

With warm regards and good wishes for your forthcoming visit to Havana from the NAM Summit.

Yours sincerely,

(K. Natwar Singh)

Dr. Manmohan Singh
Prime Minister
7, Race Course Road
New Delhi

प्रधान मंत्री
Prime Minister

New Delhi
September 6, 2006

Dear Shri Natwar Singhji,

I have received your letter of August 31, 2006. The documents referred to by you have been transferred by the Pathak Authority to the Ministry of Finance. Hence, I am sending your request to the Finance Minister for his due consideration and early appropriate response.

With good wishes,

Yours sincerely,

(Manmohan Singh)

Shri K. Natwar Singh, MP
19, Teen Murti Lane
New Delhi

EPILOGUE

Every man that comes into the world is subject to dissolution. When we have passed away, God alone survives, unchangeable. Whosoever comes to the feast of life, must, before it is over, drink from the cup of death... How much better it is to die with honour than live in infamy!

—Babur

After the Commonwealth Games and the 2G scandals broke out, a well-known journalist met me in the Central Hall of Parliament. 'Sir, you must feel like a saint now.'

I asked, 'Why?'

'You were exonerated by the Pathak Authority, yet you were hounded and crucified by the likes of me, the Congress Party and Manmohan Singh's government at the behest of Sonia Gandhi. I just wish to apologize.'

I was touched and thanked him. The hounding and harassment continue. But Sonia Gandhi can neither run nor hide.

I value nothing more than my good name. I have strong nerves. In my veins flows the blood of my ancestors. In adversity a man's mettle is tested. That test I have passed, and it proves I am not a quitter. No bitterness, no self-pity, no panic have touched me. At times I have been angry, a little depressed, but not for long. Only the guilty succumb.

My expulsion from the Congress Party was conveyed to me in a two-line note at 2 a.m. on a freezing winter night. A special meeting of the Congress Working Committee was held that evening for this. Manmohan Singh was in Moscow at the time; he was contacted and gave his consent.

The late Arjun Singh told me that at a core group meeting, then Finance Minister P. Chidambaram had told Sonia that mine was an open-and-shut case and that I would be sent to jail.

At another meeting, a decision was taken to establish the Pathak Inquiry Authority. I was told that the Law Minister H.R. Bhardwaj was in Lucknow; he was called back late at night on a special plane. He was opposed to this decision as the 'case' against me was not sustainable.

The Income Tax Department and the Enforcement Directorate filed cases against me and my son, whose name did not even appear in the Volcker Report. His passport was impounded. Stories mysteriously appeared in TV channels, newspapers and magazines, portraying me as an accomplished thief. No evidence was produced. Newspapers began turning down my articles. One Hindi newspaper editor frankly confessed that he could not publish my articles because, 'Soniaji would get angry.' Portions of what I said before the Pathak Authority and the ED were leaked to the media.

When I reminded the then Finance Minister of the assurance given by him at a meeting I had with him at Shobhana Bhartia's house, in the presence of Ahmed Patel, that my appearing before the Pathak Committee and the ED would be kept confidential, he said, 'This is democracy.' He had actually told me that my case would be closed in a couple of weeks. The couple of weeks have extended to eight-and-a-half years. Who gave the orders

EPILOGUE

is anyone's guess. In Vir Sanghvi's interview (a more detailed account of which is in my chapter on Sonia Gandhi), Sonia said I had betrayed her. It was a case of the pot calling kettle black.

My son and I held a rally at Jaipur where over one hundred thousand people came to show their support. The next day my son was expelled from the Congress. A few weeks later, chargesheets were announced against me and my son. Our 'crime'—displeasing Madam.

Manmohan Singh or any other Cabinet minister would not have touched me without Sonia's approval. The Congress tried to make me a 'non-person', but did not succeed. Those who used to hang around me for political favours—appointment to governorships, and to Cabinet and party posts—now turned their faces away on seeing me. In private, they sympathized with me, in public, I was denounced. I could go on and on. But I hold no grudges. If I did that I would go down in my own esteem.

What Sonia Gandhi has achieved is to reduce the Congress, one of the greatest political parties of the world, to a rump of forty-four members in the Lok Sabha.

No Indian could have behaved this way against me.

◆

On 4 February 2014, I met BJP prime ministerial candidate Narendra Modi at his residence in Ahmedabad. My son Jagat, a BJP MLA from Rajasthan, accompanied me. I told the PM designate that I had not come to ask for any post or office. As someone who had been involved in the foreign policy and diplomacy of India for nearly sixty years, I thought I would put some of my ideas before him.

I said to him that as Prime Minister, he would ultimately be the Foreign Minister of India too. But during the past several months, I had noticed that he had not mentioned foreign policy during his campaign. He wished to know what I had in mind. I told him that we had neglected our SAARC neighbours. As far as I could recall, Manmohan Singh had not been to Pakistan, Nepal, Bhutan or Sri Lanka. He had only visited Bangladesh in the last eighteen months of his term. I asked him, 'If you're not sensitive to the concerns and anxieties of our immediate neighbours, how can we be expected to play a constructive and meaningful role in dealing with the rest of the world?'

I pointed out that from Ahmedabad, one got a particular view of India. From Delhi, one got another view of India. Similarly with Mumbai, Chennai, Kolkata and so on. From Washington, one would get a specific view of Beijing, from Moscow, a different kind, and so on. For the past sixty-seven years there had been a broad consensus on India's foreign policy. This policy was not stuck in a time-groove but was nuanced and necessary adjustments were made to address the latest developments. No fundamental change has so far been made in our foreign policy framework. What would be the substitute?

I told him that the Muslim world extends from Mauritania in West Africa to Indonesia. The UN has fifty-four Muslim members; they could not and should not be ignored. I also mentioned where Jawaharlal Nehru had made three serious misjudgements in our foreign policy. These are yet to be resolved.

I am happy to see that our new PM Narendra Modi has opened his foreign policy innings by inviting the leaders of SAARC countries to his swearing-in. Others, too, may have given him similar suggestions. But his decision caught the imagination of a large number of people around the world.

With a commanding majority in the Lok Sabha, the PM, to begin with will, I have no doubt, restore the image of the country which for the past few years has been on a downward path.

EPILOGUE

◆

Someone wrote that man is condemned to death the moment he is born, with extended reprieve.

My reprieve could end any day. Soon I shall drift out of the harbour on a silent tide beyond the beat of time.

APPENDICES

Appendix 1: Letters from Jawaharlal Nehru to President
                 John F. Kennedy   377

Appendix 2: Letters from Authors   381

Appendix 3: A Page from K. Natwar Singh's Diary   383

Appendix 4: Letter from Prime Minister Manmohan Singh
                 Regarding the Nuclear Deal   384

Appendix 5: Letter from K. Natwar Singh to Sonia Gandhi   387

Appendix 6: Personal Explanation by K. Natwar Singh on
                 the Volcker Report   390

Appendix 7: Tribute to K. Natwar Singh   394

Appendix 1

No.24322

B.K. Nehru from M.J. Desai.

Please transmit the following message from Prime Minister to President KENNEDY.

BEGINS:

Dear Mr. President,

I am grateful for your prompt response to my two letters. Ambassador GALBRATH gave me your message this afternoon.

The Chinese statement on a cease-fire put out by the Peking radio this morning does not make any fundamental change in the situation. We will, if any official proposals are made in this connection, consider them. These do not, however, make any difference to our going ahead with our preparations.

I am grateful to you for the assurance that you are ready, in association with the United Kingdom and the Commonwealth, to be as responsive as possible to our needs.

I agree with you that the visit of a small group of top U.S. officials to help Ambassador GALBRATH in concerting with us regarding the manner in which you can help will be useful. The group should come as planned. We are making necessary arrangements for their reception.

With kind regards,

Yours sincerely,
JAWAHARLAL NEHRU

ENDS

From: Foreign, New Delhi.
To : Indembassy, Washington.
Reptd: Hicomind, London

DTG NOVEMBER 192215

MOST IMMEDIATE

No.9444.

Ambassador from Prime Minister.

Please deliver following message to President KENNEDY. I am sending a copy of this message to Prime Minister MACMILLAN.

Begins. Dear Mr. President,

Within a few hours of despatching my earlier message of today, the situation in the North East Frontier Agency Command has deteriorated still further. Bomdila has fallen and the retreating forces from Sela have been trapped between the Sela Ridge and Bomdi La. A serious threat has developed to our Digboi oil fields in Assam. With the advance of the Chinese in massive strength the entire Brahmaputra Valley is seriously threatened, and unless something is done immediately to stem the time, the whole of Assam, Tripura, Manipur and Nagaland would also pass into Chinese hands.

2. The Chinese have poised massive forces in the Chumbi Valley between Sikkim and Bhutan, and another invasion from that direction appears imminent. Our areas further north west on the border with Tibet in the States of Uttar Pradesh, Punjab and Himachal Pradesh are also threatened. In Ladakh, as I have said in my earlier communications, Chushul is under heavy attack and shelling of the airfield at Chushul has already commenced. We have also noticed increasing air activity by the Chinese Air Force in Tibet.

3. Hitherto, we have restricted our requests for assistance to essential equipment and we are most grateful for the assistance which has been so readily given to us. We did not ask for more comprehensive assistance particularly air assistance because of the wider implications of such assistance in the global context and we did not want to embarrass our friends.

4. The situation that has developed is however really desperate. We have to have more comprehensive assistance if the Chinese are to be prevented from taking over the whole of Eastern India. Any delay in this assistance reaching us will result in nothing short of a catastrophe for our country.

5. We have repeatedly felt the need of using air arm in support of our land forces but have been unable to do so as, in the present state of our air and radar equipment, we have no defence aginst retaliatory action by the Chinese.

6. I, therefore, request that immediately support be given to strengthen our air arm sufficiently to stem the tide of Chinese advance.

7. I am advised that for providing adequate air defence, a minimum of 12 squadrons of Supersonic All Weather Fighters are essential. We have no modern radar cover in the country. For this also we seek

APPENDICES

From: Foreign, New Delhi
To : Indembassy, Washington.

DTG DECEMBER 111110

MOST IMMEDIATE

No. 24392

B.K. NEHRU from M.J. DESAI

Continuation of my telegram 24387 of 10th December.

2. GALBRAITH has cancelled his visit. Please convey the following from Prime Minister to President KENNEDY. Signed copy sent by bag.

Begins:

"December 3, 1962.

Dear Mr. President,

    I am writing in continuation of the brief communication I sent on 21st November in response to your message on the visit of a small group of top U.S. officials to Delhi to help Ambassador GALBRAITH in concerting with us on our defence needs and the manner in which you and your Government could help us to meet these needs.

    Governor HARRIMAN who led the team had several talks with me and my colleagues. The members of the official team have also had close and intimate discussions with our technical experts. Some of the U.S. officials were also able to make quick trips to the eastern and the western fronts and saw for themselves the efforts that we are making to defend ourselves against Chinese aggression.

    We are grateful to Governor HARRIMAN and his team of officials for the long and arduous hours they put in to study our needs during their stay here. They indeed worked very hard.

    Governor HARRIMAN and the team of officials must have given you and the various U.S. Departments concerned their own assessment based on the spot study and discussions they have had here. In brief, our requirements fall into three categories:

a) The immediate needs of equipment to deal with the emergency situation created by the Chinese attacks since 20th October. These have been accepted and supplies have reached us or are on the way.

b) The building up of the requisite defence potential to meet the continuing Chinese threat. This project is necessarily spread over a period of 12-18 months. Your team of officials have been given details of our requirements. These are under study.

c) Preparatory work to meet any emergency that may arise from Chinese attacks before the project in (b) above is completed and we have to throw in the Indian Air Force to contain their offensive. This would consist of training facilities for

-2-

Indian Air Force personnel, radar facilities and liaison arrangements between the Indian Air Force and the United States Air Force so that U.S. Air Force can assist the Indian Air Force should an emergency suddenly arise. Our requests in this connection are being forwarded separately through our Ambassador at Washington.

The question of improving Indo-Pakistan relations and Kashmir came up during my talks with Governor HARRIMAN. We have been trying since some months to get Indo-Pakistan meetings at Minister-level started but without success. These will now begin some time before the end of this month in pursuance of the communique issued by India and Pakistan. Our differences with Pakistan particularly on Kashmir have a long and complicated history. One cannot therefore expect sudden results. The problem is difficult as it is and is further complicated by the menacing and dictatorial attitude of Pakistan vis-a-vis both India and the USA and their threat to align themselves with China. These attempts at black-mail will have to be contained by diplomatic action if the talks and discussions the two Governments have agreed to undertake are to be purposeful. We will keep Ambassador GALBRAITH informed about the progress of our talks with Pakistan.

I would, on behalf of my colleagues and myself and the people of India, like to express to you, Mr. President, our gratitude for your prompt and generous response to our request for assistance in the crisis we are facing.

With kind regards,

Yours sincerely,
JAWAHARLAL NEHRU"

Ends.

Appendix 2

Santha Ram Rau
Bombay
Sept. Something

Dear Natwar,

I am at last in decent shape. Time, distance, lack of pressure and involvement in other people's problems (for a change) all seem to have helped enormously. You'll notice the difference the moment you see me.

Santha

◆

Thakazhi Sikvasankara Pillai,
Thakazhi P.O,
Kerala, India
28 October 1964

Dear Singhji,

I started writing stories when I was 14 or 15. It was not a decision, but I wrote and wrote stories and it went on. I don't remember to have decided to write stories. I am a lawyer by profession and a writer by choice. But I stopped practicing as a lawyer in 1957 and now I have taken myself to my ancestral profession-agriculture.

Yours sincerely,
Shivasankara Pillai

◆

APPENDICES

11-A, Faran,
Hyder Ali Road,
Karachi 5
26 June 1964

My dear Natwar,

The unexpected tragedy that has overtaken India in the death of Pandit Jawaharlal, the last of the great leaders, makes one wonder if the age of intellectualism in politics has come to an end.

Yours,
Ahmed Ali
P.S. 27 June.

◆

Amaury de Reincourt
Bellevue
Canton De Geneve (Suisse)
13 March 1980

Dear Natwar,

After thirty years of writing in English, I have decided to start writing for Le Monde, in Paris, and may write something about the situation in India and Pakistan.

Amaury

APPENDICES

Appendix 3

36.7.2004.

At 4.P.M. MMS enquired if I were doing nothing then he would like to see me. I went up to his 16th floor ducal suite. He was sitting alone and somewhat forlorn.

1. The country is in deep crisis.
2. J&K. Mufti says the Cong is not treating him well & situation in J&K v.grave. J&K was slipping away. Pak. could act desperately and do something that would do immense harm. Mufti did dissolve assembly!
3. The security situation was causing deep anxiety. & st Sonia's security - after assassination attempt on life of Shaukat Aziz? (I had seen him Islamabad).
4. North East was another major worry. Manipur really has no government. Cong. govt-corrupt.

Appendix 4

प्रधान मंत्री
Prime Minister

New Delhi
May 10, 2006

Dear Natwar Singh ji,

    I have read your article on the agreement reached between India and the US on civil nuclear cooperation published in "The Asian Age" of May 1. Considering that there have been no new initiatives from our side since my March 7 *suo motu* Statement in Parliament, I should assure you that the fears expressed in your article and the resultant conclusions are at variance with the facts. In this context, I must confess to a sense of dismay at this article, since I have repeatedly referred to your own signal contributions towards making this historic agreement on civil nuclear cooperation with the United States possible.

    Nevertheless, since you have expressed your views in print, I thought I should attempt to allay your misgivings. To begin with, I would like to point out that your concerns over whether or not we are still adhering to the principle of reciprocity are unfounded. There has been no change in our position on this issue since my very first <u>suo motu</u> statement in Parliament on July 27, 2005. Pursuant to the Joint Statement of March 2, during President Bush's visit, the only development has been that we have forwarded our final Separation Plan to the United States. The US Administration has in turn, approached Congress with a draft legislation. Parallely, the United States has also established contact with the Nuclear Suppliers' Group, urging them to modify their guidelines to allow full civil nuclear energy cooperation with India. It is evident that both the Legislation in Congress and changes in the NSG guidelines will take more time to reach a conclusion. Nevertheless, until there is definitive forward movement in these arenas, we are <u>not</u> committed to taking any further action. I can therefore assure you that we continue to adhere to the letter and spirit of the July 18, 2005 Joint Statement, with which you were closely associated.

On the Proliferation Security Initiative, it is well known that the US side had raised this matter as far back as during the previous NDA Government. Once our Government came into Office, we had clearly stated that several Indian concerns relating to the PSI needed to be addressed before the question of our participation could be considered. Since that time, our concerns have increased following amendments to the Suppression of Unlawful Activities Convention under the International Maritime Organization. Currently, it would be difficult for us to participate in the PSI until our concerns are suitably addressed. While it is true that there are ongoing discussions with the US on this issue, and that our joining PSI is a matter of considerable interest to the US side, little progress has been made to date.

On the issue of an Additional Protocol with the IAEA, again we have not taken any hasty steps that could harm our national interests. As is well known, an Additional Protocol can be negotiated only **_after_** an India-specific Safeguards Agreement is finalized with the IAEA. At present, we are yet to begin formal talks with the IAEA regarding an India specific Safeguards Agreement, pending passage of appropriate Legislation in the US Congress. So far, only one round of exploratory talks on safeguards has taken place between the Chairman of our Atomic Energy Commission, Dr. Kakodkar, and the Principal Scientific Adviser, Dr. Chidambaram, on our side and the Director General of the International Atomic Energy Agency. In other words, formal negotiations with the IAEA have not commenced.

Finally, I would also like to point out that the references in your article to India **_adhering_** to the NSG and MTCR guidelines are at variance with the facts. While we have earlier **_harmonized_** our export controls with NSG and MTCR guidelines, no further steps have been taken towards adherence with these guidelines. Also, we have not unilaterally agreed to any 'conditionalities' being imposed by the NSG or the MTCR regimes.

APPENDICES

I conclude with the hope that through this letter, I will have clarified your concerns. I am confident you would continue to support our Government's initiatives as you have always done.

With kind regards,

Yours sincerely,

(Manmohan Singh)

Shri K. Natwar Singh
Member of Parliament (R. S.)
New Delhi

Appendix 5

K. Natwar Singh
Member of Parliament
(Rajya Sabha)

Res. : 19, Teen Murti Lane, New Delhi
Ph. : 23013855, 23014910, 23793704,
Fax. : 23016821

<u>CONFIDENTIAL</u>

11th July 2006

Dear Smt. Gandhi,

    I am writing this to you not as a Congressman or as a Rajya Sabha Member. I am writing as a committed and dedicated Nehruite and as a well-wisher

    The impression is gathering momentum about India becoming a junior partner of the United States. This may be at variance with facts, but perceptions are important.

    I am all for closer relations with the U.S. I am against India becoming a client State. The Americans propagate "benign hegemony", "humanitarian intervention", "export of democracy". These are sinister terminologies. Like Indira Gandhi, we should stand straight. No tilts.

<u>Nuclear deal</u>

    I remember how opposed you were to the nuclear deal. I explained to you the reasons why I went along with Manmohan Singh on the deal on July 18, 2005. I also supported his statements in Parliament on the nuclear deal on July 29, 2005, February 27, 2006 and March 7, 2006. My concerns and unease began on April 5, 2006 when Condoleessa Rice appeared before the Senate and House Committees on foreign relations. There she departed from the letter and spirit of the July 18, 2005 Nuclear Agreement. She abandoned reciprocity. She abandoned energy. She emphasized non-proliferation, permanent safeguards. I wrote about this at some length in my Columns. Having read what I had written, Manmohan Singh wrote me a letter and I replied to him why I had shifted my position. You too seem to have softened your position, both on the nuclear deal and on Iran.

You will no doubt have read the criticism that has appeared in various newspapers about the nuclear deal. Most of the criticism relates to the frequent changes of goalposts by the United States. I am, like other ex-Foreign Ministers in touch with the bureaucracy and the scientific community who have serious reservations on the nuclear deal and shifting US position. A majority of our scientific community, including Sethna are more than critical of the deal. It would be unwise not to heed what they say. The deal will undergo substantial changes (not favourable to us) when it comes before the entire Senate and the House. U.S. laws are stringent and the following will need to be altered:

(a) The United States cannot have any Nuclear Civilian Pact with any country which is engaged in civilian nuclear programmes except the Permanent 5 members of the Security Council.

(b) The IAEA will have full scope to examine our safeguards and the first waiver by the President will be based on this.

(c) US law does not allow any country beside the P-5 to have any weapons nuclear programme. Pokran II will have to get a waiver which will not be forthcoming. Waiver will be annual.

(d) The US, under its present laws cannot transfer nuclear technology to any country which has a nuclear programme. This will not only apply to nuclear technology but also the dual use technology. We have the example of the Super Computer ten years ago which the US refused to supply us.

(e) The US cannot have any cooperation with any country which has any programme for nuclear weapons activity.

(f) Even if the Senate approves the deal, the joint resolution of the Congress will be much worse. To the operational portions will be added items not to our advantage. As it is, reference has been made in the Senate for India having a foreign policy congruent with the US. This cannot and must not be accepted. There are references on Iran which we cannot accept.

We should politely but firmly tell our American friends that the July 18 Agreement should be accepted without any alterations. Otherwise an amended deal/agreement will be unacceptable to the country.

The other serious worry is the American infiltration of our Intelligence Agencies. The penetration is connived at by some of our own people whose relations have well paid jobs in America.

Election of U.N. Secretary-General

I have it on very good authority that the Foreign Office was kept out on this issue. The Foreign Secretary was asked to talk to the P-5 about the candidature of Sashi Tharoor. The Chinese were not contacted as Tharoor himself will do that. The other 4 were non-committal. It is well known that Tony Blair prefers a well known political figure like the former Prime Minister of Singapore to succeed Kofi Annan. Shashi Tharoor does not stand a chance. We shall also have rubbed Thailand, South Korea and Sri Lanka on the wrong side. All three announced their candidatures last year. Pakistan will also put a candidate. He/she will attract votes from 55 Muslim members of U.N.

Nepal

India is not playing the role it should in Nepal, It is now public knowledge that Prime Minister Koirala has written to the UN Secretary General for help in organizing aid and elections in Nepal. He did so without consulting India. This is unfortunate. It is also against the letter and spirit of the 1950 Treaty of Friendship. Sitram Yechuri has played a role. We have not. The U.N. was kept out by me. It is very active in Nepal now. So are the U.S., U.K. and Pakistan.

Palestine

Government has been careful not to criticize Israel in stronger language. Why?

There are other issues but I do not wish to inflict a longer letter on you.

With regards

Yours sincerely,

(K. Natwar Singh)

Smt. Sonia Gandhi
Congress President
10, Janpath
New Delhi

Appendix 6

Personal Explanation on the Volcker Report
By K. Natwar Singh,
Rajya Sabha, August 2006

Mr Chairman, sir, when the situation of the people of Iraq became desperate, the Congress party decided to send a fraternal delegation to Baghdad. The delegation was led by me. I visited Baghdad in January 2001. The Congress President gave me a letter of introduction to President of Saddam Hussain which letter I delivered to the Deputy Prime Minister of Iraq, Mr Tariq Aziz, on my arrival in Baghdad.

I made a brief call on the Oil Minister of Iraq as a matter of courtesy because he had been in India and a number of other dignitaries.

During my entire stay in Baghdad, no discussion or talk took place with any Iraqi authority with regard to the Oil-for-Food Programme, oil contracts, vouchers, bank accounts, etcetera. The delegation was a political delegation. The administrative arrangements and the logistics were in the hands of Aniel Matherani, who was the Secretary of the Foreign Affairs department of the party of which I was Chairman.

The delegation consisted of four members—Shri Shiv Shankar, Shri A.R. Antulay, Shri Aniel Matherani and me. Shri Vohra has confirmed and so has the Pathak Authority. My son accompanied me and I paid for his fare. There is no document approved by me to add any names to the delegation. I had no authority to do so. I have made this clear on several occasions that no names were added. The Pathak Authority has also agreed that there were only four members of the delegation.

On my return I briefed the Congress President about our discussion in Baghdad and nothing was concealed or held back.

The Oil-for-Food Programme was started under the auspices of the United Nations. When complaints arose about the misuses of this programme, the Independent Inquiry Committee was appointed to look into these malpractices and abuses by the United Nations personnel in conducting this programme.

APPENDICES

Mr Paul Volcker submitted his final report at the end of October 2005. The annexures to the report mentioned my name, and the name of the Congress party, as non-contractual beneficiaries. No evidence was produced in the Volcker report as to how and why our names were added. I repeat, no evidence was produced in the Volcker report as to how and why our names were added. And, by whom? I shall not go into it here; I will do so later. In my affidavit, I have given details of Mr Volcker's bias against those who disapproved of the US actions in West Asia and elsewhere. My affidavit and statement to the Pathak Authority have been completely ignored by the Authority.

The Permanent Mission of India at United Nations in New York, through Shri Harsh Vardhan Shingla, Minister in our UN Mission, made the following points in a communication sent to the Ministry of External Affairs on 30th October 2005, and I quote: "(1) The Independent Inquiry Committee is headed by Paul Volcker, former Chairman of the US Federal Reserve whose inclination would be to discredit the opponents of US Policy; (2) No evidence has been cited and no documentation given on most of the allegations made; (3) Due process was not observed because none of the non-contractual entities was asked, through Permanent Mission of India, to respond to the allegations."

It is not surprising, therefore, that no country in the world has taken any notice of the Volcker Report. Let me repeat, Sir. It is not surprising, therefore, that no country in the World has taken any notice of the Volcker Report.

The Pathak Authority report has not attached my affidavit that was given to it. Why then were we asked to submit affidavits and asked to make statements before [the] Authority? It has not attached a copy of the statement that I made to the Pathak Authority exposing the flaws and loopholes in the Volcker Report. Although the report of the Pathak Authority is a flawed document, but it is categorical about what matters most to me.

The Authority has in clear terms said that I and my son derived no financial gains from any source. We stand fully vindicated, and, that is all that matters to me.

I find that much has been made out of the three letters I wrote to the Oil Minister of Iraq. Normally, I would not have bothered to discuss these. However, since they seem to have been given such intense importance by Justice Pathak and my party. I would like to ask what politician in India has not written letters of introduction for constituents, friends, acquaintances, etc. at some point or the other? Are we always aware for how they are used or misused? However, in this case, I would like to point out that even if they were used for oil contracts, these were legitimate contracts under the United Nations Oil-for-Food Programme. I am entitled to ask, sir, what illegality was committed by me in India or internationally? Furthermore, if I were to have asked for a favour, I would have done so for myself or my son. At no stage did I ask for any favours for myself or my son. And, I could have asked Tariq Aziz verbally to give me whatever amount I wanted, but I did not do so.

The last nine months have been most unpleasant and disagreeable and a great strain on me and my family. Throughout this period, sir, we have acted with candor, courage, dignity and restraint. The channel to my soul and conscience is immune to the chatter and clatter of those whose links with decency, ethics and morality are non-existent.

Paragraph 15.8 of the Pathak Authority report clearly states that on August 21, 2001, the Executive Director, SOMO wrote to the Iraqi Oil Minister seeking the approval of the allocation of one million barrels of crude oil 'for the benefit of the Indian Congress Party'. After the approval by the Iraqi Oil Minister, this contract was also sent for the approval of the United Nations Overseer; Justice Pathak then says enigmatically, 'How the name of the Indian Congress Party came to be mentioned in this letter is not known.' But, sir, this is precisely what he was required to find out. Instead of doing so, he surmises, as if he had entered the mind of Iraqi authorities, that what appeared to be the reason to him was that I and my son so projected ourselves that the Iraqi authorities formed the impression that we were representatives of the Congress party, whose representative was I when I went there. This is mere conjecture on his part in order to implicate me and my son and does him no credit.

APPENDICES

Sir, clearly, therefore, Justice Pathak's conclusions dealing with the contract in which I was mentioned as the non-contractual beneficiary and the contract in which the Congress party was mentioned as non-contractual beneficiary are at best questionable. He has not explained why I would ask for one contract in my name and another in the name of the Congress party. In neither case has he produced any evidence of my linkage except through surmises and assumptions. I would like to state with all the emphasis at my command that nowhere have I signed any contract, received any voucher, signed any receipt or made any transaction whatsoever with any party.

Justice Pathak also did not examine the circumstances under which the Volcker Committee in its fifth report included my name as a non-contractual beneficiary, did not verify the documents on which such a conclusion was based and gives no explanation of how the name of many companies, mostly from the US were removed, as this was said in this House when the House discussed the report some months ago.

Mr Chairman, sir, I joined the Indian Foreign Service in 1953. I have had a reasonably successful career in the diplomatic service of India. I voluntarily left the Foreign Service and joined the Congress party in 1984 with the approval of Shrimati Indira Gandhi and Shri Rajiv Gandhi in the hope that I would in a modest way be able to serve my people and my country better. I dare say that the record of my public life has been without blemish. I was awarded the Padma Bhushan in January 1984 by Shrimati Indira Gandhi. I have the good fortune to belong to a well-known and valiant family. God has been kind to me and given me enough. I have no reason, therefore, to indulge in acts of impropriety of this nature for petty financial gains. Sir, I have placed my views before this august House and before you from a moral and ethical point of view. I have not argued from a lawyer's brief.

Sir, I am in the evening of my life and I shall meet the Cosmic Master with my head high. Clean I came into the world and clean I shall depart. Thank You.

Appendix 7

Tribute to K. Natwar Singh

I knew Natwar Singh before I met him. Two collections of his essays on E.M. Forster and Jawaharlal Nehru had been published abroad and they attracted wide notice. They showed that our Foreign Service had a young officer whose horizons were not confined to diplomacy. His reviews in *The Saturday Review* and *The New York Book Review* were knowledgeable and his prose was lively and elegant. The man had style. In 1966 we became colleagues. We both joined the Prime Minister's Secretariat when Indira Gandhi took over. Our backgrounds were very different. I was from a southern and somewhat puritanical home, had participated in the Quit India movement, wore khadi and plied what was still a harassed profession, journalism. Natwar Singh came from the erstwhile princely order, had studied in Mayo College and Cambridge, and was at home in the United Nations and all that. I was also some years older. But none of this seemed to come in the way of our striking up an instant and easy friendship. We found we had a common interest—books (come to think of it, it is not so common an interest after all). It is not unusual to find scholars among bureaucrats, but rare to encounter persons who can be called book-lovers—those who are interested in a wide variety of subjects and are at home among old books that have made a mark and cannot rest until they get hold of new books that win praise in the journals. Natwar was particularly good at getting hold of books from America and Europe before anyone else had done so. His personal library even in those early days was unusual rich. It pointed to both good taste and serious intellectual zest.

We also had a common enthusiasm—R.K. Narayan. I had been Narayan's neighbour in Mysore. Natwar had sought out Narayan on Forster's recommendation and had instantly fallen under the quiet Narayan charm. He had also played host to Narayan in New York.

Colleagues do not necessarily become or remain friends. Most offices are riven by rivalries and faction fights. If Indira Gandhi's office was noted for its team spirit, sense of purpose and vivacity, the credit must go to Indira Gandhi herself and to P.N. Haksar. Indira Gandhi was a wonderfully exciting person to work with. Apart from a forceful political intellect, she had a fine mind which was interested in everything interesting that was happening in the world in science, the arts and literature. She loved to browse through the latest books and journals. She expected her staff to send up cuttings dealing with political and literary controversies, and when they came back we could see from the markings she made and the questions she asked that she had read them closely. She was specially appreciative of a good turn of phrase. Her comments and the memos she sent her staff bore testimony to her sense of humour. Those who have cast her in the Durga image have done injustice to her. And through the Emergency she did injustice to herself.

Haksar was a very different kind of person. Even in those days he was respected for his formidable intellect and his moral passion. But he was most approachable and generous. He did not treat the people who worked with his as his subordinates. It was a team and he recognized no hierarchies. Haksar had two other accomplishments which are not usually associated with him. He was a brilliant photographer and he was a superb cook. More than once during important meetings of the Cabinet or its sub-commitees it was amusing to find the Prime Minister sending across a note to her Principal Secretary for his advice on what a visiting dignitary might be served at the state dinner that night. Indira Gandhi was not a cook herself but she was a hostess known for fine taste and she took great pains with her menus and table seating plans.

I was privileged to work with Indira Gandhi from her first day in office to her last day. Natwar Singh returned to his parent ministry within five years and steadily moved up the ladder of the Foreign Service. He had some of the most challenging assignments that an Indian ambassador could hope to be entrusted with, particularly the Islamabad and Beijing postings.

The Janata Government sought to punish Natwar for his crime of having enjoyed Indira Gandhi's confidence. The way he stood up to Morarji Desai shows his guts. The punishment posting to Zambia turned out to be a reward; it enabled Natwar Singh to consolidate his friendship with Kenneth Kaunda and other African leaders. After Indira Gandhi returned to power, Natwar was to reach the high point of his career as a civil servant when he served as the Secretary-General of the seventh Summit of Non-Aligned Nations in Delhi. After that it was only natural that Natwar Singh should go into politics. Few people in India have enjoyed the personal friendship of so many international statesmen and diplomats or seen so many countries of the world. Little wonder that today he is what the British call shadow foreign minister.

Natwar's world of friends and acquaintances is a large one. He has a fine feel for human comedy and a subtle understanding of what makes people say and do the things they say and do.

An ambassador is called upon to play host to many kinds of people. Many of them are bores. But sometimes it may be a lifetime's gain. When Natwar served in New York he had C. Rajagopalachari for his house guest. He gives an endearing picture of Rajaji [in this book].

My mind recalls the Natwar with whom I had first worked. His hair was black with not even a faint touch of grey. The impression he created was of a keen man who was conscious of being a good conversationalist and raconteur. He was full of anecdotes and witticisms. The passage of years has not by any means slowed him down but he now exudes urbanity and distinction. The voice is the same. But the wit carries a greater charge of wisdom and forbearance.

2002 H.Y. Sharada Prasad
Delhi

(Extracts from the Foreword by H.Y. Sharada Prasad in *Heart to Heart*, Rupa Publications, 2003).

ACKNOWLEDGEMENTS

This book is the result of a lifetime of experiences, and would not have been possible without the support of many others. I owe several debts, which I cannot repay. My wife Hem and son Jagat put up with me with love and patience during the long time I took to complete this book. My grateful thanks to my extremely likeable publisher, Kapish Mehra, as also to Amrita Mukerji, Anurag Basnet and the editorial, design and production teams of Rupa Publications, who laboured hard to correct and revise where that was needed.

My special thanks to my erstwhile colleagues in the IFS—Ronen Sen, Satti Lambah, G. Parthasarathi, Shyam Saran and Shankar Menon.

INDEX

Name Index

Abdullah, Farooq, 166, 330
Abdullah, Sheikh, 28, 116-117
Ackerley, J.R., 29
Advani, L.K., 161, 237, 274, 297, 328, 351
Agarwal, Arun Kumar, 355, 358
Agate, Tony, 37
Ahamed, E., 330
Ahmed, Fakhruddin Ali, 160, 213
Aiyar, Mani Shankar, 212–213, 250
Akbar, M.J., 320
Alexander, Captain, 4–5
Alexander, P.C., 218, 220, 222, 230, 289, 325–328
AlFaisal, Mrs Tojan, 363
Ali, Ahmed, 29, 94, 195
Ali, Amjad, 16
Ali, Aruna Asaf, 289
Ambedkar, B.R., 109, 159
Anand, Mulk Raj, 29, 94
Anand, R.K., 130
Andrews, C.F., 20
Annan, Kofi, 333, 346–347, 357
Annan, Kojo, 357
Ansari, Vice-President Hamid, 228, 250
Antony, A.K., 311
Antulay, A.R., 350
Arafat, Yasser, 223, 245–246, 287
Arora, Gopi, 235

Athulathmudali, Lalith, 254–256, 261
Attlee, Clement, 82, 108, 114
Aurora, Jagjit Singh, 154
Austin, Warren, 117
Ayyangar, Ananthasayanam, 50–51
Ayyangar, Sir Gopalaswami, 116
Azad, Ghulam Nabi, 330
Azad, Maulana Abul Kalam, 82,
Aziz, Tariq, 349–350

Baba-saab, 2–3
Bachchan, Amitabh, 315
Bahuguna, Hemvati Nandan, 168, 226
Bajpai, Shankar, 212
Bajpai, Sir Girija Shankar, 39
Balasingham, Anton, 253
Baldwin, James, 87
Balzac (Honore de), 228
Bandaranaike, Mrs Sirimavo, 255, 261
Banerjee, Mamata, 342
Banerjee, Sushital, 133
Bannerji, R.N., 26
Bano, Shah, 273, 274
Bardhan, A.B., 330
Barooah, D.K., 49, 160, 163–164
Bashir Ambassador, 153
Basu, Jyoti, 266, 317
Begum Zia, 207
Bhabha, C.H., 109

INDEX

Bhadkamkar, Ashok, 46, 60
Bhandari, Romesh, 241, 250
Bhardwaj, H.R., 372
Bhartia, Shobhana, 354, 372
Bhave, Acharya Vinoba, 139, 166
Bhindranwale, Jarnail Singh, 231
Bhutani, Darshan, 60
Bhutto, Benazir, 213–214, 287
Bhutto, Nusrat, 212–215
Bhutto, Sanam, 213
Bhutto, Sir Shah Nawaz, 90, 213
Bhutto, Zulfikar Ali, 90, 103, 190, 201–202, 204–205, 212
Bose, Netaji Subhash Chandra, 16
Bose, S.K., 20
Bowers, Faubion, 72
Bowles, Chester, 138
Brezhnev, President L.I., 302, 304
Brockway, Fenner, 161–162
Buck, Pearl S., 47, 93, 108
Bukov, 32
Bulganin, Nikolai, 32, 122, 248
Burnham, 225
Burns, Nicholas, 339
Bury, J.H., 25
Bush, President George, 339–340, 342
Bush, Sr., President George, 234, 285
Butterfield, Sir Herbert, 25

Callaghan, James, 161
Cameron, James, 164
Castro, Fidel, 218, 223–224, 234
Chacko, M., 71
Chaderji, Naseer, 366
Chakravarty, B.N., 38, 81
Chamberlain, 101
Chandraswamy, 242, 290
Chang, Dean, 47, 57
Chaudhuri, General J.N., 50
Chaudhuri, Nirad, C., 33–34
Chaudhuri, Sachin, 136
Chavan, S.B., 310
Chavan, Y.B., 162, 213
Chen, Peng, 51, 57, 59, 134
Cheney, Dick, 318
Chernenko, Konstantin Ustinovich, 240, 246

Chetty, R.K. Shanmukham, 109
Chidambaram, P., 252, 254–256, 310, 331, 354, 372
Chingling, Soong, 48, 50, 57
Chitnis, Leila, 16
Chona, Mainza, 175
Churchill, Winston, 77, 107–108, 111, 337
Clinton, President Bill, 294, 298–299
Coelho, V.H., 86
Columbus, 85
Comber, Leonard, 45
Confucius, 47
Coulibaly, Soli, 76
Cousins, Norman, 83, 109
Cripps, Lady, 161

Dar, Avtar, 89
Dar, Rita, 89
Dayal, Virendra, 352, 355
de Gaulle, Charles, 77, 92
Dehuai, Peng, 134
de Maupassant, Guy, 228
Deora, Murli, 318
de Riencourt, Amaury, 41
Desai, Morarji, 38, 40, 64–65, 132, 136, 143, 161, 169, 170–177, 180–184, 201, 212
Deshmukh, C.D., 25, 145
Dev, Keshav, 15
Dhar, P.N., 159
Dhawan, R.K., 230, 233, 308
Dhebar, U.N., 293
Dhillon, Ganga Singh, 208
Dickens, Charles, 16
Dickinson, Goldsworthy Lowes, 29, 30
Dikshit, Sheila, 293, 315
Disraeli, Benjamin, 22
Dissanayake, Gamini, 254–255, 259
Dixit, J.N., 254, 258–259, 262–263, 331
Dixit, Uma Shankar, 145
Dostoevsky, Fyodor, 228
Doyle, Arthur Conan, 6
Dubey, Suman, 286, 315, 319
Dutt, Subimal, 39, 61, 122
Dutt, Sunil, 238, 244

INDEX

Eban, Abba, 75
Edward VII, King, 244
Ehrenburg, Ilya, 109
Eichmann, Adolf, 86
Eisenhower, Dwight D., 63
Elizabeth, Queen, 42, 218
Elton, Sir G.R., 25
En-Lai, Chou, 43, 46–47, 48–50, 55–57, 59–60, 63–65, 117–118, 122–123, 189, 252, 265–267

Faleiro, Eduardo, 350
Farrell, James T., 72
Fernandes, George, 161, 328
Fischer, Louis, 83
Flaubert, 228
Foot, Hugh, 164
Foot, Michael, 163–164
Forster, E.M., 28–30, 33, 35, 45, 48, 94, 96, 102, 128
Fotedar, M.L., 234–235, 276, 286, 288, 292–293, 317, 330
Freud, Sigmund, 228
Frost, Robert, 107
Fu, Tu, 58

Gandhi, Feroze, 42, 157
Gandhi, Gopalkrishna, 317
Gandhi, Indira,16, 37, 42, 71, 73,96, 97, 102, 113, 128, 130, 132–136, 138–150, 154, 157, 159–162, 165–169, 171, 173–175, 177, 179, 182, 185–186, 189–191, 198, 201, 209–215, 217–218, 223–226, 230, 232–234, 273, 288, 295, 307, 316, 333, 353
Gandhi, Mahatma, 9, 16–18, 20, 58, 82–83, 94, 107–109, 119, 141, 144, 162, 165, 173, 244, 280
Gandhi, Maneka, 191
Gandhi, Rajiv, 143, 166, 174, 220, 230, 233–235, 237–238, 240–241, 243–251, 253–256, 259, 261–262, 266, 269–271, 274–288, 290, 307–309, 310, 313, 316
Gandhi, Sanjay, 160–161, 165–166, 168, 212, 288, 295, 316

Gandhi, Sonia, 143, 166, 233m 234, 241, 246, 249–250,279, 286–289, 294, 296–297, 307–315, 318–326, 328–331, 335–337, 341, 346–348, 350–351, 371
Geingob, Hage, 281
George V, King, 244
Gharekhan, Chinmaya, 257–258
Ghisingh, Subhash, 273
Ghosh, Atulya, 132
Gillani, Yousaf Raza, 342
Giri, V.V., 145
Goethe, Johann Wolfgang von, 102
Gogol, Nikolai, 228
Gopal, Sarvepalli, 38, 42, 63, 112, 119, 266
Gorbachev, Mikhail, 241, 246–251, 268, 304–306
Gowda, H.D. Deve, 295
Greene, Graham C., 34
Griffiths, Eldon, 164
Grigg, John, 161
Gromyko, Andrei, 32, 139
Guevara, Che, 73
Guha, Panu, 46
Gujral, Inder Kumar, 132, 148, 295
Gujral, Satish, 49
Gundevia, Y.D., 38–39
Gupta, Atul, 22
Gurpal, 5

Habibullah, Wajahat, 355
Haksar, Parmeshwar Narain (P.N.), 139–140, 143–145, 149, 213, 248, 279, 288–289, 297, 304, 376
Halim, 19
Hammarskjöld, Dag, 70
Hancock, Sir C.P., 4
Hanut, 299
Hassan, Aley, 18
Hazari, Lt Gen., 276
Hemingway, Ernest, 49
Henri Giraud, 77
Himmat, 299
Hitler, 101–102
Howard, Anthony, 163

INDEX

Hugo (Victor), 228
Hull, Cordell, 335
Hume, A.O., 244
Husain, M.F., 37, 92–93, 191
Hussain, Zakir, 4 135, 144, 307
Hussein, Saddam, 222, 284, 329, 345–346, 349–350, 363–364, 366
Hutheesing, Ajit, 16, 27
Hutheesing, Harsha, 16, 27
Hutheesing, Krishna, 16, 27, 36–38, 42, 61, 69, 88–90

Il-Sung, Kim, 222
Isherwood, Christopher, 29
Ivanov, Sergey, 32

Jagmohan, 220
Jayewardene, President J.R., 234, 252, 256, 259, 261–264
Jenkins, Roy, 34
Jha, C.S., 76, 97
Jha, L.K., 133, 136, 139, 150
Jinnah, Mohammad Ali, 18, 109, 115, 195, 199
Joshi, P.C., 48

Kakodkar, Anil, 339–340
Kalam, A.P.J. Abdul, 328–329
Kamaraj, K., 132–133, 136, 146
Kant, Krishan, 326–328
Kao, Rameshwar Nath (R.N.), 64, 153
Kapadia, E.R., 210
Kapoor, Yashpal, 145
Karanjia, R.K., 307
Karunanidhi, M., 161, 330
Karzai, Hamid, 320
Kasliwal, Ravi, 300
Kasuri, Khurshid Mahmud, 333
Kaul, B.G., 124
Kaul, Pratap, 242
Kaunda, President Kenneth, 172–173, 175–177, 179–184, 225, 234, 281, 316
Kaur, Heminder (Hem), 128, 130, 142, 156–157, 170, 172, 183–185, 187, 206, 230, 235, 286, 313, 315, 323, 331

Kaur, Maharani Mohinder, 130
Kaur, Prayag, 2
Kaur, Rajender, 206
Kennedy, Mrs Jacqueline, 91–92
Kennedy, President John F., 73–74, 83–84– 87, 91, 96, 123–124
Kennedy, Robert, 92
Kesri, Sitaram, 295–296
Keynes, John Maynard, 182
Khama, President Seretse, 172-173
Khan, Arif Mohammad, 274, 280
Khan, Badshah, 143
Khan, Begum Liaquat Ali, 195
Khan, Khan Abdul Ghaffar, 82, 109, 143, 244, 310
Khan, Nawabzada Liaquat Ali, 115, 195
Khan, Sahabzada Yaqub Ali, 193
Khan, Sir Muhammad Zafarullah, 19, 83, 116
Khan, Ustad Amjad Ali, 194
Khan, Ustad Hafiz Ali, 16
Khan, Wali, 197–199
Khan, Yahya, 151
Khanna, S.P., 40
Khomeini, Ayatollah, 246
Khrushchev, Nikita, 32, 70, 76, 84, 101, 121, 248, 302, 304, 336
King, Martin Luther Jr., 87–88, 108
Kinnock, Neil, 283
Kissinger, Henry, 268
Klerk, F.W. de, 282
Kohli, Sunita, 315
Kumar, Ashok, 7
Kumar, Santosh, 197

Lakshman, Kamala, 59
Lal, Arthur, 70
Lal, Bansi, 165
Lal, Devi, 284
Lama, Dalai, 56, 61–62
Lambah, S.K. (Satti), 187, 197, 212, 220, 223
Lanfang, Mei, 59
Laski, Mrs, 161
Lavrov, Sergey, 346

INDEX

Lean, David, 29
Lenin, Vladimir, 47, 51, 108, 120
Linlithgow, Lord, 7
Lisulo, Daniel, 183
Lung, Ho, 59

Mahajan, Pramod, 328, 329
Màino, Edvige Antonia Albina. *see* Gandhi, Sonia
Maksimovna, Raisa, 249, 251
Malaviya, H.K., 49
Malenkov, G.M., 302
Malhotra, Inder, 161
Malhoutra, Moni, 179, 205
Malihabadi, Josh, 190
Mallik, Meira, 60
Mandela, Mrs, 280
Mandela, Nelson, 172, 280, 282, 320
Mansingh, Lalit, 318
Marquez, Gabriel Garcia, 224
Marx, Karl, 51, 228
Masani, Minoo, 22
Mathai, John, 109
Mathai, M.O., 37
Mathrani, Aniel, 349-350
Mathur, K.P., 149
Mathur, Shiv Charan, 292
Maudling, Reginald, 163
Mayo, Lord, 8
Mazari, Sherbaz Khan, 195
Mboya, Tom, 100
McCarthy, J.K., 97
Mehta, Ashok, 161
Mehta, Jagat, 179-182
Mehta, Ved, 93
Mei, Jin Ping, 47
Menon, K.P.S., 259, 267, 269
Menon, Narayana, 29, 94
Menon, P.A., 100
Menon, V.K. Krishna, 16, 25, 42, 56, 70–71, 85, 117, 120, 123, 303
Mishra, Brajesh, 313–314, 326–328, 331
Mishra, Dwarka Prasad, 145
Mishra, Shyam Nandan, 181–182
Modi, Narendra, 373, 374
Mody, Russi, 239

Mohammad, Yunus, 37, 310
Molotov, V.M., 302
Montessori, Maria, 16
Mookerjee, S.P., 109
Mother Teresa, 225, 227
Mountbatten, Edwina, 42, 119
Mountbatten, Lord, 18, 42, 82, 114–115, 120, 146, 162
Mugabe, Prime Minister Robert, 185, 245
Mukherjee, Pranab, 293, 317, 321, 330
Mulgaonkar, S., 37
Musharraf, General (Pervez), 333

Nagast, Negusa, 77
Naidu, Chandrababu, 327–328
Naidu, Leelamani, 36–37
Naidu, Padmaja, 16
Naidu, Sarojini, 36
Naipaul, V.S., 86
Nair, T.K.A., 331
Najibullah, President, 276
Namboodiripad, E.M.S., 48, 266
Narain, Raj, 160
Narayan, Jayaprakash, 16, 22, 56, 80, 82, 144, 163, 169
Narayan, R.K., 29, 35, 71–73, 93–94
Narayanan, President K.R., 296, 301, 317, 325–327
Nash, Ogden, 192
Nasser, President Gamal Abdel, 135, 140, 150–152
Nassir, Jammal Abdul, 363 *see also* Nasser, President Gamal Abdel
Nazimuddin, Khawaja, 25
Nehru, Arun, 235, 238, 274, 280
Nehru, Braj Kumar, 74, 85, 91–92, 124, 161–162, 166, 170–171
Nehru, Fori, 166, 170
Nehru, Jawaharlal, 9, 16, 18, 20, 22, 27–28, 32–33, 38, 41–42, 49, 56, 61, 63–65, 67, 71, 73–74, 81–85, 92, 103, 107–126, 135, 140, 144, 146, 162, 164–165, 174, 190, 252, 288, 293, 324, 378
Nehru, Motilal, 146

INDEX

Nehru, Mrs Rajan, 40, 46
Nehru, R.K., 38–39, 46
Nguyen, General, 268
Niazi, A.A.K., 154, 212
Nicolson, Harold, 31
Nijalingappa, S., 132, 142, 145
Nixon, President Richard, 51, 150
Nkomo, Joshua, 173–175, 179, 184
Norman, Dorothy, 165
Novotný, Antonin, 145
Nujoma, Sam, 282
Nyerere, President Julius, 79, 181, 225

Obama, Barack, 306
Ola, Sis Ram, 294, 331
Oppenheimer, Robert, 83
Osterling, Anders, 227
Owens, Jessie, 101

Pai, Nath, 130
Pai-shih, Chi, 58–59
Pandit, Vijaya Lakshmi, 69, 88–92, 102, 113, 124, 195
Pant, K.C., 147
Pant, Pandit Gobind Ballabh, 62–64
Paranjpe, V.V. (Pai), 46–47
Parmar, Chief Minister, 130
Parthasarathi, G., 103, 104, 218, 220, 241, 266
Pasternack, 227
Paswan, Ram Vilas, 330
Patel, I.G., 291
Patel, Rajni, 132, 161
Patel, Sardar, 82, 109, 115–116, 120, 146–147
Pathak, G.S., 353
Pathak, R.S., 352–355, 368
Patil, R.K., 49–50
Patil, Shivraj, 330–331
Patil, S.K., 132, 136
Paul, Augustine, 211–212
Paul, Lord Swraj, 163
Pawar, Sharad, 288, 330
Peck, Gregory, 86
Peng, Prime Minister Li, 267–269, 271

Pillai, Sir N.R., 39
Pillai, Thakazhi Sivasankara, 228
Pindling, Sir Lynden Oscar, 242
Pirzadas, Hafiz, 195
Plimsoll, Sir James, 97
Po, Li, 58
Powell, Colin, 332
Prabhakaran, Velupillai, 253, 255, 258–260, 262
Prasad, H.Y. Sharada, 133, 149, 224, 233
Prasad, Rajendra, 23, 28, 42
Premadasa, Prime Minister Ranasinghe, 255, 261, 264
Priyanka, 286, 312, 314–315, 319
Puri, Lakshmi, 207
Putin, Vladimir, 306, 336, 343, 346
Pyarelal, 17

Qureshi, I.M, 195

Radhakrishnan, S., 42, 56–57, 62, 64, 108, 135
Rafsanjani, President, 250
Rahman, Sheikh Mujibur, 155
Rahul, 286, 319, 320
Rajagopalachari, C., 16, 81–84, 136
Rajpal, 210–211
Rajwade, 78–79
Ram, A.R., 46
Ram, Babu Jagjivan, 168
Ram, N., 259–260
Ram, Principal Raja, 21–22
Ramachandran, M.G. (MGR), 253, 255, 260
Ramanujan, Srinivasa, 35
Ramesh, Jairam, 312, 314, 318
Ramphal, Shridath 'Sonny,' 163, 179–180, 205, 225, 283
Ramsden, 22
Ranganathan, 173
Rani, Devika, 7
Rao, N.T. Rama (NTR), 239
Rao, P.V. Narasimha (P.V.), 203–204, 207, 216, 231–232, 235, 240, 256, 259, 261, 266, 280, 289–295, 309, 311–312

INDEX

Rao, Raja, 29, 72, 94, 108
Rao, Rajeshwar, 266
Rao, V.H., 197
Raphaeli, Dr Nimrod, 349
Ratnaswamy, Colonel Vincent, 45
Rau, Benegal Rama, 72
Rau, Santha Rama, 29, 72–73, 94, 108
Ray, Siddhartha Shankar, 160
Reddy, N. Sanjiva, 145
Rehmani, 19
Rice, Condoleezza, 318, 339–341
Richardson (US representative), 151
Ritu, 142, 172, 313
Roach, John, 25
Rodriguez, Carlos Rafael, 220
Roosevelt, Franklin D., 77, 108, 320
Rousseau, 26
Rowland, Tiny, 283
Rudra, Principal, 20
Russell, Bertrand, 109

Sadat, Anwar, 150–151
Sagari, 23
Sahadev, Kuldip, 259
Sahay, Subodh Kant, 350
Sahiba, Sardarni, 5
Saideen, 191
Sanghvi, Vir, 322–323, 373
Saran, Shyam, 322, 339–340, 351
Sathe, R.B., 215
Sathe, Vasant, 240
Satpati, Nandini, 149, 169
Sattar, Abdus, 188, 193, 277
Saud, King Saud bin Abdulaziz Al, 31
Scindia, Madhavrao, 275, 288, 293
Sehgal, Andaleeb, 350
Selassie I, Haile, 77–78
Sen, Gaur, 142
Sen, Nirupam, 347
Sen, Ronen, 259, 279, 285
Senanayake, Dudley, 25
Seshan, T.N., 286
Shah, K.K., 148
Shah, Sardul Vikram, 129
Shahi, Agha, 193
Shakespeare, William, 16, 107
Shamim, Air Chief Marshal, 209–210

Shankar, P. Shiv, 240, 292, 350
Shankar, Uday, 59
Shankaranand, B., 267
Shankland, Ian, 21
Shaoqi, Liu, 47–51, 56, 134
Sharif, Nawaz, 287, 298–299, 342
Sharma, Anand, 280
Sharma, P.N., 48–49
Sharma, Satish, 315
Sharma, Shankar Dayal, 289
Shastri, Lal Bahadur, 88, 102–103
Shaw, Bernard, 80
She, Lao, 47
Sheen, Vincent, 83
Shek, Chiang Kai, 64
Shekhar, Chandra, 146, 250, 284–285, 291, 351
Shekhawat, Bhairon Singh, 356
Shengkun, President Yang, 269
Shevardnadze, Edward, 281
Shukla, Principal, 18
Shukla, Rajiv, 250
Sihanouk, Norodom, 31
Singh, Amar, 319
Singh, Arjun, 238, 276, 288–290, 292–294, 314–315, 317, 319, 330, 372
Singh, Arun, 234–235
Singh, Badan, 14
Singh, Bhagwat, 14, 24, 26, 93
Singh, Bharat, 6, 23, 104
Singh, Bhawani, 162
Singh, Bheem (Bhim), 348, 351, 365
Singh, Brajesh, 138
Singh, Captain Amarinder, 232
Singh, Chaudhary Charan, 161, 181
Singh, Colonel Ghamandi, 3
Singh, Dinesh, 128–129, 132, 267
Singh, Girdhar, 105–106
Singh, Giriraj, 15
Singh, Govind, 1
Singh, Havaldar Bhole, 6
Singh, I.J. Bahadur, 46
Singh, Jagat, 142, 172, 331, 350, 356
Singh, Jagjit, 208
Singh, Jaswant, 299, 328
Singh, K.N., 292

INDEX

Singh, Karan, 32
Singh, Kewal, 167
Singh, Khushwant, 35
Singh, Kishan, 105
Singh, L.P., 279
Singh, Maharaja Brijendra, 4
Singh, Maharaja Jaswant, 2
Singh, Maharaja Kumar Hanwant, 8
Singh, Maharaja Ranjit, 1
Singh, Maharaja Yadavindra, 130, 156–157
Singh, Maj Gen. Shahbeg, 232
Singh, Manmohan, 291, 318–319, 322, 325, 330–332, 335, 337,239–344, 347, 351, 368, 371–372, 374, 376–377
Singh, President Giani Zail, 232–233, 238, 278
Singh, Sardar Baldev, 109
Singh, Sardar Swaran, 148, 160
Singh, S.P., 384
Singh, Swaran, 102–103, 213
Singh, Thakur, 3
Singh, Vishwanath Pratap (V.P.), 240, 264, 280, 282, 284, 330
Sinha, Justice Jagmohanlal, 160
Sinha, Yashwant, 351
Siqueiros, David Alfaro, 49
Smith, Brian Abel, 30
Smith, Ian, 172–173
Snow, Edgar, 43–44
Soames, Sir Christopher, 185
Soni, Ambika, 322, 348
Spasowski, Romuald, 152
Spengler, Oswald, 41
Stalin, Joseph, 51, 57, 119–120, 138, 302
Steinbeck, John, 49
Stevenson, Adlai, 73, 84, 88, 109
Stow, Harry, 76
Stow, V.A.S., 8–9
Subramaniam, C., 136
Suhrawardy, Huseyn Shaheed, 195
Sukarno, President Ahmed, 50–51
Sukhia, 21
Sundarayya, P., 48
Sundarji, Lt Gen. Krishnaswamy, 231, 276

Suri, Lalit, 316
Surjeet, Harkishan Singh, 319, 330–331
Suyin, Han, 44–45, 61
Svetlana, 138

Tagore, Rabindranath, 9, 20, 141, 228
Taimur, Said Fahar-Bin, 8
Tang, 28
Teh, Marshal Chu, 43, 47, 49, 50
Thakar, N.G., 16
Thant, U., 70, 83, 109
Thapar, Romesh, 132
Thappatham, Kunchi, 35
Thatcher, Margaret, 181, 225, 234, 241, 243, 283
Tho, Chen Chen, 58
Thompson, Sir George, 24
Thorndike, Dame Sybil, 161
Tilakaratne, Bernard, 258
Ting, Chen Pan, 58
Tito, Josip Broz, 135
Tiwari, N.D., 261, 276–277, 279, 288, 292–293
Tlas, Firas Mustafa, 363
Tolstoy, 228
Toynbee, Arnold, 109
Trehan, Naresh, 300, 313
Trevelyan, George, 25
Trotsky, Leon, 49
Tsang, Hieun, 47
Tse-hi, Pau, 123
Tung, Mao Tse, 43–51, 52 53, 55–57, 59–60, 62, 108, 118, 134, 193, 268, 302–304
Tyabji, Badar, 40–41
Tzu, Sun, 268

Ustinov, Peter, 233

Vadra, Robert, 315, 350
Vaizey, John, 30
Vajpayee, Atal Bihari, 161, 237, 266, 297–299, 317–318, 326, 328
Venkataraman, President R., 285–286
Venkateswaran, A.P., 278–279

INDEX

Verghese, B.G. (George), 133, 136–138
Verma, Lt Gen., 85
Victoria, Queen, 244
Volcker, Paul, 333, 335, 346–347, 357

Wachuku, Jaja, 85
Wadajo, Kifle, 79
Wavell, Lord, 16, 17
Wijemuni, Vijitha Rohana, 262

Xiaoping, Deng, 50, 60, 269–271, 303

Yadav, Lalu Prasad, 330

Yadav, Mulayam Singh, 317, 341
Yakunin, Vladimir, 321, 335–337
Yeltsin, Boris, 305–306
Yew, Lee Kuan, 96, 225
Yi, Chen, 64
Yunus, Muhammad, 37

Zemin, Jiang, 293
Zia-ul-Haq, President, 186, 189–191, 193–200, 201–204, 206–207, 209–211, 213–215, 223, 234, 241, 277
Ziyang, Zhao, 269
Zorin, Z.A., 74, 84
Zukov, 32

Subject Index

African National Congress (ANC), 172, 280, 283
All India Congress Committee (AICC), 110, 137, 146, 240, 244, 309, 312, 349
American civil rights movement, 86–88
Amnesty International, 161
apartheid regime, 172, 243

Bangladesh, crisis, 142
 war, 205
Bharatiya Janata Party (BJP), 237, 266, 284, 373
Bharatpur, 1-8, 102, 231, 237, 286
 Bharatpur estate in Shimla, 5
 Bharatpur annual duck shoot event, 7
Hindu–Muslim relations, 7–8
book reviews and editing, 37–38, 72, 88
 Maharaja Suraj Mal, 185
 tribute to Forster, 94–95

Central Information Commission (CIC), 355

childhood years
 Baba-saab's death, 3
 in Bharatpur, 4–5
 Braj Yatra, 3
 relationship with Maharaja Brijendra Singh, 6
 schooling, 3–4
 in Shimla, 5–6
 watching Hindi film *Achut Kanya*, 7
China. *see also* Indo-China War of 1962; Sino-Indian border dispute
 cultural life, 59
 Cultural Revolution in, 44, 134, 269
 education at Peking University, 60
 Gang of Four, 270
 Hsin Chiao Hotel, 44
 Mao's, 45, 48-49, 193
 Master Chi's paintings, 58
 meeting with Chou En-lai, 58–59
 meeting with Han Suyin, 44–46
 Sino-Indian relations, 265, 267, 293–294
 Chinese diplomacy, 267-68
 cipher code, 85, 153
Committee on Decolonization, 76,

INDEX

96–100, 172-173, 282
Commonwealth Heads of Government Meeting (CHOGM), 217–218, 225-227
Commonwealth Summit, 160, 170, 178–182, 225–227
  holding of 'investiture' for Mother Teresa, 225–227
Communist Party of India (CPI), 48, 239, 266, 304
Communist world, 302–304
Congress party, 49, 112, 122, 133, 136, 137, 142, 146, 163, 168–169, 232, 237
  centenary session of, 244–245
Congress Working Committee (CWC), 109, 137, 145, 289, 308, 330, 372, 375
  Lok Sabha Election, 1996, 294–295
  Lok Sabha Election, 2014, 343
  Rajiv Gandhi's policies, impact on, 274–279
  split of, 146
CPI (M), 239, 317

Darjeeling, agitation, 273–274
Deeg, 1–2, 15
Delhi Declaration, 224, 248–249
Delhi-Lahore bus service, 298
diplomatic bags, 171
diplomatic career, K. Natwar Singh
  as chief coordinator for CHOGM. *see* Commonwealth Heads of Government Meeting (CHOGM)
  as Deputy High Commissioner in London, 170–171
  end of, 229–230
  at Foreign and Commonwealth Office in London, 30–31, 188
  foreign delegations, 31–32
  as High Commissioner to Zambia, 172
  as IFS probationer, 27–28
  as IFS trainee in Tamil Nadu, 35
  as Indian Ambassador to Pakistan. *see* Pakistan, diplomatic career in

  as liaison officer to Chou En-lai, 265
  as liaison officer to Dalai Lama, 62–63
  Mongolia, 54
  posting to Peking. *see* China; China, diplomatic career in
  at Prime Minister's secretariat, 132–134, 139, 145, 152
  as private secretary to R.K. Nehru, 38–42
  Undersecretary (IFS (B)), 36
  in United Nations. *see* United Nations, diplomatic career in
Discretionary Grant, 171

East Pakistan and India's role therein, 152–155
Emergency period, 1975, 159–169
  arrest of leaders, 161
  critics of, 162–163
  difficulties in justifying, 165-169
  impact of, 168–169
Escorts Heart Institute, 300

father's death, 104–105
Five Principles of Peaceful Coexistence (Panchsheel Treaty), 118, 252, 271
foreign delegations
  Cambodia, 31–32
  Saudi Arabia, 31
  Soviet Union, 32

Gorkha National Liberation Front, 273
Green Revolution, 139
Gymkhana Club, 37, 38

Hindu-Muslim riots, 18–19
Hindustan Times, 9, 37
Hiroshima and Nagasaki bombing, 18
Hungarian Revolution, 303

Ijlas-e-Khas, 4
Indira Gandhi Memorial Trust, 309, 310

INDEX

Indo-China War of 1962, 65, 123, 266
Indo-Pak no-war pact, 215–216
Indo-Soviet relations, 33, 120–121, 138, 151, 246–251
Indo-Soviet Defence Cooperation, 306
Indo-Soviet festival, 249
Indo-Soviet Friendship Treaty, 306
Indo-US bilateral cooperation, 338–341
Indo-US civil nuclear agreement, 338

Janata Party, 169, 172, 184

Kamaraj Plan, 182–183
Karachi, 194–195
Kashmir issue, 114, 117, 192, 204, 298

Lahore Declaration, 298
Liberation Tigers of Tamil Eelam (LTTE), 253–254, 256, 258–260, 262–264
Lusaka, 172-173, 178

Mao–Radhakrishnan talks, 56–58
marriage and family, 128–131, 142
 father-in-law's death, 156–157
 grandsons, 299
McMahon line, 266
Miranda House, 22–23
Missile Technology Control Regime (MTCR), 338

NAM Summits, 218–221, 245
 accomodation issue, 219–220
 delegations, 220, 222
 diplomatic issues, 223–224
 eighth, 1986, 245–246
National Democratic Alliance (NDA), 297, 317, 325
National Front, 280
Nehru Memorial Fund, 309
New International Economic Order, 271
Next Steps in Strategic Partnership (NSSP), 338

Non-Aligned Students' Youth Organization (NASYO), 350
Non-Proliferation and Comprehensive Nuclear-Test-Ban Treaties, 298
Nuclear Suppliers' Group (NSG), 338

Pakistan, diplomatic career in, 187–216
 Bhutto family, meeting with, 212–215
 credentials ceremony in Islamabad, 189
 East Pakistan issue, 188
 economic situation in Pakistan, 192–193
 hijackers, issue of handing over, 209–210
 Indian Airlines flight, hijacking of, 206, 299
 Indo-Pak relations, 187, 191, 196–197, 202–203, 212–213, 333
 Kashmir issue, 192, 204
 Narasimha Rao's visit, 204
 Pakistani diplomats, 193
 re-entry of Pakistan in Commonwealth, 205
 residual problems of Partition, 192
 Sikh delegation, 207–208
 Stephanians, visit by, 210–211
 Urdu press, 191–193
Panchsheel Treaty agreement, 118, 252, 267, 271–272
Perestroika, 248–249, 305
Permanent Mission, 69, 85, 93, 101, 348, 394
political career
 as Congress candidate from Bharatpur, 231, 233, 235
 delegation to Moscow, 240–241, 250
 diplomatic mission to Sri Lanka, 254–256
 as External Affairs Minister, 265, 319, 331. *see also* Sino-Indian border dispute; Sri Lankan crisis
 Mandela, felicitatation of, 280

INDEX

as Minister of State for Fertilizers, 241
as Minister of State for Steel, 238–240
Namibian independence, celebration of, 280–282
as principal foreign affairs adviser to Sonia Gandhi, 319–320
representation at President Reagan's funeral, 332
state visit to Thailand, 332
political events
American invasion of Iraq, 329
Babri Masjid-Ram Janmabhoomi issue, 274, 292
Bofors case, 273–275
'Brasstacks' crisis, 276–277
differences with P.V.'s style of functioning, 292–293
Golden Temple incident, 231–232
Gujral Doctrine, 295
Gulf war, 284, 345
India-China Border diplomacy, 294
Indira Gandhi's assassination and attacks on Sikh community, 233–234
Indo-US bilateral cooperation, 338–340
Kargil War, 299
Mandal Report, 284
Nuclear Bill, passing of, 341
Pokhran nuclear tests, impact of, 297–298
political crisis (1996–1998), 295
Rajiv Gandhi, assassination of, 286–288
Shah Bano case, 273–274
Sino-Soviet border dispute, 304
privy purses, abolition of, 146
Constitution Amendment against, 147–148

Rajiv-Chandra Shekhar partnership, 284–285
Rajiv Gandhi Foundation, 309
Red Guards, 134
Research and Analysis Wing (RAW), 139, 153, 254, 257, 259, 262–263

SAARC Summit, 248, 252
school and college days
Chinese language training, 28, 57
at Corpus Christi College, 24–25, 28
debating contests, 23
Forster, meeting with, 28–29
Mayo college days, 8–9
ragging, 21–22
at Scindia School, Gwalior, 9, 14–18
scrapbook, 9–13
Senior Cambridge examinations, 19
at St. Stephen's College, 20–23
UPSC interview, 25–26
Simla Agreement, 201–202, 204, 213
Sino-Indian border dispute, 63–67, 84–85, 117–119, 121–122
anti-China activities by Tibet, issue of, 272
anti-China lobby of MEA, interference of, 266
Deng–Rajiv meeting, 271
Maintaining Peace and Tranquillity on the Line of Actual Control, 293–294
Sikkim issue, 266
working groups for resolving, 266
Six-Day War, 1967, 140
Sonia Gandhi's life, phases of, 307–324
Southern Rhodesia, 172
South West Africa People's Organization (SWAPO), 172
Soviet invasion of Hungary, 303
Soviet Union, dissolution of, 302–306
Soviet Union under Gorbachev, 246–248
Sri Lankan crisis
'December 19th Proposals,' 255–256
economic impact of conflict between government and LTTE, 256
ethnic problems, 253–254
humanitarian supplies into Jaffna

409

INDEX

and Sri Lankan reaction, 256–258
Indo-Sri Lanka Agreement, 258–264
IPKF arrival in Jaffna peninsula, 262–263
LTTE's proposals for ceasefire, 258–260
Rajiv Gandhi, attack on, 262
Sri Lanka Airways plane, attack on, 254–255
The Statesman, 9
Suez Canal issue, 55–56
Svetlana incident, 138

Tiwari Congress, 292, 293

UN Charter, veto provision of, 334–335
United Arab Republic (UAR), 150–151
United Nations, diplomatic career in, 68–71
    African journey, 78–80
    art of multilateral diplomacy, 75
    Committee on Decolonization, 76, 96–100, 172, 173
    Cuban Missile Crisis, 84–85
    efforts to prepare Papua New Guinea for self-rule, 98–100
    General Assembly, 1961, 70, 73–75
    General Assembly, 1963, 88–91
    General Assembly, 1970, 149

German visit, 100–102
India's liberation of Goa, 74, 122
Kashmir issue, 96, 103, 114–117
Kennedy's death, 91–92
Rajaji's visit, 81–84
round-the-world trip, 102–103
Trusteeship Council, 76–77
United Progressive Alliance (UPA), 320, 329

Vijaya Lakshmi Pandit–Krishna tiff, 69, 89–91
Vladimir, 321–322, 335
Volcker Report, 322–323, 346–358
    Al-Meda article, 363–365
    Commission of Inquiry Act, 352–353
    impact on family, 355–356, 375
    Iraq probe into allegations, 366
    Justice R.S. Pathak Inquiry report, 354, 359–361, 367–369
    Mathrani interview, 349–350

Zambia, diplomatic career in
    abortive meeting of Morarji Desai with Nkomo, 173–175
    Commonwealth Summit, 178–182
    confrontations with Morarji Desai, 175–178, 182–184
    Mishra's intervention in Commonwealth Summit, 181–182
Zimbabwe African People's Union (ZAPU), 172